SIR JOHN BEVERLEY ROBINSON

Bone and Sinew of the Compact

John Beverley Robinson (1791–1863) was one of Upper Canada's foremost jurists, a dominating influence on the ruling élite, and a leading citizen of nineteenth-century Toronto who owned a vast tract of land on which Osgoode Hall now stands.

The loyalists had founded a colony firm in its devotion to the Crown, with little room for dissent. As a true loyalist son, educated by John Strachan, Robinson attempted to steer Upper Canada toward emulation of what he perceived to be Britain's ideal aristocratic society.

As a young ensign in the York militia he defended his sovereign at Queenston Heights, and as acting attorney-general he prosecuted traitors who threatened to undermine the colony. Later, as attorney-general and de facto leader of the assembly during the 1820s, he tried to mould the government to the British form. But factors he never understood – the influence of American democracy and liberalism in the Colonial Office – ensured that Upper Canada would never be a 'new Albion.'

Robinson was appointed chief justice in 1829, and his judicial career spanned thirty-three years. During his tenure, he insisted the courts were subservient to the legislature; precedents were established which made it clear that their role should be limited to the enforcement of existing laws, with no independent creative function. Robinson's long service on the bench represented both a preservation and a strengthening of the British tradition in Canadian law.

In this biography early Toronto comes alive through the eyes of a powerful man – firm in his beliefs, attractive to women, respected by his fellows – who sought to mould society to his own ideals. For historians, lawyers, and students of jurisprudence who seek an understanding of the roots of legal practice in nineteenth-century Ontario, it is essential reading.

PATRICK BRODE practises law in Windsor, Ontario.

The Honourable J.B. Robinson, Chief Justice, C.W.,
painted and drawn on stone,
Scobie & Balfour, Lith., signed G.T. Berthon

Sir John Beverley Robinson: Bone and Sinew of the Compact

PATRICK BRODE

Published for The Osgoode Society by
University of Toronto Press
Toronto Buffalo London

©The Osgoode Society 1984
Printed in Canada

ISBN 0-8020-3406-3 (cloth)
ISBN 0-8020-3419-5 (paper)

Canadian Cataloguing in Publication Data

Brode, Patrick, 1950–
Sir John Beverley Robinson

Includes bibliographical references and index.
ISBN 0-8020-3406-3 (bound). – ISBN 0-8020-3419-5 (pbk.)
1. Robinson, John Beverley, Sir, 1791–1863.
2. Judges – Ontario – Biography.
3. Ontario – Politics and government – 1791–1841.*
4. Family Compact.*
I. Osgoode Society. II. Title.
FC3071.1.R6B76 1984   971.3'02'0924   C84-098723-4
F1058.R6B76 1984

Picture credits: *The Three Robinson Sisters* – Art Gallery of Ontario, lent by Mr and Mrs J.B. Robinson, 1944; *Sir John Beverley Robinson*, portrait of five judges, lithograph of Robinson as chief justice – by permission of the Law Society of Upper Canada; Beverley House – by permission of Mrs John Strachan Robinson; Robinson in 1816, Robinson in the 1850s – from Major-General C.W. Robinson, C.B., *Life of Sir John Beverley Robinson* (Toronto 1904)

Contents

Foreword

THE OSGOODE SOCIETY

The purpose of The Osgoode Society is to encourage research and writing in the history of Canadian law. The Society, which was incorporated in 1979 and is registered as a charity, was founded at the initiative of the Honourable R. Roy McMurtry, Attorney-General of Ontario, and officials of The Law Society of Upper Canada. Its efforts to stimulate legal history in Canada include the sponsorship of a fellowship and an annual lectureship, research support programs, and work in the field of oral history. The Society will publish (at the rate of about one a year) volumes that contribute to legal–historical scholarship in Canada and which are of interest to the Society's members. Included will be studies of the courts, the judiciary, and the legal profession, biographies, collections of documents, studies in criminology and penology, accounts of great trials, and work in the social and economic history of the law.

Current directors of The Osgoode Society are Brian Bucknall, Archie G. Campbell, Martin Friedland, Jane Banfield Haynes, John D. Honsberger, Kenneth Jarvis, Laura Legge, Allen M. Linden, James Lisson, R. Roy McMurtry, Brendan O'Brien, and Peter Oliver. The Annual Report and information about membership may be obtained by writing The Osgoode Society, Osgoode Hall, 130 Queen Street West, Toronto, Ontario, Canada, M5H 2N6. Members receive the annual volumes published by the Society.

It is appropriate that Patrick Brode's biography of Sir John Beverley Robinson should be published in the year that marks the 200th anniversary of the coming of the loyalists to British North America. Robinson, as

Patrick Brode demonstrates, embodied much of the loyalist tradition and worked to give form to important aspects of that tradition in the body politic of Upper Canada. In many respects, Brode argues, Robinson's achievements in this regard fell short of his aspirations; yet the efforts of Robinson and of like-minded Upper Canadians had important consequences for the future development of Canadian institutions in general and the nation's legal heritage in particular.

John Beverley Robinson was, arguably, the greatest Upper Canadian, and Patrick Brode offers a thoughtful and effective study of a career that had few if any parallels in the societies of British North America. The Osgoode Society is pleased that this book has involved the participation of a practising member of the legal profession in the writing of Canadian legal history, and it is hoped that other members of the profession may see fit to emulate Patrick Brode's example.

Brendan O'Brien
President

Peter Oliver
Editor-in-Chief

14 April 1984

Preface

In an annex to Queen's Park, several rooms are devoted to exhibits illustrating the growth of parliamentary democracy. The display begins with Magna Charta and continues through Upper Canadian times with copies of the *Colonial Advocate* and other voices of reform. The exhibits give the impression that in the early nineteenth century Ontario escaped from the oppression of Family Compact rule and entered into that best of all possible worlds, liberal democracy. If it is true that governments need some myth to act as the foundation for their authority, then this memorial to responsible government in Queen's Park is a superb manifestation of the prevailing myth. Myths are, of necessity, simple; even worse, they imply an inevitability of events that may not have existed. The complexities of political growth are not easily explained by myths, and the persons who took part in that growth were certainly not simple people.

Undertaking a study of the life of a major Upper Canadian historical figure is difficult. There is a tendency in such works to raise up the humble or beat down the proud. My intention in this biography is to view John Beverley Robinson simply as a child of his time. He was guided by the thoughts of revolution – American and French (which he detested) and Glorious (which he revered) – and also by the ideas that had arisen in reaction to those revolutions. Upper Canadians were inheritors of opposing views on the rights of the people to direct their government. John Beverley Robinson saw the world of the United Empire Loyalists succumb to the ideas he hated most – democracy and secularism. The story of his life is one of conflict and, in retrospect, defeat. His influence has never been completely expunged, however, and it is still worth examining to what extent the values of John Robinson and the loyalists played a part in the development of Ontario's political myth.

My thanks are due to the Osgoode Society and its editor-in-chief, Peter N. Oliver, whose encouragement and support made this work possible. I also acknowledge with gratitude the help of Robert L. Fraser, Graeme Patterson, Paul Romney, and S.F. Wise for the valuable comments. The interest of Ontario's attorney-general, R. Roy McMurtry, in this study of his predecessor is most appreciated.

Throughout the preparation of this manuscript I received the kind co-operation of the following persons and institutions: Catherine Shepard, Eugene Martel, and Terrence Campbell of the Archives of Ontario; Patricia Kennedy of the Public Archives of Canada; Andrew Johnson of the judges' staff of the Supreme Court of Ontario; the staff of the Metropolitan Toronto Library; and Theresa Dupuis of the Windsor Public Library. Peter Mackenzie assisted me in researching this book, and he may find some of his thoughts reflected on its pages. I am also indebted to J.D. Blackwell, Leah Sinclair, Jane Banfield Haynes, Ruth Dales, J. Lovatt, Rachel Grover, the late Lady Maud Robinson, Mary Stewart Bagnani, and Stephen C. Kamen.

I would also like to acknowledge the care and accuracy of my typist, Joan Reid. Finally, I thank my wife, Maureen, for her patience and encouragement under trying circumstances.

John Beverley Robinson, Solicitor-General, Upper Canada, after a miniature by
Hervé, London 1816

Sir John Beverley Robinson, by George Theodore Berthon

Portrait of five judges by George Theodore Berthon. Left to right: William Henry Draper, Sir James Buchanan Macaulay, Sir John Beverley Robinson, Jonas Jones, Archibald McLean

Beverley House, Toronto

The Three Robinson Sisters (Emily, Augusta, and Louisa) by George Theodore Berthon, 1846

Sir John Beverley Robinson in the 1850s

Sir John Beverley Robinson

1

The Loyalist Tradition

John Beverley Robinson was born into a family that keenly felt its exile from kin and country. Although the Robinson name was to become synonymous with established power and influence, John Robinson would not forget the meanness of his early life and the circumstances that caused it.

Ensign Christopher Robinson, the father of the future chief justice of Upper Canada, left his studies at William and Mary College in Williamsburg, Virginia, in 1780 to join the loyalist forces in New York. Through three years of war, Robinson fought with the First American Regiment, commanded by Colonel John Graves Simcoe. The regiment was involved in a number of actions in the Virginia area and formed part of Cornwallis's forces, which surrendered to Washington in 1781. Despite the elevation of the First Americans to the status of a regular British regiment in North America, the unit was evacuated to New Brunswick at the end of the war and was disbanded in October 1783.

The loyalist Christopher Robinson was a descendant of a Yorkshire yeoman family.[1] The earliest luminary of the family was John Robinson, Bishop of Bristol. The bishop had pursued a career as a commercial envoy to Sweden, and had attained prominence not so much for his clerical piety as for his skill as a diplomat. He acted as envoy to Charles XII of Sweden, and in 1713 was England's plenipotentiary at the drawing-up of the Treaty of Utrecht. Bishop Robinson, a controversial and influential cleric, faithfully attended upon Queen Anne until her death in 1714. The first of the family to emigrate to America was the bishop's elder brother, Christopher, who, by the late seventeenth century, had established a successful plantation, 'The Grange,' in Middlesex County, Virginia. The Robinsons became a prominent Virginia family, and Christopher Robinson himself became a member of the House of Burgesses, as did many of his descendants. The loyalist Christopher Robinson was not descended from one of the wealthier branches of the family, however. He was wholly dependent on his uncle, Beverley Robinson, for his support and education. When Christopher joined the British forces, he deliberately broke all family bonds with the Virginia Robinsons. For the most part the family sided with the new republic, thereby retaining their substantial land holdings and social position. With the coming of peace in 1783, Christopher Robinson was left without an inheritance and, no doubt, with an antipathy toward the American republic and its ideals.

The precarious position of a half-pay officer with no immediate prospects was not enhanced when, in 1783, Robinson married Esther Sayre, the daughter of a loyalist clergyman. This marriage was very much against the wishes of his uncle and only remaining financial benefactor, Beverley Robinson. Robinson, at the age of twenty-one, was considered too young for the match, and in any case the raw frontier of New Brunswick offered little employment for ex-dragoon officers. After the birth of a son, Peter, in 1785 and a daughter, Mary, in 1787, Robinson left for the town of L'Assomption in Lower Canada. Shortly thereafter, he moved to Berthier where, in 1791, his second son, John Beverley, was born. Despite his growing family and meagre income as a half-pay officer, Christopher Robinson was unable to find any government position commensurate with his social status. Even for those loyalists who were content to work the land, the times were harsh. The year 1789 was known among the loyalists as the 'starving time,' a period when failed crops made a subsistence-farming existence precarious. The hard-pressed Robinson family was therefore greatly encouraged when Colonel John Graves Simcoe was appointed lieutenant-governor of the new colony of Upper Canada in 1791. Robinson reported glowingly that Colonel Simcoe was

the First and Best Friend I ever met with since I left my Virginia Connections, having arrived Gov. of this Province, found me in Canada in the greatest distress. He recognized me, the spark of Friendship remaining in his Breast rekindled at the relation of my past misfortunes, he offered me anything in his Power.[2]

Robinson moved his family to Kingston in order to be closer to the heart of a benevolent administration. He continued to remind Colonel Simcoe of his unflagging and as yet unrewarded loyalty to the Crown. Robinson told Simcoe that he had no influential relatives, 'having forfeited their friendship by my political principles ... I was born to better prospects.'[3] His prospects brightened when Simcoe appointed him deputy surveyor-general of woods and reserves. In addition, he received a certificate for 2,000 acres of virgin land.

The Canada Act[4] (referred to as the Constitutional Act) of 1791 had established a separate government for Upper Canada with British law and land tenure. As in England, property owners could elect members to a House of Assembly. The other branch of the legislature was to be composed of an appointed legislative council, and it was assumed that a native aristocracy would arise from the members of this council. (The prescient whig critic, Charles James Fox, warned against an appointed council; he felt that a colonial aristocracy would contrast unfavourably with the representative government of the United States.) The third element of the colonial government was to be a small advisory body called the executive council. While the role of this body was only vaguely defined, it apparently was intended to advise and be answerable solely to the lieutenant-governor and to have no connection with the assembly. A provision of the act that was to cause future conflict called for 'a permanent appropriation of Lands ... for the support and maintenance of a Protestant clergy.' This appropriation was to include one-seventh of all lands granted in each township. While the Constitutional Act did not necessarily establish a state religion, it did lay the foundation for future disputes between the diverse communions.

One of Simcoe's primary tasks was to promote settlement; through liberal grants of Crown land, he encouraged disaffected Americans, the 'late Loyalists,' to come to the province. Simcoe hoped that he would be 'instrumental to the *Re-union of the Empire,* by sowing the Seeds of a vigorous Colony ...'[5] By diversifying and strengthening the province's economy, the enterprising 'late Loyalist' farmers were themselves instrumental to Upper Canada's movement out of the wilderness stage.

The French civil law still prevailed in the province through the Quebec Ordinances. The English common law was established in Upper Canada by the first act of the new assembly; by it, in 'all matters of controversy relative to property and Civil Rights,' resort would be had to English law.[6] Simcoe also wished to erect a central superior court, and this he accomplished through his chief justice, William Osgoode, who drew up the first King's Bench Act.[7] The formalities of English law were made mandatory and the Court of King's Bench, with a chief justice and two puisne justices, was instructed to sit from time to time at local assizes.

It was also necessary to have a legal profession well versed in the common law to plead before the courts. After the creation of King's Bench in 1794, the lieutenant-governor was authorized to license certain educated individuals to practice law. Christopher Robinson seized the opportunity to enter the profession. He applied to Simcoe for a licence, and in 1795 his benefactor obliged him. This somewhat haphazard way of licensing lawyers repelled the attorney-general, John White, who wished to establish a self-regulating legal profession. Therefore, in 1797, the Law Society of Upper Canada was founded on the model of the English Inns of Court to control the legal profession and provide practical experience for young law clerks. Ten licensed attorneys met in Newark to organize the new body. Although he had been practising only since 1795 and had no formal legal training, Christopher Robinson was sufficiently senior to be elected one of the benchers, or directors, of the neophyte Law Society. Only a few of those original barristers had formal legal training. Most, like Robinson, were simply educated men, and no doubt it was presumed that professional competence would result from practice.

In addition to his legal pursuits, Christopher Robinson had obtained another government post. Sir John Wentworth, the Crown surveyor of British America, granted him the Crown surveyorship of woods in Upper Canada. Better prospects were finally accruing to the Virginia loyalist.

Christopher Robinson was elected to the assembly in 1796. Ironically, the first Robinson to enter political life began his career in opposition to the government. Many wealthy loyalists had brought their Negro slaves into exile with them. Simcoe was in the vanguard of those English reformers who sought to abolish slavery. Before he left Upper Canada he brought a measure before the second session of the first legislature to prohibit the importing of additional slaves and to manumit all Canadian-born slaves at the age of twenty-five.[8] This act was highly unpopular among those loyalists who considered their slaves to be their most valuable and mobile chattel. Despite the fact that he was working against his benefactor Simcoe's fondest dream, Robinson moved a bill to allow persons coming into the province to bring their slaves with them.[9]

Christopher Robinson's legislative career was doomed to be brief. He had never completely recovered from wounds suffered during the Revolutionary War, and he was continually plagued by the gout. In 1798 he moved his family to the new capital, York, in order to attend the assembly and take an active role in the administration. After only three weeks in the capital, he suffered a reoccurrence of gout and died. Christopher Robinson was buried in the garrison grounds of York. His son, John Beverley, was seven years old. One of young John's earliest memories was of following his father's coffin along the Indian path underneath the tall maples bordering the Don River.[10]

Esther Robinson was left alone with six children to provide for. She petitioned the government to appoint her eldest son, Peter, then thirteen, to his father's position of deputy surveyor of woods. The petition failed, and the family faced the new century with dismal prospects. Their financial plight was not alleviated until 1805, when Esther married her late husband's executor, Elisha Beman, a prosperous York tavern-keeper. Meanwhile, the one friend of influence remaining to the Robinsons was the Reverend Doctor John Stuart, a former Virginian, who was the Bishop of London's commissary in Upper Canada. Dr Stuart, realizing Esther Robinson's desperate situation, accepted John as his ward and undertook to educate him. His generosity proved to be its own reward; John became an affectionate son and Dr Stuart, in turn, a doting foster-father. Determined that John should receive a proper education, Dr Stuart enrolled him at the grammar school operated by John Strachan, who had arrived in Upper Canada in 1799. Young John had met Strachan in Kingston and had helped him prepare a log house for his first dwelling. Strachan, only thirteen years older than the young loyalist, discovered in John an impressionable protégé and offered to accept him without the payment of any fees.[11] However, Robinson's stepfather, Elisha Beman, and Dr Stuart did arrange for John's lodgings and tuition while he attended the new grammar school in Cornwall.

In recommending John to Strachan's care, Dr Stuart noted Justice William Dummer Powell's interest in John's early education. Justice Powell, a Boston loyalist, had become a lawyer in Quebec and the first puisne justice of Upper Canada's King's Bench. In Quebec Powell had been the first signatory on a petition to repeal the Quebec Act and establish English judicial institutions. The King's Bench Act undoubtedly satisfied his ambition of seeing the common law supreme in Upper Canada. In the absence of a chief justice, Powell had organized the King's Bench and laid down the first rules of practice. Moreover, he had earned the gratitude of the loyalists by certifying their land titles and granting deeds. Justice Powell was a prominent figure in frontier society, and his interest in John Robinson's education was of considerable significance. While he may have favoured young Robinson because of his acquaintance with Christopher Robinson, Justice Powell also saw in the sons of the loyalists the key to preserving the British heritage in North America.

John Strachan's school offered an excellent background in the classics and humanities. According to a contemporary account, education at Cornwall Grammar School consisted of

the Latin classics, Arithmetic, Bookkeeping, Elements of Mathematics, Elements of Geography, of Natural and Civil History ... The whole was interspersed with different pieces of poetry and prose, many of the most humourous cast, composed for the occasion.[12]

At Cornwall, Robinson met John Macaulay, George Markland, Henry John Boulton, and others who would later be his partners in the provincial executive. Macaulay's family in particular possessed the wealth and social connections in Kingston that would assure their son a respectable future. Despite the fact that Robinson lacked such advantages, the two boys became close companions and formed a bond that lasted throughout their lives. Robinson later looked back on their school life as rigorous and demanding: 'We used to take our hats and mittens and hammer away at the wood. Many a cold finger we had in those days and many complaints we made of our hard times.'[13] These trials were more than compensated for by the affection Robinson came to feel for John Strachan and his wife. He expressed his youthful admiration for Strachan by composing a birthday ode in his honour.

Robinson completed his grammar-school work in August 1807. With Strachan's direction and encouragement, he sought training in the law. At that time a young clerk was required to attend on a senior barrister for five years before admission to the Law Society. At the recommendation of John Strachan, Robinson was placed in the office of G. D'Arcy Boulton, a prominent York attorney. John had wished to live with his brother Peter, but Boulton, anxious to save on time lost in commuting, insisted that Robinson live in his house near the office.[14] This familiarity may have served another purpose, for Robinson's sister, Sarah, met and married D'Arcy Boulton Jr, the eldest son of the family. Boulton Sr had recently been appointed solicitor-general, and Dr Strachan was quick to note the opportunity this union presented to Robinson: 'The marriage of your sister with young Mr. Boulton may be of some advantage to you; this is especially true if the young couple reside at the Solicitor General's.'[15] Robinson could not fail to understand Strachan's hint. By virtue of his developing family and school relationships, Robinson was becoming familiar with the leading circles of provincial life. Personal loyalties determined careers, and it was no exaggeration to say that 'the smallest government job involved the interest of one of the great ones in York.'[16]

During his tenure as an articled clerk, Robinson demonstrated an active mind and substantial critical faculties. Besides absorbing treatises on law, he read Shakespeare, Wilkes, and even two volumes of *Eccentric biography*. He read extensively in the great literature of the day, and at times regretted the fact that he was also obliged to study the law: 'Master Blackstone steps in now and then with his doctrine of entails.' Robinson carried on a lively correspondence and exchange of books with John Macaulay and described to him his brother law clerks. While Macaulay might display his virtuosity by writing in French, Robinson described one fellow who wrote in Greek – a device, Robinson suspected, that enabled him to 'write nonsense without fear of detection.' Robinson begged Macaulay to come to York and join him in the 'good company' of lawyers.[17] This 'Friendly Society' of Cornwall graduates and law clerks included the daughters of York's better families, and Robinson added a further inducement to Macaulay by mentioning that 'there are some pretty Girls here and that is something.' Apparently, some of his friends were quick to take advantage of that situation. Robinson complained that Jonas Jones, another Cornwall compatriot, wrote of 'nothing but what he calls *pieces*.' As for himself, Robinson modestly stated, 'but as to the *Demoiselles*, I disclaim all connection with them.'[18] Still, his eye remained keen enough to note that 'Miss Cartwright is a sweet girl.'[19] In the small society of York, the handsome law clerk flirted with the available young ladies. Undoubtedly, he met Anne Powell, whose acquaintance would only serve to improve his already rewarding relationship with her father, Justice Powell. Robinson also continued to correspond with his mentor, Dr Strachan, who primly corrected Robinson's composition and encouraged him in the parsimonious habits in which he himself revelled.[20]

As an accompaniment to and an extension of his social life, Robinson took the serious step of becoming an ensign in the York militia. To Macaulay he confided his enthusiasm at becoming a militiaman and his intention 'if occasion requires to fight like a man.'[21] During the parades on the York garrison grounds, John Robinson was quite unaware that he would shortly be put to just such a test.

While in York, Robinson met the 'enlightened' Christopher Alexander Hagerman. A young tory destined to become a leader of the conservative faction, Hagerman was not a graduate of the Cornwall Grammar School and was not immediately accepted as a member of the adolescent élite of

York. Still, he was of good loyalist background and unreservedly proud of his talents.[22] Robinson rather patronizingly referred to him as 'a youth whose bashfulness will never stand in his way.'[23] The clash of personality was already apparent between these two able men of similar views and conflicting ambitions.

The little capital of York fostered some pretensions that had already been discarded in the mother country; for example, the gentlemen of York powdered their hair even after the custom died out in England. Fox hunts were still carried on, although with a Canadian twist – the chase crossed the ice of York harbour.[24] Above all else York was a government town, and a fraction of the imperial treasury was dispensed to the loyal administrators. From the province's beginning, small cliques had monopolized this patronage and had striven to be as intimate as possible with the source of all influence, the lieutenant-governor. Because advancement was tied to personal connections, the gentry were jealous of their prerogatives and struggled to preserve their all-important status.

The elected and appointed representatives of the settlers met and debated at the foot of Parliament Street in the only brick building in York. In 1808 Robinson attended a session of the assembly. 'The house,' he remarked, 'appears nearly equally divided between Blackguards and Gentlemen. It might I think be stiled [sic] after the Parliament of Henry 4th.'[25] The debates he found 'more amusing than you can conceive.' Dissent in the colony was weak and largely confined to the old loyalist complaint of insufficient reward for service to the Crown and displeasure at the wealth of the new immigrants, both British and American. In the pre-war assembly there existed no unified opposition with a clearly defined set of grievances.

Robinson had already developed a low opinion of the American system of government and its 'Democratic levelling principle.'[26] His disdain for popular institutions coincided with his esteem of the permanent Crown offices. He would later add to his early distrust of democratic government an enduring faith in the executive, led by capable and loyal individuals, as the only institution capable of providing good government. The legislature was an integral part of the British constitution, but the existing assembly seemed burdened by rustics and ill-educated republican malcontents.

In addition to his displeasure with the membership of the assembly, the self-assured Robinson even expressed mild criticism of his former master. On the occasion of the King's birthday, Dr Strachan had written a flattering pamphlet entitled 'A Discourse on the Character of King George III.' Robinson, who shared the prevailing opinion that the king was a less than perfect monarch, feared that the pamphlet would probably provide cause 'to make disaffected among us loyal and contented.'[27] In a letter to Macaulay Robinson wrote, 'We surely require to be most determinately loyal to believe that the Duke of York is the pillar of state or His Royal Highness the Prince of Wales the pride of the nation.' Strachan had previously discovered one of Robinson's satirical letters and had severely reproved him: 'I must ask your promise never to write Satyrs upon anybody – the empty laugh of the malignant is but a small gain for hurting the feelings of your neighbour.'[28] Strachan also warned Robinson that he was displaying a 'want of severance ... you give a thing up because it is difficult.'[29] After these sharp exchanges, a temporary silence descended between master and student.

These transgressions were probably a reflection of Robinson's increasing restlessness as a law clerk. Three years of copying documents and delivering deeds had dulled his spirit and made him yearn for a more exciting career. Now he reversed his original recommendation to Macaulay and warned him, 'Your high conceptions in favour of the profession of the Law are not warranted by the reality.'[30]

The tedium that seemed to be suffocating him ended abruptly. By 1811 the Napoleonic wars, which were engulfing Europe, intervened in Robinson's life when his principal, Solicitor-General Boulton, was captured on his way to England by a French privateer. Boulton's incarceration placed several of the Cornwall Grammar School graduates in desperate situations. Samuel Jarvis, Archy McLean, and John Robinson were left without an employer, and worse, with no avenue of gaining admission to the Law Society. One York resident noted, 'John Robinson is likewise adrift; and as if fortune had a mind to sport with and tease Mr. Strachan's flock settled at York.'[31] In order to complete his clerkship, Robinson was articled to John Macdonell, a successful young barrister only five years older than Robinson. Macdonell belonged to the leading family of Glengarry and was soon to be elected to the assembly from that county.

The last year of peace, 1811, was a year of personal tragedy for Robinson. In January, Dr Stuart died 'with decency and comfort' and left his foster-son grief-stricken. Robinson confided to Dr Strachan the extent of his sorrow: 'The unbounded kindness with which he has always treated me would have compelled me to love him ... I can hardly reconcile to my mind the idea of never seeing him again.'[32] Later in the year Esther, Robinson's sixteen-year-old sister, died. These tragedies were compounded by the international conflict that was about to overwhelm the tiny province.

Shortly before the outbreak of hostilities, Robinson was called upon to perform his first public function as clerk-assistant to the assembly. After the competent performance of his duties, the assembly 'of Blackguards and Gentlemen' voted him an award of fifty pounds. The older generation of loyalists saw in him a capable and enthusiastic standard-bearer for their embattled ideals. His appointment as clerk was connected with the rise in eminence of one of his earliest benefactors, Justice William Dummer Powell. Lieutenant-Governor Gore recognized Powell as a respected individual who had been an integral part of the colonial administration ever since its creation. Powell, also a close friend of Dr Strachan, could now use his influence to have his loyalist protégés appointed to vacant government offices.

Powell's influence flowed from his association with the lieutenant-governor, and this association worked to their mutual advantage. Gore desperately needed competent advisers familiar with Upper Canada's frontier situation. In one instance, after Gore quarrelled with the English-appointed attorney-general, William Firth, Powell exerted his influence and had John Macdonell appointed attorney-general. John Robinson's close personal connection with the powerful clique of Powell, Strachan, and Macdonell assured his availability for appointment to any recent government position, and his selection as clerk-assistant demonstrated that he possessed the confidence of the ruling group.

While cliques were forming to control government office in Upper Canada, international events were about to render those petty struggles inconsequential. The Napoleonic wars caused Britain and the United States to be locked in a bitter dispute over the trade rights of neutrals, and the Royal Navy's impressment of American seamen aroused national resentment in the United States. That resentment was angrily expressed by a militant group of western and southern senators called the 'war hawks,' who sought to strike back at Britain through Upper Canada and to sever permanently the colony from the Crown.

Christopher Robinson had originally fled from his Virginia home in order to establish new roots in a land governed by British institutions. Now even this refuge was threatened by the aggressive republic. The loyalists had sought to erect a new British American nation, loyal to the Crown and confirmed in the British constitution. Whether this vision would persevere was now up to the younger generation of loyalists and, as was always the case in a general conflict between Britain and the United States, the strength and will of the British Army.

2

'This Outpost of England'

For Upper Canada, the American declaration of war on Great Britain on 18 June 1812 signalled the beginning of a desperate struggle for survival. In view of the overwhelming numbers of the American forces, the commander-in-chief, Sir George Prevost, advised the administrator (in Gore's absence) and military commandant of Upper Canada, Isaac Brock, to avoid all offensive action. This seemed appropriate advice, for Brock had a mere 1,600 regular soldiers at his disposal. But Brock was not content to wait. He realized the need for quick thrusts in order to inspire confidence in a largely defeatist population, and he resolved to strike at the earliest opportunity.

In August Brock called out all available militiamen and addressed the assembled soldiers on the Garrison Common in York. Standing in the ranks of the Third York Regiment was a newly commissioned lieutenant, John Beverley Robinson. Brock informed the troops that General Hull had crossed the Detroit River and was occupying the town of Sandwich. Would the Upper Canadians permit the occupation of their country? Brock intended that the company of 40 regular and 260 volunteer soldiers who made up the York militia should join Colonel Henry A. Procter's force of 1,000 regular troops, militias, and Indians at Fort Malden and drive out the invaders.

A substantial majority of Upper Canadians may have doubted that this was possible or even desirable. Nevertheless, on 5 August Brock's attack force set out from York and amassed more volunteers on the march from

Burlington Bay to Long Point. From there, the militiamen travelled by bateaux to Fort Malden. They rowed day and night along the north shore of Lake Erie. When they finally made a bivouac, persistent rain made rest almost impossible. Robinson later recalled the privation of the forced march:

This body of men consisted of farmers, mechanics and gentlemen, who, before that time, had not been accustomed to any exposure unusual with persons of the same description in other countries. They marched on foot, and travelled in boats and vessels, nearly 600 miles in going and returning, in the hottest part of the year, sleeping occasionally on the ground, and frequently drenched with rain; but not a man was left behind in consequence of illness.[1]

Brock had persuaded the Indian leader, Tecumseh, that an attack on Fort Detroit could be successful, and was assured the support of several hundred bellicose Indians. The general had also joined the militia forces to regular units, thereby creating three miniature brigades. In order to make these brigades appear formidable, the regulars were told to give their spare red coats to the militiamen. Thus attired, the men of Upper Canada took on the appearance of the soldiers of the mighty British Army. Shortly before Brock's arrival, Hull had abandoned Sandwich and retreated into Fort Detroit. Seizing the initiative, Brock demanded Detroit's surrender, and on 16 August moved his three brigades and the Indians across the river to attack the fort. After a perfunctory bombardment, General Hull obligingly surrendered his command of over 2,000 troops. Together with an officer of the Forty-first Regiment, Lieutenant-Colonel John Macdonell, Brock's provincial aide-de-camp, and his retainer, Lieutenant Robinson entered Fort Detroit and negotiated the terms of capitulation. As was due his rank, Robinson received ninety pounds in prize money for the capture of the fort and its supplies.

The day following the surrender, Robinson breakfasted with General Brock and Tecumseh. While basking in the aftermath of victory, Robinson encountered his elder brother, Peter, who had arrived overland with a party of militia. Together the brothers escorted their prisoners to the depot at Chippewa. While this first effortless victory may have made the militia confident of ultimate success, such confidence was not warranted by the overall situation. Sir George Prevost, by an ill-advised armistice with the American commander, General Dearborn, had defeated Brock's intention to maintain the initiative by attacking Fort Niagara. This lull enabled the Americans to regroup and prepare to attack somewhere on the frontier. The Third York Regiment, reinforced with new men and regular army officers, was sent to garrison the Niagara frontier at Brown's Point. American troops had been assembling on the Niagara River during the summer and fall of 1812, and their thrust finally came on 13 October near the town of Queenston.

The crash of artillery at Queenston resounding along the Niagara River alerted the British garrisons that the attack would be directed against the centre of the Niagara frontier. The York militia were only a few miles north of the Queenston Heights and, after an initial hesitation, they began a march south to the battle. The regular troops at Fort George had a longer distance to travel, so Brock left his command and raced ahead to take charge of the combat. As he galloped past the militiamen trudging into their first pitched battle, Brock waved encouragement and Godspeed to them. The militiamen expected a decisive battle. As Robinson reported, 'Their spirits were high, and their confidence in the General unbounded.' On 14 October he recorded his impressions of the face of battle, with 'its novelty, its horror and its anxiety ... fresh and perfect in my imagination.'[2]

Lieutenant Robinson arrived in Queenston to see the Heights ablaze with artillery duels and the American forces embarking across the Niagara River toward the Canadian shore. Their crossing was opposed by all available artillery and infantry, and they suffered heavy casualties. Robinson, encouraged by the number of American soldiers already taken prisoner, was shocked by the ghastly wounds inflicted by grapeshot: 'The spectacle struck us, who were unused to such heart-rending scenes, with horror.' The Americans, however, were far from defeated. Their commander, Van Rensselaer, again launched troops across the river in an attempt to create a foothold on the shore; to counter them, Brock ordered his men down from the Heights to oppose the landing. No sooner had these troops left their positions than American soldiers captured the Heights above them. General Brock, after narrowly escaping from the Americans himself, immediately grasped the seriousness of this new situation and made plans to regain the Heights. Gathering about one hundred men of his own regiment, the Forty-ninth, he made one counter-attack against the American position. When this was repulsed, he retired and organized a larger force to attempt to outflank the Americans. That assault almost forced the hard-pressed Americans off the Heights, until a rifleman shot the general at close range. As the men of the Forty-ninth gathered around their fallen leader, the attack faltered and finally fell back.

At the instant of Brock's death, when British fortunes were at their lowest, the York militia arrived in Queenston. In the absence of any senior

British officer, John Macdonell took control of the militiamen and prepared to make a flank attack on the American position. Macdonell had been appointed lieutenant-colonel and aide-de-camp largely because of his knowledge of the province and its people. He had no formal military training, and there was probably no intention that he should succeed to field command. Nevertheless, he assembled fifty militiamen in an attempt to dislodge the Americans who by now were firmly entrenched on the Heights. The American fire proved to be far too intense and, after one fusillade, the Canadians retreated. They bore with them the body of their fatally wounded commander. Robinson bitterly commented that this ill-conceived sally had been 'dictated rather by a fond hope of regaining what had been lost by a desperate effort than by any conviction of its practicability.'

After these attacks and counter-attacks, both sides were forced to pause and regroup. It was only ten o'clock in the morning, and the Americans were in control of the strongest position on the battlefield; fresh reinforcements would certainly have ensured their victory. General Van Rensselaer began to evacuate his dead and wounded back across the Niagara River. The sight so unnerved the militia reserves that they refused to join their comrades on the Heights. While the same exhausted Americans remained on the artillery site, the British forces were replenished with the Forty-first Regiment from Fort George, a brigade of artillery, and a new commander, General Roger Sheaffe. By three o'clock in the afternoon, Sheaffe had sufficiently mustered his forces to resume the offensive. A light company of the Forty-ninth and Robinson's company of militia attacked from the woods. A brigade of Indians and the Niagara Company of Blacks made a flank assault while the regular troops carried out a frontal attack. Robinson described the denouement:

In this manner we rushed through the woods to our encamping ground on the mountain, which the enemy had occupied. The Indians were the first in advance. As soon as they perceived the enemy they uttered their terrific war-whoop, and commenced a most destructive fire, rushing rapidly upon them. Our troops instantly sprang forward from all quarters, joining in the shout.

The Americans stood a few moments, gave two or three general volleys, and then fled by hundreds down the mountain. At that moment, Captain Bullock, with 150 of the 41st and two Militia flank companies, appeared advancing on the road from Chippewa. The consternation of the enemy was complete ...

Three days after the battle, Robinson acted as pallbearer for his former employer and commanding officer, Lieutenant-Colonel Macdonell. The ironies of war again intervened in Robinson's behalf. Sir Roger Sheaffe, who succeeded Brock as the civil and military commander of Upper Canada, appointed Robinson to the position of acting attorney-general, the office that had gone to the unfortunate Macdonell. General Sheaffe may have been impressed with Robinson's display of valour and leadership at Queenston Heights. Robinson's narrative of the battle modestly failed to note that his superior, Captain Heward, was on leave and that Robinson had commanded his flank company during the battle. James Coffin, Sheaffe's aide-de-camp, recalled John Robinson's conduct during the battle. Coffin remembered Robinson as 'a lawyer from Toronto, and not the worse soldier for that,' whose 'light, compact, agile figure, handsome face and eager eye, were long proudly remembered by those who had witnessed his conduct in the field.'[3]

In recognition of his bravery, Robinson was brevetted to the rank of captain, a rank he retained for the duration of he war. He remained at his military post through November and consequently missed an opportunity to be called to the bar that month. Dr Strachan chided his protégé for his tardiness: 'All your friends are astonished that you have not come over to the term in order to be admitted to the Bar.'[4] But Robinson was well aware that in this time of crisis duty took precedence over personal advancement.

Neither Robinson's fidelity nor his battlefield heroics account entirely for Sheaffe's appointment of a twenty-one-year-old clerk to the office of chief prosecutor. General Sheaffe, an intimate friend of Justice Powell, had confidence in Powell's suggestions on the conduct of the civil administration and concurred in his proposal to appoint Robinson acting attorney-general.[5] The appointment did not meet with universal approval. The Boulton family was taken aback by the sudden promotion of their former law clerk. One of the scions of the family, Henry Boulton, then studying in England, wrote to the colonial secretary, putting himself forward as a more suitable candidate.[6] Powell's influence prevailed, however, and Robinson held civil office for the remainder of the war.

Robinson seemed not to regret the return to civilian endeavours. Despite his initial eagerness for battle, he had very little military training and was of more use to the Crown as a legal officer than as a military officer. Although not officially a member of the bar, Robinson's office entitled him to be heard in all criminal cases, and he enlarged his jurisdiction by occasionally acting in civil actions.

A government under siege and troubled by a restive population made great demands on the resources of its civil officers. One of the first problems presented to the acting attorney-general concerned the occupation of the Michigan territory. Brock's proclamation of 16 August 1812 stated that the territory was 'ceded to the arms of His Britannick Majesty.'[7] This declaration made it appear as if the citizens of Michigan had become British subjects. Sheaffe asked the acting attorney-general whether the Michiganders were now liable to bear arms for the Crown. Robinson responded, 'I am of the opinion that they cannot. By the capitulation of the 16th August 1812, Fort Detroit only, with the troops regulars as well as militia, were surrendered to the British forces.'[8] Mere conquest could not turn Americans into British subjects.

The fluctuating frontier and disaffected population presented serious problems to the administration. The Niagara peninsula was a no-man's-land in which American and loyal guerrillas operated at will. It was difficult to tell which citizens were assisting American fighters and which were merely disenchanted with British rule. As early as July 1813 the new administrator, Francis de Rottenburg, had asked the commander-in-chief to give him the authority to establish special tribunals to ensure the summary punishment of apprehended traitors. Not only did these individuals merit punishment, but their trials 'from the Ordinary course of the law' would serve 'to awe the disaffected.'[9] The military obviously considered swift retribution more important than impartial justice. The officers entrusted to enforce these stern measures would eventually have to justify their actions before regular courts, however. Robinson himself characterized his role as that of aiding those 'military officers [who] had to be sustained in the Civil Courts against actions brought by the inhabitants of the country for acts done, not always very discreetly, under the pressure of the public service.'[10] Under the constant threat of foreign occupation, the authorities of an embattled colony came to place great reliance on the Crown law officer in order to sanction activities that were only marginally lawful.

The disaffection of the civilian population and the unwillingness of the assembly to enact war measures exasperated General de Rottenburg. The greatest threat to his forces was the reluctance of purveyors to accept army bills, a form of specie issued by the Lower Canadian government. By August 1813 the supply situation for the Kingston garrison had become critical. In November, de Rottenburg declared partial martial law 'as far as necessary to procuring provision and forages' in the Johnstown and Eastern districts. The assembly angrily denounced this proclamation as 'arbitrary and unconstitutional and contrary to and subversive of the established laws of the land.'[11]

General Sir Gordon Drummond, de Rottenburg's successor, had more success in persuading the assembly to adopt war measures. The supply situation forced him to impose partial martial law in March 1814.[12] One disgruntled farmer, Jacob Empey, decided to challenge the government. In May he sued a commissary clerk, Edward Doyle, for having committed a trespass. Doyle had ordered his men to collect grain from the local farmers and pay them off according to a scale used by the magistrates. While the administration wished to protect its servant Doyle, the lieutenant-governor's secretary asked Robinson whether the Crown should be directly involved in the proceedings.[13] Robinson advised against any such involvement, saying 'The Proclamation [of partial martial law] can be no legal justification to Mr. Doyle.' In his opinion, if the Crown law officer was seen to be defending the indefensible, 'it will be reducing itself to an awkward dilemma, avowedly espousing what it has no right to enforce.'[14] The acting attorney-general believed that if the war was to be successfully prosecuted Crown officers must be able to take harsh but necessary steps. If Empey was successful, he would be followed by many other supposedly aggrieved litigants. Robinson was well aware that Empey's lawyer, Levius Sherwood, had introduced the assembly's motion condemning the partial imposition of martial law; he lamented, 'Men discontented and malignant like Mr. Empey and Mr. Sherwood may be found in many parts of this Province.'[15] Robinson hoped to make a 'silent arrangement' on behalf of Doyle, thereby forestalling an avalanche of litigation and leaving the legality of the martial law proclamation unchallenged.

Drummond, however, insisted that Robinson represent the Crown in defeating the challenge to the King's authority. Patiently, Robinson explained to him that the lieutenant-governor simply could not, without the assembly's approval, dispense with the rule of law.

The King is but one branch of the Legislature, and cannot dispense with the law of the Land. This conviction induces me to say that the Proclamation is no *legal justification* tho' an *equitable defence*, that it cannot be pleaded *in bar to the action* tho' it may be urged in mitigation of damages.[16]

None the less, Robinson was quite prepared to represent Doyle if the action came before the courts. While Robinson had successfully defended other government officers by pleading that the proclamation justified their actions, Sherwood proved far too shrewd to permit such a plea in this case. After the commencement of the proceedings, Sherwood filed a demurrer that questioned whether the proclamation was a defence to a charge of trespass. Robinson managed to postpone the hearing of this motion until the spring of 1815, at which time Sherwood proved his point, the proclamation was declared unconstitutional, and Empey was awarded damages. By then the war was over, and the emergency that had given rise to the proclamation had evaporated. The acting attorney-general's discreet handling of the problem proved that even in the midst of war Upper Canada was a society governed by law. Significantly, his actions merited the approval of the justices of King's Bench. Chief Justice Scott and Justice Powell both petitioned Sir George Prevost to confirm Robinson as attorney-general;[17] but in deference to the imprisoned D'Arcy Boulton, and in view of Robinson's relative youth, the appointment remained temporary.

The war presented unique opportunities to the young loyalists of Upper Canada. Many of them, notably John Robinson and Christopher Hagerman, were able to capitalize on their war records in order to further their civilian ambitions. The adversities of war proved to be a test not only of the young loyalists but of the province itself. The British success in 1812 gave way to American victories in 1813. In April, American forces surprised and overwhelmed the York garrison. Captain Robinson, the company paymaster, along with other militia officers, surrendered the capital to General Dearborn. During this brief enemy occupation, a number of government structures, including the Parliament buildings, were destroyed. Those citizens who were less than loyal took the opportunity to join in the plunder, and republican sympathizers revealed themselves by their open support for Upper Canada's enemies. While the American fleet was still visible in the harbour, the executive council met and reminded the populace 'that it is equally now as before this invasion, high treason to aid, assist, counsel or comfort the enemy.'[18] Later, the council advised General de Rottenburg to station a company of infantry in York to suppress any civil unrest. The officer in charge of the force was to be empowered to arrest 'such persons as may be pointed out to him in writing by some confidential person in the Commission of the peace as justly suspected of any treasonable practice ...'[19]

Justice Powell, a member of the executive council, helped draft this recommendation to de Rottenburg. In a personal letter to the lieutenant-governor, Powell advised him to appoint magistrates to detain suspected traitors. He further assured de Rottenburg that Robinson could carry out any instructions: 'In official intercourse with the acting Attorney General Your Honour must have witnessed qualities of firmness, discretion, and honourable frankness at least equal to expectation in so young a man.'[20]

With Justice Powell in the council, John Robinson would never lack for enthusiastic support. Powell also proposed that Peter Robinson be granted a commission to assist the military. The appointment of special magistrates was considered essential to arrest the considerable degree of co-operation and sympathy for the enemy on the part of American-born residents. Benajah Mallory and Abraham Markle, both former assembly-men, were fighting for their native United States against the colonial government. Another former assemblyman, Joseph Willcocks, organized a company of 'Canadian Volunteers' to harry the frontier. In July 1813 American forces again seized York, although this time Captain Robinson was instrumental in hiding the militia's ordnance stores.

The second invasion created a near panic among the citizens when it became clear that the Americans had been informed that there were government stores in the town. Although the number of disaffected and traitors was probably exaggerated, strong pressure was now placed on de Rottenburg to apprehend all possible spies. The administrator in turn delegated this responsibility to the acting attorney-general, who was instructed to report 'the names of such persons as in the present situation of the country are dangerous to the public security and evidently hostile to our cause.'[21] Robinson had full authority to use military force to apprehend those individuals whose hostility 'to our cause' marked them as subversives.

Robinson doubted the efficacy of these measures, however. Despite the extraordinary nature of the situation, he boldly told the administrator that in his capacity as Crown law officer he would have nothing to do with the enforcement of military law: 'I am not giving any official direction to a step which considered in the abstract, is illegal ...'[22] Robinson could easily have condoned the arbitrary enforcement of martial law, and thereby earned the gratitude of the military and assured the security of the capital. Yet he realized that martial law arbitrarily imposed by the executive without the assembly's consent was a violation of the British constitution, the constitution Robinson and his comrades were fighting to preserve. He warned de Rottenburg that not only would he not assist in the enforcement of martial law but that he was 'obliged to acknowledge its illegality and to say as I now do that measures of the nature contemplated must rest entirely upon the responsibility of Your Honour's military command.'[23]

Moreover, the acting attorney-general took the view that many of the individuals who had been seized by the military and who were currently wasting away in the York jail were probably the victims of private vendettas. Indeed, when Colonel Thomas Talbot, a prominent Upper Canadian and founder of a large settlement in the Western District, asked that one of his settlers be released, Robinson was quite willing to grant his request. Robinson also informed the administrator's secretary, Major Robert Loring, that the jails contained four other men against whom there was not the slightest evidence of treason. 'I have no evidence,' he reported, 'against Sam'l Carson, Noah Force, Luther Cooly, William Carpenter confined here – I know nothing of their character or what grounds those who committed them acted upon.'[24] Rather than recommending the release of these individuals, he merely passed along their petitions. If innocent men were to suffer, the responsibility would lie with the military authorities. Even though he condemned the government's extralegal activities, he was willing to concede that the threat of American domination excused some irregular practices:

The Country must not be lost by too scrupulous attention to forms and when the civil administration of justice is found inadequate to our protection in times perilous and unusual as the present, recourse must be had to measures more efficacious and the necessity *must* and *will* justify their adoption.[25]

While Robinson publicly dissociated himself from the illegal seizure of individuals, he was prepared to work with the military when their actions had the force of law. He assisted the government in the enforcement of the Alien Act by taking part in the selection of commissioners. Rather than rely on prominent local leaders such as assembly members (or 'Knights of the Shire,' as he contemptuously referred to them), the acting attorney-general suggested that the regular magistrates be used to implement the act. Those men, already familiar with court procedures, would give confidence to the people that the Alien Act was being prosecuted within the normal course of the law by responsible officers.[26]

More urgent to the military than the apprehension of suspected traitors was the swift punishment of those already seized in open rebellion against their sovereign. The prompt execution of traitors and the expiation of 'their abominable crime on the altar of justice'[27] would, in the administrator's sanguine opinion, deter any further treasonous activity. Acting on Drummond's instructions, Robinson received informations for treason against a number of persons and eventually preferred indictments against seventy of them. While many of the accused had been seized in a brief skirmish at Nanticoke in the London District, most of the indicted traitors remained safely behind American lines. In December 1813 the administrator's civil secretary, Foster, instructed Robinson to prepare a special commission to hear the trials in the London District. At that time, judges could not hear capital charges without first receiving a 'commission of oyer and terminer and general gaol delivery.' That commission enabled them to prefer indictments and try the issue of the indictment. All three justices of King's Bench and several supernumerary magistrates were granted special commissions to hear the treason trials.

Drummond feared that American sympathies in the western half of the colony would lead to acquittals and, because it was necessary to impress the citizens with the harsh and inevitable consequences of treason, he originally proposed that the trials be held in York itself. In February 1814 the assembly finally suspended habeas corpus and permitted the Crown to try treason cases in any district of Upper Canada.[28] Most of the accused had committed their treasonous offences in the London District. However, the district courthouse on the shores of Lake Erie was at the mercy of the American navy, and Drummond's request that the trials be held within a secure garrison was not unreasonable. But the acting attorney-general disagreed with him and insisted on trying the prisoners at Ancaster in the Niagara District. Ancaster provided a large courtroom relatively safe from enemy interference. Robinson was quick to grasp that a show of justice, as well as a display of force, was essential to retain local sympathies:

It is wished, and very wisely, to overawe the spirit of disaffection in the Province by examples of condign punishment by laws of the Land – Executions of traitors by military power would have some – practically little influence – the people would consider them as arbitrary acts of punishment, but would not acknowledge them as the rational effects of justice.

Now if these offenders are tried out of the proper District by virtue of this Statute it will be said, and perhaps with some appearance of reason, that the law was drafted entirely with a view to try them out of the ordinary course.[29]

These sentiments reveal the underlying philosophy of Robinson's later judicial actions. His concern with 'the rational effects of justice' was pure whiggism, derived from Blackstone's *Commentaries on the Laws of England*. The *Commentaries* constituted the only summation of English legal theory available to a pioneer law clerk such as Robinson. Through the *Commentaries*, the Enlightenment's belief in law as an outgrowth of the social compact between rulers and ruled dominated English constitutional thought. Blackstone's teachings that 'municipal law ... is a rule, not a transient, sudden order from a superior to or concerning a particular person, but something permanent, uniform and universal'[30] denied the validity of arbitrary executive courts, such as the Star Chamber. Blackstone's abhorrence of uncontrolled and vindictive government power remained a guiding principle for Robinson throughout the Ancaster proceedings.

Before commencing the treason trials, Robinson reviewed the facts against each man and carefully marshalled the evidence.[31] Three of the men captured at Nanticoke and a number of other traitors agreed to testify for the Crown. Robinson pressed the judges to clear their schedules and proceed with the treason trials, 'for I shall enjoy very little rest or comfort until these prosecutions are ended.'[32] Robinson's clerk, Henry John Boulton, was dispatched to Ancaster to prepare a courtroom and secure provisions for the court officers.

The acting attorney-general was proceeding with all due dispatch, and he was dismayed to learn of the administrator's displeasure with the slow pace of justice. In Drummond's opinion, 'the Chief object of a Special Commission, namely, that of making an immediate example of those convicted under it appears to have been lost through unavoidable delay.'[33] While the military authorities may have been interested in setting examples, Robinson was duty-bound to render justice. His task was not made easier by the inexperienced staff at Ancaster. In a letter to Major Loring, he wrote, 'you have no idea of the difficulty of carrying on public prosecutions here ... every man stands in his place – like a chess man waiting to be shoved.' Their inertia was more than inconvenient; it could render the entire proceedings void, 'for if anybody commits an error, the effect as regards the prosecutions may be fatal.'[34] This delay and the difficulty in provisioning the court officers led Drummond to suggest postponing the trials. Robinson rushed to assure him that 'the objects contemplated by [the special commissioners] are likely to be no longer delayed.'[35] The justices of King's Bench also wrote to Drummond in support of Robinson's pleas that the trials go on as scheduled.[36] Under this judicial pressure, Drummond acquiesced. On 23 May 1814 nineteen men were arraigned on bills of treason.

After the required pause of ten days, Robinson initiated the proceedings before each of the justices in turn. Although Chief Justice Scott acquitted the first accused for lack of evidence, it soon became clear that the Crown's case against most of the accused was overwhelming. After two weeks of trials, fourteen convictions and one plea of guilty were entered by the court. While the justices condemned all the convicts to death, Drummond stayed execution until he could examine recommendations from Robinson and the chief justice as to whether clemency should be granted.

Robinson recommended clemency for a number of the condemned, the most notable among these being the two Hartwell brothers. The Hartwells were American citizens who had taken the oath of allegiance upon obtaining a land grant in Upper Canada. With the outbreak of war, they returned to the United States, joined the Michigan militia, and were captured at Fort Detroit. There was no question that they were technically guilty of treason and liable to hang. Robinson, however, considered it expedient 'not to strain the law to its utmost rigour.'[37] He even suggested that it might be sufficient to hang one or two of the traitors and banish the rest. After consideration of the two reports, eight of the accused were put to death on 20 July 1814. The remainder, including the Hartwells, were incarcerated for the duration.

While the treason trials later came to be called the 'Bloody Assize,' there is no evidence that Robinson acted in a vindictive fashion. Given his duty as Crown counsel to enforce the law, and the seriousness of the threat that the accused and their at-large compatriots posed to Upper Canada, prosecution was essential and the penalties inevitable. The Ancaster assizes did not endear Robinson to the local gentry, who petitioned the government to pardon most of the condemned. None the less, Robinson's persistent efforts achieved two objectives: his meticulous attention to the proper forms and procedures made it apparent to all that the condemned had not been judged by a harsh or hasty tribunal, and the ultimate outcome of the trials satisfied the military's desire to make examples of those who committed treason. Robinson's capabilities as an administrator and a jurist were duly noted by the administration. Drummond reported to the secretary of state for the colonies, Lord Bathurst, that 'in the arrangement of these prosecutions, the conduct of Mr. Robinson, the Acting Attorney General, has been highly meritorious and praiseworthy.'[38]

The end of the war in December 1814 left Upper Canada intact, although large parts of the Niagara peninsula had been devastated. Some of the changes that resulted from the conflict were less obvious, though their effects were more enduring. During the war, many residents who had pronounced American sympathies abandoned the colony. The raids on Canadian farms had generated considerable bitterness toward Americans. The potentially American character of Upper Canada was effectively stifled by 'purging it of the small minority who were incorrigible republicans and by corralling within the British fold the great majority who were not.'[39] Robinson recognized the role that the war had played in strengthening the British character of the province:

It is scarcely less certain that the war of 1812, which was engaged in by the United States, mainly for the purpose of subjugating the Canadas, has had the effect of binding them, as well as Nova Scotia and New Brunswick, much more strongly to the Crown.[40]

With the coming of peace, young John Robinson was left in a position of considerable authority and influence. For the previous two years he had filled a senior executive role and had acted as a bencher of the Law Society. Moreover, he had had the heady experience of actually participating in government decision-making at the highest colonial levels. In 1814, Robinson was even appearing, on an occasional basis, before the executive council.[41] The lesson that judicial officers could play a significant role in government was not lost on the acting attorney-general. Robinson had achieved this level of influence at the age of twenty-three and before he was properly a member of the Bar. His status was similar to that of a number of clerks who had completed their legal training but, because of war service, had not been called to the bar. By a special statute, all such clerks were admitted to the Law Society of Upper Canada in Hilary Term 1815.[42]

For a colonial lawyer with ability and ambition who aspired to high office, it was essential to be recognized as a barrister by one of the great Inns of Court in London. Robinson's success in handling colonial affairs had added to his confidence and undoubtedly made him dream of becoming an English barrister. He had worked hard and capably during the war and was now 'desiring to see England.' News of the release of Solicitor-General Boulton and Boulton's appointment as attorney-general probably contributed to his decision to leave Upper Canada. The relationship between Boulton and Robinson was not warm. Perhaps this was to be expected in a situation in which the long-absent Boulton had claimed the attorney-generalship from its previous steward.[43]

In order to attend an Inn of Court, Robinson needed a considerable amount of money. He asked Drummond to make him an award of additional fees for his work and disbursements during the Ancaster treason trials.[44] There is no record that this request was granted. But Robinson had another favour to ask, one that gained Drummond's enthusiastic response. In April 1815 Robinson requested a five-year leave of absence in order to pursue his goal of becoming an English barrister. Before leaving the province he asked for a letter of introduction to the new provincial administration so that his claim on the government for war services could be redeemed at a later date.[45] He need have no fear of the Crown neglecting its loyal sons. In return for his services as acting attorney-general, he was granted 1,000 acres and was confirmed in the office of solicitor-general on the understanding that he could draw his salary while he was in England. With this as insurance, Robinson obtained a leave of absence from the temporary lieutenant-governor, Sir Frederick Robinson, the son of Christopher Robinson's old benefactor, Beverley Robinson.

John Robinson's desire to go to England may have been motivated by long-term considerations. He was beginning to discover that influential patrons in Upper Canada did not necessarily guarantee success. In order to have real influence it was also necessary to have imperial support. The leaders of Upper Canada had realized, from the earliest years of the province's existence, that their power could be measured by their ability to influence the Colonial Office. Already factions in York and Kingston were beginning the struggle to control patronage and public office. If these cliques were to be effective, they must have their leadership recognized and confirmed by the imperial government itself. In order to cement their control and give it legitimacy, it was important to establish relations directly with the Colonial Office.

John Robinson put himself forward as the man to establish those relations. While his appointment as acting attorney-general had been the direct result of Powell's influence, his record of prosecutions had demonstrated that he was a young man of rare ability. Now that ability was to be put to the test at the seat of imperial power. In September 1815, with letters of recommendation in hand and the office of colonial solicitor-general as his security, Robinson took ship for England.

3

Gentleman of Lincoln's Inn

In London, as he had in Upper Canada, Robinson attracted influential patrons and allies. Shortly after arriving in England he called on Sir Samuel Shepherd, the solicitor-general. With Shepherd's approval, and with the bond of Sir William Garrow, the attorney-general, Robinson was admitted as a student to Lincoln's Inn Hall. His formal legal training began in November 1815 with a dinner at Lincoln's Inn. Throughout his English narrative[1] Robinson made little reference to time spent at the Inn. This is hardly surprising, given that the four Inns of Court did not teach their articling students any of the intricacies of the law. Students had to attend a number of dinners over a course of years and be in attendance at the law courts and chambers, but no attempt was made to provide them with a formal legal education. Walter Bagehot, the Victorian man of letters, described his training at Lincoln's Inn as consisting principally of a moot or debate given during dinner. A student received part of a problem scrawled on a piece of paper. He then argued for the plaintiff, the defendant, or both. By 1850 the trial case had dwindled down to the everlasting question, 'whether C should have the widow's estate.' Bagehot noted that 'the animated debate had become a mechanical reading of copied bits of paper which it was difficult to read without laughing.'[2] Robinson's own account of his daily activities at Lincoln's Inn is mostly an assessment of the daily menus.[3]

Attendance at the law courts did enable Robinson to evaluate English procedures, however. In November 1815 fresh from the frontier where taverns usually served for courtrooms, he went to the opening of the ancient Westminister Courts:

We found the hall full of gentlemen and ladies and men and women waiting in anxious expectation to see the Judges and Chancellors pass to their respective Courts. The young lawyers, with their wigs and gowns, parading through the hall with a lady on each arm, made rather a grotesque appearance.

Westminster Hall, which was very much a part of London's exciting life, was not well maintained. Robinson was impressed with its size, but

everything about it seems to be tumbling into ruin – the first impression it occasions is melancholy and gloomy, but in the present instance the gay tripping belles and the sly old serjeants with their gowns and full bottom wigs eyeing them.[4]

Robinson also made rather critical appraisals of the English judges. He found Sir William Grant to be a man of calm intelligence who 'decides promptly, without, however, any appearance of haste, and with perfect composure and good temper.' Sir Samuel Romilly also impressed Robinson with his 'respectful and gentlemanlike manner'; but the lord chancellor was all but asleep as an able advocate laboured vainly before him.[5] Robinson noted that the intimidation and mocking of witnesses was common among lawyers and judges: 'The style is to browbeat and insult, and uniformly to question the witnesses' veracity, without respect to his feelings.'[6] He did not think that this achieved any measure of justice and it detracted from the proper decorum of the court. Already Robinson was forming a fixed opinion of the court and its role; for him, the courtroom was a dignified forum in which the judge presided over an orderly inquiry. The proceedings at Westminster Hall left their mark on the young Upper Canadian. As much as he admired English institutions, he determined that frivolity and rowdiness would not be permitted in any courts that might come under his administration.

Robinson did not allow attendance upon the law courts or Lincoln's Inn to interfere with his enjoyment of London. He frequently went to the theatre and the public boxing matches. As a youth he had lain awake at nights picturing London and the 'wonderful sights which are the admiration of the world.'[7] The city lived up to his expectations, and he became a regular spectator at Covent Garden and Drury Lane. It was characteristic of his quiet, subtle personality that he thought the overacting of the great Edmund Kean to be directed to the mob and not to the mind. The young Upper Canadian also found English manners rather strange after his upbringing in the rough straightforwardness of America. He described a typical group of English youths who visited one of the fashionable houses:

The gentlemen drop in, *ad libitum*, with their hat in their hand, or under their arm, as if they should say, 'I am all ready to go off if I don't like you,' and their behaviour speaks this exactly. They saunter, snuff and stare about as if they were all strangers to one another, look at the ladies dresses, and when they have satisfied their curiosity, make a bow and go out again. The tone seems to be a striking and laboured affectation of indifference to everything.[8]

Viewing the boxing matches, a spectacle he considered 'so purely English,' Robinson observed that the 'coachmen, butchers, innkeepers, and gentlemen' who attended the matches 'affect to talk in the genuine slang style.'[9] Gentlemen used these occasions to pretend to be what they were not, and the lower classes were permitted to behave in a manner above their station. None of this conformed to Robinson's idea of how Englishmen should conduct themselves.

One aspect of British life did live up to Robinson's expectations. Very much in contrast to York's assembly, Parliament favourably impressed the young colonial. The decorous speeches in the House of Lords were 'the first specimens of speeches anything in fact like orations, that I have heard.'[10] Prepared to believe the best of English institutions, Robinson found no rustic 'Knights of the Shire' within the confines of Westminster.

Throughout the winter of 1816, Robinson moved easily in English society and renewed his acquaintances with a number of the officials under whom he had worked in Upper Canada. Sir Frederick Robinson, in England for the court-martial of Sir George Prevost, put his cousin in touch with the English Robinsons and introduced him to the permanent under-secretary for war, William Merry. At the Merry household, Robinson became familiar with the under-secretary's niece, 'an exceedingly fine, pretty little girl – a Miss Walker.'[11] Regular visits to the Merry household and Emma Walker soon dominated Robinson's London activities. The Merrys approved of John Robinson and encouraged his familiarity, although his Sunday walks with Emma took place under the protective eye of an elderly relative.

During this time, Robinson continued to see Anne Powell, the daughter of Chief Justice William Dummer Powell. Anne, aided by other young ladies of quality, had embroidered the flag of the Third York Regiment. Lieutenant Robinson had managed to spare time from his military duties to entertain the ladies in the sewing room with his recital of the epic poem, 'Battle of Talavera.' The melodrama of an embattled province defended by its gallant militiamen probably added to Anne's infatuation with one of the regiment's young officers, John Robinson. As Dr Strachan observed, all York knew that Anne Powell was 'distracted after' Robinson.[12] Anne had clearly fallen so in love with him that she managed to follow him to London in 1816. Although it would have been politically fatal for Robinson to have spurned her completely, it is not apparent that he in any way reciprocated or encouraged her affection.

The possibility of a liaison between Robinson and Anne Powell delighted Dr Strachan, and he endeavoured, at a distance, to guide his pupil's fortunes. Soon after Robinson's arrival in England, Strachan warned him that he might have to return to the colony within nine months. Apparently, the lieutenant-governor was not entirely satisfied with D'Arcy Boulton's performance,[13] and might require Robinson to take up his duties as solicitor-general. However, in a few months Strachan was able to reassure his protégé that the issue of his recall had been put to rest;[14] no doubt the doctor had used his good offices on his friend's behalf. Strachan began to urge Robinson to consider seeking a career at the English bar. He advised him to publish an account of the Ancaster assizes as 'state trials.' His ensuing fame, added to his obvious abilities, would undoubtedly result in his being 'better introduced than a Peer's son.' However, if the young barrister insisted on returning to Upper Canada, then 'a tempting offer will be made you, or it will be attempted – viz, to place Mr. Boulton on the Bench and make you Attorney General.'[15]

While Robinson may have been a minor curiosity in London, he was not the only British American in the capital. Henry John Boulton, the Honourable D'Arcy's son, was also touring England and occasionally he and John attended divine services together. No great camaraderie existed between the two young men. When Robinson had a miniature portrait of himself commissioned in 1816, Boulton thought this affectation to be 'unparalleled impudence.'[16] Dr Strachan, never an advocate of Boultons young or old, felt that the 'faults of the Attorney' [D'Arcy Boulton Sr] would soon lead to Robinson's appointment to that office.[17]

Dr Strachan's career was itself in the ascendant. Ever since his forthright defence of the rights of York residents before the American invaders of 1813, he had played an increasingly prominent role in the colony. Not long after the war, in May 1815, he was appointed an honorary member of the executive council; he could now debate and vote in the body that advised the lieutenant-governor. His marriage to a wealthy widow had made him a rich man, and his new office was a further foothold on power. Robinson rejoiced in his mentor's advancement, but remained aware that his pre-eminent patron was still Justice Powell. Powell, the dominant figure in the executive council, was the obvious choice to succeed Thomas Scott as chief justice of Upper Canada. In writing to Powell, Robinson continued to pay homage to his benefactor: 'I must rely, my Dear Sir, upon that friendship which I well remember has put me in a situation to entertain the views I have.'[18]

By this time, Robinson was adding imperial connections to his colonial contacts. Sir Frederick Robinson, in addition to introducing his cousin to the charming Miss Walker, had provided him with a letter of introduction to Lord Bathurst himself. Bathurst, secretary of state for war and the colonies since 1812, was to remain in this office until 1827. A confirmed tory, he shared many of the convictions prevalent among Upper Canada's élite. By January 1815 Bathurst had already instructed the colonial government to refuse land to any American immigrants and to reserve available land for British settlers.[19]

This directive indicated that the Colonial Office would take an increasingly direct role in the administration of the dependencies. Originally added as an afterthought to the secretariat of war in 1801, the Colonial Office had played a subservient role during Britain's struggle against France. With the coming of peace and with a greatly expanded empire, Bathurst had insisted on increasing the staff of the Colonial Office. The Second British Empire had amassed vast new colonies of French, Dutch, and Asiatic cutures. Those colonies were considered to be ill-suited to the representative institutions that had been granted to British America and the West Indies, and their administration must be directed from London. It was up to Bathurst and his under-secretary, Henry Goulburn, to create the bureaucracy to administer these colonies. Through the efforts of the energetic Goulburn, the central machinery was set in motion both to inform Parliament of colonial affairs and to effect imperial policy in the colonies.[20] Colonial authority would be placed in the hands of the governor, who would be controlled from the grey walls of the Colonial Office. Instructions to the governor could be made directly to him or by orders-in-council, and recourse to Parliament could usually be avoided.

John Robinson frequented the corridors of the Colonial Office and soon became familiar with its leading figures. While Bathurst and Goulburn had created an impressive bureaucracy to handle imperial administration, they themselves remained unfamiliar with the exotic peoples and situations that confronted them. Ignorance of colonial life pervaded England, as Robinson discovered when a gentleman asked him whether Canadians 'drove reindeers in [their] sledges.'[21] This was especially galling to Robinson, who considered himself an Englishman who lived in a far-off and often neglected colony. He thrilled to the speeches in Parliament and the 'references to the history of our country.'[22] Passionately, he described his feelings as he stood at the place of the execution of Charles I: merely standing within those dark walls, he wrote, 'has more than once brought tears into my eyes.'[23] Yet his English pride was coloured by his colonial background, and he was forever conscious of the difference in manners, and especially in political outlook, between himself and his imperial counterparts.

Henry Goulburn, for one, showed no great interest in Canadian affairs. Robinson bitterly observed, 'I have discovered on several occasions in conversation in this [Colonial] office the most disgraceful ignorance on the subject of the Canadas.'[24] Robinson's pique might also have been the result of the colonial authorities' reluctance to pay him his regular salary. By October 1816 Robinson had had to ask for three extensions of his leave, and the government had decided arbitrarily to reduce him to half-pay. He protested vigorously and commented acidly on the under-secretary's treatment of him:

I very much doubt whether that tenacious obstinacy shown by *Mr. Undersecretary Goulburn* on this *important* occasion, if evinced by *Mr. Plenipotentiary* Goulburn at Ghent might not have preserved to us Niagara and Mackinac.[25]

The reference to Goulburn's part in drafting the Treaty of Ghent, which ended the War of 1812, reflected a widespread Canadian disenchantment with British policy. The northern and western parts of Michigan, which the British had held throughout the war, were returned to the United States. By this concession, direct access to the western frontier was forever lost to the Upper Canadians. Robinson deplored the Colonial Office's lack of informed opinion and firm resolution. Enlightenment from the proper British Americans was necessary to direct the Colonial Office to the policies that alone could preserve the colony for the Crown.

During his trip to England, Robinson was called upon to act as the provincial executive's unofficial ambassador to the Colonial Office. At the time, a proposal to move the capital of Upper Canada from York to

Kingston was being seriously considered by London. Strachan instructed Robinson on the position of the York executive, which was, naturally enough, opposed to any change.[26] Robinson sent Strachan's note to Lord Bathurst and added his own comments against the proposed move. Making Kingston the capital, Robinson argued, would be interpreted by the Americans as the beginning of a British withdrawal from Upper Canada.[27] Whatever his view of such reasoning, Bathurst accepted this position and York remained the provincial capital. This first success with the Colonial Office laid the foundation for Robinson's later diplomatic service in the cause of Upper Canada.

Despite his acquaintance with Lord Bathurst and the leading English jurists, Robinson seems not to have considered seriously the prospect of staying in England. For the moment he was determined to enjoy Regency society to the fullest, and he participated in the rich social–theatrical milieu that Upper Canada was unable to provide. But London's principal attraction was the Merry residence and Emma Walker. Through the spring of 1816, John and Emma exchanged long, passionate letters. Even when a death in the family prevented him from being received, Emma arranged for a rendezvous on a nearby street corner.[28] By July their relationship had reached a critical stage, and John begged for the opportunity 'of coming to those interesting explanations necessary to our mutual satisfaction.'[29] Emma made it clear that before any proposals were made or accepted, John must declare himself with regard to Anne Powell. 'It is rather an *arduous undertaking* for you,' she wrote, 'and will require penetration to discover her meaning and *nice* consideration *politely* to tell her *yours.*'[30] After this ultimatum, John met with Anne Powell and told her to abandon any hope of marriage with him. When this distasteful duty had been performed, the relationship between John Robinson and Emma Walker blossomed in only a few months into a deep affection. But even Emma's company could not keep him from leaving England in the fall of 1816 to tour the Low Countries and France. Before his departure, his engagement to Emma became public knowledge in both York and London.

The Continental tour of those days encompassed a trip to the Hague, the museums of Antwerp, and the battlefield of Waterloo. One of the most fascinating aspects of Dutch life was the *trekshuyts*, or canal boats. Robinson noted that the cities of the Netherlands were connected by a canal system and that regular boat service made travel and commerce most convenient. This aspect of European life would certainly impress any Upper Canadian who had to cope with the rapids and nonexistent roads of the new world. While in Paris, Robinson joined the locals in paying homage to Louis xviii. Ever a supporter of monarchy, he bared his head and joined in the cries of 'Vive le Roi.' He did notice, however, a singular lack of enthusiasm in the crowd: 'Poor Louis can't feel much elevated by the shouts of this Paris mob.'

Shortly after his return to England, Robinson was confronted by the 'inconsiderable example of a London mob.' With the restoration of peace the Continental demand for English products subsided, and unemployment became widespread. Poor harvests and the protectionist Corn Laws resulted in exorbitantly high prices for bread. While the poor sought work and cheap food, their more articulate spokesmen began to make political demands for a representative Parliament. Agitators such as the pamphleteer Cobbett and 'Orator' Hunt were organizing meetings and petitions in aid of parliamentary reform. Hunt's meeting at the Spa Fields on 15 November 1816 degenerated into a riot. Robinson, as a curious spectator, was on hand for this demonstration and was caught up in the mob that marched on Castlereagh's house and smashed the windows. Robinson did not conceal his disgust: 'I was in the midst of them, and greater cowards I never saw. They were in continual fear of the military, and two dragoons could have put them to flight.'[31]

It is indicative, perhaps, of Robinson's insensitivity that not once in his English narrative did he mention the mass unemployment and near famine that existed in England in 1816. To the contrary, he became even more attached to what he considered to be the ideal social hierarchy of yeomen and aristocrats. Robinson did write to Justice Powell describing the 'horrors of starvation' that the English lower classes were enduring. In his view, however, social unrest was caused by 'despicable declaimers' playing upon the wretchedness of the poor.[32] The distribution of wealth and the hierarchical social structure were not at fault. Yet the Spa Fields riot was more than an isolated incident; it was indicative of the evolution that was sweeping British society and that would eventually transform toryism into the pragmatic conservatism of George Canning and, later, Robert Peel.

The evolution of toryism in the Age of Reform did not come soon enough to influence Robinson greatly. When he visited a reform-oriented debating society in April 1816, he dismissed it as 'a blackguard audience and a set of low factious declaimers.'[33] John Robinson had left Upper Canada with a hearty dislike of 'mobocracy' and republican ways. The Spa Fields incident had served to increase his fear of any idea that threatened the established order. Added to Robinson's hatred of American egalitarianism was a fear of 'declaimers' bringing popular pressure to effect reform. This intransigent toryism, with its disdain of democracy and dogmatic certainty of the right of the few to govern, would later become evident when Robinson and his colleagues struggled against reform movements in Upper Canada.

Leaving behind the turbulent streets of London, Robinson continued his travels with a tour through the English Lake Country and Scotland. After observing a storm over Lake Windermere, he wrote to Emma Walker in a 'poetical fit':

Where hills and dales and meads are seen,
Like Albion's in eternal green,
Say – do'st thou ever rise to cheer
A brighter scene than Windermere?

Before leaving London, John Beverley Robinson and Emma Walker had confirmed their marriage plans. While marriage to the under-secretary's niece was an advantageous union, Robinson's letters confirm his deep and genuine affection for his 'fine, pretty little' Emma. After Robinson made his intentions clear to Anne Powell, Emma began to address him fondly as 'My Dearest Boy.' During John's travels they maintained a lively correspondence.

While in Scotland, Robinson enjoyed the enlightened society of Edinburgh. There he met a number of celebrities, including the poet Thomas Campbell. As usual, Robinson was accepted into their rarefied company; at the end of his stay, Campbell recommended that he visit their friend, the novelist Walter Scott. Robinson made the pilgrimage to Abbotsford and shared a bottle of madeira with the 'great laird.' Scott took Robinson for a walking tour of the grounds, and they exchanged anecdotes concerning their travels. Robinson greatly enjoyed Scott's company and found him 'good humoured and replete with recollections of every kind ...'[34] Both men were romantics with a strong compulsion to preserve traditional hierarchical structures. Scott, like Robinson, ignored the misery of the countryside and, on hearing of the Spa Fields riot, expressed views similar to Robinson's.[35] Although Scott invited him to remain a while longer, Robinson returned to London.

Not all the news in the capital was favourable. Justice Powell, who had ventured to London in pursuit of the chief justiceship, had heard of Robinson's engagement to Emma Walker in the summer of 1816. When Dr Strachan learned of this romantic commitment, he wrote Robinson a stern note, reminding him of the desirable match he had spurned. With considerable annoyance, Strachan grilled Robinson on his London activities:

The Judge [Powell] surprised me with intelligence that you were going to be married to an English Lady, and appeared much surprised to learn that I knew nothing of it before. ... I want to ascertain if you were under any engagements, directly or indirectly to Miss P.[36]

Strachan's concern to amend Robinson's relationship with Justice Powell went beyond merely patching up a quarrel between parishioners. Had Robinson antagonized Powell, he might have forfeited his chances of advancement. Strachan reminded Robinson that Powell was a powerful figure who had 'given himself up for some time past as much to your affairs as to his own,' and urged Robinson to repair his relations with the justice as soon as possible. Robinson wrote a conciliatory letter to Powell in which he explained that he had never entertained any hopes of marrying his daughter.[37] The Powell family seemed not to resent Robinson's marriage, and upon his return to York Mrs Powell referred to him as 'a young man of uncommonly good talents.'[38]

Despite the fact that he was unable to stay in England long enough to be called to the bar, Robinson's trip resulted in impressive achievements. He had succeeded in establishing relations with a number of colonial officials who would be of use to him. His memorandum to Lord Bathurst concerning the moving of the provincial capital had served to introduce him to that powerful figure, and his able advocacy substantiated the favourable reports the colonial secretary had received. Moreover, he was now a known quantity to the officials who determined colonial policy; henceforth his correspondence from York could be used by them as reports from a capable and trustworthy source.

On 5 June 1817 John Robinson married Emma Walker in the New Church of St Marylebone in London. Robinson apparently had no intentions of practising law before the English bar. In the fall of 1817, several terms before he had completed his articling and before he could properly be called to the bar, he returned to Upper Canada to claim his position as solicitor-general.

4

Public Life

Soon after his arrival in York in November 1817, John Robinson purchased the pre-war residence of D'Arcy Boulton and renamed it Beverley House, a somewhat pretentious name for little more than a stone cottage. In the coming years, however, Robinson would construct a west wing on the house and erect a veranda and stables, transforming Beverley House into a mansion and one of the social centres of little York.[1] Enlargement of the house was all the more necessary since within a year of the couple's arrival in Upper Canada their first child, James Lukin, was born.

Robinson was bursting with enthusiasm after his experiences as a student at Lincoln's Inn. Within days of his return, he began to discuss measures to find a permanent home for the Law Society.[2] It was not fitting that the benchers should be reduced to meeting in whatever chambers were available. A new structure would enhance the prestige and add to the respectability of the struggling legal profession. Early in 1818, Robinson was elected treasurer of the Law Society. As the formal head of the society, he could now effectively convey his enthusiasm for a permanent edifice to the rest of the membership.

The ambitious solicitor-general was also dissatisfied with his minor role in the judicial establishment. Before Robinson left England, William Merry had advised him of efforts that were being made on his behalf to remedy that situation.[3] Powell's appointment to the chief justiceship had created a vacancy in King's Bench, and D'Arcy Boulton Sr hastily put himself forward as the most appropriate candidate to fill it. Lord Bathurst had delegated to Francis Gore the task of appointing judicial officers. Gore, a friend of both Merry and Robinson, was willing to approve Boulton's promotion as long as Robinson became attorney-general and Henry John Boulton solicitor-general.[4] Somewhat tactlessly, the elder Boulton had informed the Colonial Office that he would accept the advancement to King's Bench only on the condition that young Henry was appointed solicitor-general.[4] Bathurst was not used to being dictated to by colonials, and he told Gore that the appointments he made would have no conditions attached.[5]

Gore himself was exasperated by Boulton's insistence on Henry's advancement, and he told William Merry that he was even prepared to recommend appointing John Robinson to King's Bench.[6] There was little chance of this coup, however, given D'Arcy Boulton's seniority and Robinson's youth. Merry advised Robinson that the attorney-generalship was within his grasp, if only 'you exert yourself at the bar, perhaps make a little money.' Elevation to the bench would not be far behind; Robinson's friends at the Colonial Office would see to that: 'There [is] no need to apprehend that you would be superseded.'[7]

The manipulations to which Merry alluded eventually succeeded, and in February 1818 D'Arcy Boulton finally dropped his insistence on Henry's promotion and was elevated to the bench. John Robinson succeeded him as attorney-general of Upper Canada. The personal power struggle between Henry John Boulton and John Robinson ended with Robinson gaining Bathurst's favour and the attorney-generalship, while Boulton was left to languish in private practice. According to Dr Strachan's master strategy, Boulton, another of his former pupils, should have moved into the solicitor-general's office. Never willing to accept defeat, Strachan immediately began to marshal support behind his protégé. He informed his collaborator, Francis Gore, that

Mr. John Robinson writes me that the failure of the arrangement respecting Mr. Boulton was owing to the Condition that Henry should succeed him as Solicitor General. At this job as it appeared to be Lord Bathurst took fire. But it is whispered in the office that were your Excellency inclined an arrangement may take place without this.[8]

With this covert assistance, Lord Bathurst's fire was banked and Henry Boulton was finally appointed solicitor-general in September 1819. These machinations illustrate the ability of the province's leaders to manipulate even the Colonial Office in order to secure positions of authority. The control of public offices with the ultimate goal of private gain (or 'jobbing,' as Dr Strachan accurately described it) resulted in John Beverley Robinson's being prominently established in York society and in possession of an enviable appointment at the age of twenty-seven.

In those days the office of attorney-general was not a ministerial position. The attorney-general was the king's attorney and represented the Crown's interest before the courts. As chief judicial officer, he exercised his discretion in the conduct of public prosecutions. He was free to maintain his own private law practice to supplement his stipend. In Britain, because of the fear of legal sanctions being used for partisan purposes, the attorney-general was not permitted to sit in the Cabinet. In Upper Canada, the attorney-general assumed a number of executive responsibilities, such as reviewing the final version of colonial legislation before it was signed by the lieutenant-governor and transmitted to England. From his advisory duties grew the attorney-general's role as confidant to the lieutenant-governor. During his tenure Robinson commented on criminal sentences, Crown conveyances, and the rights of the clergy.[9] Robinson's cautious and sound advice soon earned him the confidence of the lieutenant-governor. But the trust of the Crown's representative did not in itself explain the prestige that accrued to the office. The leading source of the attorney-general's importance arose from his pre-eminence as government spokesman in the assembly.

Ever since Simcoe had entrusted his attorney-general, John White, with conducting government bills through the assembly, the attorney-generalship had been a significant political position.[10] Overshadowing the less educated members, the attorney-general introduced measures which the chamber knew had the approbation of the lieutenant-governor. Almost invariably during the 1820s and 1830s, the attorney-general sat in the assembly as the de facto government leader. Though he was not an executive councillor, the attorney-general regularly advised the lieutenant-governor and saw that his projects received the necessary legislative approvals. No executive councillor combined these advisory and legislative functions. It was not surprising, therefore, that the attorney-general was called on to represent the province in London, making him, in effect, the principal officer of the Crown in the province. The prominence of the office was even more apparent when it was occupied by as capable and energetic an individual as John Robinson.

Robinson's prospects were bright, but he had returned to a province mired in depression. Army bills were no longer being issued, and consequently there was not enough currency in circulation. Most of the British regulars had been withdrawn, and their absence as major consumers of Canadian produce contributed to the economic malaise. Moreover, the colonial secretary was reluctant to provide compensation for war losses; Bathurst advised the colonial government to pay war claims from the confiscated estates of traitors, which were not adequate to satisfy the claims.

The chief cause of post-war controversy was Lord Bathurst's directive of January 1815, which was intended to stop the granting of land to Americans. The Colonial Office and the provincial government agreed that one of the great difficulties in the prosecution of the war had been the presence of so many American settlers in the colony. Bathurst's dispatch did not specifically empower the lieutenant-governor to take any measures to prevent the influx of Americans. Francis Gore, who had returned to the province after a wartime absence, interpreted it as enabling him to order commissioners to refuse to administer the oath of allegiance to recently arrived Americans. British immigration was negligible, and Gore's policy restricted the number of new settlers entering the province, worsening the economic lassitude. The large landowners protested that the policy retarded the growth of the province. One of those land barons, William Dickson, was a prominent political figure and a legislative councillor. Dickson, who depended on a steady influx of Americans to buy his land, simply ignored Gore's instructions, and continued to use his commissioner's authority to administer the oath to those Americans who wished to buy land from him.[11]

Despite its economic difficulties, the province remained politically tranquil for a brief period after the war. However, the election of 1816 revealed a growing popular discontent with the government's land policies. One member, Robert Nichol, a former quartermaster-general of militia and a representative of the unrewarded veterans, called the assembly into committee of the whole to discuss the state of the province. In the ensuing debate, the government was condemned for permitting valuable land to lie fallow in clergy reserves and refusing to sell land to American settlers. Another resolution noted that the statute under which Americans were first encouraged to come into the province was still in force and that the government had no right arbitrarily to suppress their entry. Nichol's resolutions were supported by a substantial majority of the members, and it began to appear as if the assembly would question the legality of the government's land policies before the Crown itself. Faced with this threat, Lieutenant-Governor Gore hastily prorogued the assembly and wrote to the Colonial Office seeking confirmation of his policies. If the policy of excluding Americans was not maintained, then, in Gore's opinion, 'the next declaration of Hostilities by America, will be received by Acclamation, and the Loyal population of the Colony, will be reduced to defend themselves from the disloyal.'[12]

In his reply, Bathurst chastised the provincial executive for having ordered commissioners to refuse to administer the oath of allegiance.[13] The commissioners had no discretion in the matter; they had to permit qualified Americans to swear allegiance. Bathurst also reminded the assembly that the mere taking of the oath did not entitle Americans to hold land. A statute of 1740 was still in effect, which prohibited any alien with less than seven years' residence under the Crown from owning land. This revelation cast doubt on the legitimacy of virtually all of the land transactions that had occurred in Upper Canada. An apprehensive executive council asked the attorney-general to give his opinion on how the government could comply with Bathurst's instructions without precipitating a rebellion.

In April 1818, after only two months as attorney-general, Robinson was called upon to draft a proclamation to conform to Bathurst's instructions. In giving his opinion to the executive council, Robinson knew that the proclamation would create a 'great sensation' in the colony.[14] But his analysis of the problem revealed that it was hardly as straightforward as Bathurst had concluded. Prior to 1783, the year in which Britain formally severed the American colonies from the Crown, all inhabitants of America were British subjects. If severance meant that those inhabitants were no longer British subjects when they entered Upper Canada, then they must necessarily be naturalized by the act of 1740. Did this mean that the loyalists, many of whom had come to British America after 1783, had forfeited their rights as British subjects? But if Americans born before 1783 were still British subjects, then a 'monstrous absurdity' presented itself. Many of the residents of the United States – indeed, many of the soldiers who had invaded Upper Canada in 1812 – were by this definition subjects of the Crown. And what of the Americans born after 1783 who had settled in Upper Canada? Many of them had served in the militia during the war, and were under the impression that they were British subjects. Were they now to be deprived of their lands and rights because they had not been properly naturalized under the act of 1740?

The issue was enormously complex, and the attorney-general readily admitted that no simple solution existed. If Americans arriving in Upper Canada after the war had to be naturalized after seven years' residence, it was obvious that those who had arrived in the province before the war were under the same obligation. Moreover, if those individuals had been granted or transferred land, the transactions were void. A sizeable proportion of Upper Canadians stood to be dispossessed of their lands. In Robinson's opinion, the question of allegiance was 'not fit, I humbly conceive, to be decided in a Colony' and could only be resolved by the mother country. He wisely urged the executive council to put off any decision until the Colonial Office issued a definitive judgment. The council agreed. Unfortunately, the Crown law officers dallied over the issue and failed to take any remedial measures. The inability of the Colonial Office clerks to recognize the 'great sensation' would have tragic consequences for Robinson and the provincial administration in the 1820s.

The land speculators' dissatisfaction with the government policy of keeping Americans out of the province had raised a crucial question. The civil and property rights of all American settlers were now in serious jeopardy. The fuse on the alien question had been lit; although the issue was set aside for the moment, it would blaze across political debate in the coming decade. The question of the status of American settlers would prove to be a momentous one, not only because it affected the lands and rights of so many Upper Canadians but because it became the means of uniting a reform movement against the colonial oligarchy.

Almost immediately after the young attorney-general had explored the depths of the alien problem, he was plunged into one of the great public trials in Canadian history. Although he had not practised law since 1815, he would need all his skills as an advocate for the litigation concerning the Earl of Selkirk and the Red River massacre.

In 1811 the Earl of Selkirk had obtained title to the vast Red River territory, where he established a colony of highland crofters. The earl was an important figure in the Hudson's Bay Company, and his settlement soon came into conflict with the rival North West Company. The Nor'westers, as they were called, had based their prosperity on the fur trade, and the agricultural settlement of the northwest threatened their survival. When Selkirk's governor, Miles Macdonell, issued a proclamation forbidding the removal from the settlement of pemmican, the dry food used by the trappers on their journeys, the Nor'westers feared that their trading empire was threatened. They considered the pemmican embargo the opening shot in a war for the fur trade. Throughout 1815, the settlement was subjected to harassment from the trappers. Settlers were killed or injured in clashes, and most of them eventually gave up and accepted the North West Company's offer of resettlement in Upper Canada.

Undaunted, another of Selkirk's agents, Colin Robertson, reorganized the settlement, and governor Robert Semple led a new band of Highlanders to the northwest. Robertson obtained documents that indicated that the Nor'westers planned another assault; against Robertson's advice, the settlers seized the North West Company's post at Pembina. This provocation, and the burning of a Nor'wester fort, caused the company's trappers to prepare for war. One war party converged on the settlement and confronted Governor Semple and his settlers outside their fort. Tempers on both sides were on edge, and violence broke out. In the ensuing skirmish twenty settlers, including Semple, were killed, and once again the settlement at Red River was razed. The Nor'westers had successfully cleared their lines for trade, and Selkirk's innocent settlers had paid with their lives for this convenience.[15]

While the North West officers toasted their triumphs at their Fort William headquarters, Selkirk was making his way up the Great Lakes to visit his colony. He had arrived in Sault Ste Marie when he learned of the massacre; he immediately resolved to seize Fort William and exercise his authority as a justice of the peace to collect evidence for later use against the Nor'westers. He invited two local magistrates to accompany him, but they declined. On his arrival in Fort William, Selkirk learned the details of the massacre. He then had William McGillivray and several other North West Company officers arrested for treason and conspiracy. Selkirk conducted a formal enquiry and seized all the available official papers. The Nor'westers attempted to detain him in Fort William by having a warrant issued for his arrest. The warrant, for the illegal seizure of Fort William, had been refused by Chief Justice Powell and Justice Campbell; it was finally signed by a frontier magistrate of dubious reputation, Dr Mitchell. Selkirk refused to recognize the warrant, and on the basis of this refusal was indicted on criminal charges in Upper Canada.

John Robinson had heard details of these events while he was in England. In a memorandum written in December 1816, he noted that 'Gov. Gore has lately put up a sheriff with orders to bring down Lord Selkirk by fair or foul means – I don't understand all this, but if the matter is to be decided in Upper Canada, I shall probably know more about it in time.'[16] In fact, he was to receive his indoctrination into the North West dispute while still in England. Dr Strachan, by his marriage to the widow of Andrew McGill, had acquired a substantial financial interest in the

North West Company. Strachan had already stated the establishment's view that the Red River Colony was a frivolous venture undoubtedly doomed to failure, and that all immigration should be directed instead to Upper Canada.[17] While Robinson was still in London, the doctor was already shaping his pupil's judgment as to the liability for the disturbances in the northwest:

The crimes committed in the Indian Territory can only be tried in Lower Canada, and there you ought to send the Prisoners. Peter Robinson will explain the transactions on both sides. There should be no Magistrate in the Indian country who is a trader there or wishes to establish settlements. Your good sense will direct you, but I thought a hint on the subject the duty of one who has so often thought for your advantage.[18]

The York establishment held the fixed idea that once British America was denied access to the American midwest, there was no further room for westward expansion.[19] Selkirk's settlement, they felt, was therefore only a sham to mask his plans to destroy the Nor'westers. While Strachan's prejudgment of the issue set the tone for later proceedings, Selkirk was assured by his own lawyer that Robinson was a man of 'strict probity.' In a letter to Selkirk, Robinson reassured him:

I can only say, what I trust is scarcely necessary, that I will on this, as on other occasions, do my duty to the Crown in the prosecution of the offenders, as well as I may be enabled from the means of preparation placed within my reach, without any consideration of any interests but those of public justice.[20]

Selkirk was left to ponder one disquieting factor: Robinson, who had been approached in London by North West Company agents, had accepted a retainer to be their counsel in civil matters.[21] Despite the fact that he had returned the retainer when it became apparent that he would have to prosecute some North West employees, Selkirk's attorney warned him that '[Robinson] would no doubt find it difficult to divest himself of his first impressions as to the innocence of his present clients.'[22] The company had influential friends not only in the Canadas but within the heart of the British administration itself. Besides Robinson, Henry Goulburn was also a London agent for the Nor'westers. Whatever their moral failings, the officers of the North West Company attracted powerful advocates.

Apparently, the colonial secretary, Lord Bathurst, viewed the Red River disaster as yet another incident in the trade war, for when Selkirk resisted a magistrate's warrant Bathurst stormed, 'Lord Selkirk has rendered himself doubly amenable to the laws ... the determination of the government to enforce the law with respect to all, and more particularly with respect to Lord Selkirk, should be effectually and speedily evinced.'[23] The founder of the Red River Colony was about to find himself the primary object of prosecution, while the killers of settlers became only secondary villains. The charges of resistance to arrest had been filed against Selkirk in the Western District, and Selkirk and his attorneys travelled to Sandwich, the district town, to answer the charges of the Nor'westers.

Robinson had spent the summer of 1818 in preparation for the proceedings, aided by the report of a royal commissioner, W.B. Coltman, on the North West dispute. Robinson also had the counsel of a number of North West officers eager to precipitate Lord Selkirk's downfall. Principal among these men was Simon McGillivray, William's brother and the North West agent in London. The Sandwich proceedings called for a grand jury of between eleven and twenty-three men to hear the prosecutor's evidence and decide whether or not to present a true bill against the accused and refer the charge to a petit jury for trial. If the evidence was insufficient, the indictment would be quashed and no further proceedings taken. The attorney-general was to present evidence of several charges, including Selkirk's refusal to heed Dr Mitchell's warrant. In addition, Robinson cryptically warned Selkirk that he would have to face charges for 'various acts of injustice and oppression' committed by him at Fort William.

By September, the time of the grand jury sittings, the entire Western District was alive with excitement over the issue. Selkirk's attorneys protested that two of the grand jurors were North West agents. The presiding judge, Chief Justice Powell, a former friend of Selkirk's, overruled the objections and permitted the two men to remain on the jury. Surely, reasoned the chief justice, they would withdraw from the jury 'if they thought [it] proper.'[24] Robinson laid the charge of resistance to arrest; the grand jury, whose frontier sentiments seem to have been with the earl, quashed the indictment after only a brief deliberation. Robinson then postponed the remaining charge and preferred what he hoped would be a crushing indictment.

Selkirk now stood accused of various acts of 'injury and oppression' in a conspiracy to destroy the fur trade of his rivals. Powell had advised Robinson against preferring the new charge, and had urged him to proceed with the existing ones. Conspiracy was, after all, a difficult offence to establish. Robinson, however, had almost forty Nor'westers willing to substantiate the charge and he was confident that the grand jury would accept it. Before the attorney-general began his statement, Powell counselled the grand jurors on the nature of conspiracy. Powell later confessed that his reference to 'overt acts' and 'circumstances without direct proof' confused the grand jury. Robinson did not simplify matters when he suggested that Simon McGillivray introduce evidence for the Crown. The jurors, forewarned that McGillivray was one of the active participants in the North West dispute, refused to have him as an expert examiner. While it was not unheard of for a prosecutor to employ a special examiner to assist him in reviewing complicated evidence, Robinson's introduction of McGillivray seems to have convinced the grand jury that the Crown prosecution was anything but objective. They insisted that Robinson himself conduct the prosecution, and the chief justice concurred.

For three days, Robinson was confined with the grand jury, tediously explaining evidence and examining witnesses. On the second day, Lord Selkirk appeared in court and approached the bench. He demanded to know why Nor'westers were allowed on the grand jury and why Robinson was able to closet himself with the jurors and poison their minds. Robinson was called into the courtroom, and there followed an angry exchange between the attorney-general and the peer.

Perhaps in response to Selkirk's outburst, Powell permitted other irregularities to take place. Although it was not the proper procedure before a grand jury, Selkirk's attorneys presented defence evidence. The introduction of this material probably resulted in the grand jury becoming hopelessly confused, for they could neither find nor dismiss the charge. On the following Monday, the chief justice asked whether they would be able to find a true bill. The grand jury refused to reply, and the puzzled Powell concluded that the jury was stalemated. He adjourned the court and left the conspiracy indictment in limbo.

The young attorney-general had hardly given a convincing performance. After months of preparation and after amassing reams of evidence, he had failed even to get a charge laid by the grand jury. Yet he remained sure of the rightness of his position. It was indicative of Robinson's personality that he chose to pursue the conspiracy charges even after he reviewed the gruesome evidence of the massacre at Seven Oaks. When Selkirk's attorney asked Robinson to lay perjury charges against the men who had filed the rejected warrant, the attorney-general refused on the ground that the evidence against the men was tenuous; he would not single them out for 'a mistake of the laws, which, in my opinion, is general throughout this unfortunate contest.'[25] Perhaps subconsciously the attorney-general was expressing his concurrence with the Colonial Office's view that all the crimes committed in the northwest – the seizure of pemmican, the massacre of settlers, and the arrest of Nor'westers – were part of a continuous chain of offences. This bland equanimity brought an angry retort from Selkirk's physician, John Allan:

It was probably by an equal mistake of the law, though of another kind, that the houses of the Colonists with the Schooner at Red River, were burned; that Governor Semple and twenty others were put to death; and that nearly two hundred men, women and children, were driven to encounter the horrors of famine in a desert.[26]

Robinson was somewhat taken aback by the tone of these remarks, which he considered to be 'the first thing resembling an insult ... which I had received in six years professional duty.'[27] He immediately sensed a personal attack and revealed his inability to accept that parties on the opposite side of a lawsuit passionately believed in the validity of their cause.

There was little doubt that the correspondence with Allan and the shouting match in Sandwich had increased the antipathy between the attorney-general and the earl's faction. Selkirk had no expectation of seeing the Nor'westers successfully prosecuted. The venue of the proceedings was changed to York, where two of the trappers who were implicated in the massacre were under charge of murder. Robinson had little confidence that he could persevere in these prosecutions, and even Selkirk's attorney, Samuel Gale, advised him to drop some of the charges. When Robinson asked Gale to put this request in writing, he declined to do so and Robinson proceeded on all charges.[28] Selkirk later charged that Robinson conducted the proceedings without consulting his lawyers or permitting them to take part in the trial. The inaccuracy of this charge was proved by Robinson's working with Gale to arrange the evidence.[29] Gale was unable to take part in the proceedings because he was not a member of the bar of Upper Canada, not because of Robinson's preferences.

On 26 October 1818 the trial of Brown and Boucher for the murder of the Red River settlers began in York. The tough, lined faces of the trappers were an unfamiliar sight in the court of King's Bench, and were very much in contrast to the refined visage of the attorney-general. Robinson's high forehead and fine features marked him as one of the handsomest men in

York and his suave manners placed him above his rougher colleagues. Described as 'very erect and of medium stature'[30] Robinson was not physically imposing, but his aristocratic features were 'decidedly prepossessing' in the courtroom.[31] With the Crown's authority to add weight to his words, he announced before Chief Justice Powell, 'I am ready, My Lord, I take the charge of murder against Boucher and Brown ... The charge which I now propose to try them on is for the murder of Governor Semple.'[32] The flow of Robinson's presentation was suddenly interrupted as one of the defence counsel, Samuel Sherwood, interjected a motion to grant bail. This tactic of obscuring the Crown's case was developed as a continuing ploy by the North West attorneys. Opposing Robinson were some of the most able counsel in the Canadas, including Levius and Samuel Sherwood and Dr W.W. Baldwin. The presence of these senior counsel arrayed against the relatively inexperienced attorney-general was an unfavourable omen for the prosecution.

Robinson opened the Crown's case by detailing the events leading up to the massacre. He noted that the settlers had fired only one accidental shot long before the parties confronted one another. While courtroom observers may have been impressed with the attorney-general's eloquence, counsel for the defence were not swayed. Sherwood condemned Robinson's presentation of the facts, particularly his reference to Robert Semple as governor. Sherwood laboured the point that Semple held no official position and was simply another British subject. Already attention was being drawn away from the details of the killings to subsidiary questions. Nevertheless, Robinson pressed on with his prosecution, examining eyewitnesses to the massacre and eliciting their dramatic recollection of the slaughter of the settlers. Sherwood's clever cross-examination discredited their testimony and substituted another version of these events. Sherwood could usually find something in the past characters of the witnesses, who were trappers themselves, to detract from their credibility. Moreover, his questions began to show the massacre as an inevitable result of the fur-trade war. Overriding Robinson's objections, Sherwood revealed the defence's case: the massacre at Seven Oaks was only a 'great riot,' not murder. He referred the chief justice to the common law of early England when, during the time of Edward I, feuding earls killed their opponents' supporters in private wars. These acts were not individual murders; rather, they were misdemeanours, committed in a general pattern of uprisings and disturbances. Robinson's objections became less frequent as Sherwood developed and substantiated this remarkable line of defence.

While confidence in the defence's case grew, the Crown prosecutor was hard-pressed even to establish that the Nor'westers had fired the first shots. Even the attorney-general seemed to fall under Sherwood's spell. When Robinson attempted an occasional interjection, Powell consistently overrode his objections. Samuel Gale knew that Robinson was the chief justice's protégé and acidly commented on his perfunctory objections: 'It is by such tricks that appearances are to be saved.'[33]

On the second day of the trial, Robinson presented his most persuasive evidence. He summoned two witnesses who attested both to the brutal killing of helpless and wounded settlers and to the fact that the killers were acting under the instructions of North West Company officers. Despite this damning testimony, the defendants' guilt was not proved beyond a reasonable doubt and defence witnesses succeeded in shattering Robinson's case. They testified that Brown had not even been at Seven Oaks and that Boucher had taken no part in the killings. Both of the accused were acquitted.

Yet the prosecution of the earl did not cease. In the spring of 1819, Robinson acted as counsel for two Nor'westers who brought civil actions against Selkirk for false imprisonment. The earl was again indicted on the conspiracy charge, this time in York where a true bill could be more readily obtained. The additional charges could have little effect on Selkirk, for by 1819 he was a worn and broken man. He abandoned his emigration schemes and was residing quietly in France at the time of his death in 1820.

Before leaving the province, the earl sent Lieutenant-Governor Gore an angry letter condemning the judicial system and particularly the judicial officers of Upper Canada.[34] Robinson hastily drafted a reply to this slur on his character. After explaining his account of the proceedings, he added his opinion as to the main cause of the dispute:

A mature consideration of the evidence before me left no doubt in my mind, that the proper mode of proceeding upon it was to consider all the violences and wrongs it stated, as proofs of a combination or conspiracy in the Earl of Selkirk and his followers, to injure the trade of a rival company, by open violation of the liberty and property of its members, and by an oppressive perversion of legal power and authority to interested ends.[35]

Indeed, on the face of it there is good evidence that Robinson prosecuted Selkirk with considerable intensity while making only a half-hearted effort to convict the Nor'westers. Why, in Robinson's 'mature consideration,' was the Earl of Selkirk so liable for the seizure of Fort William, while the Nor'westers, who murdered innocent settlers and then sent their booty to Fort William, were comparatively blameless? The accusation of partiality against Robinson is not easily answered or even explained in the light of his usually high ethical standards. Perhaps the answer lies in the influence the North West Company exercised over Robinson. From his first contact with North West agents in London and in conversations with Dr Strachan Robinson had been exposed to the North West Company's version of events. Moreover, his conduct of the proceedings indicated that by and large he accepted that version, as did many other Upper Canadians. It is also important to note that his prosecution of Selkirk was a direct order from the colonial secretary and had to be undertaken with all appropriate zeal. While these factors can perhaps explain Robinson's behaviour, they hardly constitute an excuse for his apparent lapse in objectivity.

The reason for Robinson's unusually partial conduct may be found in his later recollections of these events. Writing in 1854, he reiterated his belief in every item in his charge of conspiracy against Lord Selkirk:

On a view of the whole immense mass of evidence, it appeared to me to be obviously the proper course, instead of indicting, as Lord Selkirk desired me, for murder and larceny and arson, to look upon all that had been done by his Lordship and his associates, in a high-handed contest of this nature, as so many efforts on their part to ruin their opponents, by possessing themselves of their effects and supplanting them in their trade.[36]

It remained Robinson's honest conviction that Selkirk was guilty of the charge of conspiracy. This honesty was apparently obvious to all, for even after the Sandwich proceedings, Selkirk asked Robinson to defend him against civil charges. Robinson refused to do so only because he had been retained by the plaintiffs.[37] While Selkirk may have been the victim of a partial prosecution, he certainly considered the attorney-general to be an upright adversary, one he would employ if ever the opportunity arose.

Even though Robinson believed that Selkirk was the principal offender, his belief was not the result of a mature analysis of competing interests, which would have been the mark of an experienced advocate. Nor was his prosecution of Selkirk any more effective than his prosecution of the Nor'westers. Instead of prosecuting Selkirk on existing charges, Robinson, against the advice of the chief justice, launched into the murky depths of conspiracy. Powell had also observed Robinson's failings, his inability to display 'that dispassionate tone which is so desirable in his station … His expression is too warm & he gives offence.'[38]

It was obvious that John Beverley Robinson was not a born advocate.

Despite his intensive preparations, he suffered from a painful shyness and an unwillingness to force his viewpoint. In his first actions before the bar, Robinson admitted that he was so nervous that he never saw any of the jurymen.[39] The pressure of conducting public prosecutions eventually resulted in his attaining pre-eminence in the courtroom, however. As later events proved, Robinson also became a forceful advocate of his own opinions.

The Selkirk trials brought Robinson to the attention of the Colonial Office once again. In the opinion of the colonial secretary, Robinson was achieving note as a responsible lieutenant whose 'temper and judgment' could well serve imperial interests.[40] Despite the embarrassments that had been part of the Selkirk proceedings, the trials had brought John Robinson a step closer to prominence in the provincial administration.

No aspirant to leadership in Upper Canada could attain power without first enjoying the confidence of the lieutenant-governor. The latest holder of that office, Sir Peregrine Maitland, arrived in York in August 1818. Maitland was a distinguished general and a veteran of the Peninsular War and Waterloo. Of Scottish descent and tory persuasions, he had become the head of the Upper Canadian government largely through the influence of his father-in-law, the Duke of Richmond, governor of the Canadas. Maitland's wife, Lady Sarah Lenox, added a graceful, aristocratic touch to the rustic capital of Upper Canada. Together, they attended St James Church. A member of the congregation noted that the Crown's representative was a 'tall, grave officer, always in military undress; his countenance ever wearing a mingled expression of sadness and benevolence.'[41] Maitland's views were conservative and entirely in agreement with those of Strachan and Robinson. Even more encouraging to the provincial executive was Maitland's distaste for politics and his tendency to leave day-to-day administration to his trusted subordinates.[42]

Prior to Maitland's arrival, another Scot had burst upon Upper Canada's political scene to present a challenge to the attorney-general's skills. Robert Gourlay, a trained agronomist and a man of violent and unpredictable emotions, had arrived in Upper Canada in the summer of 1817 with the intention of initiating a resettlement scheme for impoverished British yeomanry. He conferred with several prominent Upper Canadians, including his wife's cousins, William Dickson and Thomas Clark. Those land barons had been antagonized by Gore's policy of excluding Americans, and they readily supported Gourlay's plans to encourage British emigration, as did the York executive. Chief Justice

Powell even helped Gourlay publish a questionnaire in the *Upper Canada Gazette*. The encouragement of British emigration was very much a government objective. Robinson believed as strongly as Gourlay that the poor yeomanry of England could advance both themselves and the Empire by emigrating to the Canadas. In 1816, Robinson's observation of British paupers had led him to speculate on the possibility of turning 'this stream of emigration produced by this overflow of misery from the U. States to Canada.' Not only would such a diversion relieve Britain of its poor, it would 'people a colony with useful subjects and accelerate its growing means of internal defense.'[43]

Gourlay and Robinson pursued radically different approaches to their shared objective. In order to initiate his settlement plan, Gourlay requested a substantial tract of land. He was, however, anything but diplomatic in his approach to a project. In a published address to resident landowners, he indiscreetly praised Colonel Nichol's resolution condemning the government's policy of excluding Americans and maintaining Crown and clergy reserves. Dickson warned Gourlay against antagonizing the government at this early stage in his career, but Gourlay felt it his prerogative to condemn corruption wherever he found it, and he managed to find it at every turn and every level. His readiness to rush into print to expose government malfeasance, real or imagined, ensured his acquisition of powerful enemies. Gourlay eventually was denied the large land grant he sought and was offered only the average settler's allotment. In response he published a more vitriolic address calling on the assembly to inquire into the present state of the province.[44]

The legislative assembly had more important matters to consider than the visions of a recently arrived Scot. The assembly session in the spring of 1818 was preoccupied with gaining control of the civil list and the regulation of trade with the United States. The assembly also was embroiled in a controversy with the legislative council over the right of the council to amend supply bills. Faced with endless arguments and no legislation, the assembly was prorogued on 1 April. This early dismissal spurred yet another address from Gourlay.[45] This time he condemned the assembly as well as the government and called for township meetings to elect delegates to a convention to examine the state of the province. To those in government, this suspiciously resembled some kind of continental congress, a popular movement that must be stopped at all costs.

Colonel Samuel Smith, the interim administrator of the colony, did not consider Gourlay to be a serious threat. The attorney-general, however, after examining Gourlay's increasingly inflammatory addresses, decided that some independent action was necessary to curb this incipient sedition. He confided to the provincial secretary, Samuel Peters Jarvis, that Gourlay's address of 2 April

contain[ed] passages which are, in my opinion so plainly and grossly libellous, and so entirely subversive of that respect which the Government of every Country should vindicate to itself ... that I consider that I cannot in the proper discharge of my duty as Crown officer refrain from prosecuting the author and publishers of them.[46]

Robinson tempered his righteous indignation by considering the possibility of jurors acquitting a popular figure like Gourlay. Robinson's skills as an advocate may have been lacking, but his instincts as a politician were remarkably acute. He understood that any government prosecution would raise Gourlay as a 'Champion for liberty' in the public mind. But John Robinson was a young man unafraid of a fight, and urged the government not to 'sit tamely under every insult.'[47] Robinson informed Colonel Smith that he would order the arrest of Gourlay on a charge of criminal libel. Gourlay was arrested in Kingston in June 1818, and released on bail. He was subsequently arrested in Brockville and again released until trial there later in the year. His release permitted Gourlay to prepare for his convention, which was to be held in York in early July. Robinson feared that Gourlay's 'Convention of Friends to Enquiry' would, at the very least, result in another Spa Fields incident. Yet he noted that the convention was legal, and any suppression of the meeting probably would strengthen Gourlay's position. With his usual thoroughness, the attorney-general examined the principle of freedom of assembly and found that only one statute of questionable legitimacy could be said to prohibit such conventions. Robinson counselled against employing a 'harsh construction' of the law to prohibit meetings on the ground that doing so would only arouse sympathy for Gourlay's cause.[48] These fears proved to be groundless; the convention was a staid affair, attended by some of the most respected men in the province, including several landowners whose interest in encouraging American or British emigration was more pecuniary than patriotic. After a few sessions, the convention petitioned the lieutenant-governor to call for a new assembly, and then quietly adjourned.

In the following month Sir Peregrine Maitland took up his post as lieutenant-governor. Maitland was already aware of the grievances that motivated Gourlay's followers. His visit to the Highlanders of Glengarry county convinced him that they still languished in poverty amid the uncleared lands of absentee landowners that divided the small settlements and precluded any consolidated growth. With all the enthusiasm of a new administrator, Maitland promised that he would pressure the land office to start efficiently processing land patents and assisting settlers in gaining title to their lands. True to his tory instincts, however, Maitland had no tolerance of radicals like Gourlay. He informed Bathurst that Gourlay, 'half Cobbet [sic], and half Hunt' had been stumping the province and arousing the discontented, and he expressed the hope that the prosecutions for libel would 'cripple him.'[49]

Gourlay was arraigned in Kingston on the charge of criminal libel, and the offending passages of his pamphlet petitioning the prince regent were read to the court. He accused the government of being 'palpably ignorant of existing circumstances' and claimed that 'radical change' was necessary to eliminate corruption.[50] The prosecution of these libels was left not to the attorney-general, who had originally sought their prosecution, but to Solicitor-General Boulton. This change might have been more than coincidental, since there was no great expectation that the local juries would convict their flamboyant champion. Boulton's prosecution, while conducted with considerable fervour, did not sway the Kingston jury; after only half an hour of deliberation, they dismissed the charge. The proceedings at Brockville took much the same form, and Gourlay was acquitted by a sympathetic jury.

Despite his ability to evade criminal conviction, Gourlay's crusade was losing its fervour. He had antagonized every major figure in Upper Canada, even those who had originally supported his cause. It was becoming apparent that his meetings and petitions could not bring about change. If there was to be any alteration in government policy, it could only be brought about by the exertions of the popular assembly. In late 1818, the governor of the Canadas, the Duke of Richmond, accurately reported to Lord Bathurst that 'what appeared to be rather serious will turn out of small consequence.'[51]

During the fall session of Parliament, Maitland refused to receive the convention's petition and asked the assembly to forbid any future conventions. Jonas Jones, one of Robinson's school friends, expressed the assembly's 'just indignation' over Gourlay's machinations. With the help of Peter Robinson, now assemblyman for the east riding of York County, a bill was introduced to prohibit 'certain meetings.' In three days the statute was approved with only one member dissenting.[52]

For its part, the provincial government was about to weave a web in which Gourlay would find himself neatly ensnared. In November 1818

Maitland sought the opinion of the judges as to whether someone in Gourlay's circumstances could be banished under the Seditious Attempts Act of 1804. They replied that if a person failed to take the oath of allegiance in the province after six months' residence and then left the province, upon his return he was liable to prosecution as a seditious alien.[53] Isaac Swayzie, a government operative in Niagara, reported to Maitland's secretary that he was monitoring Gourlay's movements.[54] On 21 December the trap closed; Gourlay was arrested and accused of being a seditious alien. Taken before magistrates William Dickson and William Claus, Gourlay was ordered to leave the province forthwith. When he refused to comply, he was imprisoned.

The case against Gourlay was a strong one, and the attorney-general was determined to be rid of him once and for all. After being denied habeas corpus, Gourlay was bound over for trial. During the stifling August of 1819, Robinson proved conclusively that Gourlay had failed to obey a valid court order. The attorney-general carefully built his case around Gourlay's refusal to obey the order and avoided engaging him in any debate as to whether his conduct was seditious. Robinson's caution was unwarranted. Either the long imprisonment or a pre-existing mental condition had left Gourlay baffled by his surroundings and unaware of the charges against him. Prosecutor Robinson put the question to the jury as one of law, and they were forced to return a verdict of guilty. Chief Justice Powell, one of Gourlay's many former supporters, banished him forever from Upper Canada.

Was it necessary to secure a conviction against this unbalanced, impetuous Scot? Sir Peregrine Maitland claimed that he was indifferent to him and that Dickson and Claus had 'perplexed me' by giving Gourlay 'a new interest for a short time.'[55] Why had the government sought the opinion of the judges in November? Why had Swayzie been instructed to follow Gourlay? The administration, keen to rid the province of Robert Gourlay's presence, went to considerable lengths to secure his banishment.

Robinson's dogged prosecution of Gourlay revealed another aspect of his personality. On the one hand, he was loath to interfere with Gourlay's convention because he knew that the law was on his side. In Robinson's opinion, nothing could give more consequence to Gourlay's 'wild measures' than an 'attempt to suppress these meetings by any harsh construction of Law.'[56] As he had done at the Ancaster assizes, Robinson displayed a dispassionate objectivity that exasperated his more emotional colleagues. On the other hand, when he had the law fully behind him he could be ruthless in using it to crush his enemies. It is not entirely accurate to state that Robinson had determined 'if necessary, to strain the law'[57] to banish Gourlay; but he did not hesitate to apply the law as it existed to drive him from Upper Canada. As Barnabas Bidwell and Francis Collins would later discover, when the law favoured his position Robinson would use it with all the ferocity of a religious zealot to defeat those who stood against him. This combative aspect of his character made his opponents wary of any compromises he offered, and added to the bitter, vindictive tone of Upper Canadian politics in the 1820s.

In this first crisis of Maitland's administration, the attorney-general had proved himself a capable lieutenant. His dispatch of Gourlay had been accomplished efficiently and with little comment. Executive Councillor Dickson gushed to the lieutenant-governor that Robinson's 'luminous exposition of the Law and facts in every case with his suavity of manner' had won the day.[58] Dr Strachan's influence in the executive council had also increased, and now his protégé had shown himself useful in carrying out the government's policies. The Gourlay proceedings also enabled Robinson to make his first contact with Maitland's secretary, Major George Hillier, who proved to be more than a conduit for information from Strachan and Robinson to the lieutenant-governor. Hillier shared their conservative views and was able to work with the locals in advancing his commander's policies.

In 1819 Maitland again called on Robinson to assist him in a project. In the preceding year an assembly committee had discovered that government spending was not always authorized by the assembly. The committee recommended that the matter of supply be reviewed and that the administration's budget be submitted to the assembly. Maitland informed the Colonial Office that if these restrictions were imposed, he would have difficulty governing the province. He noted that most of the government revenues came from a British grant to the civil list and administration of justice. The only other revenues received were from king's rights (rents and fees) and monies raised by provincial statutes. Maitland had no quarrel with the assembly reviewing the expenditure of the latter; however, he advised the assembly that henceforth the British grants and king's rights would be spent as he saw fit and that he would account only to the imperial treasury.[59]

The attorney-general advanced Maitland's plan to gain control of part of the provincial purse by drafting a legal opinion to the effect that fines and forfeitures could also be applied directly to the Crown revenue without being placed at the disposal of the provincial legislature.[60] In so doing, Robinson displayed a greater awareness of the fiscal and constitutional nature of the colonial government than did his reform-minded adversaries. Besides bearing the cost of Upper Canada's defence, the British taxpayer was also financing the province's civil administration. In these circumstances, it was inevitable that Upper Canada's government would be an outgrowth of the imperial administration. Even if the assembly refused supplies, the government could continue to function; furthermore, it would be responsible to London, not the York assembly. As the provincial legislature assumed more of the colony's financial obligations during the 1820s and 1830s, it would correspondingly seek more control over government administration. Robinson would be among the first to point out that despite this change in circumstances, the Canada Act was an inflexible document, and the subservience of the legislature to the lieutenant-governor and Colonial Office remained in effect until altered by the imperial Parliament.

By 1819, Robinson was becoming interested in electoral politics, and his old comrade John Macaulay helped him gain recognition. Macaulay had passed up Robinson's offer to join him in legal practice in York and instead had pursued a mercantile career in Kingston. In 1818, in partnership with Alexander Pringle, he founded the *Kingston Chronicle*, which soon became one of the most prominent journals in the province. Macaulay was an intelligent and effective publicist for the tories, but he was no sycophant, and had originally intended to keep his newspaper aloof from any factions.[61] He refused to print Dr Strachan's attacks on Gourlay and considered Gourlay's banishment to be an unwarranted persecution. Eventually, however, the *Chronicle* was brought into the government fold by Dr Strachan, who assured Macaulay that his newspaper would be the recipient of substantial government advertising.[62] Major Hillier even offered to pay Macaulay out of the province's secret service fund.[63] As a result, the *Chronicle* became a major vehicle for the advancement of tory issues, and in 1819 Macaulay published a number of essays (attributed to Robinson) on public improvements and commerce.

Robinson did not seize on the issue of public improvement merely as a likely vehicle to propel him into politics. While in England, he had warned Lord Bathurst that Canada would remain at the mercy of an unpredictable foe and dependent on Britain for protection until Upper Canada's 'own internal increase in opulence, and population, and that every thing which aids the growth of prosperity of this infant Colony is, in its peculiar Situation, of most important consequence to its security.'[64] Economic prosperity and political survival were inexorably linked. Robinson warned Upper Canadians that if they did not adopt American business practices, American republican institutions might well be forced upon them. A series of articles thought to be contributed by Robinson in 1819 praised the American 'anticipating' spirit and the American willingness to build 'on a scale which could perhaps be premature several centuries hence.'[65] Upper Canada was a land of rich promise, and if Canadians were to 'shew a little public spirit and rational enterprise, [they] will assuredly not be disappointed in the result of what they undertake.'[66]

The expansion of the assembly to forty seats in 1820 made it possible for John Robinson to stand for election to the new constituency for the town of York. At first, Major R.R. Loring, the former civil secretary, stood for the York seat. When he was recalled to active service, John Robinson was left as the sole candidate. Though Robinson donated a fine bell to St James Church on the day before the polling,[67] other contributions made by the attorney-general and his partisans probably assured his victory. One of Upper Canada's cheapest commodities, and one most likely to influence vacillating voters, was the whisky blanc distilled throughout the province. A candidate with serious hopes of winning usually had his barrel of whisky stationed near a polling booth. The head of the barrel would be staved in and a tin dipper made available for prospective supporters to help themselves. After generous helpings, the voter would be led out to the polling platform where he could, before the rest of the assembled electors, declare himself for his candidate.[68] With whisky a staple of Upper Canadian campaigns, elections were rarely sedate affairs. Moreover, unlike Great Britain, most Upper Canadians possessed the necessary property qualification. In rural ridings, an elector had only to show that he owned unencumbered property valued at forty shillings. Most residents were landowners and therefore eligible to meet this standard no matter how mean their origins or educations, and much to the attorney-general's distaste, popularity was an important element in Upper Canadian elections.

Already there was some opposition to the attorney-general running for the assembly. An anonymous broadside urged the electors to oppose Robinson and keep the assembly free of the influence of the administration.[69] On the day of the York election, one hardy individual even nominated another candidate, George Ridout. But since Ridout was not present and there was no seconder, John Beverley Robinson was declared elected by acclamation.[70] This was a propitious beginning for what Robinson hoped would be government by consensus. While the Selkirk and Gourlay proceedings had brought Robinson to prominence in the

administration, his election to the legislature would enable him to take part in public debate and represent the government in the assembly. With the assistance of like-minded colleagues who had also been elected, Robinson would try to instil the American 'anticipating' spirit into Upper Canadian commercial life. The greatest test of his political mettle, however, was to come when the smouldering discontent whose root cause was the alien problem burst into flame.

5

Parliamentary Life

'Politics I am not fond of,' Robinson yawned to Macaulay before the opening of the Eighth Parliament, 'and as to anything very abstract, I have neither time nor talent for it.'[1] The attorney-general's spirited activity on behalf of the government made that disclaimer difficult to believe. Events would prove Robinson's fondness for debate and his aptitude for solving problems.

In January 1821 the new session began in the Parliament buildings on Front Street. Built to replace the structures destroyed by the American invaders, the plain brick buildings overlooking Lake Ontario reflected the austere tastes of the province's settlers. Yet, despite the buildings' unrefined architecture, their inhabitants had inherited the ancient forms of British government, and Parliament was ordered to assembly by the Gentleman Usher of the Black Rod. The members heard Chief Justice Powell, the speaker of the legislative council, deliver the lieutenant-governor's message. Sir Peregrine Maitland admitted that Upper Canada was undergoing a mild depression, but added that it would not impoverish the population; the province's natural abundance assured all its citizens an adequate living. In the circumstances, Maitland's words were excessively optimistic. The prosperity of the war years had yielded to a depression that discouraged investment and drew the province's more ambitious settlers off to the American midwest. The situation was due in large part to the British Corn Laws, which permitted the importation of Canadian wheat only when British prices were high. In

1820, a good harvest in Britain closed off Upper Canada's only market for export. The province was forbidden by mercantile restrictions from selling grain in Europe and could not compete with local producers in the American market. Lacking markets for its wheat, Upper Canada was hard-pressed to get the foreign currency necessary to import the manufactured goods it needed. Maitland glossed over these hardships, remarking only that 'the present, like all other periods of tranquillity, may be unfriendly to the enterprise of commerce.'[2] To his military mind, one of the unfortunate side-effects of peace was widespread poverty.

Some members of the assembly were not so complacent about the province's situation. Robert Nichol, the feisty member from Norfolk, called for a debate on the throne speech and condemned the government for failing to pay militia pensions to war widows and the disabled. Robinson, a member of the committee assigned to draft a reply to the lieutenant-governor's address, succeeded in having an innocuous answer prepared and accepted by the assembly over Nichol's objections.[3] Nevertheless, Nichol was the dominant figure in the first session and was held in high regard by a number of members who enjoyed his continual sniping at the government. So that the York executive would not forget the Gourlay episode, Nichol introduced a measure to repeal the Seditious Attempts Act. This measure received overwhelming approval, and only eight tories joined the attorney-general in supporting the bill that had banished Robert Gourlay.[4]

Within the assembly there existed a loose and ill-defined organization of government and opposition factions. The diminutive Robert Nichol, 'Samson' to his partisans, headed the opposition, and Dr Baldwin served as his adjutant.[5] It soon became obvious that the attorney-general spoke for the government. Colonel Nichol was his most prominent adversary, and Robinson considered some of his speeches to be personal attacks. Nichol opposed a bill that would have had the effect of denying remuneration to parliamentarians; if members were not paid, he argued, only wealthy lawyers or civil servants could afford to hold office. Robinson thought that the gentlemen of the assembly should be independent of government support, and argued against 'any person in office under the government [receiving] the wages of prostitution.'[6] (He was not as selfless when it came to his own salary as attorney-general.) Robinson suspected an insult in Nichol's comment on lawyers and he wrote to Macaulay complaining that

the little Colonel is as troublesome as he could be and throws all the obstacles he can in the way ... There are many good members in the House, and I trust it will be found that a majority will discountenance anything like factious opposition. Without that little animal however, all would certainly be harmony.[7]

The Assembly boasted a number of members, such as Jonas Jones and Mahlon Burwell, who were able to assist the attorney-general in upholding the government, and the 'enlightened' Christopher Hagerman had won election in Kingston. The members of the York executive, who had favoured George Markland's candidacy, were disappointed by Hagerman's victory. Yet, after observing him in the House, Robinson wrote enthusiastically to Macaulay that '[Hagerman's] conduct is manly, correct and sensible and shews in everything that kind of independence most rarely met with ... His speeches gain him great credit.'[8] Hagerman in turn considered Robinson to be 'a very able debater, but he loses his temper.'[9] Together, Robinson and Hagerman proved to be a powerful match for Colonel Nichol and his supporters.

The attorney-general and the little colonel clashed again in early February over Robinson's bill to reform the marriage laws. The existing penalty for conducting a marriage without legal authority was transportation for fourteen years. Because of this harsh punishment, juries were usually unwilling to enter convictions. Robinson was already fully aware of the problems created by the itinerant preachers. In 1820, an Anabaptist minister, Reuben Crandall, was charged in the London district with unlawfully solemnizing a marriage. Crandall was convicted and given the mandatory sentence for the crime, fourteen years' banishment. Robinson had previously acted for Crandall in a civil case, and in deference to his former client he reported Crandall's plea of ignorance to the lieutenant-governor. Robinson hinted that he did not believe the preacher's explanation, although 'the law seems to be thought severe and he goes to York I believe with much interest made in his favour.'[10]

The attorney-general adroitly sought to turn that interest in his favour; to that end, he proposed a bill to make the solemnizing of illegal marriages a misdemeanour. Colonel Nichol's solution was to grant the privilege of solemnizing marriages to ministers of all Christian denominations. The attorney-general stated that he would support Nichol's bill if the definition of 'Christian denomination' was clarified and if fringe sects were excluded from the operation of the statute. He was willing to grant the power of conducting marriages to Methodist and Baptist preachers, since 'they did not differ materially ... from the established Church in their beliefs or doctrines.'[11] Even Christopher Hagerman thought that the attorney-general's tolerant sentiments were 'going far enough' and that Nichol's comments that Upper Canada did not have an established

Church had motivated a vandal to break into and desecrate St James Church.[12] To Robinson and Hagerman, the existence of an established and therefore privileged Church in Upper Canada was beyond question.

Another contentious religious issue, that of the clergy reserves, had not yet aroused much public animosity. Plenty of land was still available for settlement, and even those farmers who had leased reserve land found little difficulty in avoiding payment of rents. In order to establish some system for obtaining a steady income for the Church of England, Robinson drafted legislation to create a clergy corporation. In describing the structure of this new entity to the lieutenant-governor, Robinson explained that it was proper to delegate the authority for the management of reserve land to the party most concerned with their productivity, that is, the Anglican clergy.[13] The attorney-general pointed out the advantages of incorporation: the land remained vested in the Crown and a renter could obtain his lease at a district office without having to travel to York.[14] The clergy of the Church of England, under the firm direction of Dr Strachan, now had an official means of controlling their reserve land. The creation of the clergy corporation gave the Anglican Church an elevated status and confirmed the Church's direct control of certain Crown land. In the vital area of public lands, Robinson and Strachan neatly amalgamated the interests of the Church of England and the government, and, to outward appearances, confirmed the existence of an established Church in the face of a legal opinion from the Colonial Office that the Church of Scotland was as eligible for reserve revenues as the Anglican Church.[15]

The attorney-general was beginning to present a considerable amount of legislation in the House. Robinson realized that ever since army bills had ceased to be issued, one of the province's chief commercial difficulties lay in providing an adequate currency. He drafted a bill to provide for a uniform currency and saw it safely through the assembly.[16] Another important matter left to the attorney-general's expertise was the arrangement of commercial affairs with the United States. Several years earlier Robinson had advised Major Hillier that the Navigation Act, which had regulated American trade and inland navigation, was not within the legislature's authority and could be disallowed by the imperial government.[17] Nevertheless, trade acts had been passed to limit the amount of foodstuffs imported from the United States. Robinson and Hagerman introduced amendments to the Intercourse Bill to protect Canadian wheat and to tax imported luxuries while permitting beef to be sold without any tariff. Robinson sponsored this measure, but remarked in an aside to Macaulay that 'we have no right to legislate at all concerning [tariffs] –

however that trifling circumstance seems by general assent to be overlooked.'[18] Still, there was precedent for believing that a province could legislate to control its internal navigation; moreover, the measure encouraged the local shipbuilding industry and provided the province with a merchant marine in the event of war.

The assembly was about to embark on an even more momentous course of action. On 5 February Dr W.W. Baldwin moved to create a committee to examine the state of the province.[19] The use of committees to study an issue and present a policy for the assembly's consideration was still a novel procedure, but its usefulness was becoming apparent. The committee, was chaired by Robert Nichol, was composed of some of the most important commercial figures in the province. Nichol's final report left no doubt that the key to Upper Canada's prosperity was the expansion of its agricultural economy.[20] It was essential that the Corn Laws be modified to permit Upper Canada's surplus to be sold in Britain. Even more important than obtaining markets was the opening up of the hinterland to navigation. The treacherous rapids and falls of the St Lawrence system made the economic shipment of grain to Europe all but impossible. A concerted program, supervised and financed by the government, was the necessary first step to securing the province's prosperity.[21] The assembly acted on Nichol's report by appointing a commission to examine and recommend improvements to internal navigation.

Robinson supported the creation of the commission. This new spirit of co-operation reflected his desire to help further the province's development and thereby secure its loyalty to the Crown. Calling Nichol's report 'comprehensive,' he advised Macaulay to write of the report in the highest terms. The improvement of inland navigation was an issue that was 'not by any means political in the narrow sense of the word.'[22] While Robinson and Nichol agreed on the necessity for internal improvements, they were somewhat at odds over the possible extent of expansion. The committee's report alluded to the 'limited power and deficiency of pecuniary means of the Provincial Legislature [which] almost precludes the possibility of legislating on the subject.'[23] Nichol was aware that the recently completed Erie Canal of New York State could serve the vast fertile lands of the midwest, and that in Upper Canada, the barren Canadian shield covered most of the northern part of the province. Nichol therefore cautioned the assembly to limit its vision. The young tories, however, downplayed these warnings, and Hagerman boasted to Robinson that Nichol's warnings were unwarranted.[24] To them, Upper Canada was a province of boundless potential.[25]

The solution to the problem of financing these ambitious internal navigation projects came from a committee, chaired by the attorney-general, that was examining militia pensions. The committee realized that the only manner in which the pension funds could be raised was by issuing a debenture. The attorney-general steered the necessary money bill through Parliament in March 1821, and announced that the security for the debt would be the amount of arrearages owing to Upper Canada from the duties collected at Quebec.[26] If money for the pension funds could be raised in such a simple manner, it was obvious that public works could also be financed by issuing government notes. The prosperity created by the canal projects would undoubtedly be the source for future revenues to repay the debentures. The Debenture Bill of 1821 was the first step in the government's plan to mortgage the province's future with the security of an efficient navigation system. Many years later, after Upper Canada had borrowed extravagantly to finance the canal projects, John Robinson faced the cold reality of the province's limited ability to support such projects, ruefully admitting that he had had 'the *glory* of laying the foundation of our public debt.'[27]

Sir Peregrine Maitland remarked at the prorogation of the legislature that the first session of the Eighth Parliament had been one of the least fractious and most productive in the province's history. The commitment to internal navigation was certainly of the utmost importance and would inevitably enhance Upper Canada's greatness.[28] John Robinson had lent his enthusiastic support to this measure and had shown how the contemplated projects could be financed. Moreover, he had begun to implement the 'anticipating' spirit described in Macaulay's newspaper. Robinson had also drafted and seen to the passing of the Uniform Currency Bill, the Bank of Upper Canada Bill, and the Commercial Intercourse Bill. He had remained responsible, as attorney-general, for certifying the constitutionality of his own legislation before it was signed by the lieutenant-governor. His public duties as well as his private law practice allowed him little time for other pursuits. In response to Macaulay's request for an article, Robinson encouraged his friend to continue publishing in the 'good cause' because Robinson '[prized] anything anti-radical beyond measure.' In explaining to Macaulay his inability to contribute articles to the paper, he described his working day:

I declare I have not time for sleeping or eating but I have a good constitution and fear nothing but the loss of my sanity ... It is now 5 minutes before 12, I have to write a speech on the election for Gore, to draw a Report for a Committee &

present an Act of Parliament, get my sleep and my breakfast and be at the House at 10.[29]

The attorney-general seemed to thrive in this hectic atmosphere and apparently enjoyed being the government's prime mover in the assembly. His temper was as quick as ever. In one incident, which should probably have remained inconsequential, Robinson had Robert Horne, the printer of the assembly's debates, brought before the bar of the House. Incensed at what he considered to be a partisan report of a debate, Robinson put forward a motion to make Horne insert a notice in the *Upper Canada Gazette* that owing to the 'incompetence or negligence' of his reporter, Francis Collins, the reports of the House debates were unreliable.[30] Robinson's motion was defeated and the printer received a more moderate admonition. This incident once again revealed Robinson's tendency not just to defeat his opponent but to crush him entirely. While he was a tireless worker and an able legislator, Robinson's temper sometimes blocked his judgment and made his actions appear harsh and oppressive.

After this taste of government authority, Robinson returned to the relatively prosaic duty of going on circuit with the Court of King's Bench. The trips were hardly luxurious. Roads were maintained, if at all, by statute or compulsory labour and were little more than trails through the bush. Coach service was irregular, and tree stumps were usually left in the right-of-way. Small wonder that Robinson usually travelled by horseback, as he later reminisced, with his saddlebags filled with legal texts, files, and, if time permitted, his volumes of Shakespeare.

Robinson's approach to public financing mirrored his conduct of his own affairs. He had had to borrow enormous sums from his brother Peter to finance his education and travels in Europe. The purchase of Beverley House and a house for his mother had left him heavily in debt. In 1819 he told Chief Justice Powell that he could not lend money to him, saying that it would take 'some years to extricate myself.'[31] Fortunately, his successful legal career was enabling him to satisfy his debts and support a growing family.

Although Robinson was occupied with his practice, politics was not completely forgotten during the summer and fall of 1821. In November 1821 a by-election was held in the Lennox and Addington riding to fill the seat vacated by Daniel Hagerman's death. The York clique was disgusted when a reputed republican and Gourlay sympathizer, Barnabas Bidwell, put himself forward for election. Strachan fervently hoped that Bidwell would be 'hissed off the hustings' during his first campaign.[32]

The two anti-Gourlay candidates split the vote, however, and Bidwell was elected by a small margin. The gentlemen of the assembly would be in the company of the democrat Bidwell and his vulgar associates, David Pattie and Robert Randall. Robinson advised Macaulay that those men 'represent[ed] the rascals of the Province – I feel so squimish [sic] I assure you, as you could about the prospect of sitting in such Company.'[33] Nevertheless, as a gentleman Robinson doubted whether it would be 'quite correct and proper to withdraw & leave the field entirely to such scum.'

Robinson shared the social and political prejudices of the eighteenth century. The honourable gentlemen, the gentle-born, had a natural right to govern; the lesser-born, the yeomen, had a duty to obey. According to Robinson, gentlemen were 'possessed of that degree of intelligence, respectability, & property which naturally confers upon them a salutory influence in Society.'[34] Of those qualifications, by far the most important was property, and 'property' meant tracts of land. Colonel Talbot and William Dickson were men of influence because their vast land-holdings set them far above the average settler. But landowners such as Talbot and Dickson were exceptions; there did not exist a class of land barons sufficient to constitute an aristocracy. The absence of great landed estates and the prevalence of small landowners was an early indication that Upper Canada would be unable to emulate Britain's hierarchical class structure.[35] Of course, as in Robinson's case, birth to a landless family of rank, or former rank, gave one the potential of admission to the upper class. Education at a gentleman's school was also important, and until élite public schools were established, Cornwall Grammar School fulfilled this function. In their adult careers the sons of the gentry were able to call upon the friends of their adolescence for political and financial support.

The early Upper Canadians were obsessed by status. For the privileged, life was a struggle for the favourable attention of one's superiors.[36] At the other end of the spectrum, among the settlers whose assets were roughly equal, little in the way of class distinctions existed.[37] Yet the gentlemen were acutely conscious of the gulf between the settlers and themselves. The question was whether the gentry could survive in a society in which the mass of small landowners would render such distinctions meaningless.

The fortunes of the Robinson family illustrate the hopelessness of implanting gentle society into Upper Canada. John Beverley's rise to prominence was based on his administrative ability, not on his land-holdings. Nevertheless, the Robinsons and others of the ruling group tried to make good their landless deficiency. By 1820 John Robinson owned a considerable amount of land around York. The illusion of the existence of a landed gentry enabled Robinson and his colleagues to maintain their belief in the right of the gentry to govern.

Within this refined sphere, the customs and biases of the past century flourished in Upper Canada. A distinguishing feature of the gentleman was adherence to the gentle code. A man's reputation was more important than his life, and gentlemen still resorted to the duel as the ultimate way of defending their honour. While on his first trip to England, Robinson had stopped in Montreal and attempted to exchange his American funds for British currency. When he was taken to a broker's house, the man dismissed Robinson brusquely and told him to return at a later date. Young Robinson was not used to being treated in this off-hand manner, and he considered that 'as a Gentleman, even tho' a Stranger I was entitled to an answer in rather a cooler strain.'[38] He wondered whether a challenge was in order and decided against it only when he realized that the broker must have been unaware of his position in society.

Among gentlemen, the consequences of failure to maintain civility could be fatal. John Macdonell, Robinson's senior and the leader of the ill-fated charge up Queenston Heights, had duelled with Dr W.W. Baldwin, then the treasurer of the Law Society, on York Peninsula (now Toronto Island) in 1812. The tempestuous Macdonell had publicly insulted the doctor, and Baldwin explained that a duel was the only way 'to protect me from insults which as a gentleman I cannot submit to.'[39] In the event, Macdonell refused to fire, Baldwin purposely fired wide, and the matter was settled honourably.

On other occasions, the gentle code resulted in the affair being settled by blood and death. In 1817, the young men of the Jarvis and Ridout families quarrelled, and their duel left young John Ridout dead. Samuel Peters Jarvis, the surviving principal, was charged with murder. Jarvis was found to be an aggrieved party and, since the duel had been conducted in a proper manner, was aquitted.[40] Though even Blackstone's *Commentaries* noted that duelling was illegal, it remained the accepted way for gentlemen to resolve their disputes. If conducted fairly, a duel could not lead to a murder conviction; as Robinson himself later stated from the bench, 'juries have not been known to convict when all was fair.'[41]

Into this refined world of gentlemen came a republican and democrat, Barnabas Bidwell. John Macaulay, convinced that Bidwell was not fit to be a member of the king's legislature, organized a petition of freeholders of Lennox and Addington asking that Bidwell's election be declared void. Bidwell had been a representative in the Massachusetts state legislature and later, as treasurer of Berkshire County, had renounced allegiance to the British Crown. In 1810, he had been indicted on charges of embezzlement; rather than face a trial, he had settled in Upper Canada. He turned to pedagogy, and his grammar school flourished. During the War of 1812, Bidwell took the oath of allegiance, although it was rumoured that he felt that the oath was of no effect because it was taken under duress. The petition alleged two grounds for Bidwell's expulsion: it declared that he was an alien in that he had abjured the King's allegiance and that his low moral character disqualified him from sitting in Parliament.[42] Macaulay forwarded a copy of this petition to Robinson, who seized upon it as a tool to expel this dangerous republican.

Robinson wrote to his co-conspirator, Macaulay: 'If you have reason to believe that the old vagabond has solemnly sworn to renounce forever all allegiance to the King of Great Britain & that proof can be obtained of it, I will go you halves in the expense of procuring a certificate of it, properly authenticated – but this is, of course, as Judge Boulton says *sub-rosa*.'[43] Macaulay concurred and dispatched one of his employees to Boston to collect as much evidence as possible to be used against Bidwell. Robinson defrayed the investigator's expenses and arranged for Henry John Boulton to present the collected evidence to the Assembly.[44]

On 22 November 1821, the day after Parliament was called into session, Robinson tabled the petition of the freeholders of Lennox and Addington. While the attorney-general's attempt to have the petition reviewed by a committee was rebuffed, the assembly voted overwhelmingly that if the allegations in the petition were proved, then Bidwell must be expelled.[45] Robinson wished to proceed with the work of the House and defer further debate on the matter until the end of the session. Jonas Jones, Robinson's somewhat overenthusiastic associate, brought a counter-motion to declare Bidwell an alien and therefore incapable of election to Parliament.[46] Although Robinson felt obliged to support his friend's motion, the question was soundly defeated by a vote of twenty to twelve. Even if some of the members agreed with Robinson that Bidwell was a low character, unfit for the company of gentlemen, declaring him to be an alien would, by extension, threaten the citizenship and property of a substantial number of their own constituents. For this reason the assembly was reluctant to support Robinson's plans to expel Bidwell. The attorney-general had no great hope that the assembly would back the expulsion; he wrote with little enthusiasm to Macaulay that 'we must wait until the 29th and dispose of old Barney one way or the other.'[47] In the meantime, Bidwell revealed his radical colours. He consistently voted with the reformers and himself proposed a bill for the relief of religious societies. However, he could not obtain the support of the assembly to introduce a bill to amend the distribution of intestate estates by abolishing the right of primogeniture.[48] Significantly, it was Dr. W.W. Baldwin who led the fight against this levelling measure, which he was certain would destroy the 'principles of Aristocracy' in the colony. For once, Robinson was compelled to agree 'with every word that had fallen from the hon. gentleman.'

In his eagerness to expel 'the old vagabond,' Robinson overlooked an important principle of law. At that time, British subjects could not renounce their allegiance; any attempt to do so was void. The question was not whether Bidwell had renounced his allegiance, but whether he was a British subject because he had been born in the American colonies prior to 1783. Thousands of other Upper Canadians had also remained in the United States after 1783 and migrated to the colony only in later years. Their citizenship, as well as Bidwell's, was at stake. It was this crucial question, which Robinson had wisely deferred in 1819, that he now unwisely resurrected.

As the end of December approached, Bidwell marshalled evidence of his innocence of the Massachusetts embezzlement charges, and a group of his supporters filed a petition attesting to his superior moral qualities. The trial of the Lennox and Addington election finally began on 29 December with Solicitor-General Boulton presenting the case against Bidwell. Boulton filed evidence of Bidwell's malfeasance in Massachusetts, and Bidwell filed evidence that he had satisfied whatever debts he owed in that state.[49] Colonel Nichol, who had missed the earlier part of the session, rose to champion Bidwell's cause. He argued that the assembly had no right to take cognizance of matters relating to a member's character that had occurred outside the province. He spoke with such vehemence that the speaker frequently had to call him to order. On Wednesday, 2 January, Nichol moved that the allegations in the petition were not proved and therefore should not be taken into account in deciding the issue. That motion passed, and the case against Bidwell began to seem hopeless. The only matter remaining before the House was the question of his citizenship; because that question was so complicated, Nichol suggested that it be deferred until the next session. The colonel understood the deeper implications of the question: if Bidwell was declared an alien, then 'every person who did not withdraw from the U. States, according to the stipulation in the treaty, was in the same predicament.'[50]

The debate raged on. Hagerman and Robinson passionately condemned Bidwell's character, maintaining that since he had renounced the Crown, he had no right to enjoy full liberties under the Crown. Robinson's lengthy address relied as much on emotion as on legal reasoning. He noted that Americans born in the United States before 1783 had engaged Canada in a war and had been treated not as traitors but as foreign belligerents. 'If aliens in war,' he declared, 'they must be aliens in peace.' Robinson then appealed to the assembly:

Was it to be supposed that the citizens of the United States who involved Great Britain in war, and the people of this Province in ruin, as soon as their hands were washed of the blood of our fellow subjects should be allowed to cross the river and enjoy all the privileges of British subjects?[51]

This emotional rhetoric brought the debate to such a pitch that Dr Baldwin urged that future speeches be more moderate in tone. According to later reformer accounts of the Bidwell debate,

Mr. Attorney-General Robinson went beyond any former effort of his life in the way of vituperation, and overleapt the bounds of the commonest decency. He proclaimed himself to be the son of a United Empire Loyalist who had fought and bled for his country, and as therefore being no fit company for runaway felons and pickpockets. His sympathy with himself was so great that the tears chased one another down his cheeks as he was speaking.[52]

While the reformers probably exaggerated the attorney-general's passion, his arguments seemed to be having some effect. On 4 January, at the end of a week of turbulent debate, Dr Baldwin moved that the petition be dismissed for want of proof. After a roll call, the motion was declared defeated, although an examination of the transcript indicates that in fact it passed by one vote.[53] A mere clerical error probably kept the Bidwell case from being dismissed altogether.

In any event, the government members seized the opportunity to introduce another resolution which stated, somewhat cryptically, that 'sufficient of the allegations' in the petition had been proved to void Bidwell's election. One of the reformers, McDonell, was induced to join the government, and the resolution was passed by a majority of one. There was no comment on the fact that this result was in direct contradiction of Colonel Nichol's resolution of 2 January. This confused and vague measure finally secured Barnabas Bidwell's expulsion from the assembly, and a new writ of election was issued to Lennox and

Addington. To ensure that the assembly would never be divided by a similar issue, Nichol introduced a bill to prevent a person who had served in an American legislature from being elected to the assembly.

Bidwell's expulsion was a hollow victory. In his intemperate haste to rid the assembly of one republican, Robinson had again called into question the status of the late loyalists, those Americans invited to Upper Canada by Governor Simcoe. The dilemma of alien status, touching as it did the property, voting, and citizenship rights of thousands of Upper Canadians, was squarely before the province. The debate had aroused great anxiety among the American-born settlers. They feared that if the attorney-general's opinion was correct 'it will disfranchise a large proportion of the freeholders of every district.'[54]

Another unfortunate result of the Bidwell affair was that it gave a harsh and combative tone to the alien debate. John Macaulay, writing in the *Kingston Chronicle*, condemned Bidwell as 'an unprincipled peculator and a notorious refugee from justice.'[55] According to the *Chronicle* of 11 January 1822, Bidwell's supporters were 'apostates' and nothing could erase the province's shame that 'it was a majority of *one* only that saved the Province from appalling disgrace, and its House of Assembly from indelible pollution.' Such venom did much to poison political life, and provoked equally vituperative reform rhetoric.

While Bidwell's prosecution might have been politically inexpedient, Robinson was legally correct in his assertion that Bidwell was an alien and therefore incapable of sitting in Parliament. Later opinions of the Crown law officers confirmed that the American-born were not British subjects until naturalized, and that the attorney-general's arguments were completely correct. Yet Robinson's bitter personal speeches against Bidwell seemed to vindicate the suspicions of many that the government was run by a harsh and oppressive oligarchy. Hagerman had already noted that Robinson's temper could cloud his judgment and lead him into politically harmful personal attacks. The tenor of the Bidwell proceedings ensured that the alien debate would be a rancorous one with little hope of compromise.

It became apparent during the Bidwell debate that the attorney-general exercised only a limited control over the assembly. The cliques that existed in the chamber were based more on personal loyalty than on any party affiliation. Without party discipline, it was possible for reform-minded members to advance their own causes. The Sedition Law Repeal Bill, which had been rejected by the legislative council, was raised again in the assembly, and passed with only Robinson, Hagerman, and three others in opposition.[56] Charles Jones, the member from Belleville, challenged the attorney-general over a measure to hire parliamentary reporters to record the debate. Robinson objected that this was not the custom in Britain and that it was improper for Parliament to advertise itself. The attorney-general's speech was more vitriolic than necessary, and Jones made a mock apology for having left a 'disgusting and undignified impression on the learned gentleman.'[57] The assembly overruled Robinson and voted to hire a reporter.

The fundamental issue facing the assembly, far more important than Bidwell's expulsion, was the embarrassing state of provincial finances. In order to keep the civil government operating during the summer of 1821, Sir Peregrine Maitland had had to borrow money from the military appropriation. In the throne speech, Maitland reported that because the government had failed to reach an agreement with Lower Canada as to the distribution of customs duties there was no expectation of receiving any of the essential revenues. Without those funds, normal government activity would be halted and any public improvement projects would have to be postponed indefinitely.[58] The dispute with Lower Canada over the distribution of customs revenues had its origins in the division of Quebec in 1791. Upper Canada had no ocean port, and all imported goods other than those coming through the United States had to be transported through Lower Canada. It was inequitable that Lower Canada should be able to collect a duty on goods destined for Upper Canada, and in 1797 the provinces agreed to place an inspector at Côteau du Lac to render an account of the goods passing into the upper province. Inevitably, a large proportion of goods imported from Lower Canada escaped the inspector, and the system expired in 1817. In that year the provinces reached a new agreement by which Upper Canada was to receive one-fifth of all customs duties collected at Quebec. The agreement expired in 1819, and Lower Canada appeared reluctant to appoint commissioners to negotiate a new arrangement. When commissioners were finally appointed in 1821, they refused to recognize Upper Canada's right to arrears of duties for the years from 1819 to 1821 and suggested that each province establish its own custom-house. The two delegations parted with no agreement in sight.

The legislature acknowledged the seriousness of the financial crisis, and the attorney-general was appointed chairman of the assembly's delegation to the joint parliamentary committee on the customs problem. Robinson spent long hours working on the committee's report and complained to Macaulay that 'the war of words in the House from 10 to 6 left me only from 10 to 3 at night to work up my report.' Robinson took the leading role in writing the report, noting that 'it is a ponderous document of 43 pages of my crabbed hand.'[59] The final draft detailed the history of the customs dispute and concluded that the province could no longer function without sending a commissioner to appeal to the imperial government.[60]

Even before the committee had completed its report, the members discussed who should be selected as commissioner. The assemblymen, who formed a majority of the committee, felt that their leader and the architect of the report, John Robinson, was the natural choice. Dr Strachan, who also sat on the committee, was aware that Maitland had anticipated the necessity of appointing a commissioner and that he had already approached Chief Justice Powell. Powell, who had assisted in drafting the final report, was widely considered to be the most eminent Upper Canadian. Strachan did not divulge this information, and to his undoubted satisfaction the committee concluded that 'the Attorney General and no other was qualified to go.'[61] Robinson's appointment was put forward as a government measure and the legislative council concurred in his selection. Strachan felt that the chief justice 'would very gladly (as was his duty) relieve the L. Governor from any private pledge.'[62] But Strachan was rather too quick to suppose that Powell would meekly step aside and defer to the legislature's choice. As speaker of the legislative council, Powell registered his opposition to the appointment of Robinson, the 'popular choice,' as commissioner to England. While his remarks were later expunged from the record, Powell was now convinced, with some justice, that he had been sabotaged by Strachan, Robinson, and company.

The commissioner's appointment precipitated the final breach between the aging chief justice and John Robinson. Powell felt that Strachan had used his influence in the executive council to shunt him aside, and that Robinson, now that he could draw on the support of the assembly, no longer needed his assistance. When Robinson's appointment was confirmed in January 1822, Powell sent him an abusive note. Robinson replied angrily, denouncing Powell for his 'injurious and dishonourable imputation.'[63] So great was the chief justice's ire that he confronted the lieutenant governor and accused him of reneging on a promise.[64] Powell hastily apologized to Maitland for his unseemly conduct, but he had violated the cardinal rule for political survival in Upper Canada by antagonizing the lieutenant-governor.

As Powell's star waned, the attorney-general prepared himself for one of the greatest challenges of his career. He felt obliged to point out to the assembly that he did not have the independent financial resources necessary to conduct himself adequately as a commissioner in England.[65] His friends, Hagerman and Jones, saw to it that a bill was passed to provide £2,000 for the commissioner's remuneration.

Robinson's appointment marked his ascension to a new level of government authority. In addition to his executive role in internal affairs, he was about to take a leading part in negotiations with the imperial administration concerning Upper Canada's future. The time Robinson had spent in England as a student and observer was long past. He now travelled to England not as a student, but as a practitioner of political strategy; not only as a representative of Upper Canada, but as an advocate of the loyalist tradition.

6

An Advocate in England

Commissioner Robinson's voyage to England in the spring of 1822 was marred by bizarre and tragic events. In the society of Little York, Robinson was renowned not only for his political accomplishments but also for his suave and distinguished manner. His education and travel had given him a savoir faire which in Upper Canada passed for Continental charm. Anne Powell's infatuation with the young ensign of the York militia had not abated during the years following his marriage. Miss Powell had little use for the usurper of John Robinson's affections, and in her letters she referred to Emma's 'romantic history' and the mysterious, 'tragical way' in which her father was lost.[1] Was such a strange creature a proper mate for her beloved John?

If anything, Anne's affection for John Robinson flourished after his marriage. She accosted him in public with protestations of her affection and sent him notes which his brother William described as 'some of the d——ndest letters you ever saw.'[2] Miss Powell attempted to be received at Beverley House, but was consistently turned away. On one occasion she was discovered alone in the mansion caressing the infant Lukin. However, she was faced with Emma Robinson who 'never faltered in the vigilance of her guard, or in her determination that Miss —— should be to her a myth or a nullity.'[3]

Yet Anne Powell was determined. Upon learning that Robinson had been appointed commissioner, she made arrangements to travel with him to England in hopes of regaining his affections. On the evening before

Robinson, Emma, and their daughter, Emily, were to leave for London, Anne Powell came to Beverley House begging for permission to join the official party. The attorney-general described this embarrassing situation to Anne's brother, Grant Powell. Neither he nor her mother could reason with her, so they consented to her departure. In deference to the Robinsons, Mrs Powell promised the attorney-general a two-day head start. However, the resourceful Miss Powell coaxed one of the servants into monitoring Robinson's movements, and when it was apparent he was about to leave York, she escaped. After chartering a sleigh, she tracked down the attorney-general's party in Albany, New York. Anne's escape triggered an uproar in York; her mother feared that this latest adventure would be the 'subject of conversation from the Government House to Forest's Stable.' From Albany to the very piers of New York City Anne Powell travelled with the Robinsons, and boasted that she 'was always considered the *Lady* of the party.'[4]

In New York, Robinson wrote to Major Hillier that he was uneasy over more than Anne Powell's unwanted companionship.[5] The chief justice, after indicating that he was going to Bermuda for his health, had taken ship for England. He was undoubtedly going to London to plead his case before the Colonial Office. Because he was still a well-known and respected Upper Canadian, his bitter comments against the provincial government could do serious damage to John Robinson's reputation. Added to this annoyance was the fact that Emma had become seriously ill and had to be carried on board ship. With these mounting concerns, the last thing the attorney-general wished to endure was a trans-Atlantic voyage in close confinement with Anne Powell. She had attempted to book passage on Robinson's ship, the *Panthea*. However, Robinson approached the ship's captain and explained to him that if he accepted Anne Powell as a passenger, he would lose the large official party from Upper Canada. The captain understood this kind of persuasion and refused to let Anne Powell board the vessel. She was compelled to take a later ship, the packet *Albion*.

The *Albion* was caught in a gale off the south coast of Ireland and was lost, along with most of the crew and passengers. Anne Powell's body was washed ashore and was identified by a brooch that had been given to her by her father. Even though the chief justice had been mortified by his daughter's erratic behaviour, he was disconsolate when he learned of her death. Powell had arranged for London lodgings for Anne and no doubt had planned several stern lectures on decorum. He sought out the surviving master of the *Albion* and from him learned of Anne's last moments as she took her turn on the pumps with the men when the ship, its masts down and rigging fouled, foundered off the Head of Kinsale.

While the Powell family had been aghast at Anne's 'vain folly,' after her death a feeling grew up that somehow Robinson had led her on. One of Anne's sisters confided, 'I do indeed pity J.B.R. I think he ought never to make an idle or insincere speech again, for from that we date all this misery.'[6] Prior to this affair, Robinson had never been accused of more than the occasional honeyed word. Now, the Powells believed that the object of Anne Powell's obsession had actually played a part in her death. Whatever affection had existed between Chief Justice Powell and John Robinson was now completely lost. In later years, the Robinsons and the Powells would be at pains to avoid each other at social gatherings.[7]

The chief justice still had influential friends in London, and Robinson believed that one of them, Francis Gore, was now actively working against him.[8] Yet it was not Robinson's intention to let 'sullen sentiment' forever mar the relationship between himself and Powell. Eventually, the two men met in the waiting room at Downing Street and had a strained conversation.[9] While relations between the chief justice and the attorney-general were outwardly civil, there was never again any degree of rapport between them. Powell, in a deliberate insult, neglected to call on the Robinsons before he left London. But Powell was now an impotent enemy. He had lost much of his influence in Upper Canada, and even with Gore's assistance he held little sway with the Colonial Office. In contrast, the attorney-general was just beginning to exercise his authority in London.

'I am here in the very thick of it,'[10] Robinson reported to Major Hillier shortly after his arrival. The ocean voyage seemed to have greatly improved Emma's health, and Miss Emily was 'fat as a little cub.' On his arrival in Liverpool on 20 March 1822, Robinson noted that there was nothing in the British press concerning Canadian affairs.[11] Yet influential persons were already at work in London altering imperial policy toward the Canadas.

Edward Ellice, a member of Parliament and the owner of a large seigniory in Lower Canada, had begun to lobby the Colonial Office to effect a legislative union of Upper and Lower Canada. Ellice had had frequent contact with colonial officers during the negotiation of the liquidation of the North West Company and its merger with the Hudson's Bay Company. At that time he had advanced his opinion that the feudal restrictions of seigniorial title held back commercial development in Lower Canada. Ellice received the enthusiastic support of Lower Canada's solicitor-general, Charles Marshall, and receiver-general, John Caldwell. Marshall and Caldwell, who were both in London when the union measure was proposed, represented the English minority of Lower Canada who longed to be part of a larger English entity.

The union also recommended itself to the British government. The Lower Canadian legislature had been reluctant to vote yearly supplies for the civil list, and consequently the government was hard-pressed to keep the administration functioning. Perhaps if the French Canadians were submerged in a union with English settlers, the French influence would abate. Ellice, Marshall, and Caldwell met frequently with Colonial Office officials and had all but convinced them of the merits of union. After they learned that Robinson had been appointed commissioner, they suspended discussions pending his arrival. The attorney-general would undoubtedly add his own comments on the union question, and with any luck he might be won over to the proposal.

Even before he left Upper Canada, Robinson was aware that some project to unite the Canadas was under consideration. Prior to his departure, he had approached Sir Peregrine Maitland for instructions on the issue. Sir Peregrine, who had not seriously considered the matter, refused to advise him.[12] Left to his own judgment, Robinson was susceptible to the blandishments of Edward Ellice. When he learned the details of the union plan as envisaged by Ellice, he was favourably impressed. Yet he stopped short of endorsing the measure until he had had time to reflect on its long-term effects. In the meantime, he set to work on his appointed task, the settling of the customs dispute.

Upon his arrival in London, Robinson went directly to the Colonial Office. There, in Number 14 Downing Street, he first met the politician who was to have such a great effect on his career, the under-secretary for colonies, Robert John Wilmot. Wilmot, a cousin of Lord Byron, was married to the heiress Beatrice Horton, who had placed her considerable fortune at her husband's disposal to finance his political ambitions. At the time of Wilmot's appointment in December 1821, Bathurst's secretary, Charles Greville, had warned Wilmot that the under-secretary's job was 'beyond belief lonesome and laborious – nothing can equal the stupidity and prolixity of your Colonial Correspondents.'[13] Despite the unpromising introduction, Wilmot approached his duties with vigour and a high degree of intelligence. Soon after their first meeting, Robinson found Wilmot to be 'exceedingly civil and even attentive and what is of much more consequence he seemed really desirous of being thoroughly informed of Canadian affairs.'[14] Throughout April, Robinson and Wilmot met frequently for breakfast to discuss Canadian matters. Together with Marshall and Caldwell, they discussed the merits of Canadian union. Yet it was Robert Wilmot whom Robinson regarded as the leader of these discussions. While neither would subordinate his ideas to the other's, the morning conversations developed an enduring respect between the two men.

Some historians have denigrated Wilmot's role in the early Colonial Office. It is usually assumed that after Henry Goulburn's departure from the Colonial Office, Lord Bathurst assumed the dominant role.[15] This analysis does not conform to Robinson's observations. During their conversations, Robinson found Wilmot to be 'candid, straight-forward and intelligent,' possessed of a 'quickness of mind,'[16] and genuinely concerned about colonial affairs. Here at last, thought Robinson, was an English official who was informed about the colonies and solicitous for their welfare. Lord Bathurst, in contrast, avoided the confines of the Colonial Office whenever possible. His Lordship was in the habit of taking lengthy vacations, and Robinson was compelled to arrange for interviews at opportune moments. Even when they did meet, Robinson did not find Bathurst particularly interested in Canadian affairs. While he considered Bathurst to be 'a very good man, and an upright minister ... there is a coldness about him, an evident desire not to be troubled, and in fact a very prevailing determination to let the Colonies alone as long as they will let him alone.'[17] Robinson was not the only one to comment on Lord Bathurst's practised lack of interest in imperial concerns. On one occasion, he was alleged to have said to a departing governor, 'Joy be with you and let us hear as little of you as possible.'[18] Most of Robinson's correspondence and reported conversations were with Wilmot, not Bathurst. The evolution of policy rested more on the under-secretary than the colonial secretary himself.

The year of Robinson's arrival, 1822, also marked a distinct alteration in the course of the administration of Lord Liverpool. A new Cabinet was formed, and there was a move toward a more liberal policy.[19] Eager to get on with his mission and seek a resolution of the trade dispute, Robinson finally arranged a meeting with Bathurst in April. At this meeting he made it clear that interprovincial negotiations had failed; only the British government could resolve the issue. When Caldwell and Marshall joined the discussion, they clashed with Robinson over a proposed resolution. Wilmot resolved the impasse by instructing Robinson to draft a trade bill and send it to Marshall and Caldwell for comment. After reviewing the bill, Caldwell and Marshall reported that they had no objections to any of the material points in it. With their concurrence, Robinson was assured that 'Mr. Wilmot must be with me'[20] and that parliamentary approval would be forthcoming. Less than a month after his arrival, Robinson had succeeded in his delegated task.

The proposed trade bill guaranteed Upper Canada one-fifth of the duties collected at Quebec, and allowed for the percentage to be readjusted every three years. The amount of arrears owed to Upper Canada would be determined by a board of arbitrators. Each province was to appoint one official and the imperial government would appoint a third if the provinces failed to agree. The trade act also stipulated that no Lower Canadian bill affecting duties was to come into effect until it had been transmitted to the Upper Canadian and imperial governments. By that act, Lower Canada lost the authority to alter arbitrarily the rates of duty, and Upper Canada's future revenues were assured.

It appeared likely that both Robinson's trade bill and the act to unite Upper and Lower Canada would be presented to Parliament together. The proposed union measure went well beyond merely uniting the legislatures of the provinces. The bill provided that each province would have equal representation, despite the fact that Upper Canada's population was less than half that of Lower Canada's. In this English-dominated legislature, the journals would be kept in English and, after fifteen years, debate would be conducted exclusively in that language. Not only was the union bill a blatant attempt to undermine the French-Canadian nation, it also contained provisions to stop the spread of American egalitarianism in the Canadas. The new property qualification for elected members was to be £500, and the governor was empowered to appoint two non-voting members to the assembly. With these measures, the assembly would promptly join the legislative council as a preserve of the conservative gentry. Ellice had held several conversations with Wilmot and Bathurst and had convinced them of the merits of union. He had also assured them that the bill could be passed by Parliament without any serious opposition.[22]

By this time Robinson had lost his original enthusiasm for the project. He now felt strongly that the Colonial Office had not carefully reviewed the consequences and that a union of the provinces at this time would be 'an inconvenient and rather dangerous experiment.'[23] Until Robinson's arrival, Wilmot had been meeting exclusively with Ellice and the other promoters of union. One Sunday in April, Wilmot and Robinson spent the day discussing the union project. At the end of their discussion, Robinson felt that Wilmot's firm conviction in favour of union was shaken at least a little. Two days after this meeting, Robinson wrote to Wilmot detailing his arguments of the previous Sunday.[24]

He began by recounting that the division of Quebec in 1791 had been initiated because of the differences in language, religion, and origin of the settlers in the upper and lower areas. In the years since the division, these differences had become more acute. The British government should be aware that if it moved to unite Upper and Lower Canada, it would be wedding a French Catholic community to an English Protestant one. If the two communities were forced into union, violent confrontations would undoubtedly occur. Robinson readily admitted that Lower Canada's policies were perverse, but there was no guarantee that those policies would be righted in a union. Unfortunately, the Lower Canadians 'cherish prejudices which confine them to a narrow line of policy and make them hostile to improvements which would advance the welfare of the Colony.'[25] It was hardly in the imperial interest to tie the backward millstone of Lower Canada to the progressive commercial province of Upper Canada. While a union of the St Lawrence system might appeal to commercial interests, there were political, linguistic, and religious barriers to the scheme.

Robinson's memorandum seemed to have little effect in halting the momentum toward union. Lord Bathurst read Robinson's comments, and he discussed the issue with him in a personal interview. Nevertheless, the secretary remained determined to present a union bill to Parliament. While his fellow tory ministers were reluctant to put a contentious colonial issue before Parliament so late in the session, Bathurst was counting on Ellice's assurances that the bill would not encounter any opposition. Having instructions neither to oppose nor to advance the bill, Attorney-General Robinson determined to lobby on behalf of Upper Canada's best interests as he saw them. Despite his misgivings about the union, Robinson met with Marshall and assisted him in preparing a draft of the necessary legislation. Yet he was anxious to dissociate himself from the project: 'I am yet too doubtful of the wisdom of the change to be desirous of being thought the author of it, tho' to prevent worse measures I have taken a great deal of trouble to modify and may be so far considered to have countenanced these.'[26]

Robinson was left with little choice but to sit back and contemplate the great changes planned for his country. While Emma passed the summer visiting with her family, he spent his time in Westminster listening to the debates. On 20 June 1822 his trade bill and the bill to unite the Canadian legislatures were joined together and presented to Parliament as the

Canada Government and Trade Bill. To the government's surprise, one of the leading whigs, Sir James Mackintosh, rose and protested that this measure was of such importance to the people of the Canadas that it should not be passed without consulting them. Wilmot replied that 'he did not think it was necessary to apply to the people of the provinces for their consent to the measure, since their present constitution was derived from an act of the British legislature.'[27] The English newspapers, while not stating an opinion on Canadian affairs, condemned the under-secretary's cavalier treatment of colonial constitutions. The government's confidence was shaken, and the union bill was deferred to July.

While Parliament debated, Robinson transmitted news of the government's latest opinions to Major Hillier, and Hillier passed the information on to John Macaulay for publication in the *Kingston Chronicle*. This efficient system meant that Upper Canadians were receiving news of the latest events in London from a suitable tory source.[28]

While he was at the Colonial Office, Robinson also devoted himself to other matters of Canadian concern. He circulated Dr Strachan's memorandum on emigration, which put forward the idea of having the government send British paupers to Upper Canada. The attorney-general himself submitted a proposal on this subject which he thought would reduce the English poor-rates and increase Upper Canada's loyal population. But the British were reluctant to invest in their colonies, even to the extent of sending their poor overseas. One of the most popular themes advanced by the opposition whigs was the ultimate futility of maintaining colonies. Their arguments that colonies were a drain on the mother country and would declare independence as soon as they became self-reliant were generally accepted in liberal circles. Robinson found those ideas, as expressed in the *Edinburgh Review*, to be all-pervasive and the British government reluctant to accept any idea that might increase the colonial budget. Why spend money on colonies that would soon become independent (and probably hostile) republics? Robinson considered this attitude to be unwarranted but so widespread as to be beyond refutation: 'The people of this Country are opposed to the expenditure of a farthing for the Colonies.'[29]

Perhaps British disenchantment with colonies was increased by the publication of Robert Gourlay's *Statistical Account of Upper Canada*. In his diffuse and rambling tome, Gourlay condemned Upper Canada's government as utterly corrupt. Robinson refused to purchase any of the volumes, and instead glanced through a bookseller's copy. He reported to Strachan, 'such trash you never saw – It is a miserable compilation of all sorts of matter without order or connection – a great deal of abuse of course of you, the Chief, William Dickson, me and of all Governors that have ever been.'[30] Fortunately, Gourlay was almost unknown, and his book was so incoherent that it could be dismissed as the scribblings of a lunatic. Gourlay used his *Statistical Account* as the basis for a parliamentary petition to be presented by a leading whig, Henry Brougham. The petition alleged that Gourlay's banishment had been improper and that an inquiry into the system of government in Upper Canada was necessary. Because the petition was to be presented during the Canada bill debate, Gourlay and Robinson were forced to rub elbows in the parliamentary gallery. When Brougham failed to introduce the petition on the day Gourlay's supporters were present in Westminister, Gourlay stormed out of the gallery in feverish pursuit of Brougham. Robinson, who observed the scene, casually commented that the radical Mr Gourlay was obviously drunk.[31]

In Upper Canada, Dr Strachan was afraid that Robinson's prolonged absence would bring down criticism on his favourite pupil. Strachan advised Robinson that Maitland considered the attorney-general duty-bound to return to Upper Canada and report to Parliament on the customs dispute. Failing to report, in Maitland's opinion, would be 'a blot on yourself and a departure from the manly and direct course.'[32] At the same time Strachan and Maitland both agreed that Robinson should exercise his political and legal skills in a larger and more significant arena than Upper Canada. But Robinson was not eager to try his luck in England. He wrote to Strachan that he now had a growing family to consider and that on his slender finances beginning a new career in England was a risky proposition.[33] Strachan chastised Robinson for his caution and lectured him: 'As to your not having 100£ that is nothing with your talents.'[34] Nevertheless, Robinson remained unwilling to leave Upper Canada without the guarantee of a position at least equal to the one he currently held.

About the union measure, however, there was no disagreement between Robinson and his mentor. Strachan imagined the new joint legislature as 'a Babel, half roaring French, half English.' It was obvious to anyone who lived in British America that Upper and Lower Canada were two distinct communities that should remain separate. Strachan was so fearful of an association with the French Canadians that he predicted that a 'dismal explosion' would rend Upper Canada. Moreover, Britain had no right to impose union on the colonists without even consulting them. In revolutionary language more appropriate to John Adams than John

Strachan, he warned that 'it cannot be endured on constitutional principles that it should pass into law without any reference to those who are principally concerned.'[35]

From his London vantage, Robinson was beginning to have second thoughts about the undesirability of union. The bill contained provisions that favoured English Protestants and Upper Canada over French Canadians and Lower Canada. While union would undoubtedly result in temporary inconveniences, Robinson speculated, 'I trust it will in the end be found productive of much good – I think it will.'[36] Yet on the following day he wrote to Hillier that the project was an 'unnatural union of John Wilson and Jean Baptiste. I doubt not John will consider it most monstrous.'[37] These contradictory sentiments not only indicated Robinson's ambivalence on this issue but also reflected the delicate role he was forced to play in London. As a Crown officer he was expected to support a government measure, even if he found it to be ill-conceived.

Such vacillations did not afflict the British government, which remained convinced of the project's merits. But despite Ellice's assurances the bill encountered stiff opposition from the whigs. The government house leader, Lord Londonderry, finally agreed to an arrangement whereby the union bill would be postponed and the trade bill, which was necessary to resolve Upper Canada's financial crisis, would be passed during the session.

The task of drafting a new customs bill fell upon Robinson. He was given only a few days to redraft the legislation in a form acceptable to both government and opposition. He applied himself diligently, and on 5 August the revised Canada Trade Act was passed by Parliament.[38] Robert Wilmot knew that in order for an important colonial measure to have 'moral effect' in a colony, it required the full support of Parliament.[39] Nevertheless, no one was more disappointed than the under-secretary who had just seen his first major project go down to ignominious defeat.

In contrast, John Robinson had thoroughly enjoyed his first major triumph in London. Not only had he gained his objectives, but his Lower Canadian adversaries, Caldwell and Marshall, had been aware of his proposals and had given their approval. Despite their misgivings, Robinson had convinced them of the merits of Upper Canada's claims. In so doing, he had impressed colonial authorities with his diplomatic skills, and Lord Bathurst had invited Upper Canada's spokesman to dine with the government members, including the Duke of Wellington and Lord Liverpool.

In August 1822 Robinson gave Sir Peregrine Maitland a full report on his London activities.[40] He apologized for having acted without official authority, and explained that as commissioner for Upper Canada he felt obliged to represent the province's interests. He acknowledged that his ultimate authority was derived from the Colonial Office, and that he was therefore reluctant to 'fly in the face of the measure which His Majesty's Government proposed.'[41] Necessity dictated that Robinson's opposition be private. One sure measure of his diplomatic success was the fact that his cautious opposition had not antagonized Wilmot; during the debate they had maintained frequent personal contact. Their meetings 'prevented the necessity of written correspondence.' Robinson's ability to discern the limits of his opposition and his lucid defence of his own proposals had earned him considerable esteem in government circles.

In Upper Canada, however, the attorney-general's prolonged absence had created some anxiety. Since the beginning of the Eighth Parliament, Maitland had come to rely on Robinson's adroit handling of the assembly. Strachan informed Robinson that Maitland had anticipated Robinson's quick return to Upper Canada and an early resumption of his leadership during the next session: 'His Excellency seemed to think it necessary that you should attend the next Session of Parl't and that without your assistance he would be placed in an awkward situation.'[42] While this message indicated that Maitland placed a high degree of confidence in the member from York as the de facto leader of the government in the assembly, it also served as a clear reminder of Robinson's duty not to neglect his responsibilities in Upper Canada for diplomatic intrigues in Britain.

A far more serious threat to the soundness of the government than the attorney-general's lengthy absence was the split in tory ranks over the union question. In York, Dr Strachan was convinced that union would be disastrous, and that without guarantees of English Protestant supremacy the French Canadians would inevitably overthrow the society the loyalists had so painstakingly created. In Kingston, the gentry were enthusiastic supporters of union; both John Macaulay and Christopher Hagerman were in favour of a federation that would place them in a larger province with an ocean port and ready access to European markets. Even before the measure was debated in Parliament, Macaulay wrote an editorial in which he gave early approval to the proposed union.[43] The Kingston merchants, who felt that Robinson's trade act had not solved the province's revenue problems, were certain that union would bring prosperity. Macaulay and Hagerman addressed a huge meeting held in Kingston to demonstrate popular support for the union. 'Nature intended us to be one people,' Hagerman cried out to the receptive gathering. Macaulay, who disliked public speaking, described in more subdued tones the likely benefits of joining resources with Lower Canada.[44]

The differences in opinion between York and Kingston remained a discreet dispute between gentlemen. Strachan praised Macaulay for giving his honest opinion on a matter of such grave importance.[45] Robinson thought that his friend's speech was 'a fair argument & extremely creditable to him.'[46] No lasting hostility resulted from the difference between the York and Kingston factions over the union question, but the incident revealed that there were disagreements within tory ranks about the future course of Upper Canada. Nevertheless, while one might respect the opinions of another gentleman, Robinson also thought that 'he [Macaulay] does not look eno' at the consequences as he will find if the measure carries.'[47] Robinson did not oppose the union because he 'instinctively distrusted centralization and control,'[48] but rather because he remained convinced that union was inimical to Upper Canada's best interests. If possible, he wished to see union deferred until the English population could form a majority in a united province. Until then, Robinson warned, the Lower Canadians in a united assembly would regard the Upper Canadians with 'perfect contempt,' as if they were 'yankees or Indian traders.'[49]

Although Robinson was certain of the correctness of his stand, he was uneasy about the possibility of the provincial establishment repudiating his arguments. Robinson's anti-union stand reflected his opinions and Dr Strachan's. He had had no directives from either Hillier or Maitland instructing him to oppose the measure. After Robinson had made his report to the lieutenant-governor in August, he was left to wonder whether the provincial government supported him. When he received no word from Upper Canada he began to fear that Hillier and Maitland had dissociated themselves from their presumptuous commissioner. This frightening uncertainty was dispelled in November when Lord Bathurst read one of Sir Peregrine Maitland's dispatches to Robinson. The dispatch indicated, in Maitland's usual cautious tone, that he too entertained 'stubborn scruples' about the union project.[50]

Other than this dispatch, Robinson received no indication that the lieutenant-governor supported his activities. Two events entirely unconnected with public affairs induced the attorney-general to remain in England. Emma had heard of the horrors of making an Atlantic crossing during the winter, and insisted on staying with her family until the spring; Robinson had been attending Lincoln's Inn, and stood ready to be called to the English bar early in 1823. Frantically, he wrote to Hillier, begging for directions. In strong language (for which he was later to apologize) Robinson expressed his 'annoyance, to use a gentle word' for having been left without instructions.[51] Finally, in November, Robinson received his orders from Maitland to return to Upper Canada.

At this critical point, with the union question still pending, Robinson decided to defy Maitland and seek authority to remain in England. Outflanking the lieutenant-governor, he referred his orders to the Colonial Office. Robert Wilmot had a great deal of confidence in Robinson's opinions, and instructed him to stay.[52] 'It is very important,' Robinson explained to Maitland's secretary, 'that there should be someone on the spot between this and the next session capable of informing them [the Colonial Office] as I believe I am, how to appreciate the representations [on the union question] they receive from various quarters.'[53]

The attorney-general now had the authority to tarry in England until the next session of Parliament. The reliability of the advice he had already given ensured that he would be consulted on any new Canadian legislation. This respite also gave him the opportunity to reconsider his personal position and to reflect on the advantages of abandoning the colonies for a career in English politics.

The break between sessions of Parliament enabled Robinson to return to Lincoln's Inn and be admitted to the English bar. The interval also freed him to cultivate his English friends, and he frequently breakfasted with Wilmot. During one of their meetings, Robinson suggested that the British government should be looking beyond the mere union of Upper and Lower Canada to a general confederation of all the British North American colonies. Robinson was not the first to envisage a federation of the British North American colonies. Chief Justice Sewell of Lower Canada had advanced the idea in 1807. Wilmot was intrigued by the idea, and when Robinson mentioned it to him again in January 1823, he asked his Canadian colleague to write down his visions of this larger union. Robinson set to work outlining a plan for a general confederation. He envisaged the united British America becoming 'effectually an integral part of the Empire.'[54] Through a general union, British America could transcend colonial status and merge into the United Kingdom as a trans-Atlantic component of the British nation.

Robinson's despondency over the anticipated federation with the French Canadians was swept away as he contemplated the exciting possibility of confederation. Early in 1823 he submitted his plan to the Colonial Office.[55] By uniting the two Canadas with Nova Scotia, New Brunswick, and Prince Edward Island in one 'grand confederacy,' British America would become indelibly British and Protestant. The French Canadians would be in the minority and could not object to being junior partners in the arrangement. This was, to Robinson's mind, a more equitable solution, and one that could be accomplished 'without injustice, or appearance of injustice.'[56] In the confederation, the general legislature would have authority over trade, revenue, defence, and religion, would dispense money to the provinces to pay their civil lists, and would even serve as a court of appeal. Provincial legislatures would remain, but their authority would be limited to matters of local concern. The desired effect of this centralization would be to 'bind more closely the allegiance of the whole.'

Robinson, who sincerely hoped that British America would become a 'New Albion,' saw the united legislature as only the first step in its ultimate absorption into the United Kingdom:

By making these provinces actually a part of the *United Kingdom*; by bringing nearer to their view the true nature and spirit of those monarchical institutions which they sincerely respect ... In due time, the semblance of monarchy might be made more exact.[57]

To cement the imperial tie, Robinson suggested that British Americans be elected to sit in the Westminster Parliament. British America would cease to be a colony and would eventually evolve into a functioning part of the United Kingdom.

Robinson kept the proposal for a confederation before the Colonial Office, and added his own thoughts on allying the confederation more closely with the British Crown. Perhaps the most attractive part of the plan, at least as far as the attorney-general was concerned, was the probability that union would inhibit the growth of American institutions in Upper Canada. The upper provinces would be submerged in a federation with the Atlantic provinces, which maintained closer contacts with the mother country. The direction of the single province's growth would be steered toward Britain and the ties to the United States held to a necessary minimum.

It is believed that to unite the British North American Provinces by giving them a common legislature and erecting them into a Kingdom, would be gratifying to all those colonies: that it would add to their security, confirm their attachment to the present government, and make wider the distinction between it and the republican institutions of their neighbours.[58]

Robinson's suggestion of a general confederation of British America was more than an attempt to distract the Colonial Office from the question of the union of Upper and Lower Canada. he foresaw that a federation would increase the self-reliance of the colonies while strengthening the imperial bond. The colonial officers, however, thought Robinson's projections far too optimistic. A report by a member of the Colonial Office's legal staff dismissed the plan as impractical.[59] The report accurately noted that British America covered a vast expanse, and travelling between the colonies was a time-consuming task. It would be impossible for a member to travel to the capital to attend a session and still keep abreast of his constituents' opinions. The report also noted that the germ of independence existed within all the British American colonies. How was it possible to retain the loyalty of a people 'whom every day removes further from us in consanguinity, customs, habits and opinions. It may be a strong expression, but it had appeared to me that our colonial principle retains within itself the germ of separation.'[60]

The discussion of a 'grand confederacy' remained mere speculation so long as the Colonial Office was wedded to the project of uniting the Canadas. By January 1823, however, reports of violent French-Canadian opposition to the union were reaching London. Even in Upper Canada, the measure was receiving little support. While the Kingston merchants anticipated some advantage from the union, the York officials were afraid of losing their government positions. In rural areas, the union bill was condemned as anti-democratic, and it was said that in some counties not one person possessed the minimum property qualifications to stand for election. Lord Bathurst told Maitland in January 1823 that in view of this uproar the union bill would not be reintroduced in the next session of Parliament but would be postponed until it had greater support.

During the winter of 1823, Robinson and Wilmot speculated whether Upper Canada could be the solution to the serious problems afflicting the Empire. In the years prior to 1823, the British Isles had witnessed the exodus of a number of impoverished people. The eviction of the Highland crofters had resulted in thousands of them making their way to the United States and the provinces of British America. English emigration was not as great, although the parish poor-rates which supported the paupers added a heavy burden to an overtaxed middle class. The most dire poverty existed in Ireland where the densest population in Europe struggled to survive on a single staple crop. With a population reduced to tenantry, and the tenantry subject to high rents, there was civil unrest throughout rural Ireland. Wilmot was beginning to believe that it would be to the Empire's advantage to spend the money to send those paupers to the colonies; they would no longer be a burden on the finances of the mother country, and their labour would fortify the Empire.

The problem of British overpopulation intrigued Robinson, and he prepared an article for the *Quarterly Review* on the merits of supervised emigration. When Wilmot expressed an interest in the subject, Robinson put aside his writing and concentrated on working through the government. He advised Wilmot that it would be to the benefit of the colony and the Empire to establish 'a regular system of sending out to Canada as many of the labouring poor as you have land to hold – at the charge of the Govt. and under their superintendance ...'[61] Wilmot enthusiastically seized on this idea and began preparing an emigration scheme for the Cabinet's consideration. Robinson had confidence that Liverpool's government could be persuaded to support the scheme as a novel way of reducing the poor-rates. The project would need considerable government financing to get underway. Even though Robinson was aware that Lord Bathurst was continually preaching economy in colonial spending, the attorney-general gleefully reported that 'the benefits I anticipate from this system are very great particularly in the great consumption in provisions it will occasion for which the Govt. will pay in money.'[62] The colonial secretary's sermons on frugality clearly were lost on the attorney-general.

In January 1823 Wilmot presented his emigration plan to the Cabinet. He had prepared the groundwork by circulating the plan among several government leaders and getting their cautious approval. On 13 January the Cabinet discussed the issue and consented to the introduction as a government measure of a supervised scheme of emigration to Upper Canada. This was not the first such project sponsored by the British government: the government had settled disbanded soldiers in Lanark and Perth counties in the hope of creating a military settlement to protect the canals. Those projects had proved to be costly failures that did not improve Upper Canada's defences. Wilmot and Robinson were now planning on a grander scale to use not just soldiers but civilian emigrants to settle unpopulted areas. This new approach would also address the problems created by Irish overpopulation and make the emigration project a truly unique experiment.

It was not enough merely to set aside money for the project. In order to transport hundreds of paupers from one continent to another and keep them from starving until they could fend for themselves, a leader must be found who could not only organize this massive project but also maintain the respect of the Irish. It was felt that John Robinson's brother Peter might be the right man for the task. Peter, not content to live his life in offices and courtrooms, had followed his stepfather, Elisha Beman, to a trading post north of York. The market was accessible to the outlying settlers and eventually developed into a flourishing business. By the early 1820s, the 'New Market' was the main distribution point for goods traded with the Indian tribes. Peter also owned farming tracts, several productive flour mills, and a tavern. His success in business had brought him prominence in frontier society, and he had preceded his brother in gaining entry to the assembly. Peter, in London as a tourist, was interested in his brother's emigration scheme, and was happy to advise Robert Wilmot on conditions existing on the frontier.

The under-secretary was impressed with Peter Robinson's business acumen and his understanding of provincial conditions. John Robinson acknowledged that while 'Quille driving ... is to be my vocation' his brother was a man of action.[63] Wilmot advised him that the government had decided on a plan to settle five or six hundred Irish peasants in Upper Canada, and the experiment, if successful, would be the model for future projects. In order to succeed the project needed a capable administrator. Would Peter Robinson be willing to undertake the task? When John brought the proposal to his brother, Peter declined, saying that he would be forced to neglect his prospering businesses for 'what appeared to be a limited experiment requiring his full attention, and offering few financial rewards.'[64] Wilmot, convinced that Peter was the only man for the job, approached him personally to request that he organize the emigration. Peter replied that he doubted whether he could control the 'South Irish.' John Robinson applied further pressure to his brother by telling him that if he did not accept the assignment, the project would be abandoned and Peter would later regret having acted solely in his own self-interest. Under this pressure, Peter Robinson finally conceded and agreed to take charge of the emigration project.

In May 1823 Peter Robinson arrived in Cork and began the process of selecting emigrants. The local gentry put forward their least desirable inhabitants; but Robinson, after gaining the trust of the local priests, eventually received applications from more respectable paupers. Peter worked quickly and by July had organized a party of 568 settlers to be sent to Upper Canada.

In addition to the need for new settlers, there were other serious difficulties in Upper Canada's land settlement policies, ones that had to be remedied without imperial assistance. Settlers were widely dispersed and large blocks of Crown and clergy reserves separated one small village from another. In the early years of the province, land had been granted with a too generous hand, and large estates now lay idle in the possession of speculators or government officials. The government itself retained millions of uncultivated acres of Crown and clergy reserves in townships throughout the province, making it by far the largest speculator. Sir Peregrine Maitland aware of the defects of the system, had initiated steps to ensure that granted lands were cultivated and not merely held for speculation.[65] Robinson and Strachan also were unhappy that the clergy reserves were not providing financial support for the established Church and the Crown reserves were not materially assisting the government. As he had done many times during his English sojourn, Robinson discussed the future of the reserves with Wilmot, who then asked Robinson to set down his thoughts in a formal memorandum.

Robinson's essay on land policy began by conceding that the leasing program was a failure.[66] It was obvious that with free grants of land available, few settlers were interested in leasing land and fewer still were interested in paying their rents. In many ways the Crown reserves were more of a liability than an asset. They were the main cause of the dispersed form of settlement and had become a focus for settler's grievances. However, Robinson cautioned against disposing of the Crown reserves when the ready availability of land made real estate such a cheap commodity. He thought that the solution lay in a limited sale of reserve lands. Demonstrating a shrewd knowledge of local land prices, probably gained from his travels through the province, Robinson suggested that leased reserve land be sold to the tenants for twenty shillings per acre. While he realized that the current price for an acre of such land was five shillings, Robinson thought that many tenants would grasp an opportunity to increase their holdings.

While Robinson advocated a limited sale of Crown reserves, he was quick to deny that the government should sell any clergy reserves, which, he felt, 'at present form but an insignificant provision for the invaluable object they are intended to secure.' According to Robinson, clergy reserves were protected by statute and should remain at the disposal of the established Church. This single-minded devotion to the preservation of clergy reserves, while undoubtedly a result of his association with Dr Strachan and their mutual understanding that an orderly society required an established Church to preserve moral order, had little support in the province. The religious loyalties of most settlers seem to have been with the Methodists, Presbyterians, or Baptists.[67]

Robinson felt that the limited sale of Crown reserves would solve the problem of dispersed settlement and provide an independent source of income for the provincial government. On his copy of the report, Robinson noted that it 'led to the formation of the Canada Company – as it seems – by Mr. Galt.' This was no immodest boast; the Colonial Office would very shortly see the necessity of selling Crown lands in order to finance the imperial administration. Within a few years, Wilmot would be administering a vast system of Crown land sales in Australia and New Zealand as well as in Upper Canada. If John Galt was the actual founder of the Canada Company, then Robinson and Wilmot were its 'spiritual fathers.'[68]

In January 1822, however, the British government was not particularly receptive to any suggestions to sell off Crown lands in the colonies. The clerks in Treasury Chambers found Robinson's projections to be 'too sanguine.' Wild lands could not possibly be sold for the sums the attorney-general suggested; instead, the Treasury clerks wished to see an improvement in the leasing system.[69] The clerks doubted that anyone would be willing to invest in the forests of the Canadas, and they dismissed Robinson's plan as altogether impractical. John Robinson was unable to convey to the London bureaucrats his boundless faith in the future prosperity of Upper Canada.

During his prolonged stay in England Robinson maintained some contact with Canadian events by becoming a regular patron of the New England Coffee House. Most days, Robinson could be found in the New England, taking his leisure and reading the latest newspapers from the Canadas. The news from York in the spring of 1823 was mixed. In the attorney-general's absence Dr W.W. Baldwin had emerged as a leading figure in the legislature. While Christopher Hagerman introduced the government measures, it was the eloquent and reform-minded Baldwin who seemed able to dominate the House. Yet the doctor occasionally struck an independent stance. On the all-important question of union, Colonel Nichol had said confidently that a majority of the members would support the measure to unite the provinces.[70] Baldwin, however, condemned the 'great evils' in the bill, saying that the proposed union had 'little regard for the principle of the British Constitution.'[71] The union question was referred to a joint parliamentary committee, which found itself unable to reach a conclusion. No doubt to the attorney-general's relief, the Legislature of Upper Canada refused to endorse the proposed union.

Although Dr Baldwin might join with the government on some important issues, one cause bound all the reformers together. Robinson had advised the government in December that he had exhausted his grant and that he had suffered a serious financial loss as a result of having neglected his legal practice.[72] The lieutenant-governor recommended that Robinson be voted additional remuneration. The resolution authorizing the additional sum cited Robinson for having performed 'with a zeal, ability and fidelity highly honourable to himself.' Holding this flattering resolution up for ridicule, Baldwin pointed out that it was the commissioner's sworn duty to perform to the limits of his ability.[73] Other reformers downplayed the attorney-general's efforts: Robert Randall considered him to be a man of 'alarming talents,' but 'did not wish to make an idol of him.' Fortunately for Robinson, he had two able advocates in Christopher Hagerman and Jonas Jones. Hagerman pointed out that John Robinson had saved the province from the threat of bankruptcy, and for this invaluable service he deserved to be recompensed to the extent of his lost legal fees. Jones told the house that he had received a communication from Robinson in which the commissioner admitted to being so reduced in funds that he and his family were living at a friend's residence.[74] The reformers' sniping at the attorney-general could not stop the government members from voting him an additional remuneration of £1,000.

Even more than during the previous session of the legislature, the question of alien status occupied the assembly's attention. Marshall Spring Bidwell, the son of the expelled Barnabas Bidwell, had stood as a candidate in the Lennox and Addington by-election. The returning officer refused to accept his candidacy, reasoning that Bidwell, born in the United States, was as much an alien as his father. When the matter was brought before the assembly, Nichol moved that the election be declared void and that Bidwell be proclaimed 'in so far as allegiance is concerned ... eligible to a seat in the house.'[75] This motion passed despite the objections of Dr Baldwin, who noted that a mere resolution of a provincial assembly could not change the imperial naturalization laws.

Robinson made a point of seeing the imperial attorney-general, Sir John Singleton Copley, and advising him on the serious implications of the naturalization laws. Copley could only tell Robinson to be patient; a case currently before the English Court of King's Bench would decide definitively the issue of alien status. In private conversation, however,

Copley assured Robinson that Bidwell's expulsion was quite proper, as Bidwell was 'an Alien as much as a Frenchman.'[76] But the government still had no desire to remedy the situation; Robinson observed that with the union bill pending, the ministry had no inclination to place any other contentious colonial matters before Parliament.

Robinson was aware of the seriousness of the alien problem and the threat it posed to the government's authority. American settlers took great offence at being deprived of their civil liberties and blamed what they perceived to be an intransigent York oligarchy. They would have been surprised to learn that Attorney-General Robinson was as concerned about their predicament as they were. Robinson knew that aliens could not hold land and that most of the land in Upper Canada had been owned, at one time or another, by aliens. If all those deeds were void, then Robinson's work in encouraging emigration and rationalizing land settlement was in vain. Anarchy would result, and no doubt the American-born would see rebellion as the only way to secure their land holdings. In order to avoid this chaos, Robinson urged Lord Bathurst to insert a clause in the union bill recognizing the rights of American-born settlers to vote and convey land.[77] Robinson was aware that Upper Canada was legally impotent to remedy the situation and that it required an act of the British Parliament to naturalize the American settlers. However, Robinson found that a 'repugnance was felt to introducing any matter which might seem to bear however indirectly upon the Alien Laws of England.' The Colonial Office refused to act, and the imperial attorney-general waited for a decision from the courts. The alien issue remained unresolved, fostering controversy and attracting disciples to the cause of reform.

Still, the Assembly of Upper Canada naively believed that the problem could be neatly solved by provincial decree. Once again there was an election in Lennox and Addington, and this time it appeared certain that the younger Bidwell would win. Robinson, discouraged by this prospect, wrote to urge John Macaulay to run against Bidwell.[78] Robinson's warm and often humorous correspondence with John Macaulay indicates that the Kingston publisher was foremost among Robinson's few close friends. Now he advised Macaulay of a sure way to victory: 'You have full liberty to abuse me if that will help you as no doubt it would – You know I am a most tyrannical and corrupt fellow and don't let old acquaintance make you shy of opposing me.' Robinson was well aware that his position as leader of the government in the assembly had made him the obvious target for popular discontent. Macaulay, however, could not be persuaded to run.

With the government's acceptance of the emigration scheme and its abandonment of the union project, Robinson's work in London was complete. His mission to England from 1822 to 1823 was the most outstanding success of his career. He had negotiated a favourable trade bill, played a part in the defeat of a potentially disastrous union, and had worked with much success to dispel the notion that colonies were futile enterprises. He had given a convincing demonstration of the deep desire of British Americans to remain part of the Empire. Beyond that, he had helped to initiate the supervised emigration scheme of 1823 in an important attempt not only to benefit Upper Canada but to tie the colony even closer to the mother country. His one major failing was his inability to convince the Colonial Office of the significance of the alien question. That failure would eventually bring disaster to the provincial oligarchy.

As a result of his mission, Robinson, in British eyes, was much more than a minor colonial official. The influential men of Westminster were impressed with his legal skills, and the friendships he made could be easily translated into power. 'It is really fortunate I suppose to be here,' he remarked, 'for vols. of dispatches would not instruct so satisfactorily as I can do personally or rather have done.'[79] Robert Wilmot remained an intimate friend, and Lord Bathurst's regard for Robinson was such that he offered him the vacant position of chief justice of Mauritius. This was a high honour for any colonial, and especially for one who was only thirty-two years old. To have accepted the chief justiceship would have assured John Robinson – the son of an impoverished soldier – wealth, a knighthood, and a status superior to anything he could achieve in Upper Canada. Robinson declined the offer, explaining to Lord Bathurst that 'attachments of a public and private nature ... lead me to prefer my present situation in Canada.'[80]

A major factor in Robinson's refusal of the appointment was his rise to prominence in Upper Canada. He not only represented the government in the assembly, but also acted as the provincial government's intermediary between York and London. His unquestioned abilities made him the lieutenant-governor's most trusted adviser. Even John Strachan, his former master, bowed to the views of the attorney-general. In a statement made years later, but which might well have applied to 1823, Strachan admitted that Robinson was 'wiser than I am – to him I give up in most things, but to no other tho' it would commonly seem that we arrive even without communication at similar conclusions.'[81] With the assistance of Strachan and Hillier and the compliance of Sir Peregrine Maitland, Robinson was now in a position to direct the future course of Upper

Canada's government. The chief justiceship of Mauritius could not replace status and power already achieved.

Before he left London, Robinson was informed that the initial surveying work had begun for a canal on the route from Kingston to the Ottawa River. Estimates were also being tendered for a canal to connect Lake Ontario with Burlington Bay. The great improvements to the province's internal navigation were at last underway, and the projects would undoubtedly result in a dependable transportation system that would ensure Upper Canada's future prosperity. As he prepared to return home, John Robinson was determined to play a part in guiding this exciting era of economic development. 'One day or another,' he prophesied, 'we shall be a great people – That is certain – My boys may live to see it.'[82] For once, John Robinson was not sufficiently optimistic; he himself would live to see a great and prosperous Upper Canada.

7

'He Serves the King, Sir'

After an uneventful Atlantic crossing, the Robinsons arrived in New York to a warm welcome from their friends in the British community. Families like the Robinsons regularly passed through New York on their way to or from England, and the British residents of the city welcomed their company and, of course, their gossip. The Robinsons travelled by steamboat up the rivers of New York State, while their baggage was sent via the slower Erie Canal. John Robinson arrived at the Niagara, and called on Sir Peregrine Maitland at Stamford Park.

During the summer months the lieutenant-governor all but abandoned the unhealthy lowlands of York and resided at his 'cottage' at Stamford. On a lovely escarpment overlooking the Niagara River, Lake Ontario, and the lush farmland of Niagara, Maitland had built a twenty-two-room mansion. The four hundred acres surrounding the house were carefully laid out, and even the occasional English visitor was impressed with Stamford Park's natural beauty and orderly arrangement.[1] After 1822, Maitland preferred to spend more and more of his time at Stamford Park, and it became the site for the transaction of government business. Robinson spent two days reporting to the lieutenant-governor on the resolution of the customs dispute, the union question, and the emigration projects. Maitland was excited by the prospect of increased emigration, and he ordered a surveyor to lay out farm lots for the expected arrivals.[2] Robinson continued on to York and from there travelled by horseback to Newmarket.

York had become John Robinson's home and the focus of his ambitions, but Newmarket was the centre of the rest of the Robinson clan's activities. The youngest Robinson brother, William, had joined Peter in the fur-trading business and was now running various enterprises in Peter's absence. William Robinson was cast in Peter's mould – the not very bookish but lively and talented frontier entrepreneur. During John's absence, William had married, and he and his new wife looked after Robinson's mother, who now resided permanently in Newmarket. William's marriage had been a gala affair, well attended by the province's leading families. In Newmarket, John retrieved his two boys, Lukin and John. After his lengthy absence, he was dismayed to find that 'they did not seem to remember much of me.'[3]

The family retainer, Howard, had taken care to see that John Robinson's garden was tended in the family's absence. Robinson returned to find his asparagus beds in tolerable condition and his apple trees in fine health. Indeed, he found York in the summer of 1823 to be 'as healthy as anywhere in the world can be.' There had been little change in the capital, and York remained a sleepy government town of fewer than two thousand persons.

After spending the early part of the summer attending to his legal cases, by late August Robinson was travelling with King's Bench in the eastern districts of Upper Canada. Soon after, he was required to act as Crown prosecutor in another set of assizes. Travel on the court circuit was still laborious. On one occasion he wrote to Macaulay, 'Pray for good weather for me'[4] as he prepared to travel the 250 miles from York to Sandwich.

In the early 1820s, the legal profession was still in its infancy, and the Law Society did not yet own a building. Robinson had already served one term as treasurer and had been a member of the committee that had discussed the plans to build a hall. In 1821, he had removed an obstacle to the construction of a legal chambers when he introduced a bill in the assembly to permit the Law Society to own land.[5] In addition to incorporating the Law Society, this statute enabled Robinson to put some of his English experiences into effect.

The distinction between barristers, who represented parties before judges, and attorneys, the 'lower branch of the profession' who prepared files and pleadings, was made clearer. Barristers were to be supervised by the Law Society; attorneys were placed under the direct jurisdiction of the courts. In practice, most Upper Canadian lawyers were both barristers and attorneys. Many British attorneys were applying to practise in the province, and Robinson insisted that because they were not barristers in

England, they should not be entitled to be barristers in Upper Canada. The attorney-general also hoped to raise the standards of the legal profession by requiring articling clerks to serve under a senior lawyer for a fixed term of five years before being admitted to the Law Society. Dr Baldwin, another former treasurer of the Law Society, agreed with Robinson's plans but asked, tongue in cheek, why the government felt it necessary 'to make the profession respectable.' Baldwin noted that Britain abounded with 'petty foggers' who engaged in law practice, and that it would be an injustice to the young lawyers of Upper Canada to permit such persons to have access to the provincial bar.[6]

Not all members were enthralled with Robinson's amendments to the Law Society Act. Some feared that the society would become a wealthy, self-serving institution. Charles Jones proposed an amendment to limit the amount of money the society could charge a student for admission.[7] The amendment was soundly defeated. The attorney-general reminded the House that in thirty years of existence, the Law Society had accumulated assets of only £600. His plan to leave the legal profession free from government interference as a self-regulating society remained intact. In addition to gaining the gratitude of the legal fraternity for preserving its independence and raising professional standards, Robinson resolved a long-standing dispute concerning fees. The old tariff prescribed by the Judicature Act of 1794 was abolished, and judges were given the responsibility of establishing counsel fees.[8] This flexible approach proved to be a popular and efficient solution to fee scheduling.

Robinson's primary responsibility, however, was to ensure that the routine tasks of the attorney-general's office were performed. He investigated criminal activity and made the necessary decisions to lay charges.

In addition to undertaking criminal prosecutions, Robinson was often consulted by local sheriffs about personal disputes. In one such case, the Niagara sheriff reported that an elderly resident had died in debtor's prison with his debt unsatisfied. The sheriff asked Robinson to relieve him of the unpleasant duty of having to seize the estate property left to the deceased's family. Robinson expressed his sorrow that any man should have to die in debtor's prison and ordered the sheriff not to proceed against the estate.[9]

In addition to conducting the prosecutions during the criminal assizes, Robinson maintained a sizeable civil practice. The size of his clientele was due, in part, to his stature in the government. To have the attorney-general, the lieutenant-governor's adviser, as one's advocate added credibility to the weakest of cases. Perhaps because of his official and unofficial influence, Robinson acted as counsel to Upper Canada's foremost citizens. In 1818, he had been retained by William Dickson in a case concerning the ownership of almost 90,000 acres of land on the Grand River. The case consumed most of a year and involved a number of complicated motions. The parties finally went to trial in November 1818. On the first day, the court sat until four in the morning. After a second exhausting day, Robinson had the satisfaction of noting 'a verdict for the *Plaintiff*.' His triumph was sweetened when he submitted a bill of costs for £699.[10] Robinson also had been retained by another wealthy Niagaran, Thomas Clark, in a successful suit against a reformer, Robert Randall. but retaining the attorney-general was not in itself a guarantee of success; in 1819, Robinson defended Samuel Peters Jarvis in a suit in which Dr Baldwin successfully presented the plaintiff's case.[11]

In most cases, settlements were amicably arrived at without the necessity of going to trial; in those situations the attorney-general still collected a respectable fee for his services. Robinson's legal practice undoubtedly gave him one of the highest incomes in his profession and enabled him to discharge the heavy debt he had accumulated during his student days. The seizure of contraband goods by revenue officers also helped Robinson augment his salary. The smuggling of tobacco and beef into the province was a regular practice, and smugglers, when detected, often abandoned their goods only to slip back across the border and try their luck another day. These 'persons unknown' were then sued by the attorney-general and their goods forfeited to the Crown. The fees from these proceedings netted Robinson a modest but regular supplement to his ordinary income.

During the attorney-general's sojourn in England, a system of reports of the leading court cases was begun. Ironically, in the first reported case in which the attorney-general appeared, he acted as a defence counsel. As he had done during the War of 1812, Robinson again defended government officials accused of misusing the authority of their office.

In the case of *The King* v *McKenzie and McIntyre*,[12] Robinson successfully defended two magistrates who had been charged with contempt. He then asked that they be granted the costs of their defence. Robinson presented his case by using a series of arguments, all leading to the conclusion that his opponent's argument was unprecedented and, if followed, would lead to serious public harm: 'There are two substantial reasons for giving costs, namely, to protect magistrates where there is no proof of intentional misconduct, and to discourage vexatious attacks upon them.'[13] This argument met stiff resistance from Robinson's opposing counsel,

Solicitor-General Henry Boulton. Boulton reminded the court that it was also their duty to protect citizens from the arbitrary acts of local magistrates. Two of the justices split their decision, and the deciding judgment was left to Chief Justice Powell. He held that there were substantial grounds for the prosecutor's actions, and the motion for costs was dismissed.

English precedent dominated legal reasoning in Upper Canada, but Robinson relied on precedent only when it served his purposes. Acting for a plaintiff who had neglected to state in the pleadings the place where a promissory note was to be paid, Robinson argued against the application of precedent.[14] According to the strict rules of procedure of that time, pleadings on a note had to specify the place of payment in order to be valid. While this was undoubtedly the common law as it existed in Upper Canada, Robinson argued on behalf of his client that a statute had recently been passed in Britain which annulled this requirement. In dismissing Robinson's argument the court held that any British statutes passed after 1792, the year Upper Canada adopted English law, would have to be specifically adopted by the province in order to be effective.

As a sign of his growing maturity as an advocate, Robinson was undertaking increasingly difficult files. At the Niagara Assizes of 1824, he acted for a young woman who had been seduced and had borne a bastard child. At trial, he had the unfortunate girl testify while rocking her child. This tactic had little success, and the jury awarded minimal damages. Even though Robinson could not promise success, his presentation of cases was thorough and intelligent and even one of his political enemies admitted that in court 'his conduct was marked throughout with a degree of politeness to all who had to do with him, which joined to his leniency as a public officer, deserves commendation.'[15]

Although he was a prominent figure in the reported cases of the period, Robinson never towered above his colleagues. Perhaps even more notable was James Buchanan Macaulay, a capable advocate who often argued against and prevailed over the attorney-general. One of the new attorneys appearing before the courts was Robert Baldwin, the son of the leading reformer, Dr W.W. Baldwin. In the first clash between Baldwin and the attorney-general, Robinson argued that his client, a debtor, should be freed from jail because of a release from debtor's jail that he had received in the United States.[16] Baldwin successfully countered that this was not in accordance with English custom and that the man's imprisonment was valid. In this instance, Robinson was forced to argue the persuasive value of American law while Baldwin defended the English way. Even though Robinson was a leading member of the small Upper Canadian bar, he was not predominant; even in eulogy a spokesman for the provincial bar remarked that '[Robinson] surpassed his contemporaries at *nisi prius* [trial of civil causes] we are not prepared to affirm; we think he had certainly his equals; but in soundness and depth of legal knowledge, he was preeminent.'[17]

John Robinson was certainly an impressive figure in the courts. His aristocratic features, his high forehead, and his prominent, narrow nose gave him an air of authority. As events would soon reveal, he would not shrink from the attack of anyone, even a judge. The unsure attorney of the Selkirk hearings, the shy young barrister who admitted that in his first cases he had never even seen the jury, was becoming a mature and able advocate. Other advocates might be better orators, but it was generally conceded that the attorney-general's thorough preparation made him a formidable opponent. One of his most persistent political adversaries, Marshall Spring Bidwell, who occasionally acted as his junior solicitor, observed,

His appearance was striking. His features were classically and singularly beautiful, his countenance was luminous with intelligence and animation; his whole appearance that of a man of genius and a polished gentleman, equally dignified and graceful.

I heard him frequently at the Bar, and on some occasions I had the honour to be junior counsel with him. He was a consummate advocate, as well as a profound and accurate lawyer.[18]

His growing maturity was never more apparent than when he undertook a difficult case and succeeded against the odds. In *Emery* v *Miller*,[19] Robinson's client sold land and was then sued by the purchaser because the title was invalid. Despite the fact that there was evidence that the defendant knew beforehand that the title was invalid, damages were awarded to the purchaser. On appeal, Robinson claimed that the purchaser's tactics were 'mere plundering' and even though he knew that the law was probably against him, he asked the court to apply equitable rules of justice: '... it must not be inferred, because courts of equity are so often called upon that courts of law have not equally the power of relieving against fraud, suppression of truth or false assumption...'[20] The Attorney-General convinced the court that fraud may have played a part in the transaction, and a new trial was ordered.

Robinson still maintained a lucrative civil practice, but as attorney-general his foremost responsibility was the conduct of criminal prosecutions. The criminal law was a particularly harsh instrument of justice. In November of 1823, three men were publicly hanged in York; one was a horse-thief and the other two burglars.[21] In 1820, two horse-thieves sentenced to die had petitioned for clemency. The chief justice advised against granting mercy on the ground that 'example is necessary.'[22] After the Midland assizes of 1826, a woman convicted of petty larceny was sentenced to be whipped and imprisoned for twelve months. A man convicted of grand larceny was imprisoned for a year and publicly whipped. At the same assizes, however, a man convicted of assault with intent to commit rape received a ten-pound fine, three months' imprisonment, and one hour in the pillories.[23] Convictions for violent sexual assaults merited far less punishment than did crimes against property. This attitude was clearly evident at the Niagara assizes of 1826, where a man convicted of cattle theft was sentenced to be hanged while a man convicted of attempted rape received a fine of twenty-five pounds and three months' imprisonment. Little allowance was made for mitigating circumstances, and many crimes carried a mandatory death penalty.[24]

The inflexibility of this system was called into question as a result of the case of Mary Thompson. A serving girl in the McNabb household, young Mary had given birth to an illegitimate child. When the child disappeared, Mary was forced to admit that the baby had died and that she had buried it in a makeshift grave.[25] She was charged under the statute of 21 Jac. I, c. 27, with having concealed the death of her bastard child. The court record, however, lists her charge simply as 'murder.'[26] Conviction under that statute required the judge to pass a sentence of death. During the October assizes of the Home District (covering York and surrounding areas) Robinson conducted the prosecution of Mary Thompson before Chief Justice Powell. He called only seven witnesses, including the accused's sister and the two doctors who had performed the autopsy on the infant. Thompson was convicted, but the jury urged royal clemency. The chief justice sympathized with the girl's plight and asked the lieutenant-governor to delay the hanging in order that a review of the case could be conducted.

On 24 October Powell wrote to Major Hillier that while 'part of the evidence was hypothetical and all circumstantial' the jury was justified in returning its verdict.[27] Only four days later, after having reviewed the medical evidence Robinson had presented for the prosecution, the chief justice came to a different conclusion. In order to prove that the child had been born alive, Robinson had presented the evidence of medical examiners that the child's lungs could float. Powell now understood that for many years that evidence had been disallowed in England and was not considered conclusive proof that the child had been born alive.[28] Powell even doubted that Robinson had proved an essential element of the offence, that is, whether the child had been born a bastard. Robinson defended his actions by stating that it was 'unnecessary to charge against the form of the statute.' This was not a satisfactory defence, considering that a charge that carried a capital penalty should strictly comply with proper form. Yet Robinson also pointed out that the accused's sister, during the course of her testimony, had related facts relevant to the illegitimate birth; these facts had enabled the attorney-general to establish evidence of the child's illegitimacy before the court.

In his final report on the Thompson case, the chief justice concluded that the evidence was 'strongly circumstantial' and that a conviction was probably not warranted by the evidence.[29] Powell also suspected that Upper Canada's inherited criminal law was hopelessly outdated; the offence for which Mary Thompson was tried had been reduced to a misdemeanour in Britain. In 1824 Thompson was granted a general pardon. The harsh fate she had narrowly avoided made many Upper Canadians realize that drastic reform of the criminal law was necessary. That reform was to come, in part, from the established gentry.

In 1823, George Markland, a Kingston tory, introduced an act in the Legislative Council to abolish 21 Jac. 1 and substitute another penalty. The bill was passed by the council, but failed to get past the assembly's committee. John Robinson was also concerned about the unwarranted harshness of the criminal law. He later drafted and steered through the assembly a bill to allow judges a discretionary power to impose a lesser sentence in certain capital cases.[30] Not only was the government active in trying to reform the criminal law, but the opposition members also proposed debate on altering the judicial system. In the early 1820s, the movement to reform the criminal law was barely gaining momentum; but cases such as Mary Thompson's would make reform inevitable.

No sooner were the Home District assizes over than the attorney-general was forced to begin preparations for the fourth session of the Eighth Parliament. He probably looked back with longing at his idyllic year in London. There was no longer the opportunity to take long breakfasts with Wilmot Horton (as the under-secretary now styled himself)[31] and discuss grand plans for the future of the Empire. Now the attorney-general had to devote himself to the details of local administration and the incessant verbal assaults of the reformers.

Before the session began in mid-November 1823, Robinson concerned himself with drafting a new statute to consolidate the election laws.[32] Ever since 1792, the assembly had passed numerous enactments concerning the qualifications of members and electors, and these had led to contradictions and confusion.

Indeed, one of the first issues presented to the fourth session was yet another contested election in Lennox and Addington. In this enactment of an almost yearly ritual, the by-election was again challenged for irregularities. This time the polling officer had breached the regulations by closing the polls on Good Friday and the sabbath. Marshall Spring Bidwell, who had lost by a narrow margin, protested that this irregularity voided the contest. The attorney-general tried to defend the polling officer's actions by pointing out that his error had not necessarily changed the results of the poll.[33] That argument was contemptuously rejected by the opposition, and the election was declared void. None of the members, not even Robinson, pointed out that Bidwell was an alien and therefore ineligible for election; the confrontation of that problem was put over for another day.

In some ways, the fourth session was a tiresome repetition of complaints that had been raised in the preceding sessions. The Sedition Law Repeal Bill was again passed and again rejected by the legislative council. The question of dissenter marriages was reopened when Colonel Nichol proposed a Methodist Relief Bill to permit Methodist clergy to solemnize marriages. He thought it absurd that young Methodists had to travel to the United States in order to be married by their own clergy. The colonel noted that Catholics, who acknowledged a foreigner as their spiritual leader, were permitted to conduct their own marriages. The attorney-general replied that the Catholic clergy were usually British subjects, while most of the Methodist preachers were aliens. Although Robinson had no objections to Methodists performing marriage ceremonies, he did object to this important power being vested in non-British subjects. The assembly disagreed, and the Methodist Relief Bill was approved, only to be defeated by the legislative council.[34]

In addition to participating in the usual conflicts between government and opposition members, Robinson again took the lead in drafting executive legislation. After presenting his consolidated statute on the election laws, Robinson, with Hagerman's assistance, introduced bills to levy road taxes, regulate trade with the United States, and, perhaps most important, reinforce the tax on idle lands. The vast tracts of idle lands lying between settlements presented one of the greatest obstacles to growth. Farmers who had cleared their lands often found themselves surrounded by wild lands held for speculation. Robinson had drafted the original wild-lands tax in 1819, but the bill of that date was limited in effect to eight years. Most landowners never expected it to be enforced. As a measure of the government's determination to fight land speculation, Robinson introduced an amendment to make the 1819 assessment permanent. If tax arrears were not paid within eight years, then the land could be seized and sold. Although Robinson considered the tax essential, it was by no means popular among the landed class.[35] The legislative council was under the influence of land barons who would just as soon have done away with the tax altogether. Sir Peregrine Maitland, however, regarded Robinson's wild-lands tax as an important part of the campaign to rationalize land settlement, and he instructed his executive councillors to support the bill in the legislative council. Because of this pressure the tax was made permanent.[36]

The legislature was not the only source of change in Upper Canada. One of the main problems afflicting the province and one of the reasons for Upper Canada's slow growth was the isolation of the western half of the province. If this fertile bread-basket (the 'better half of our country,'[37] according to Robinson) could be connected to British markets, then, in the optimistic opinion of Robinson and his associates, Upper Canada could even surpass its American rivals. The spirit and soul of this project, the most crucial development in early Upper Canada, was a most unlikely entrepreneur.

William Hamilton Merritt was a failed shopkeeper who combined a loyalist background and a deep attachment to the British Crown with an admiration for American commercial skill. Merritt was determined to compete for the traffic on New York's Erie Canal by building a canal to circumvent Niagara Falls and thereby join Lake Erie and Lake Ontario. At first, Robinson considered Merritt to be a 'wild visionary projector.'[38] His scheme to bypass the Falls by connecting the Welland River to the Twelve Mile Creek ignored a government survey which had favoured a canal from Burlington Bay to the Grand River. Merritt succeeded in obtaining American financing for his company, and was astute enough to leave the directorship in the hands of the provincial gentry. The attorney-general concluded that Merritt's motives were 'pure and disinterested and highly patriotic.' Robinson's confidence had been earned by Merritt's diplomatic choice of company directors, a choice which eventually included the attorney-general himself. 'It seemed your earnest wish to have the direction of the Company committed to gentlemen whom you could not hope to bend to anything unworthy.'[39] With the assurance that the project was in the hands of those unbending gentlemen, Robinson introduced the Welland Canal Bill to the assembly. The legislature, delighted to find that this important work was to be financed by a private institution, passed the bill with little debate.[40]

During the session just completed, one member, William Morris of Perth, had begun to stir up trouble. He had drafted a petition asking the King to regard the Church of Scotland as an established church in Upper Canada. According to Morris's petition, the Presbyterian Church was a 'true Protestant Church' within the meaning of the Canada Act and was therefore eligible to receive funds from the clergy reserves.[41] Morris's challenge struck at a fundamental belief of the York élite. Religion and government were mutually supportive; as Robinson later wrote, religion was 'the only secure basis on which civil authority can rest.'[42] The moral force of religious belief had to be linked to the temporal power of the government. This view was not mere political expediency. Men such as Robinson, Strachan, and Maitland held profound Christian beliefs which influenced all their personal actions. John Robinson began each day by gathering his family for morning prayers. Sir Peregrine Maitland resigned the highest military command of his career when his orders conflicted with his Christian scruples.[43] To the gentry, it was beyond question that the established church, the Church of England, was a cornerstone of civilized society; it alone deserved government assistance.

In London, the petition from the aroused Presbyterians was not the only complaint to upset Lord Bathurst's equanimity. The question of uniting Upper and Lower Canada was raised again in 1824 as a possible solution to the Colonial Office's continual financial wars with the Lower Canadian assembly. Robinson reminded Wilmot Horton that a union of the Canadas was no remedy. By joining the provinces, Lower Canada's radicalism would be sure to infect the upper province. Robinson used this opportunity to return to his proposal for a 'grand scheme of a *British-American anti-republican confederacy.*'[44] His advocacy of a general union was no mere diversion from the Colonial Office's plans to unite the Canadas. He repeatedly pressed his plan for a confederation, but to no avail;[45] Lord Liverpool's administration remained unwilling to undertake any radical experiments in colonial government. Although he was consulted on imperial affairs in 1824, Robinson was now content to leave diplomatic intrigue to others.

Upper Canada was on the verge of initiating important internal improvements, and one of the institutions necessary to finance those improvements was a secure banking system. Reliable banks would undoubtedly assist commerce by issuing bills and discounting promissory notes. It was also possible that the banks might provide funding for the Welland Canal and other development projects. Unfortunately, provincial banking was in its infancy and its first steps were awkward failures.

The Bank of Upper Canada was unable to subscribe the full limit of its capital and was therefore capable of undertaking only modest financing. The businessmen of Kingston had established their own bank, which fared even worse than the official Bank of Upper Canada. After only a few months in operation the Kingston establishment had floundered, and by 1822 it was unable to honour its debts.[46] The bank's failure wiped out so many creditors that the assembly ordered an investigation. During the spring session of 1823, the assembly committee reported that the bank's inability to pay its debts was probably due to the criminal activity of its officers. As a result, all bank assets were vested in a committee empowered to satisfy any outstanding bank debts from the assets of the former owners. The former owners could not even transfer any of their personal property without the approval of the commissioners.[47]

Revolted at this statute, Robinson advised Macaulay that had he been in the province he would have lectured the assembly that it was 'wrong and indeed monstrous to fine a man by an *ex post facto* Statute ... [to] beggar him for life for a general imputed negligence of which he has never been convicted – that may be the effect of the Act of 1823.'[48] The commissioners' report on the affairs of the 'Late Pretended Bank of Upper Canada' noted that the directors of the bank were suspected of fraud. Among the directors were several prominent Kingstonians, including Christopher Hagerman. Even after being implicated in the affair, Hagerman suggested that the bank's assets be vested in the former directors instead of the commissioners. Perhaps to deflect criticism from himself, Hagerman also named a former fellow director, Thomas Dalton, as a likely culprit in the bank's failure. Dalton struck back at this slur and publicly ridiculed Hagerman's accusations. Robinson considered Hagerman's suggested amendment to vest the assets in the directors as nothing less than ridiculous. In Robinson's opinion, Hagerman was now suspect of conduct unbecoming a gentleman.

In the spring of 1823, Thomas Dalton and another former bank director, Bartlet, were sued by the trustees for the amount of two of the bank's bonds. Somewhat to his dismay, Robinson was retained by Dalton and Bartlet to defend them. The case was enormously complicated and raised ten separate points of law. Despite his reservations about taking the case,

Robinson prepared a substantial defence. He was not convinced of his clients' innocence; he confided to his brother, Peter, 'I hope I may fail but I apprehend I cannot.'[49] His apprehension became fact; his case succeeded on a technicality and his banker clients were released from liability.[50]

Although Robinson may have considered Dalton and Bartlet to be shady characters, he approved of the principle of limited liability. Investors in banks or canals should only be liable to the extent of their investment and they should not be compelled to risk their personal holdings.[51] This attitude was in conflict with the prevailing public distrust of financiers. Frontier settlers, whether in Upper Canada or Indiana, demonstrated a marked dislike of banks that issued paper notes. All too often those notes became worthless and a farmer's lifetime of effort was wiped out. Even if the notes retained their value, a farmer might be so burdened with debt that he might have to work a lifetime to repay the loan that financed his pioneer days. One political faction in New York State, the Loco-Focos, condemned the use of credit to finance ventures and accused the banks of being the source of the evil of credit. The Loco-Focos were 'hard money' men who were opposed to banks issuing currency not backed by silver or gold. American currency at the time consisted mostly of bank notes, which were so unreliable that a prudent merchant would have to hire a 'banknote detector' to determine the value of the paper. Upper Canada did not suffer from the unreliable currency or the multiplicity of banks that made American financing so chaotic. The Bank of Upper Canada held firm control of provincial finances, and the bank itself was under the authority of the York government. Among the executive and legislative councillors who sat on the bank's board of directors, John Strachan was perhaps the most prominent.

The merchants of Kingston and Niagara resented York's control of the bank. If they had been given the opportunity, they would have copied the American example of a number of small, unstable banks. Populist spokesmen mirrored the anti-bank sentiments of the Loco-Focos. One of the most bitter opponents of the Bank of Upper Canada was a recently arrived Scot, William Lyon Mackenzie. Mackenzie had been a merchant in Dundas until he developed a fondness for radical politics. He founded a newspaper, the *Colonial Advocate*, and made it his chief instrument in a crusade against the government. Eventually, he concluded that the Bank of Upper Canada, a 'great monied engine, the only one in the colony, is entirely under the thumb of parson Strachan and his pupils to wield at their discretion.'[52]

Mackenzie, like the Loco-Focos, saw the credit system as a positive evil.

'Labour is the source of all wealth,' he was fond of repeating; by this he meant that labour should be the only source of private gain. The real wealth of Upper Canada was being created by its farmers, and that wealth was being translated into bank notes. According to Mackenzie, the oligarchs who controlled the bank had done nothing to create the wealth they administered. Yet did this stop the directors from offering generous dividends to themselves? Mackenzie hoped that Upper Canada would become a simple egalitarian community of farmers and merchants who conducted their transactions in metal coins and whose currency was forever sound.[53]

Mackenzie's vision of Upper Canada's future was radically different from John Robinson's. Although Robinson envisaged Upper Canada as an agrarian community, he also saw it as a hierarchical society in which the landed gentry ruled the common yeomen. As the province advanced commercially, it was inevitable that a wealthy merchant class would arise to oversee economic expansion. Robinson abhorred egalitarianism, and could only conceive of a society in which the well-born and meritorious ruled and all others obeyed. With such opposing views of Upper Canada's future, it was not surprising that the attorney-general and the Scottish printer soon found themselves in political combat.

Mackenzie wasted no time courting the great men of the province. In the second issue of the *Colonial Advocate* he dismissed the attorney-general, stating that '[Robinson's] abilities are greatly over-rated; his flippancy has been mistaken by some for wit; but not by us ... We account him to be a vain ignorant man.'[54] Mackenzie later referred to the attorney-general of Upper Canada as 'the most jesuitical, equivocal character in the Province.'[55] In addition to attacking government policies, Mackenzie never neglected an opportunity to slander the character of government officers. His continual venom brought Upper Canadian political comment to new lows and diverted criticism of government from policies to personalities. Mackenzie's vicious attacks did not leave the attorney-general indifferent; writing to Major Hillier, he complained that

another reptile of the Gourlay species has sprung up in a Mr. Wm. Mackenzie of Dundas ... a conceited red-headed fellow with an apron. He publishes a weekly pamphlet and has begun *secundum artem* by attacking the Lt. Governor ... He said that I am the most subtle advocate of arbitrary power ... what vermin![56]

The appearance of Mackenzie and his radical newspaper in the spring of 1824 was especially unpleasant for the government. The provincial election was to be held in July and the *Colonial Advocate* was sure to expound the grievances of many of the common people. A month before the election, Robinson wrote an anxious note to John Macaulay in which he excoriated the editor of the *Colonial Advocate* as 'a blackguard and a fool.' Robinson was aroused because Mackenzie had dared to question the propriety of the assembly's grant to him of £1,000 as remuneration for his extended stay in England: 'The ill-starred scoundrel has seized, tho' weakly eno' upon the only thing connected with my name upon which I could fancy it necessary to set myself right in the opinion of the world.'[57] Ever since the Ancaster assizes, the attorney-general had been sensitive to any adverse public criticism. Anyone, even the insignificant Scot, who besmirched Robinson's name before the 'opinion of the world' had made a powerful enemy.

Robinson had been forewarned that personal vilification was the way of provincial politics. One reason Strachan had urged him to seek a career in England was to direct his protégé away from the petty aggravations of colonial affairs: 'You will have all the Bills to draw, your best motives will be questioned and belied, your words and expressions twisted, your conduct slandered, and all this without any redeeming advantage.'[58] Despite this warning, Robinson still had confidence that the government would be vindicated and that evil reptiles such as Mackenzie would slink away. 'The Government of Sir P. is strong and unassailable & every district does contain men who would not forget the experience of former demagogues.' Once again, Robinson urged John Macaulay to stand for election against the reformers. This time, his call was tinged with an appeal for Macaulay to do his duty on behalf of his fellow gentry. 'You are one of the *regularly bred*,' Robinson reminded him, 'and you owe the state some service.'[59] But Macaulay could not be persuaded to run.

John Robinson's uncontested election in 1820 was not repeated in 1824. The attorney-general was now highly visible as the government leader, and those who opposed his views eagerly seized the opportunity to eject him from the assembly. Yet Robinson, as the chief Crown law officer, the successful negotiator of the trade bill, and the supporter of the Welland Canal, had impressive political credentials. The tory press boasted that 'it must be evident that the talents of the Attorney-General cannot be dispensed with.'[60]

A significant new force was about to enter York politics. Robinson's opponent in the 1824 election was George Duggan, a former cabinet-maker and now a shopkeeper. Duggan, although otherwise a political nonentity, was an Orangeman with powerful connections in the new

Orange Lodges. For the first time, Orangeism became a factor in a York election. Yet Robinson was the embodiment of loyalty to the Crown, and he contrasted favourably with his unlettered rival. According to one of his broadsides,

We liked the last we chose, but still
A Lawyer's not the thing, Sir –
He's done some good, but may do ill;
Besides, *he serves the King, Sir!*'[61]

The attorney-general may have underestimated his opposition. 'We amuse ourselves anticipating troubles,'[62] he casually commented to Macaulay in June. This easygoing attitude was not warranted by the strength of his challenger. Despite Duggan's conservative stance, he would inevitably garner the votes of those radicals who wished to see the attorney-general removed from the assembly.

Both candidates began the polling day by gathering their followers together on a public street and delivering election addresses. According to the government newspaper, Robinson gave one of the most 'eloquent, energetic and electrifying orations' ever heard in York.[63] None the less, his speech failed to make much of an impact on the electorate. After the first day of polling, Robinson and Duggan were tied with thirty votes each. On the second day, Robinson pulled ahead and completed the polling with sixty-two votes to Duggan's fifty-one. The reformers and Orangemen claimed a moral triumph and attributed the attorney-general's victory to his generous distribution of whisky to the voters. In reality, Robinson's victory was probably attributable to York's dependence on the government. Public officials, from the chief justice to the doorkeeper of the Parliament building, had all obtained their positions through their loyalty to the government; naturally, they sought to uphold that government. Moreover, the Orange lodge was hated by the Catholics of York, and even those Catholics who favoured reform rallied to the attorney-general's banner.[64]

Local issues and personalities dominated the election in York and those in most other parts of the province. In Kingston, Christopher Hagerman's reputation had suffered as a result of the bank scandal, and even Robinson advised John Macaulay to remain neutral in the contest.[65] Hagerman, who had lost the confidence of a number of conservatives, was defeated by an old tory, Colonel John Cumming. In Middlesex, the government member for the previous twelve years, Mahlon Burwell, was turned out in favour of two renowned reformers, John Rolph and Captain John Mathews. The reform victory in Middlesex was the result of local discontent over the autocratic rule of Colonel Talbot rather than a demonstration of popular sympathy with provincial reform. However, in one county riding, a provincial issue had a decisive effect on the election. In Lennox and Addington, M.S. Bidwell had at last gained election, as had another reformer, Peter Perry. The victories of Bidwell and Perry can be attributed primarily to displeasure with the naturalization laws.

The election of 1824 was largely a series of regional contests. But in Lennox and Addington the reformers had shown that a candidate could run successfully on an issue of provincial concern.[66] The alien question was an issue that sustained popular interest, and by raising the issue at township meetings the reformers eventually would be able to mount province-wide campaigns to replace regional contests. In time, tory candidates would also respond to popular issues to support their candidates. One of the side-effects of the alien question was its role in fostering the growth of political parties in Upper Canada.

The Ninth Parliament found the government members in a decided minority. Having to present a government program for internal improvements to a hostile assembly might have dismayed the attorney-general; during the summer of 1824 he contemplated leaving politics altogether. His wife's uncle, William Merry, had used his considerable influence in the Colonial Office to have Robinson put forward as Chief Justice Powell's successor. However, Robinson told Merry that he was not interested in appointment to the bench.[67] Wilmot Horton, dismayed that Robinson had refused an offer to step into the higher echelons of imperial affairs, asked him to explain why he had declined such an enviable appointment.[68] There is no record of Robinson's reply. One reason for his refusal probably was the loss of income that would have resulted from his acceptance. Robinson, as the foremost advocate in the province, commanded high legal fees. With the expenses of raising a young family and the cost of seasonal entertainments at Beverley House, he probably considered his present income a necessity.

Robinson also seemed to gain considerable satisfaction from his legal and political careers. He was playing a vital role in the development of Upper Canada, from advancing the canal projects to encouraging emigration. Still, he found the necessary intrigues of everyday political life distasteful. In anticipation of the first session of the new Parliament, he complained that 'the Gov't is every now and then in hot water.'[69] The large number of reformers in the assembly meant that the next session was unlikely to be a placid one. As an apocalyptic sign, on the second-last day of 1824, the new Parliament building was destroyed by fire. The handsome little brick building had been the pride of York, and its loss left Parliament without a permanent residence. The attorney-general would meet the new assembly in unfamiliar surroundings accompanied by men who did not share his vision of an agrarian Upper Canada being led to its prosperous future by its upright gentry.

While Robinson prepared to face this hostile assembly, an obscure case was being argued in the English courts that would fundamentally alter the future of Upper Canada's government, a case that would reveal the problems inherent in the alien question and eventually drag the province's leaders down into a maelstrom of controversy.

8

The Alien Debates

Unfortunately for the chronicler of the period, political life in Upper Canada during the 1820s was not so sophisticated as to consist of interparty struggles. Although it is possible to speak of government and reform factions the terms are somewhat misleading, since members were usually independent of actual party affiliations. Patterns did exist in assembly voting; some members consistently supported the government and some voted against any administration proposal. But there was no cohesive organized group of reformers. Many members, for diverse reasons, could be classified as opponents of the government. The motives for their opposition ranged from indignation at the naturalization laws to personal pique. Most of the opposition members were rough-hewn settlers or merchants who had little education and no social graces. An obvious example was Peter Perry, who was almost completely uneducated but who combined common sense with a natural eloquence. Another capable new opposition member was Marshall Spring Bidwell of Lennox and Addington. Only twenty-six, Bidwell possessed keen intellectual and legal skills. But neither Bidwell nor Perry offered the leadership the effective opposition needed to embarrass and obstruct a government. Even Mackenzie once commented, in his usual acidic manner, that it was a great effort for most members to sign their names and that framing a bill was absolutely beyond their powers.[1] The opposition needed a champion to articulate their complaints, someone who would be a match for the smooth, articulate John Beverley Robinson.

The reformers found their paladin in John Rolph of Middlesex. Rolph, born in England, emigrated to Upper Canada in 1812 and returned to England in 1818 to pursue degrees in law, medicine, and divinity. Armed with this varied education, he returned to Upper Canada in 1821 and began to practice law and medicine. His dual career was not unusual in the early nineteenth century; Dr W.W. Baldwin also combined a legal and a medical practice. Rolph's professional activities in the London area made him a well-known figure, and in 1824 he won election in Middlesex County. Although at one time he had been on good terms with the arch-tory, Colonel Talbot, Rolph now decided to join the opposition. His education and breeding set him apart from his rustic colleagues, and he was soon renowned as an eloquent speaker and a formidable debater.

Rolph was inexperienced in Parliament, and in his first encounter with the attorney-general he fared badly. Speaking to a bill to permit religious societies to hold land, Rolph denounced the measure as vague and claimed that it was dangerous to permit some denominations, notably the Roman Catholics, to hold land. Robinson pounced on the bigotry inherent in Rolph's comments and defended the Catholic Church as 'a learned body, and no more to be dreaded than any other sect.'[2] Robinson not only succeeded with the legislation but emerged from the debate as the defender of religious minorities. As the session wore on, however, Rolph was more successful in discovering ways to embarrass the government. On the issue of granting a permanent salary to the receiver-general, Rolph denounced the custom of the government operating on fixed salaries and warned the assembly that it could only retain its 'dignity and consequence by keeping a firm hand on the purse strings.'[3] Although Robinson prevailed and the receiver-general was granted a salary, the assembly was obviously becoming more reluctant to vote supplies to a government over which it exercised little control.

Rolph began to focus his attacks on Robinson as the leader of the government in the assembly and the de facto prime minister. Robinson denied the allegation that he was government leader, a denial that is hard to accept in view of the amount of government legislation he introduced.[4] The measure to create the first east–west provincial road was popularly termed the 'Attorney-General's Road Bill' in honour of its patron.[5] Robinson also introduced bills to set definite terms for the Court of King's Bench and to permit sects such as the Quakers to swear oaths. If not officially a prime minister, Robinson was effectively leading the government in the House. Rolph insisted on calling him 'Prime Minister' and Robinson countered by addressing Rolph as 'Mr Fox' in a reference to the great whig leader of the opposition.[6]

On perhaps the most important issue facing the first session, Robinson and Rolph clashed in heated debate. The Welland Canal Company had applied for government assistance, and Robinson chaired the committee that reviewed the company's petition. In submitting his report, Robinson noted that the proposed canal would be of immense economic benefit and would facilitate military communications in wartime. This last reason struck a hollow note, since the province had made no contribution to the construction of the Rideau canal, which was primarily of military value. The Welland canal lay only a few miles from the United States, and it was first and foremost a mercantile venture. Robinson moved that the province buy £25,000 of stock in the company to give it the working capital it needed. Rolph opposed taking stock in the canal company; he felt that the government should not become directly involved in a commercial enterprise.[7] Robinson defended the government purchase of stock, saying that 'he did not like foreigners to have a preponderance of management in such a concern'[8] and that the stock would be a necessary security for the assembly's loan. On 25 February the assembly resolved to lend the company £25,000.

The government became even more committed to canal projects in April 1825, when the Welland Canal's charter was amended. The amount of authorized capital was expanded, and the new investors in the company included D'Arcy Boulton, William Allan, and John Robinson. The Welland Canal was now supported by individual members of the government as well as by the government itself. It was not unusual for a private company involved in a development project to have such close ties to the government. The Burlington Bay canal project was also to be financed by public money. Unable to obtain the capital they needed from private investors, the canal builders had to turn to the government to supply public capital. As a result, the canal company ceased to be run as a private concern and began to consider matters of public policy; money was spent to improve the canal even when profits appeared unlikely.[9] Writing in 1833, Robinson described the new public nature of the Welland Canal: 'The grand object was to overcome a great natural impediment to the prosperity of the better half of our country ... As to its being a work that will pay, I never laid stress on that branch of the question'.[10] The canal company was a 'mixed corporation,' a form of corporate structure common in the midwestern American states; it was a development company that depended upon public capital, had legislators on its board of directors, and had public objectives. In all other respects it was operated as a business in the hope that it might eventually turn a profit. By suggesting that the province actually hold shares in the company,

Robinson was advancing the concept even further. It is interesting to note that later development projects (such as the interprovincial railways) would similarly combine private entrepreneurial energies with public capital-raising powers.

A significant document produced by the Ninth Parliament was the report of the Robinson–Strachan joint committee on internal navigation. The report concluded that the Welland Canal was the most important project underway in Upper Canada and that prosperity was sure to result from the opening up of the Western District. The Robinson–Strachan report recommended a rapid program of canal building, for 'it is greatly in the interest of the present generation to submit to some temporary sacrifice in the prospect of a very rapid recompense.'[11] While Rolph and a few reformers might object to government-financed ventures, there was broad agreement in Upper Canada, especially in the western half of the province, that the projects were necessary. Even Mackenzie came as close as he ever would to complimenting John Robinson. Writing in the *Colonial Advocate*, he noted that 'the warm and hearty support which he [Robinson] offers at so early a date to a measure eminently calculated for the benefit of the province will be a firm base to the pyramid of popularity he is anxious to build in Upper Canada.'[12]

Mackenzie's admiration of Robinson was short-lived. By the end of the session, the little Scot was gloating that the attorney-general's budget had been severely slashed by the assembly and the government's supply cut from £7,370 in 1824 to £6,710 in 1825.[13] Near the end of the session, the opposition overrode the attorney-general's objections and passed a bill to prevent the government from tampering with any non-appropriated funds.

After the end of the first session, Mackenzie rejoiced in the government's discomfiture: '[Robinson] was literally overwhelmed – his measures, whether good or bad; whether the fruit of an enlightened mind or of an arbitrary and tyrannical disposition shared one common fate.'[14] This was hardly an objective analysis; Robinson had seen to the passage of a number of significant measures, including the Law Term Bill, the Road Bill, and the loan to the Welland Canal Company. Including the joint committee's report on internal navigation, the first session was one of the most productive legislatures in Upper Canada's history. Admittedly, one disquieting factor was the ability of the assembly to obstruct money bills. It would not be long before reformers would seek to join control of the civil list with actual control of the government.

Those problems, however, could be dealt with in the future. A more immediate threat presented itself to the government during the autumn of 1824. The decision which Sir John Singleton Copley had told Robinson would definitively solve the alien question was finally received from the imperial courts. In *Thomas* v *Acklam*[15] the English Court of King's Bench decided that all persons, whether loyalists or revolutionaries, who had remained in the United States after the peace of 1783 had ceased to be British subjects. According to the colonial law officers, the alien question 'which has been so long and so frequently agitated may at length be considered as finally determined.'[16]

This might have been an adequate solution for the Downing Street clerks, but it only aggravated the problem on the Canadian frontier. American settlers who had been invited to the province by Simcoe could no longer consider their land patents valid, and even some loyalists whose forebears had left the American republic after 1783 began to fear that they were now aliens within the British Empire. The York government would be hard-pressed to restrain the rising feelings of anger among the American-born.

The reform press was already expressing indignation over the alien controversy. A letter to the *Colonial Advocate* remarked that 'the titles to three-fourths of the landed estates in this country are a nullity, from either now being in the hands of, or once having been in the hands of persons born in the United States.'[17] Sir Peregrine Maitland, aware of the dangers in the situation, hoped to avoid controversy by naturalizing those settlers who 'had lost their status as British subjects by the recent decision of the courts.'[18] Maitland was succumbing to the reformers' insistence that the decision in *Thomas* v *Acklam* had somehow disfranchised the Americans. In fact, the York government had known since 1817 that the American settlers were aliens and that their land titles were void. *Thomas* v *Acklam* only confirmed this fact and made it public. Maitland wrote to Lord Bathurst in April 1825, asking him to pass a statute in the current session of Parliament to naturalize the American settlers.[19] In order to impress Lord Bathurst with the urgency of the matter, Maitland resolved to send an emissary to London to explain the situation directly to the colonial secretary. Not surprisingly, he chose the attorney-general, whose legal knowledge of the alien question and diplomatic ability made him the obvious messenger. The first session of the Ninth Parliament was hardly prorogued before Robinson was on his way to London to plead the government's case directly to Lord Bathurst.

Robinson quietly left York in April 1825. He was accompanied by the elderly Justice Boulton, and there was speculation that Robinson was leaving as attorney-general only to return as chief justice. While no official reason was given for Robinson's mission, Mackenzie hinted that it 'is more intimately connected with the decision of the alien question than with any immediate claim upon the centre seat of justice.'[20] John Beverley Robinson was faced with the challenge of his career. Fortunately for him, he was going to seek a solution from men who were his intimate colleagues and who, he hoped, understood the problems of the Canadian frontier.

On the voyage to England, Robinson was accompanied by young George Mountain, the Archdeacon of Quebec and the son of Bishop Mountain. To the archdeacon went the duty of informing the Colonial Office of the Canadian Anglicans' fear that the government was about to dispose of their most valuable asset, the clergy reserves. The government had determined to raise revenues by selling Clergy and Crown Reserve lands to the Canada Company.[21]

Robinson carried to London a petition from Upper Canada's Clergy Corporation which requested that the clergy reserves be excluded from the Canada Company lands. Robinson, on orders from Major Hillier, gave the petition to Mountain, who was to carry on negotiations with the Colonial Office. Entrusting these vital pleas to an inexperienced and diffident young man no doubt weakened Robinson's resolve to remain aloof from the clergy reserves controversy. Nevertheless, immediately upon his arrival in May 1825, Robinson disclaimed any intention to take part in the Canada Company dispute and expressed a desire 'to avoid all interference with his [Mountain's] agency.'[22] The feebleness of this disclaimer was demonstrated by Robinson's activities in subsequent weeks: he visited the Bishop of London and gave him a letter from Strachan asking the bishop to use his considerable influence with Lord Bathurst in the cause of the Church of England.

The fortunes of the established Church did not fare well under George Mountain. He accepted Lord Bathurst's arguments in favour of the sale of clergy reserves and even began to question the legality of Upper Canada's Clergy Corporation. Bathurst explained to Mountain that the petitions would greatly embarrass the government, and pointed out that the Colonial Office would thereafter be at odds with the Church. At this point it appeared inevitable that the government would sell at least one-half of the clergy reserves. Robinson intervened and hastily advised Mountain to obey Bathurst and withhold the petition. This did not mean, however, that the attorney-general was prepared to abandon the clergy reserves.

He had learned in 1822 that it was futile to oppose openly the imperial government and that results could best be achieved by quiet persuasion. After stating his official position that the provincial executive was 'at one with H.M. Government,'[23] Robinson then entered into a series of discussions with colonial officials that significantly altered their views of the Canada Company.

He reported to Upper Canada that the colonial officers were 'most confoundedly vexed at any opposition being made to the Canada Company Project.'[24] Nevertheless, he managed to instil doubt by challenging the findings of the special parliamentary investigation (the Cockburn Commission) and the proposal to sell all reserves for 3s 6d an acre. Robinson forced the issue by insisting that the suggested selling price was entirely inadequate and that 'the reserves in the London, Gore Districts are actually worth as much as the Company gives for the whole.' He reversed his previous advocacy of a corporate sale of the reserves and instead questioned the legitimacy of the entire transaction. The sale became 'a reward for the very easy transaction of transferring to American Speculators what the Government could have sold to subjects for double the price they pay for it.'[25] Robinson revived a counter-proposal, originally suggested by Sir Peregrine Maitland, that the Canada Company should be sold the Indian tract in the western section of the province instead of the clergy reserves.[26]

The Colonial Office weighed Robinson's comments and suggestions against the evidence of the parliamentary committee. The decision was not an easy one. Both Lord Bathurst and Wilmot Horton trusted Robinson's judgment and hesitated to disregard his proposals. Robinson confidently told Hillier that 'my lamentations were so touching' that Wilmot Horton finally decided to 'look this whole matter manfully in the face & to put me against the Commissioners.'[27] The firm resolve of the Colonial Office to sell the clergy reserves was rapidly failing. In June the Cockburn Report was sent to Robinson, who was asked to comment on all aspects of the proposed sale. His criticisms made the Colonial Office even more unsure of the transaction which had at first seemed designed to solve so many problems. Robinson reported to the special arbitrator, Sir Giffin Wilson, that the Cockburn Commission could not possibly have accurately valued two million acres in just six weeks. The commissioners had never left York and had not even seen 90 percent of the land records.[28] Applying his own knowledge of property values, he stated that sales of similar lands ranged between ten and twenty shillings per acre. In response to the Canada Company's request for a price abatement because of the vast extent of the purchase, Robinson noted that the price was already too low to allow for any further reduction. Although Sir Giffin's report accepted some of Robinson's criticisms, it failed to resolve the issue.

With matters in this state of confusion, Robinson was recalled to York to resume his official duties. After further discussions during which the Canada Company threatened to cancel the land purchase altogether, the government agreed to the sale of the Indian tract at a reduced price of 2s 9d per acre. The clergy reserves were effectively removed from the settlement plan and remained the privileged domain of the Church of England. Robinson had again used his diplomatic skill to achieve what seemed an impressive triumph.

On later reflection, Robinson may have doubted the efficacy of his victory. He had delayed and diminished a scheme to settle large numbers of British immigrants in Upper Canada. He had opposed this worthwhile project because it had detracted from one element of the tory plan to create an ideal English society by establishing the Church of England. Moreover, while the clergy reserves remained intact, they constituted a major source of friction between the citizens of Upper Canada and their government.

In the midst of the confusion created by the Canada Company and the clergy reserves, Robinson was having difficulty in getting the colonial secretary to discuss the alien issue. On top of his mounting colonial worries, Lord Bathurst was reluctant to allow an issue to arise that might give his enemies the opportunity to ask awkward questions in Parliament. An imperial act of naturalization was the only way, argued Robinson, to reverse *Thomas v Acklam*. Bathurst thought it was too late in the session to introduce any new colonial measure, and Robinson lamented that the 'reluctance to legislate upon the subject in England seemed not much diminished.'[29] Bathurst insisted that if the provincial government wanted to address the problem they should pass a local naturalization act. Robinson replied that the question of British citizenship was so fundamental that it should be decided in London; it would be 'better not to *agitate* the question in the Colony.' The colonial secretary was adamant, and so, on the eve of Robinson's departure, Bathurst instructed him to send a dispatch to Maitland. Working with George Baillie, the Colonial Office clerk responsible for British America, Robinson prepared the instructions for a naturalization bill and forwarded them to the colonial secretary for amendments.

Bathurst's letter to Maitland of 22 July 1825 authorized the provincial Parliament to pass an act to confer civil rights on Americans who had been 'declared by the judgment of the Courts of law in England and by the opinion of the Law Officers to be Aliens'.[30] When Robinson examined the dispatch after his return to Canada he was appalled by the 'too general language' in which the instructions were framed.[31] Having taken part in the drafting of the document, he accepted some of the responsibility for its failings. It was now his unwelcome task to take the July dispatch and put it into legal form. What elements of citizenship could the province bestow on resident aliens? The province could grant them property rights, but it was legally estopped from granting civil rights to the same persons. The Constitutional Act of 1791 provided that only British subjects by birth or a 'subject naturalized by act of the British Parliament' could exercise civil rights. Although their rights could be confirmed, it was constitutionally impossible for the province to grant the American settlers voting privileges. Robinson prepared the legislation with those principles in mind, knowing tht any legislation dealing with political rights must be more than legally correct; it must be perceived to be fair as well as constitutional.

Until John Robinson's return from England in the autumn of 1825, his career had consisted of a succession of political triumphs. Beyond doubt he had inherited no small measure of the political acumen of the Bishop of Bristol. Lacking both wealth and position, he had forged a career that made him a close adviser to the administrators of the greatest empire in the world; he was still a young man of thirty-four, and he could anticipate even greater achievements. Even his personal fortunes changed for the better after his return from England. In November 1825 he registered his purchase of the south half of York's park lot number 11. This acquisition cost the attorney-general £1,000, an enormous expenditure. Now, the Robinson family held the landed wealth that guaranteed respectability. In the pre-industrial society of Upper Canada, land provided both a source of income and proof that the Robinsons were part of the gentry.

The only disquieting feature of this picture was the mood of discontent existing in Upper Canada in late 1825. The first session of the Ninth Parliament had shown the depth of reformer dissatisfaction with many of the government's policies.

An opportunity was presented to Robinson to remove himself from political turmoil and the imminent alien debate. After the retirement of William Dummer Powell in October 1825, Robinson was again offered the chief justiceship. Again he declined the appointment. The salary of the chief justice was not substantial and Robinson was certain that he could better support his family on the income from his legal practice. He possessed 'a large practice at the Bar,' and he felt 'no disposition to lay myself on the shelf at so early a period of life.'[32] Moreover, if there was a successful resolution of the alien question, Robinson would once again find himself raised in the public esteem and possibly freed from the annoyances of fractious politics.

The second session began with the lieutenant-governor recommending to the assembly two naturalization bills to resolve the question of alien status. One conferred rights on foreign-born soldiers; the other conferred rights on American settlers. Both bills were premised on the fact that 'certain inhabitants' named therein were aliens and required formal naturalization. One clause confirmed the settlers in their property rights and the other limited voting rights to the provisions contained in 'any Law of this Province respectng the qualification of persons entitled to vote.' No aliens could vote unless they were naturalized according to the stringent requirements of the statute of 1740. Both bills were passed by the legislative council and forwarded to the assembly, along with Sir Peregrine Maitland's comment that *Thomas* v *Acklam* held that American settlers were aliens, and it was now up to the provincial Parliament to remedy their disfranchisement as far as its powers permitted.[33]

For once, the assembly debate was attracting considerable attention; the gallery of the House was filled with the curious and the indignant. Before the legislation was even presented, a rumour began to circulate that it was intended to disfranchise and subjugate American settlers. This speculation added to the public interest and huge crowds eventually filled the area outside the temporary Parliament buildings. It was in this tense atmosphere that the attorney-general rose on 4 December 1825 to present the naturalization bills.

He began by reviewing Upper Canadian settlement, and conceded that with Simcoe's approval much of the province had been settled by Americans.[34] At no time had those persons acquired British citizenship. Even though the imperial act that authorized the American entry permitted the administration of loyal oaths, the statute did not confer civil rights; in fact, it confirmed the distinction between resident aliens and British subjects. In any case, few of the Americans who had entered the province had even bothered to take the oath of allegiance. The only other legislation that affected citizenship was a provincial act that disfranchised even more Americans. As a result of their alien status, Americans had on occasion been refused the vote and it was now apparent from the interpretation in *Thomas* v *Acklam* that the American settlers did not own their land or possess any civil rights. They were foreigners in the country they had created out of the wilderness.

The situation was intolerable, the attorney-general conceded, especially in view of the loyalty of most of the settlers: 'I am happy upon this, as upon every other occasion, to bear testimony to the loyalty and good conduct of a very great portion of these people who had emigrated from the United States.' This tribute, however well-intentioned, sounded hollow coming from the prosecutor of the Bloody Assizes. The law was clear: all American settlers were aliens, and 'we can no longer, in justice to them, shut our eyes to the truth, that many of them, at least, are subject to legal disabilities, which as it is intended that they should be placed on the same footing as the other inhabitants of the Province, it is necessary to remove by some positive legislative enactment.'

If the proposed bills did not go far enough to relieve the civil disabilities of the Americans, Robinson suggested, there was yet another course that could be followed. Citizenship was an imperial matter, and the attorney-general would be agreeable to petitioning the King for further relief. Robinson's address, which lasted for four hours, was a brilliant exposition of the alien problem and the possible remedies. He proposed to confer on American residents as many liberties as the provincial Parliament was able to grant. If this was not sufficient, he was willing to take the case to London and appeal for further measures. The attorney-general considered his naturalization bills to be a just compromise, and he was unprepared for the storm of anger that broke over him.

Opposition members thundered that no matter what the law said, the American settlers were British subjects and not aliens. One member, Edward McBride, denounced the bill as a treason against the people of the province and flatly asserted that it was Robinson's intention to 'deprive of their rights loyal subjects of his Majesty, men who have thirty or forty years exercised the rights of Britons.'[35] The gallery crowd became more and more boisterous as they cheered on their champions. One government member protested to the speaker that 'shouting below the bar began the French revolution.' The English-born John Rolph led the avalanche of opposition to Robinson's proposals. American settlers were already citizens, argued Rolph, yet Robinson's insulting bills would force them to 'purchase that benefit [citizenship] by the sacrifice of feeling'; they were 'being required to register their own degradation.'[36] One government member, Jonas Jones, enraged at Rolph's pandering to the crowd, demanded that the galleries be cleared. 'Mr. Rolph's language is foul, infamous and scandalous,' fumed Jones, and then added the worst insult one gentleman could apply to another: 'He [Rolph] has a vile and democratic heart.'[37]

The attorney-general's fine legal reasoning was lost on the gallery, and even his opponents, such as Rolph, who understood the constitutional complexities of the issue ignored them and instead profited from the popular outrage against the measure. No argument could convince Robinson's opponents that the naturalization bills were intended to remedy their situation. It had been a grave miscalculation on Robinson's part to believe that a mere guarantee of property rights could satisfy the American settlers; only an unqualified declaration that they enjoyed all the liberties of British subjects would mollify them.

The increasingly bitter debate continued through December and into January of 1826. During a rambling address in praise of American residents, Rolph obliquely attacked the attorney-general's own origins: 'It is those who have American blood flowing in their veins,' he observed, 'who thus traduce the whole of the American people.'[38] Provoked, Robinson rose to his feet and in a speech described as 'thirteen yards, two feet six inches and a half' long,[39] vociferously denounced the American settlers for having been either neutral or traitorous during the war. He enumerated the atrocities committed by American forces against Canadians and the unwillingness of Americans to serve in the local militias.[40] The reformers had found the key to the attorney-general's renowned temper.

The naturalization bills were rejected, and the assembly passed several resolutions praising American emigrants and declaring their British status to be an acknowledged fact. The assembly passed its own naturalization bill, which declared that 'such persons [American settlers] have been, are, and shall be considered to be, to all intents and purposes, natural born British subjects.' After this bill was returned to the legislative council, and to Robinson's undoubted mortification, the reformers passed a resolution in favour of increased American emigration to the province.

The legislative council attempted to deal with the assembly's revised bill by holding a conference. After a thorough report on the assembly's amendments, the council concluded that the changes had no merit. Both the legislative and executive councils asked the imperial government to intervene and resolve the problem. In the wake of the acrimony left by the alien debate, this appeared to be the only solution.

It was clear from the vehement opposition that the attorney-general had encountered that his naturalization bills were seen as crude attempts to revoke the rightful liberties of resident Americans. Later observers commented that

on the other hand, they [Maitland and his advisers] were now completely convinced that the non-Loyalist American-born settlers who had come into the province after 1783 were aliens, without the right to vote or hold office until they conformed to British law or were accorded legislative relief. On the whole, they were on sound legal ground in so arguing, although everyone knew that their motives were essentially political in reaching this decision.[41]

That analysis presumes that John Robinson, a cool, methodical lawyer, reached an important constitutional decision using something other than legal reasoning. Robinson's naturalization bills were not 'political' ploys but rather were rational attempts to resolve a difficult problem. The reform opposition had to ignore the fact that the government was legally correct and that the naturalization bills were remedial measures designed to grant what relief was possible to the American-born. Far from trying to take rights away from the settlers, Maitland and Robinson had been working to grant rights to resident aliens. They did so not out of any paternal concern for Americans, but rather to keep peace and order in the province. They were defeated by an opposition eager to stir up animosity against the government. The *Kingston Chronicle* printed a succinct summation of the first alien debate:

The kind interventions of the Ministry towards the Aliens in this country are at present defeated – a victory over the laws and over the Executive is attempted – the happiness and security of the Aliens is disregarded – and the different branches of the Legislature are called upon to declare that to be the law which is not the law – that to be fact which everyone knows is not fact.[42]

In the meantime, provincial business had to proceed. In addition to the naturalization proposals, Robinson introduced road bills and a bill to incorporate the Desjardins Canal Company. The opposition contented itself with posturing, and the work of the House was left to the attorney-general. Robert Stanton, the government printer and tory wit, observed that 'it is really astonishing to me to see how much real business Robinson gets through.' Stanton also observed that Robinson was wearying of the constant strains of partisan politics: 'if I may judge from appearances [Robinson] is *sick* of the thing – his labours are not appreciated and consequently lost.'[43]

As if enough controversy had not been generated, before the assembly adjourned it passed a resolution that advocated an equal distribution of clergy reserves among all Protestant denominations. If this proved to be too cumbersome, the assembly favoured a secular solution – devoting the reserves to education and public works. That solution was unacceptable to the Anglicans, and their spiritual leader was busily working up even more controversy. At the service marking the death of Bishop Mountain, Strachan denounced the 'uneducated, itinerant [Methodist] preachers.' Where his address was made public there were outcries of disbelief and rage. Robinson underestimated the harmful effect Strachan's comments would have on public opinion, and marvelled at 'the absurd fuss they have continued to make about the Kingston address.'[44]

Dr Strachan added fuel to the fire when he travelled to London in the spring of 1826 to obtain a royal charter for a university to educate Anglican churchmen. Robinson supported Strachan, not only from old-school loyalty, but because of their shared objectives:

[Strachan] hopes to bring out a Royal Charter and if so, he may feel still more exalted above the malice of the vile shameless ruffians who honour him with their uncompromising hatred. They know they can never make *him* a convert to their cause.[45]

The image of Dr Strachan as an apostle of John Rolph and radicalism is beyond contemplation. In correspondence with Strachan, however, even Robinson admitted the futility of compelling citizens to support a national church. He cited Ireand, where 'tithes are collected from the great mass of people detesting the Church which they support.'[46] Yet Robinson also believed that the 'moral state of society' could only be upheld through a national church. To keep this objective from slipping from their grasp, Strachan and Robinson hoped that the chartered Anglican university would symbolize the entrenchment of the established church.

If the first alien debate had been an indication that the population was about to rise up against the government, the lieutenant-governor's tour put an end to the myth of public disaffection. During the winter of 1826, Sir Peregrine Maitland and his retainers visited the Midland and Eastern districts. Maitland reported to the colonial secretary that he received a warm welcome wherever he went and that the Crown was quite popular among the common people.[47] Maitland forwarded a petition from the settlers of Leeds County in which the resident aliens begged the government to proceed with the naturalization bills in order that they might be confirmed in their land holdings. In Durham, an address was presented to the lieutenant-governor in which the assembly was dismissed as a 'band of factious demagogues' who were trying to 'subvert legitimate authority.' In Peter Robinson's latest settlement, cedar boughs were strewn in the path of His Excellency's sledge. The rousing welcome the Irish gave to the vice-regal party evidenced their satisfaction with their Upper Canadian homes.

Supervised emigration was now well underway, but was only meeting with limited success. In 1823 rioting had broken out between the emigrant Irish and the local Orangemen. John Robinson observed that the 'Ems' were not to blame and that there existed 'an actual terror inspired by the very name of Irish Catholics.'[48] Nevertheless, he begged Peter to persuade Wilmot Horton to bring future emigrants from English parishes, not from the Irish counties. The results of the 1823 project were dismal. By 1824, only ninety-one acres had been cleared and 'many settlers finally had to come to terms with the land and recognize it for what it was – largely unfit for farming.'[49] In 1825, Peter tried again and settled more than two thousand Irish near the Otonabee River. That settlement prospered, and after only a year Peter was able to report that over one thousand acres of wild land had been cleared.

The success of the Peterborough settlement (named by the Irish after their benefactor) convinced Wilmot Horton of the desirability of moving paupers to the colonies. At his instigation a parliamentary committee studied the matter of emigration schemes. The committee, however, seemed more interested in investigating poverty in Britain and made no special reference to emigration in its report. Assisted emigration was an expensive proposition and Parliament was unwilling to authorize any further experiments. The Irish emigrations of 1823 and 1825 were dismissed as 'mere relief measures, which had no appreciable effect on the situation either at home or in the colonies.'[50] The emigration schemes had made no dent in British poverty, although they had benefited the colony by supplying some badly needed settlers.

While the winter tour had proved that the government was popular in many parts of the province, Maitland and his minions were forever damned in the eyes of the editor of the *Colonial Advocate*. Mackenzie had stridently supported the opposition during the alien debate, and after the session his attacks on the government members became increasingly vicious. The *Colonial Advocate*'s descent into pure venom climaxed with a tirade in the issue of 18 May 1826, directed against the entire Robinson family:

The delicacy of our York belles would be shocked if reminded that the present Attorney General is the hopeful progeny of Mother Beman who kept the cake and beer shop in King Street; that the honourable Peter Robinson, whose pranks and Peterboroughs we hear so much of, with his learned brother, the Declaimer General against the Americans, were paupers of the lowest class for whom people now in York, taking pity on their forlorn condition, went about and begged handfuls of meal and York sixpences to keep them from actual starvation. The reputed father of these worthies was likewise an original in his way; and when he took his hopeful family into the boat with him for a very remarkable purpose, it would have been no loss to society if the heart of flint in the bosom of his son had then found a bed in the bottom of the deep, where the hardest pebble has a softer texture. This Virginian descended of Virginians has not forgotten the unshakable pride of his country; has he forgotten that it was long the Botany Bay of the British Kingdom the unhallowed receptacle of thieves, rogues, prostitutes and incorrigible vagabonds? Have the Robinsons anything to boast of in their Virginian descent ... Is it a secret in these parts that many, very many, such Virginian *nobles* as the Robinsons assume themselves, were descended from mothers who came there to try their luck, and were purchased by their sires with tobacco at prices according to the quality and soundness of the article. And is it from such a source that we are to expect the germ of liberty? Nay, rather is it not from such a source that we may look for the tyranny engendered, nursed, and practised by those whose blood has been vitiated and syphilized by the accursed slavery of centuries?[51]

The antic publisher had forsaken political satire for gross and mindless insult. Perhaps as a result of this scurrilousness, his subscribers were reluctant to pay for their copies and the newspaper was on the verge of bankruptcy. On 8 June Mackenzie managed to have one final edition of the *Colonial Advocate* published before closing down his newspaper. Late that afternoon, a group of York's young bloods, including Robinson's clerk, Henry Sherwood, invaded Mackenzie's shop and destroyed his printing press. This display of adolescent temper was forthwith condemned by the tory elders, and all the 'type rioters' were put under threat of civil or criminal prosecution. Mackenzie sued for damages and received a settlement which enabled him to reopen his newspaper. In a province ruled by a government 'more fit for Russians than Britons,' the colonial court had given Mackenzie a fair and open trial. That, of course, would not alter his convictions about the tyranny of the ruling regime.

The year 1826 was an exciting one for the province. Mackenzie, who had almost faded into obscurity, was suddenly thrown back into public esteem. Dr Strachan was in London seeking a charter for the Anglican university. Sir Peregrine Maitland was making plans to move the provincial capital to Kingston.[52] Negotiations on the alien issue were again underway in London. Rolph had been sent to England by the reformers, and Henry John Boulton, who was in London representing the Welland Canal Company, advanced the government's case. Robinson took no formal part in these public events, restricting his activities almost exclusively to his law practice. Still determined to resolve the alien question when it was presented to Parliament, he seemed willing to leave partisan activities to others. Good government was, in Robinson's opinion, not the result of wild speeches in the assembly, but of quiet deliberative work such as that which flowed from the attorney-general's office or the benches of the courts.

Throughout the summer and fall of 1826 the attorney-general took no active part in political life. It was a convenience that Boulton was in London so that the provincial government's position could be reiterated. In March 1826, Boulton sought out Wilmot Horton and outlined the disastrous results of the first alien debate. Reports of the debates were reaching London and the Colonial Office was becoming desperate to deal with this embarrassment once and for all. Wilmot Horton conceded that the provincial government was entirely correct, and instructed Boulton to prepare a naturalization bill that would be 'satisfactory to all Parties.' Boulton prepared a statute to confer citizenship on those settlers who had resided seven years in the province and who had taken an oath of allegiance. When Wilmot Horton rejected this bill for 'certain state reasons,' Boulton suggested another plan. Westminister could pass an act to grant the Upper Canadian Parliament the authority to naturalize. The harassed under-secretary quickly agreed, and Boulton was instructed to prepare the imperial act and accompanying instructions to Maitland.[53] After he had drafted the bill Boulton showed it to John Rolph, who was in London at the behest of the opposition. Rolph told Boulton that he had no objections to the act, and the Canada Naturalization Bill passed through Westminster with only a perfunctory debate.[54] At last, reasonable men had prevailed and a solution to the alien question was at hand.

Or was it? The reformers had found in the alien question an issue on which to focus their opposition. The reform position was popular with the

American-born and promised to be the basis for future electoral success. The reformers had no intention of surrendering the issue until their demands were completely satisfied. When the provincial parliament reassembled in December 1826, the government was confronted with a united and aggressive opposition. the reply to the lieutenant-governor's address was not a mindless echo. The assembly rebuked Maitland for having accepted addresses critical of the legislature during his winter tour. Rolph, without waiting for any formal instructions from London, then introduced a naturalization bill that entitled all resident settlers to become British subjects unless they registered their dissent within six months.

Rolph's bill was referred to committee, and in the meantime the Colonial Office's instructions arrived in York. This time Bathurst's orders were explicit. The power was granted to the province to naturalize aliens, but the Crown would not accept any act that merely declared aliens to be British subjects: 'The subjects of the United States of America whether born before or after the treaty of Peace of 1783 are aliens, and must, in point of law be regarded in that character.'[55] Bathurst stipulated that aliens were to be divided into two classes. Those who had resided in Upper Canada for seven years could be naturalized by taking the oath and signing an alien register; all others must complete their seven years before taking the oath. In addition, the alien must renounce his former allegiance and take the oath within a specified period. The Crown also reserved the right to pass on the legitimacy of the act. These terms, while highly unpalatable to the opposition, left no doubt as to the legislation that had to be passed in order to resolve the alien question. Under Robinson's guidance, the committee revised Rolph's bill so that it met the requirements of Lord Bathurst's dispatch.

The passage of a year had not reconciled the reformers to the fact that the Americans were aliens, and again they vigorously attacked the government for abrogating the rights of loyal residents. Mackenzie published a mock alien bill; one of its provisions read:

I acknowledge I have only one leg, having lost the other leg by a cannon ball at Queenston; yet I am not only an Alien in U.C. but also a vagabond: and that you have the right forthwith to order me into the Lake, or to the land where there is no resurrection.[56]

In January 1827 Robinson gave a detailed reply to reformer allegations that the naturalization act was a repressive tool designed to disfranchise the innocent. The law and the instructions from the Colonial Office were clear: American residents were aliens and could be naturalized only in a specific manner. The Crown, as a royal favour, was permitting the naturalization of the settlers. The aim of the legislation was to do away with alien disabilities and remove any legal barrier to their ownership of land and voting rights. Further opposition to this measure was only opposition for the sake of obstruction.[57] Nevertheless, when the natural-ization bill was reported from committee on 26 January, a tie vote in the assembly forced the Speaker to return the bill to committee for further amendments. On two more occasions the bill was returned to committee, and it was at last presented for third reading on 29 January. The House was again deadlocked, and the Speaker cast the deciding vote to defeat the bill.[58] Robinson's work in London, in committee, and on the floor of the assembly had been in vain. Upper Canada was simply unable to resolve the problem and matters were left to stay as they were or await an English law to alter alien status.

Then the unexpected occurred. Rolph and Bidwell moved that the bill they had just defeated be reintroduced and placed on the order of the day. This extraordinary measure took the House by surprise, and even some of those members who supported the bill voted against this tactic. The measure had been lost and recommittal served no purpose. Nevertheless, the naturalization bill was again placed on the order paper, and was again defeated. Once more, it was resurrected by Rolph and Bidwell; finally, on 5 February 1827, Robinson's naturalization bill was passed by a vote of twenty-two to eighteen. What had possessed the reform leadership to reintroduce and, in effect, legislate a measure they so despised? The official reason given by Rolph was that the bill had to be re-examined for further amendments,[59] an explanation that lacks credibility given the fact that the bill could not be amended so that it was in conflict with Lord Bathurst's instructions. The reformers' alternatives were living with the status quo or accepting Robinson's naturalization bill. If they chose the status quo the land titles of many of their constituents would be voided. Moreover, an election was likely in 1828 and the application of *Thomas* v *Acklam* would so restrict the franchise that many reform supporters would be unable to vote. Several sitting members, including M.S. Bidwell, would be ineligible to stand for re-election. To have rejected the naturalization bill would have resulted in a temporary halt to the reform movement. The passage of the bill assured the opposition that their constituents would be confirmed both in their lands and, more important, in their voting rights.

The opposition may also have been anxious about public reaction to their continued obstruction. Petitions in support of the bill were submitted by groups of American settlers who feared that they would lose the farms they had settled.[60] But while the opposition acceded to and even assisted in the passage of the naturalization bill, they remained reluctant to part with the issue that had aroused so much popular excitement. Even Maitland did not think the measure went far enough; he asked the colonial secretary to make the citizenship benefits conferred by the province effective throughout the Empire. The reformers, after ensuring the passage of the bill, denounced it as an arbitrary and coercive measure and formed a 'central committee' to urge the imperial government to disallow the act. The reform press called the naturalization act 'the Upper Canadian or Robinson's Penal Code,' and the editor of the *Canadian Freeman*, Francis Collins, exposed the government's sinister purpose:

The Alien Question has been nothing but a snare – a hidden trap, with which to destroy the civil rights of the American emigrants in this colony – an apple of discord, with which first to divide the people, and then rule them with an iron rod.[61]

The central committee resolved to send the Virginia-born reformer, Robert Randall, to London to plead their case for the disallowance of the naturalization act.

To a great extent the tumult generated by the alien question subsided after the passage of the bill. A serious threat to the peace and order of the province had been resolved according to law and with the support of the people's representatives. Even Edward McBride, who had spoken so passionately against Robinson's bill, supported the final naturalization measure as a necessary answer to the settlers' dilemma. Mackenzie grumbled that during the last session 'the attorney-general ... carried any measure he wanted to carry ... Mr. Rolph as a minister is not quite a match for the Minister who is full of finesse and always succeeds.'[62] While it was not true that the attorney-general always succeeded, the passage of the 1827 Naturalization Bill was John Robinson's greatest political triumph. Robinson had argued since 1824 that the American settlers were aliens and required naturalization. The assembly had at last bowed to his view and accepted his solution.

By the summer of 1827, Robinson was confident that 'the stuff about the Naturalization bill has blown over.'[63] His confidence was premature, however, for events in Britain had drastically altered the character of the Colonial Office. Lord Liverpool suffered a stroke in February 1827, and

George Canning succeeded him as prime minister. Many of the older tories disagreed with Canning's policies and refused to serve in his government. Among these was Lord Bathurst, whose career as colonial secretary ended in April. Bathurst's lengthy stewardship had given a continuity and direction to colonial affairs that his successors were unable to equal. Dr Strachan lamented that 'the retirement of Lord Bathurst is most unfortunate for all the Colonies.' Fortunately, Strachan had made arrangements for the establishment of an Anglican college before Bathurst resigned.[64]

Lord Goderich, a man more interested in financial administration than colonial affairs, became colonial secretary. One of the first issues thrust upon him was the naturalization bill. Despite the fact that Robert Randall, the central committee's emissary, had not submitted his petition through the proper channels, he was politely received at Downing Street. The under-secretary was favourably impressed and in June sent an unexpected message to Upper Canada.

The 1827 naturalization bill had contained a clause requiring aliens to renounce their former allegiance. This clause had been specifically inserted by Lord Bathurst, but Wilmot Horton now took strong exception to the provision. The foreign office, now in the midst of negotiations with the United States over the question of naturalization, took the position that no subject could ever renounce his allegiance. Any British subject who was naturalized in another country was still British if he returned to any Crown territory. The Upper Canadian bill might be an unwelcome precedent that would weaken the British case. This was difficult to believe in view of the fact that naturalization laws in Upper Canada and Britain were now so radically different. Moreover, it was unlikely that the laws in one of the smallest colonies would set a binding precedent for the mother country. Wilmot Horton gave another, more persuasive reason for setting aside the provincial statute: Randall had sought and received the support of radical members of the House of Commons, and they promised to give the naturalization bill a harsh reception in Parliament. Canning's precarious government had no intention of facing a debate on colonial policy, and Wilmot Horton advised that the bill be disallowed.[65]

The official rejection of the bill came from Lord Goderich. According to his instructions for new legislation, all aliens who had received land, held office, or taken the oath before 1820 were declared to be British subjects.[66] Those persons whom the courts had ruled aliens would not be required to take an oath of allegiance in order to be naturalized. Aliens who had arrived after 1820 would have to reside in Upper Canada seven years, be placed on an alien register, and take the oath. Goderich set aside the acts of the provincial government, the executive council, the legislative council, and the assembly and substituted the opinions of one group of petitioners. This was a stunning capitulation to the reformers, and was especially surprising in view of the fact that no British government would ever have considered applying the same principles in the mother country. The success of Randall's mission also showed the opposition that the attorney-general did not hold a monopoly on influence in the Colonial Office. The first dramatic alliance of provincial reformers and British radicals had proved that together they could significantly alter colonial policy.

However encouraging this sudden shift in policy was to the reformers, Goderich's dispatch was considered by the provincial government to be a shameful betrayal of a loyal government. Sir Peregrine Maitland complained that the new imperial government understood Canadian circumstances 'but imperfectly.' The colonial secretary had committed Britain to a complete reversal of policy based on one unsupported petition, without consulting the provincial government.[67] Nevertheless, Maitland obeyed his orders and a new bill was drafted to conform with Goderich's instructions. Appropriately enough, this bill was introduced to the assembly by an alien, Marshall Spring Bidwell.

On this third and last alien debate, Robinson did not bother to mask his feelings. Americans who had driven his father from his home and later invaded the loyalist Eden and killed numbers of his colleagues were, by this act, declared to be British subjects. Although he was prepared to grant British citizenship to Americans who lived peacefully within the province, simply to proclaim that those persons who had recently invaded the province were citizens was, to John Robinson, an abomination. In this futile cause he delivered some of his most impassioned speeches. One observer remarked that 'Robinson's speeches have been most brilliant, and I never before saw him so much aroused – all in vain – he is left to battle the watch against men who have closed their ears against argument.'[68] The new naturalization bill received enthusiastic approval. Robert Stanton described the scene in the House when the bill received final reading after its amendment by the legislative council:

Rolph said it would be with three hearty cheers for the King – the *patriots* had been regularly drilled for it and hat in hand, standing, the walls of our *deliberative* Assembly rang with the hip-hip hurrah of a bacchanalian festivity.[69]

Captain Mathews then invited all members to adjourn to a bonfire lighted to celebrate the occasion. The attorney-general muttered sourly that they should all be careful – it would be such a pity if the Captain and his radical friends fell in.

This conclusion to the alien question left most Upper Canadians with the impression that their government had opposed granting civil rights to American settlers and had sought to take away existing rights. Their sinister project had only been foiled by the reformers sending Randall to London to open the eyes of the colonial administration. The success of Randall's mission was seen as proof that the imperial government was basically benevolent and that the York clique were the villains who had attempted to oppress honest settlers. That perception was fuelled by Mackenzie and eventually became part of reformer lore. Remarkably, future scholars would repeat the legend of the insidious tory plot to disfranchise reform voters and the stand of the stout hearts in the assembly who revealed to all the Tory conspiracy.[70] The durability of this legend is all the more curious since Upper Canada's government disfranchised no one and went to considerable efforts to bestow rights on American settlers. For their efforts Maitland, Robinson, and Boulton received derision at home and betrayal abroad. To the government faction, the Colonial Office's reversal was a signal that they could not depend on the support of the British government. At any time, for its own convenience, the British government could reverse any policy in favour of the opposition. This incident demonstrated both the weakness of the provincial oligarchy and the increasing futility of attempting to administer a government that was an extension of a confused and vacillating British ministry.

The betrayal by the Colonial Office, the rejection of his legislation, and the hostility of many of the people to the government poisoned the attorney-general's view of political life. His mother had died in the summer of 1827. In the fall of that year, after the rejection of the naturalization Bill had become public, Peter urged his brother to abandon Upper Canada and take up a career in England. Peter assured him that Wilmot Horton still retained strong feelings of friendship despite their differences over the alien question. Waxing enthusiastic, Peter reported that Wilmot Horton was 'preparing the way for bringing you forward' and that it only remained for John to obtain a seat in the House.[71] With the decline in his provincial fortunes, John Robinson appeared eager to follow his brother's suggestion. But Robinson's last personal contact in the Colonial Office, Wilmot Horton, had resigned at the end of 1827; the department was now staffed by men who either had no high regard for Robinson or did not know him at all. The temporary legal clerk to the office, James Stephen, was now permanent legal counsel to the department. A brilliant and able man, Stephen soon came to dominate the Colonial Office. With Stephen as the final arbiter of legal questions the department would have no need of Robinson's expertise. Stephen confidentially advised Robinson that he was considered to be next in line to become chief justice of Upper Canada. While Robinson welcomed this assurance, he protected his reputation by scribbling on Stephen's note, 'I positively declined what was suggested in this.'[72] Significantly, Stephen made no mention whatsoever of any imperial appointment. Robinson would have to reconcile himself to playing his part on the colonial stage with Rolph and Bidwell, not with Goderich and Wellington.

The final alien debate turned the balance against the provincial oligarchy. From that point on, they were constantly on the defensive, withstanding the reformers' charges of abuses and outrages. In that atmosphere, it was unlikely that Robinson could achieve much in government; he would be a mere defender of the administration and a helpless observer of Upper Canada's factious political landscape.

9

'Politics I Am Not Fond Of'

The phrase 'family compact' was first used in 1824 by Thomas Dalton, the failed banker and reform sympathizer, in reference to the tory oligarchy of Kingston, whom he labelled 'a family compacted junto.'[1] By 1828, the term took on a wider meaning and was used in reference to the York government itself. M.S. Bidwell wrote to Dr Baldwin, 'I shall be happy to consult with yourself and Mr. Rolph on the measures to be adopted to relieve this province from the evils which a family compact have brought upon it.'[2]

'Compact,' in its original meaning, refered to an agreement or understanding, not to a political party.[3] Nevertheless, in Upper Canada the term 'family compact' eventually came to refer to a distinct political faction, giving the impression that the family compact was a cohesive, self-seeking group in firm control of Upper Canada's government. Mackenzie wrote that the family compact was a vast nefarious organization, linked by blood, which held the province in its grip: 'This family compact surround the Lieutenant-Governor, and mould him, like wax to their will.'[4] Lord Durham provided the most widely known and most generally accepted version of the family compact and its activities. The radical peer admitted that there were few blood relationships between the leading members of government. Nevertheless, those men formed a closed oligarchy that possessed all the highest public offices, 'wielded all the powers of government,' and dispensed official patronage.

This rather simplistic interpretation was challenged by later historians, who substituted a more sympathetic view. Aileen Dunham, in her analysis of politics in early Upper Canada, concluded that 'the term stood for a tendency of society rather than for a definite organization.[5] It was inevitable, she argued, in a pioneer society that the few men of education and proved loyalty would head the government. Heirs of the loyalist tradition, veterans of the War of 1812, those men instinctively fought against egalitarianism and republican institutions. With the settlement of the province, the new arrivals sought to supplant the tendency to oligarchic rule with a popular responsible government. However, the early perception of the family compact has survived in popular legend and, to a degree, in contemporary historiography; some recent scholars continue to refer to the oligarchy as 'the relatively small, tightly knit group of men who dominated the government of Upper Canada in the 1820s and to a somewhat lesser extent in the following decade.'[6]

Perhaps the most obvious myth associated with the family compact was that it was bound together by blood ties. When Mackenzie tried to describe the compact's interrelationships, he necessarily had to exclude half of the executive council and most of the legislative council, since no blood ties united those men. While it was true that John, Peter, and William Robinson were all influential men, their influence was felt at different times and for different reasons. Peter was primarily a business-man, and though he sat in the executive council emigration projects consumed most of his time. John had no business ventures but was vitally concerned with public affairs from 1820 to 1829. William built up his enterprises and did not become active in politics until after John had left the arena. The careers of the Robinson brothers were not intermeshed or mutually supportive.

The family compact was not the 'family' organization Mackenzie imagined it to be, nor was it the powerful monolith of reformer lore. During the Eighth Parliament of 1821–4, when Robinson was at the peak of his authority, there had been continual opposition to the government in the House. During the Ninth Parliament, that opposition hardened into intransigence. The reformers were now able to curtail the govern-ment's spending and even stop important government measures such as the Naturalization Bill. On a number of issues that required parliamentary consent, the government was effectively stymied. Even tory members could not be relied on consistently to support government bills. The assembly began to assume a mind of its own by petitioning the King to abolish clergy reserves and erect an independent judiciary. Despite its influence in the legislative council the government was unable to manipulate Parliament, and during the 1820s the assembly became an effective organ of popular discontent.

Even though the phrase 'family compact' became a byword in Canadian history, in reality it is unlikely that such an organization could have existed in Upper Canada. To understand the province, it is essential to remember that it was a colony administered by the Colonial Office through its representative, the lieutenant-governor. Reformers usually were hesitant to attack the personage of the Crown's representative, so they vilified his subordinates, accusing them of 'moulding' the lieutenant-governor to their designs. In reality, the lieutenant-governors of the post-war period were usually strong-willed individuals of fixed conservative ideals. Sir Peregrine Maitland, Wellington's first brigade commander at Waterloo, was not a man to be led by subordinates. Maitland came to rely on Robinson and Strachan because their views coincided with his own and because of their administrative ability. As early as 1819, Maitland had bemoaned the fact that he lacked a 'confidential person in the House' to explain government measures to the assembly.[7] After Robinson established his credentials at Stamford Park as a loyal and trusted aide, he became Maitland's confidant. The men who surrounded Maitland were there not out of any inherent right to rule but simply because the lieutenant-governor relied on them. To understand with what speed that reliance could change, it is only necessary to remember how powerless Chief Justice Powell became after his fall from grace.

Of the inner circle of government, the civil secretary, Major George Hillier, was especially close to Maitland and was responsible for carrying out his direct instructions. Sir Peregrine even ordered Hillier to burn official correspondence so that the people would see orders emanating from subordinates rather than from the Crown's representative himself.[8] After Major Hillier, John Robinson was the lieutenant-governor's alter ego within the government. It was Robinson who was entrusted with negotiating the customs dispute, handling the alien question, and drafting government legislation. A year after Maitland's departure, Robinson remarked in passing, 'I knew Sir Peregrine I think, as well as almost any person did here.'[9] Robinson's outlook was similar to the lieutenant-governor's, and Maitland had implicit faith in his ability to steer the government. Strachan was perhaps the least attached to Maitland and, after Maitland's attempt in 1826 to move the capital from York to Kingston, there was an open breach between the two men.

When a new lieutenant-governor replaced Maitland, Robinson and Strachan found their influence greatly diminished. The government of

Upper Canada was not dominated by an entrenched oligarchy; rather, the imperial government founded an oligarchy to assist it in governing the colony. The Crown's representative chose men of ability, influence, and compatible ideas to assist him in the day-to-day affairs of government. Moreover, the imperial government did not hesitate to change the personnel of the oligarchy whenever it wished. Maitland's successors chose their own advisers and, on occasion, even consulted with reformers.

Though an entrenched oligarchy did not exist in the provincial government, throughout Upper Canada small 'family compacts' dotted the province and controlled local office and patronage. Upper Canadians were most directly affected by their district governments, and it was the existence of these local cabals that convinced them that a provincial family compact did indeed exist. The chief administrative unit for each district was the Court of Quarter Sessions. This court, presided over by magistrates, levied taxes, issued licences, appointed lesser officials, and received reports of the occasional township meetings.

One of the most outstanding features of gentry society in rural Upper Canada was its overrepresentation in the magistracy. In the Western District, the gentry boasted families like the Babys who, although Catholics, possessed the breeding, loyalty, and education to be the social equals of the Robinsons. Four Babys became magistrates and their sons and daughters married into the other families who monopolized the remaining offices in the Western District.[10] In Carleton County, at the opposite end of the province from the Western District, the gentry was composed of half-pay officers who controlled the magistracy and local patronage.[11] To the Carleton gentry, a seat in Parliament was less desirable than local office. Gentleman squires such as Hamnet Kirks Pinhey found appeals to the electorate to be particularly distasteful, preferring the unsullied offices of county treasurer or postmaster. The gentry's preference for staying close to home was matched by a concern for local issues and a distrust of their tory brethren in York.

These local compacts did not necessarily agree or co-operate with the government in York. During the union question of 1822, for example, the Kingston tories were in open conflict with York. Those two doughty churchmen, Strachan and Macdonell, were equally attached to toryism, but antagonistic when it came to advancing the claims of their respective communions.[12] It was not surprising that Upper Canada, with its poor roads, irregular communication, and rudimentary politics, did not erect local cells to complement a province-wide tory faction. District magistrates did not consider themselves under York's sway. Occasionally they simply ignored the attorney-general's instructions and conducted business in their own fashion.[13] It is not necessarily true that there existed a 'system of alliances' between York and the local élites.[14] In this early society, 'there was no one locus of power.'[15]

Robinson's career offers further evidence of the oligarchy's fragile grasp of power. His close association with Maitland was the primary source of his authority; that John Beverley Robinson is spoken of as a leading member of the family compact is attributable to Maitland's unusually long term as lieutenant-governor. His confidants, such as Robinson, were seen as an established 'compact' when in reality their influence was a result of their friendship with the Crown's representative. On the provincial level, it is difficult to find evidence of the all-powerful 'family compact' that ruled Upper Canada and moulded the lieutenant-governors to its will. Perhaps the phrase 'family compact' should be used in the context in which it was originally intended, as a political slur directed at local cabals.[16] If the family compact existed at all, it was at the local level of government where appointed positions enabled the gentry to dominate society.

John Robinson's career is proof of the usually high ethical standards of provincial government figures. Despite his undoubted influence over the lieutenant-governor, Robinson rarely used his authority to have his friends appointed to public office. While he did have John Macaulay named to the minor position of deputy postmaster, Robinson refused to assist him in gaining the important job of Collector of Kingston, a position that became vacant as a result of Hagerman's appointment to the bench in 1828.[17] Macaulay reminded Robinson of his previous services to the government and asked for his support. Robinson explained that he felt obliged to support Dr James Sampson,[18] who had devoted much of his time to Kingston's poor and was thought to be deserving of a government sinecure. Macaulay was deeply hurt by the reluctance of his friend to intercede on his behalf.

Whenever he was called on to recommend someone for an official post, Robinson tended to look to the candidate's loyalty rather than to personal connections. One prospective magistrate had abandoned his thriving business in the United States and had returned to Upper Canada during the War of 1812.[19] Robinson put this paragon of loyalty forward as an ideal candidate. He listed the shortcomings of candidates with cruel brevity: 'I have heard that William Anthony drinks hard' or, simply, 'C.H. Crown – corruptible.'[20] Robinson was careful to use patronage for the government's ends. On one occasion he attempted to have a trusted lieutenant appointed postmaster. London objected and insisted that the appointee have some postal experience.[21] Robinson then had his man appointed to a local position in the expectation that he would enjoy an imperial appointment later. Close attention to the loyalty of the men who filled low-level functions was a feature of Upper Canada's government.

Although patronage was dispensed mainly to the government's faithful supporters, most public officers did not abuse their positions. In addition to refusing land grants from governments and individuals, Robinson firmly rebuffed any suggestions of bribery. It was well known that he was the most influential government figure involved in the canal projects. One contractor, James Strobridge, had hired Robinson to draft a note to be used as security for a government loan. Strobridge sent Robinson four pounds in the hope of receiving 'some more favours at your hands.'[22] Robinson retained one pound for legal services rendered and returned three pounds with a terse statement that he did not dispense favours.

With the momentum given to the reform movement by its success in the alien debates, Rolph and his colleagues used any petty incident to prove their case that a family compact ruled and oppressed Upper Canada. One example of this tactic was the controversy at Niagara Falls concerning William Forsyth's fence.[23] Forsyth ran a hotel near the Falls, and in order to induce persons to view the cataract through his establishment he erected a fence that blocked other forms of access to the Falls. The military owned the strip of land along the river, and in May 1827 a group of unarmed soldiers tore down the fence where it encroached on military property. They were accompanied by a surveyor who marked off the precise limits of the military reserve. Forsyth immediately rebuilt the fence. The soldiers returned and this time threw the fence into the Falls. Forsyth then sued the captain in charge of the soldiers and the local sheriff for trespass. The captain protested that he was being sued for having performed his duty. Maitland asked the attorney-general to defend the captain. At trial, the evidence was manifestly against Forsyth; Robinson introduced surveyors who proved conclusively that Forsyth had trespassed on the military lands. Both of the suits brought by Forsyth were dismissed and a verdict of intrusion was entered against him.

Having lost in the courts, Forsyth went to the assembly where sympathetic reformers were always willing to examine a case of government high-handedness. The case was referred to a select committee composed exclusively of reformers and chaired by John Rolph. In testimony before this committee, Forsyth bemoaned the fact that Robinson was now prosecuting him after Forsyth had done him a great favour. He stated that in 1822 he had transferred four acres of land to Robinson for no consideration.[24] In fact, William Dickson had sold some land to Forsyth in 1821 with an option to Robinson to purchase one acre on the riverfront for a cottage. In 1822, while Robinson was in England, Colonel Nichol and Colonel Clark, acting on Robinson's behalf, exchanged the option for four lots in the interior which were better suited for a cottage. This was only a business transaction; Forsyth had not done any special favour for the attorney-general. Unfortunately, the truth was not revealed until after the committee hearings.

It came as no surprise when the committee reported that Forsyth had been horribly wronged, and that the 'acts of violence' committed by the government were 'justly regarded with jealousy in all free countries.' The committee ignored the fact that Forsyth had no right to build his fence on the military reserve and that the military had every right to enter on their own lands and remove obstructions. The reformers basked in the excitement aroused by Forsyth's case, and when Maitland refused to allow two officers to testify before the select committee the assembly ordered them jailed for contempt.

Another example of the attorney-general's attitude toward reformers and justice was the notorious tar-and-feathers case in Gore.[25] George Rolph, brother of John, had sheltered a Mrs Evans, who had fled from a brutal husband. This so offended local morals that a group of vigilantes dragged Rolph from his bed (which, to their surprise, he did not share with Mrs Evans) and had him tarred and feathered. Rolph sued three of the assailants and received minimal damages. This display of impromptu justice incensed Robinson, and it was his opinion that Rolph 'ought on the one hand to prosecute without delay those persons suspected of so atrocious an umbrage.'[26] The fact that some of the assailants were prominent local tories did not lessen his sense of injustice.

Robinson's devotion to the rule of law had not slackened since the Ancaster assizes. Nevertheless, he continued to be accused of instigating the foulest outrages to British justice. The most prominent of these incidents had its origins in an innocent attempt to reform the court system. To understand the proposed changes and the resulting turmoil, it must be remembered that the province's court system was the product of centuries of English law. The common law had its origins in the attempts by the English kings to impose a uniform code of law and procedures throughout the kingdom. This system was becoming inflexible by the mid-fourteenth century and subjects began to appeal for royal dispensations, or equity. By appealing to the chancellor subjects could receive justice based on equitable principles of moral correctness. These two paths to justice, common law and equity, developed separately and each developed its own jurisdiction. While common-law courts might deal with liability and damages, equity would be invoked to control the behaviour of the Crown and its subjects. In addition to issuing remedial orders, equity (or the chancery court) presided over matters of estates, bankruptcy, and guardianship.

In 1794, when William Osgoode established King's Bench as Upper Canada's common-law court, no equitable jurisdiction was created, and many claims involving equitable remedies could not be applied for in the existing courts. Since 1801 proposals had been made to create an equity court, but the province was simply unable to afford a vice-chancellor's salary. In 1825, during his discussions with Bathurst, Robinson again raised the issue of the province's desperate need for a chancery court.[27] Bathurst suggested to Maitland that an equity jurisdiction be created in King's Bench and one of the justices made vice-chancellor. In July 1827, an English barrister, John Walpole Willis, was named a justice of King's Bench in the expectation that he would shortly be named vice-chancellor. Willis was one of those imperial appointees who manifested a disdain for anything colonial and an unwarranted belief in his own superiority. His wife, Lady Mary Willis, also disturbed the social tranquillity of Upper Canada by challenging the privileged position of Lady Sarah Maitland, the only other titled lady in the province. Aristocratic feathers were ruffled when the two grande dames met at the Christmas ball of 1827; after that the ladies were kept discreetly out of each other's presence.

At first, Willis and Robinson seemed to work well together, and there was reason to believe that Willis would be a fair and competent judge. Robinson and Boulton were assigned to draft a report describing how the new equity court could be created. They concluded that it could not be established by Crown patent, but would have to be legislated by the assembly. The colonial secretary agreed and instructed Maitland to put legislation for a proposed chancery court before Parliament. In March 1828 the attorney-general submitted the resolutions to the committee of the whole. Justice Willis, a regular visitor to the Assembly, began to socialize with the reform members. Despite Robinson's wish to see if the assembly supported the principle of the measure, the reformers insisted on reviewing the proposed bill. Robinson submitted the draft legislation for Rolph's examination on the understanding that it was for his information only.[28] Rolph, still unable to resist any opportunity to embarrass the government, proceeded to make the contents of the bill public. The resolution in favour of the chancery court was defeated, and the assembly passed resolutions condemning the existing courts for their partiality. The reformers thwarted any movement toward a more effective judicial system and barred Willis from becoming Upper Canada's first vice-chancellor.

This did not dismay Willis who, knowing that Chief Justice Campbell was to retire in a few months, thought that he would be the ideal candidate to succeed him. Maitland, however, had already put forward Robinson as his candidate for chief justice. Willis boldly advanced his own cause by describing his qualifications for the office:

As an English Barrister of more than ten years standing – the Son in law of the oldest Scottish peer – & the husband of the only Titled Female in the Province with the exception of Lady Sarah Maitland I must confess I felt it *rather irksome* under the Circumstances in which I came here, to remain in an inferior situation.[29]

Was it possible to promote a mere colonial over a man with such a pedigree? Notwithstanding Willis's background, Maitland informed the colonial secretary that Willis was not a fit candidate. His flirtation with the reformers had irritated the lieutenant-governor, and while Willis might look upon reform support as helpful to his advancement, the government could form 'no favourable opinion' of him.[30]

This opinion was largely the result of Willis's quixotic behaviour in April of 1828. Francis Collins, the irascible editor of the radical *Canadian Freeman*, had printed a lurid account of the Jarvis-Ridout duel of 1817 in which he stated that Jarvis had all but murdered the defenceless Ridout. The lieutenant-governor felt that Collins's article contained 'gross Reflections' on the administration of justice, and he instructed Robinson to conduct a libel prosecution against Collins. The case was being heard before Justice Sherwood, and Willis was sitting in attendance. After Willis's repeated pleas, Sherwood permitted him to take the bench on 11 April. Almost as if the following events were prearranged, Willis motioned for the sheriff to bring additional bailiffs into the court.[31] Preliminary motions were still pending, and Robinson was outside the courtroom. Collins rose and began a tirade against the government and its partial administration of justice. He condemned Robinson for his '*gross and foul Partiality*' in not prosecuting Henry John Boulton and James Small, Jarvis's seconds in the fatal duel. Henry Sherwood, Robinson's clerk, hastily fetched his senior into court and the attorney-general immediately protested that Collins was out of order; indeed, he had not even been arraigned. To Robinson's astonishment, Willis turned on him and accused him of failing to perform his duties as public prosecutor. Robinson replied that for the past sixteen years he had properly discharged the duties of attorney-general. 'Then I take leave to remark,' said Willis, 'that you have never properly discharged your Duty, and that in the Case mentioned you ought to have prosecuted.' According to observers, Robinson turned a 'rich cream colour.' After a lifetime of service to the Crown, he was being accused of neglect by one of His Majesty's judges. With thinly veiled rage, Robinson replied, 'My Lord, I think differently; I think I have properly discharged my Duty; and I must be allowed to say, that I think I understand that Duty as well as any Judge presiding on the Bench.' Willis then informed Robinson that this last outburst would be reported to London. Robinson stormed from the courtroom muttering that he was 'Attorney General to His Majesty and not to his Lordship.'[32]

After only six months in the province, Justice Willis had succeeded in antagonizing every important person in the government. Even Henry Sherwood, Robinson's hot-tempered clerk, felt so insulted by Willis that he almost challenged him to a duel; only the impropriety of an articling student duelling with a judge restrained him. So erratic was Willis's conduct that in London James Stephen was beginning to question his mental fitness.[33] Willis, determined to complete his own self-destruction, rendered a decision that made his continued presence on the bench intolerable. At the opening of the courts in Trinity term 1828, Willis declared that after investigating the powers of King's Bench, he had concluded that the court was improperly constituted unless all three judges presided. As Chief Justice Campbell was out of the province, the court could not be assembled. The day after Willis's pronouncement, Justice Sherwood attempted to reconvene the sittings. Dr Baldwin and John Rolph ostentatiously removed their gowns as a sign that they no longer stood before a valid court. The administration of justice had been reduced to a shambles.

Technically, Willis's interpretation of the King's Bench Act might have been correct.[34] However, the fact remained that no one had ever questioned the constitutionality of King's Bench. Willis's ruling cast into uncertainty hundreds of decisions that had been reached by fewer than three judges. Those judgments had confirmed dozens of land titles, which now were all laid open to doubt. The executive council was shocked by

Willis's decision and by his failure to consult the provincial government about his plans to declare the judicial system invalid. The council concluded that Willis should be removed from office, and Maitland did not hesitate to put their recommendation into effect. Willis left his family in York and travelled to England to protest his dismissal and initiate legal action against Maitland. John Walpole Willis had left too much havoc in his wake to be found innocent of the allegations against him, and his removal from office was confirmed by the privy council. (For Willis, when matters went wrong, they did so consistently: his wife took advantage of his absence to elope with an officer of the light infantry.)

Willis's dismissal was certainly justified in view of the chaos he had created. He did not understand the function of the attorney-general's office, and refused to accept correction from a mere colonial. He insisted on prosecutions when none were warranted and declared his court unconstitutional when no one had questioned its constitutionality. Nevertheless, the reformers made Willis into a popular hero, another victim of government oppression in the long line of Robert Gourlay, Barnabas Bidwell, and William Forsyth. At a public meeting a subscription was opened to purchase a set of plate for Willis, and Maitland's government was condemned as arbitrary and tyrannical.

Was Upper Canada in the grip of tyranny? Did the government act arbitrarily and illegally? In both the Forsyth and Willis situations the government had dealt with malcontents according to the rules of Law. In return, the reform faction used their majority in the assembly and their control of certain newspapers to spread the myth that the government was perpetrating outrages against the people. If the reform leadership had been more moderate in tone, as it became in the 1840s and 1850s, the government would not have been faced with this conflict. But Maitland's government had to deal with Mackenzie and Rolph, men frustrated at their inability to gain control of the inner workings of government. The reformers of the 1820s failed to understand that it was the imperial system and not a family compact that permitted the lieutenant-governor to administer the government and choose his advisers as he pleased. The impetus toward popular control of the executive was making it increasingly difficult for the provincial administration to function. As the fourth and last session of the Ninth Parliament approached, it was apparent that the assembly was interested only in opposition for the sake of opposition and the investigation of 'outrages.' Robinson might well have remembered his earlier remark to John Macaulay: 'Politics I am not fond of.'

10

Tory Twilight

The reform faction progressed in strength and cohesion, and their authority became evident in the winter session of 1828. Rolph took charge of introducing a number of reforms, including measures to abolish the right of primogeniture and imprisonment for debt. Robinson played little part in the ensuing debates, but his few interjections were carefully timed for effect. One of Rolph's proposed revisions had been to reduce the number of militia training days to one a year. The attorney-general countered that this would dangerously weaken the province's defences, and for once succeeded in defeating one of Rolph's proposals.[1]

Although the opposition was interested in reform, they were not particularly concerned with the province's economic advancement. In the last session of the Ninth Parliament, Robinson was again the only member to introduce important developmental legislation. This time he proposed the construction of a highway to connect the eastern and western extremities of the province. Some stretches of an east–west highway could be said to exist already, but it would require government action to connect and make the provincial roads passable. The estimated cost for this work was £25,000, and the attorney-general reckoned that the sum could be raised by collecting 2s 6d from every person liable to perform statute labour. If this levy was insufficient, Robinson suggested incorporating a turnpike company or even starting a lottery.[2] Many opposition members held local biases against the provincial highway. Some claimed that their district roads were adequate, others that they lived too far from the proposed highway to benefit from it. Robinson was presenting projects of a provincial scale to an assembly that was still too parochial in its outlook to consider the advancement of the entire colony.

Even though Robinson must have been discouraged at having to preside over the defeat of most government proposals, he seems to have thrived on the responsibility and effort his office required of him. Writing to Macaulay in the midst of the session, he reported that

I am as usual at such times, full charged with weighty matters of State – Chancery, roads – assessments, aliens, canals – form an agreeable variety – and at this moment I am *totus scribus* in the cause of Mother Church.[3]

The galleries of the assembly were frequently filled with the attorney-general's constituents, and even though many of them disagreed with the government all were impressed by Robinson's leadership. Robert Stanton observed that Robinson's speeches against Rolph's Naturalization Bill were in vain, and yet his addresses were so lucid and forceful that the listener had to be impressed: 'The Atty Gen's conduct in the House & his manly speeches have gained friends for him here.'[4] Even Marshall Spring Bidwell readily admitted that when aroused to 'great exertions,' the attorney-general was the most commanding speaker in the House:

The fire of his eye, the animation of his countenance and his manner, combined with dignity, cannot be appreciated by any who did not hear him. No report of his speeches, no description of his manner and appearance can convey to others a just and adequate idea.[5]

Among the people of York, the word was that 'Rolfe & the Attorney General know how to make a bill.' There was also general agreement that 'fortunately for the House the two bill makers are of opposite parties.'[6] Most opposition members did not take this objective view, but instead devoted their energies to seeking Robinson's removal from the House.

Francis Collins acknowledged the attorney-general as the government leader and prime target of reformer venom. Collins incessantly condemned Robinson for his stands on the alien issue and the clergy reserves, and concluded that he was 'a sort of *nondescript* in politics that we would call *an old English Yankee Tory* – a sort of derivative compound character deteriorated, at least 50 per cent, below the original.'[7] In response to reformer charges of 'daring outrages,' Robinson circulated a petition among the provincial bar asking them if they were aware of any such acts. Dr Baldwin, in his reply, attributed the partiality of the judges and Crown law officers to the fact that they were required to assume too many offices. Collins's response ridiculed Robinson's circular:

An appeal from the Duke of Wellington to the common drunken soldiers for testimonials of his conduct would not have surprised us more than the Attorney General's to the worthless, unprincipled, ignorant, vagrant village lawyers of this province.[8]

The opposition began to cast about for an issue to force Robinson out of his York constituency, and they seized on the proposition that because of his government office he was not an independent representative.[9] In order to gather some public support for this idea, Collins organized a meeting for the purpose of securing the 'independent representation' of York. The convention was opened at Frank's Hotel by its chairman, Dr Thomas Stoyell, with Francis Collins sitting at his elbow. Collins introduced two resolutions reaffirming the invaluable privilege of elections and the undesirability of a public official being elected to office. Those two resolutions passed. Collins then turned to specifics and proposed a resolution declaring Attorney-General J.B. Robinson to be an unfit candidate for York. This proposal was resoundingly defeated, and Collins attempted to grab his resolution from the hands of the chairman before it was entered on the record. Robinson's supporters protested and the meeting adjourned when an apple was thrown at the chairman.[10]

Undiscouraged, Collins called for another meeting which he hoped would produce a more satisfactory result. The tories took the bait, and the *Upper Canada Gazette* expressed the wish that all true friends of the government would be in attendance. It was therefore a highly partisan crowd that converged on Frank's Hotel at Monday noon, 12 November 1827. While the attorney-general himself refused to attend, his partisans arrived en masse. Robinson's faction was composed of 'barristers by the dozen – colonels – magistrates, honourables and militiamen by the score.' Dr Christopher Widmer, a prominent physician, opened the proceedings for the government by pointing out that it was still the custom in England for high officers to run in elections and that the attorney-general was equally entitled to be elected by suffrage. This neatly answered the reformer's objections to Robinson's candidacy. Mackenzie ignored Dr Widmer and spoke at great length about Robinson's stand on public issues and how they were at variance with public feeling. Despite being called to order over fifty times, Mackenzie carried on for over an hour and a half. Most of the tory supporters grew bored and left the hall. Eventually, after much jostling on the floor, a resolution was passed which rejected John Robinson as a candidate for York. Mackenzie crowed, somewhat prematurely, that 'the cause of freedom, and of old England had here a glorious triumph,' and that Robinson would be forced to 'take shelter in a gaelic shantie and endure the highland horrors of an unfortunate Glengarry campaign.'[11] That is, he expected Robinson to abandon the York constituency and run in the ever-loyal Highland Scot county of Glengarry.[12]

The attorney-general apparently had no intention of trusting himself to the loyalty of the Highlanders, preferring again to risk the insults of Mackenzie and Collins by standing for re-election in York. A petition from his supporters begged him to remain their candidate and face the onslaught of the reformers. As the provincial election of 1828 approached, it was evident that all was not well with the reform campaign. The reformers were divided over just who should carry their standard in York. Young Robert Baldwin, the son of the senior reformer, W.W. Baldwin, was supported by Francis Collins. Mackenzie, who disliked the Baldwin family, favoured Dr Thomas Morrison, a former copying clerk of dubious integrity.[13] Much to the displeasure of many reformers, Morrison was chosen to challenge the attorney-general.

No such divisions plagued the tory campaign. When it was rumoured the radical Dalton might run in Kingston, Robinson and John Macaulay rallied to Christopher Hagerman. Robinson advised Macaulay to dissuade any other tories from challenging Hagerman and leave the road clear for this capable man to return to politics.[14] Hagerman declined, however, and instead accepted appointment to the bench. Whatever party organization existed among the tories seems to have been centred on the attorney-general. His correspondence with Macaulay was circulated among the Kingston brethren, and on one occasion Robinson instructed his friend to 'see if you cannot help him [Donald Bethune] into the right path.' Maintaining a united front among the province's tories was another of the attorney-general's many roles. Robinson's efforts show the extent to which the York executive attempted to attract prominent tory candidates in constituencies throughout the province. Just as the alien and clergy reserves issues had given the reformers cohesion and organization, the tory reaction to these assaults was creating a core of conservative partisans throughout the province.

Robinson received petitions of support from loyal citizens and even lowered himself to visit the public houses in search of a broad base of support. The campaign of 1828 was the most turbulent in memory, with a clear choice being offered to the electors. The voters of York, many of whom depended on the government for their incomes, could choose between the esteemed attorney-general, the de facto leader of the government in the assembly, and Dr Morrison, an outsider who was entirely antagonistic to the establishment. As July approached, the campaign grew increasingly vitriolic, with reformers dredging up tales of tory abuse dating back to the time of Francis Gore. According to a critic of the tories, the 1828 campaign featured 'loyal fountains of corruption' in which 'the commonest blackguards in York would drink nothing inferior to Port or Madeira!'[15]

On 12 July 1828, the morning of the election, John Robinson's name was proposed by two Catholic burghers, Alexander McDonell and Robert Meighan. The reformers apparently had resolved their internal differences, for Dr Morrison was nominated by W.W. Baldwin. Both candidates addressed the assembled electors. Robinson, never at his best when addressing the general public, spoke somewhat defensively about his part in the Gourlay and Willis episodes. Dr Morrison predictably chastised the government and the attorney-general in particular for their unprincipled administration. The polls were opened, and at the close of the first day Robinson led by seven votes. The polls reopened the following day and closed at about five o'clock. Morrison's supporters protested that they still had more electors on the way but since the York riding encompassed only the town of York their complaint was not taken seriously. Sheriff William Jarvis solemnly read the totals to the assembled citizens: for the attorney-general, 110; for Dr Morrison, 93. Despite the efforts of the reformers, Robinson had increased his plurality since the previous election. 'Little York is Little York still,' fumed Francis Collins, as Robinson was chaired in triumph through the muddy streets of the capital. That evening a makeshift band was assembled for the victory procession which ended at Howard's Hotel. Loyal toasts were drunk in abundance and York's tories stumbled home in a state of euphoria.

Despite the victory in York, the tories did badly in the rest of the province, and the legislature again was filled with men who were, according to Sir Peregrine Maitland, 'notoriously disloyal.'[16] The election of 1828 was an indication that the regional personality contests of Upper Canada's early history were giving way to province-wide factional struggles for power.[17] Reformers throughout the colony basked in their triumph and attributed their success to the popular discontent aroused by the alien debate. The township meetings had proved to be especially successful in defeating the tory Jones family, who had dominated politics in the Johnstown District for decades.[18] In Lennox and Addington, Peter Perry and M.S. Bidwell were returned with impressive majorities. Perhaps the most discouraging event for the tories was the election of Mackenzie in York county. The tory faction (which would have disdained the term) had used its occupation of government offices to preserve what seats it could. In Kingston, the loyal burghers had returned Donald Bethune. Unlike the reformers, however, the tories had yet to find an issue that would enable them to fight a provincial campaign. They had no local party organizations to assist the provincial party, relying instead on their loyal office holders. Their defeat was a signal to the tories that if they intended to wrest the assembly away from the reformers, an entrenched party organization was essential.

Although 1828 was a year for reform victories, John Rolph barely retained his seat in Middlesex. Rolph's blanket opposition to any measure proposed by the government had angered many reform supporters. The *Gore Gazette* noted that Rolph had opposed the attorney-general's Highway Bill, which 'is admitted by everyone in the country, except the few who voted it down to have embraced a larger public benefit.'[19] As well, Robinson's increased plurality, won in the face of a determined reform effort, was a sign that some individual tories enjoyed popular favour. The new reform members were held in low esteem by Maitland, who commented that only one of them, Dr Baldwin, could be considered a gentleman. Jesse Ketchum, Mackenzie's associate member for York county, was an illiterate American tanner who was 'by no means respectably spoken of as a British subject.'[20] Another new member was John Cawthra, a retailer who had become wealthy during the war. According to Maitland, neither man belonged to the 'Society of Gentlemen,' and he found it disgraceful that they should be permitted to sit as legislators. Maitland failed to see that no matter how mean their origins, Ketchum and Cawthra were men of intelligence and industry. Ketchum, as a politician and philanthropist, eventually became one of York's outstanding citizens.

The rise to wealth and political prominence of men like Ketchum and Cawthra was a sure sign of the decline of gentry society. These rustic individuals were attaining eminence, and no landed aristocracy was emerging in Upper Canada to claim authority as its birthright. Upper Canadian society, composed as it was of small independent freeholders, was beginning to resemble the egalitarian society of the adjacent states. Robinson could only lament that 'there is no longer confidence in being supported by the King's Government & public virtue seems to be barred from public counsels.'[21]

After the election, one piece of unfinished business remained. Francis Collins had continued to print his free-wheeling accusations against the government and was again charged with libel. Although Robert Baldwin successfully defended him, Collins could not restrain himself from writing further libels. He accused the attorney-general of stating 'an open and palpable falsehood in Court' to 'our old *customer* Judge Hagerman.'[22] Collins later tried to temper his accusations by calling the attorney-general's remarks merely 'untrue.'[23]

Robinson had his prey. At last one of his antagonists stood exposed as having called him a liar in the public press. Collins was charged with a libel on the attorney-general, Justice Hagerman, and Solicitor-General Boulton. This time his conviction seemed assured. But Rolph argued persuasively, and after five hours of deliberation the jury found Collins guilty only of a libel on the attorney-general. Justice Hagerman instructed the jury that they must find the accused guilty of all of the libels or of none. The jury returned with a general verdict of guilty. Rolph's and Baldwin's objections were overruled, and Collins was sentenced to a year's imprisonment and a fine of fifty pounds. According to a tory observer, the assembled reformers 'looked very blank when the Sentence was pronounced' and left the courtroom 'bearing the appearance of great consternation.'[24] For the tories, Collins's conviction was almost as sweet as electoral victory. It has been suggested that Robinson's prosecution of Collins was unduly vindictive.[25] It might be remembered that Robinson had suffered the constant insults and outright lies of the reform press and was eager to seek satisfaction through the law; but Collins's sentence was a harsh lesson and probably reflected a desire for retribution as well as for justice.

While Francis Collins accustomed himself to his new surroundings in York jail, the government he so maligned was about to undergo a significant change. In October 1828 Sir Peregrine Maitland was appointed lieutenant-governor of Nova Scotia. His successor in Upper Canada, Sir John Colborne, was a brilliant soldier who had never been promoted through purchase but had earned through merit every advancement from ensign to field marshal. He arrived in York on 3 November to find a radical printer in jail, an active reform faction set against the government, and the government seemingly unable to counteract widespread disaffection. Colborne shrewdly chose to take a middle course by dissociating himself from all cliques. The reformers immediately pressed the new lieutenant-governor to free Collins and reinstate Justice Willis; Colborne refused to interfere in the ordinary course of the law and the petitions were dismissed.

Colborne was not as quick as Maitland had been to seek Robinson's advice. An incident occurred barely a month after Colborne's arrival which signalled the decline in influence of the 'family compact.' Without warning, Colborne called a meeting of the college council, the body entrusted with putting Strachan's royal charter into effect by founding an Anglican university. The lieutenant-governor opened the meeting by declaring that a university was not called for and that the royal charter should be amended. He then asked the shocked members for their comments. Robinson rose to refute some of the points raised by the lieutenant-governor. Colborne interrupted him, flatly asserted that Robinson was wrong, and ordered the council to execute his instructions.[26]

With Colborne's arrival, Robinson lost the prerogatives of government leader and returned to being merely the Crown law officer serving at His Majesty's pleasure. These changes in Upper Canada mirrored the greater movements that were altering the colonial policies of the Second British Empire. William Huskisson, who became colonial secretary in September 1827, was a man of great ability who conducted an administration very unlike Lord Bathurst's. Energetic, efficient, and liberal, Huskisson set out to initiate reforms in colonial government. A parliamentary committee was established to study and report on the problems of the Canadas. Sir James Kempt was dispatched to Lower Canada with instructions to mollify the French Canadians by granting their legislature greater control over provincial revenues. Robinson, dismayed by the liberal attitudes now prevailing in London, found Kempt's orders to be 'conciliatory in the *extreme.*'[27] In Britain Huskisson was considered a brilliant administrator, but he had not endeared himself to the colonial tories. Perhaps his most prominent attack on the colonial status quo came from the British Parliament's Canada Committee of 1828. The committee was primarily concerned with Lower Canadian affairs, and of the nineteen witnesses who testified only William Hamilton Merritt and Egerton Ryerson were familiar with Upper Canada. The committee's finding that it was the local administration and not the constitution of the colonies which was the root cause of disaffection applied to Upper Canada as well as to Lower Canada. The committee recommended that judges be excluded from the councils, that customs revenues be put at the disposal of the assembly, and that the Anglican Church lose its exclusive claims. This report reached Upper Canada in late 1828, and its contents shocked Robinson. Had the British government disowned the principles upon which the Empire had been founded? Robinson composed a lengthy critique of the Canada Committee's report and sent it to Wilmot Horton as one loyalist's response to the liberal winds of change.[28]

Robinson heatedly denied that there was anything approaching 'agitation' plaguing Upper Canada. The real cause of unrest in Lower Canada was the fact that too much had been conceded to the French Canadians after the Conquest. English law, which was 'incomparably more certain' than the French code civil, should be used as a stepping-stone to the eventual anglicization of the French Canadians.

Addressing himself to Upper Canada, Robinson condemned the various reforms suggested by the committee. The committee's finding that the legislative council obstructed popular legislation was entirely false. Rather, that body filtered out many of the frivolous and unconstitutional bills passed by the assembly. The committee's recommendation that the local Parliament be given control of the civil list was especially repugnant to the attorney-general, since elected representatives were 'not fit to be trusted with the annual appointments.' Upper Canada was not a democracy, and Robinson wanted to preserve the independence of the government from corrupting popular influences: 'the position and character of the local Government will equally suffer from such an abandonment of it to the intrigues of a fluctuating popular assembly.' The 'bablers and brawlers' could have their assembly, but they had no right to conduct public affairs; that privilege was reserved for those select gentlemen who truly served the Crown. The danger to the system lay in a weak and liberal British government betraying its loyal sons. Perhaps Robinson was recalling the shame of the alien debate when he wrote, 'It was not firmness, it was folly that brought on the American Rebellion.'

Behind Robinson's criticisms was the knowledge that the reformers eventually intended to end the colonial system by making the provincial government responsible to the assembly rather than to the lieutenant-governor. The reformers would not be satisfied until 'the Executive Government is placed on a right footing, till the Governor is elected.' Robinson was reaching the 'painful conviction that the policy recently pursued in England is unwisely and unnecessarily accelerating the separation of the Colonies from Great Britain.' He articulated the fears of many British Americans that England was about to abandon the colonies to sectarianism, democracy, and the American republic:

The interests at stake are not secondary to us: They involve everything in this world ... I assure you that recent occurrences are going far, and have gone far to extinguish that love of Country which are delights to cherish.

To men like Robinson, the necessity of preserving the British connection was of the utmost importance: 'We have had a war here; we know in what patriotism consists.'

The report of the Canada Committee was never debated in Westminster and was not even considered for legislation. The slow pace of events at the Colonial Office helped to allay Robinson's fears. The gradual loosening of imperial control would coincide with the growing attachment of Upper Canadians to British institutions. Robinson was also reassured by the appointment of the Duke of Wellington as prime minister and Sir George Murray as colonial secretary. Murray did not exhibit any particular aptitude for or interest in colonial administration. In contrast to Huskisson's reforming zeal, Murray's neglect was a welcome relief to the tories.

When the Tenth Parliament convened in January 1829, the reformers gloried in their majority, and the reply to the lieutenant-governor's speech was a long and bitter condemnation of Sir Peregrine Maitland's administration. The assembly also expressed its desire for the lieutenant-governor to 'recognize us as Constitutional Advisers of the Crown.' Robinson was so appalled by these democratic sentiments that he and his tory associate, Bethune, absented themselves from the vote. The reply was approved thirty-seven to one.[29]

Now that Robinson was freed from the entanglements of the alien and clergy reserves questions, he was able to appeal to the province with his own astute legislative proposals. He presented a bill to remove legal disabilities from Quakers which, with some amendments, was enthusiastically endorsed.[30] The attorney-general even put himself forward as the champion of provincial rights when he advocated demanding payment from Britain for war-losses claims.[31]

The farmers of the Niagara peninsula had never been adequately recompensed for the damages resulting from the war of 1812; because the war had been waged in imperial interests, 'the empire ought to pay the losses sustained in the preserving of its unity by the people of this frontier province.' Robinson proposed that Upper Canada borrow funds, have those funds matched by a British donation, and apply the total sum to satisfy war-losses claims. The reform press pointed out the obvious flaws in the plan: the province was already heavily in debt, and there was no likelihood of Britain sending additional financial aid.

The reformers suggested that the attorney-general's War Losses Bill was a ploy to distract the members from the upcoming trial of the York election. Dr Morrison, it seems, had proved an ungracious loser. He claimed that Sheriff Jarvis had arbitrarily and illegally closed the polls before the doctor's electors had had a chance to vote, and that he had accepted improper votes for the attorney-general. The assembly debated the merits of the York election through February and, to the dismay of the radical reformers, decided that Morrison's claims were frivolous. The York tories gave further encouragement to their member by sending him a petition of thanks. Oddly, the petition was signed by more persons than had actually voted for him.[32] The attorney-general's political durability probably explained his growing popularity.

Not satisfied with their victory in the Naturalization Bill, the reformers passed another act to permit foreigners of 'good moral character' to own land. Although Robinson was unable to halt the passage of this bill,[33] as attorney-general he had the authority to comment on the implications of the legislation before it received royal assent. Robinson, using his considerable legal skills, pointed out the numerous errors and contradictions that pervaded the bill. How was the 'good moral character' of the alien to be determined? How could the bill possibly be reconciled with prevailing imperial law? In the attorney-general's opinion, 'the object of the present bill appears to be to encourage foreigners to speculate in our lands by allowing them, as no other nation does by any such general laws, to hold and transfer real estate ...'[34] Robinson effectively halted the bill, but was powerless to stop the assembly from following its anti-government course.

In 1828 one assembly committee had examined Archdeacon Strachan's university charter and his ecclesiastical chart (a document forwarded to the Colonial Office in 1827, in which Strachan implied that the Anglicans were the predominant faith in Upper Canada).[35] With few exceptions, the committee's witnesses contradicted Strachan's claims to an established Church. The dissenters were the largest religious body in Upper Canada, and they were as loyal as any other denomination. Only Robinson went before the committee to defend Strachan's chart and university charter. According to Robinson, the 'inevitable effect' of the established Church would be to 'produce attachment to the constitution, and obedience to civil authority.'[36] The struggle for the established Church seemed so fundamentally right to John Robinson that he ignored political reality and fought in defence of positions that were no longer tenable. During the session, fifty-three of the assembly's bills were defeated in the legislative council. Since the attorney-general was no longer an effective force in Parliament, only the legislative council could restrain the reformers. Writing from the tranquillity of Nova Scotia (which was firmly in the hands of an established oligarchy), Sir Peregrine Maitland observed that, 'the proceedings of your political agitators are spoken of here in terms of horror by the most liberal of our politicians.'[37]

In the early days of his political career, John Robinson had cherished his leadership of the House and his role in drafting key legislation. His brilliant success as a diplomat and his contacts in London made him the unchallenged leader of Upper Canada's administration. He used this authority to channel the government's energies into canal and emigration projects. His authority to implement his vision was not based on popular support, but flowed from the prerogatives of the imperial system. Moreover, his views were in marked contrast to the realities of Upper Canada. The province had no tradition of aristocracy, and the settlers clearly expressed a preference for self-made populists like Mackenzie instead of imperial appointees like Robinson.

Even without popular support, John Robinson's political career need not have faltered so long as he held the confidence of the imperial authorities. Against the determined assaults of the reformers, Robinson had implemented a reasonable solution to the alien question. This remarkable triumph which, given the obstacles in its way, was even more impressive than the resolution of the trade dispute, was all undone by a clumsy Colonial Office reversal of the policies of the previous administration. Robinson's political career failed not in Upper Canada but in Britain, where the authorities were no longer prepared to provide consistent support to their servants. Because he no longer held the confidence of the imperial government and the lieutenant-governor, Robinson could not presume to force his views on the province. John Macaulay would look back wistfully on these years and lament the 'decay of old fashioned loyalty.' In Macaulay's opinion, Upper Canada's early government was ideal, because 'whatever were the failings of the so-called "family compact" we had a Government of Gentlemen.'[38] The days of government by oligarchy had passed and Robinson's role in the assembly was now that of a mere critic of reform agitation. He wrote to Macaulay:

Alas these exertions seem thrown away on a population such as ours ... there are many things which though I think I could do, I cannot cause to be done. Meantime do not take quite so gloomy a view of our present state as some others – the *view* indeed, I think is rather picturesque.[39]

During the session just passed, Robinson was powerless to halt the bills to remove disabilities from religious dissenters and abolish debtor's prison and the right of primogeniture. In what must have been a time of frustration and disappointment, a new avenue of public life opened to him. Chief Justice Campbell had at last retired, and Robinson was nominated to succeed him. He hesitated to accept; he was making a substantial income from his law practice and he had every expectation that his income would grow. On the other hand, the chief justiceship was the pinnacle of a Canadian legal career, and had long been his goal. The assembly's petition foreshadowed a possible change in colonial policy whereby an English barrister could be named to the bench ahead of a worthy native son. Robinson was 'apprehensive that, by the appointment of some person from England not older than myself, I might be shut out from the judicial office when circumstances might lead me to desire it.'[40]

And desire it he did. With little fanfare, the announcement was made in York on 13 July 1829 that John Beverley Robinson had been sworn in as the seventh chief justice of Upper Canada. Robinson was the first chief justice to have been born in the Canadas, and at thirty-eight the youngest in Upper Canada's history.

Robinson's elevation may have been viewed by the reformers as something of a blessing, for it removed an able tory from political affairs. Or did it? There was no precedent that stated that the chief justice could not also sit in the assembly. This potential difficulty was resolved when Robinson accepted the post of registrar of the county of Kent and was thereby required to resign from the House. As was traditionally due his office, Robinson was appointed speaker of the legislative council and, shortly thereafter, became president of the executive council. Henceforth during the speech from the throne Chief Justice Robinson would sit at the right hand of the lieutenant-governor. Much to the displeasure of the reformers, their old tory nemesis now exercised power at all three levels of government – judicial, legislative, and executive. Robinson would be able to use his new offices to exercise considerable political authority. These circumstances and the reformers' strident demands that the judiciary become independent of the executive ensured that the chief justice's future activities would be both political and controversial.

11

A Love of Order

The chief justice of one of His Majesty's smallest but most dynamic colonies required a substantial dwelling; consequently, work was begun on a front porch, a balcony, and the impressive fanlight over the front door of Beverley House. The entire structure was elevated and a west wing attached to it. While the chief justice familiarized himself with his new duties, Emma Robinson redesigned the mansion and supervised the workmen. Despite this activity, she never forgot her duties as hostess. A visitor to Beverley House found the entire household undergoing renovation, Yet Emma herself 'received us in a little back room ... everything about it was in perfect order and she herself more than commonly ladylike.'[1] The expansion served a practical purpose; the Robinson family had now grown to include four boys and four girls. As the youngest chief justice in the British Empire, Robinson found himself in an enviable financial and social position. He took pride in the fact that he had risen from poverty to attain one of the most respected and highly rewarded offices in Upper Canada. Almost as desirable, his reputation would no longer be exposed to the attacks of the radical press.

The new chief justice would be among the first jurists to use the Law Society's own building, Osgoode Hall. Work had begun on the building during Robinson's last term as treasurer in 1829. In 1827, it was Robinson who moved to reject a proposed grant of land from the executive council on the ground that 'between fifteen and twenty acres would be more suitable to the purposes contemplated.'[2] Strange to relate, the following year the benchers voted to buy a mere six acres severed from Robinson's own park lot. The purchase price of £1,000 was about five times the value of similar properties in York.[3] No reformer chose to editorialize about this unusual transaction. W.W. Baldwin executed the necessary deeds, and John Rolph, sitting as a bencher, approved the purchase. Rolph had become a bencher in 1824 at the nomination of none other than John Robinson.[4] Politics, it seems, did not come between brother lawyers.

During his career in legal practice, Robinson had played a prominent role in the Law Society, serving three times as treasurer and remaining a bencher ex officio throughout his service as attorney-general. The construction of the Great Hall was the fulfilment of one of his ambitions; the legal community would remain English in its customs and procedures. Although Robinson fostered this adherence to the English way, he also wanted Upper Canada to develop its own traditions. At his urging, the new hall was named after Upper Canada's first chief justice, William Osgoode.

As chief justice, Robinson was called on to interpret and apply many of the provincial statutes that he had written. This familiarity probably gave him a greater understanding of the intent of the legislation than most of the advocates who appeared before him. The new chief justice also used his position to root out creeping Americanisms. The use of the American term 'Your Honor' ceased, and the traditional 'Your Lordship' was substituted. The years Robinson had spent at Lincoln's Inn were now reflected in his direction of King's Bench. The bullying and sarcasm that he found so distasteful in English courts were banished from the Canadian courtroom. Witnesses and counsel were permitted to give evidence and state their cases without interference from the bench. D.B. Read, who often appeared before Robinson, felt that as a former prosecutor the chief justice's sympathies usually lay with the Crown. However, Read added, 'I can bear testimony that while the Chief Justice was strict he was ever ready to hear what counsel had to say in defense of a prisoner, giving due weight to all counsel's arguments in his charge to the jury.'[5] Chief Justice Robinson was well respected by the provincial bar, even by those members who held opposing political sentiments. Read felt that Robinson's liberal interpretation of commercial matters was especially appreciated by the bar because it facilitated the growth of provincial business.

Robinson did not regard the chief justiceship as an authoritarian position; he hoped that the judgments of King's Bench would be collegial decisions. In one of his first reported decisions, he expressed his regret that the members of the bench were not unanimous in their interpretation of the law.[6] Robinson was not so awed by his appointment that he considered his own opinions infallible. On one occasion, he heard the appeal of a case in which he had acted as the trial judge. After reconsidering the law, he decided that he was wrong and ordered that a new trial be held.[7] His willingness to admit his own errors, his patience with counsel, and his extensive knowledge of the law gained the chief justice the respect of the provincial bar.

The Court of King's Bench was preoccupied not with deciding cases on their merits but with the application of rules of practice. Legal procedures were extremely complicated, and a claimant could easily make several errors in the course of a lawsuit that would destroy his case. For example, in one case a claim for a debt was ruled defective on the ground that the entirety of the claim had not been set out.[8] In another case the defendants to an action had a valid defence under a provincial statute; however, they failed to invoke the statute and were later barred from claiming its protection.[9] This slavish devotion to correct forms sometimes resulted in absurdities, as when an unsuccessful party objected after trial that the word 'attached' should have appeared in the other party's pleadings instead of the term 'summoned.' The chief justice thought that there might have been some merit to this objection, but because it was raised after trial he refused to recogize it.[10]

In order to understand the details of procedure, it was necessary to interpret English statutes as well as the hundreds of cases and learned commentaries that made up the English common law. In one case of a fraudulent or 'covinous' sale by a debtor, the entire question hinged on the interpretation of an Elizabethan statute.[11] In order to determine whether magistrates had the authority to build new jails, Robinson looked back to English laws from the days of Henry VIII.[12] The common law was more than a link between Upper Canada and its British origins; the great reservoir of English legal experience was at the disposal of Upper Canadians and provided an unsophisticated society with a mature body of laws.

Frontier conditions did place unanticipated strains on the common law, however. When the province's statute respecting debt imprisonment was put in issue, Robinson conceded that 'it is a question which must be decided without the aid of cases precisely in point, because in England the same circumstances cannot occur.'[13] When a land claimant based his case on a patent issued under the seal-at-arms of a governor, the chief justice rejected this approach as contrary to the 'laws of Canada.' Those laws clearly stipulated that land could only be conveyed by way of a Crown patent.[14] Even so English a judge as John Robinson realized that North American conditions required North American solutions.

The chief justice's legal work was not confined to the Court of King's Bench. In 1829, Robinson had become ex officio a commissioner of the Heir and Devisee Commission, which had originally been established to investigate the land certificates issued to the early settlers. The certificates were contingent on the pioneer having performed certain settlement duties, and the certificates themselves were bought and sold as if they were deeds. The commission reviewed all land claims based on the certificates; if the claim appeared valid, a deed was granted. Owing to the popularity and expediency of this system, a second Heir and Devisee Commission was established in 1805. The members of the commission were drawn almost exclusively from the province's oligarchy and included Robinson's brother, Peter, and his colleagues, D'Arcy Boulton and Archdeacon Strachan. Despite the commission's colouring and its wide discretion, it was remarkably objective in its administration. When Henry Boulton appeared before the commission in 1832, claiming that he was the devisee of a lot in York, his claim was turned down by the chief justice on the ground of insufficient evidence. When Boulton submitted further proof, his claim was eventually allowed. Even Peter Robinson's claim for patents to land he inherited from his father was rejected by the commission. Not until after his brother's death did the chief justice draw up a detailed memorandum of his father's land transactions and swear an oath before the other commissioners certifying the validity of the land transfer. Only then were the proper deeds issued. Although the commission met only once a year, it provided claimants with an inexpensive means of establishing title. Despite its control by the 'Compact,' the commission was a popular and impartial institution which escaped even Mackenzie's condemnations.[15]

Under Robinson's direction, King's Bench itself was no longer the cause of reformer petitions to the King decrying the inadequate state of justice in the province. While the reformers' investigations into the Forsyth and Willis episodes had led them to conclude that the judicial system was hopelessly partial, such charges could not be readily made in the era of Chief Justice Robinson. Robinson's personal record of the cases heard before him reveals a judge with a passionate sense of justice, a jurist who gave careful and unbiased consideration to each case brought before him.

He held the jury system in especially high regard, and in civil matters he usually was content to present the facts to the jurors and leave the ultimate decision to them. In a libel action, for example, he explained the law to the jury and left it to them to decide on the facts whether the newspaper in question had breached the law.[16] In contrast, on one occasion in which a debt was in question, the chief justice strongly advised the jury that there was no evidence of the debt and that judgment should be for the defendant.[17] There was no guarantee that the chief justice's opinion on the evidence would be accepted by the jury, however. In a case involving the seduction of a serving-girl, Robinson doubted whether there was sufficient evidence that the girl had conceived before she entered the defendant's service. He instructed the jury that if they wished to find a verdict of seduction, they must conclude as a fact that when the defendant hired the girl, 'he contemplated a seduction & took her with that view.' Though the chief justice saw no such evidence, the jury returned with a verdict of seduction against the defendant.[18]

In civil matters, success depended as much on the credulity of the jury as on the persuasive powers of an advocate. In criminal cases, it was the court's duty to direct the jury to acquit the prisoner if there was any doubt as to guilt. If the evidence against a prisoner was not persuasive, Robinson 'left all the evidence to the jury, telling them to acquit if they had any doubts.'[19] If the evidence against a prisoner was overwhelming, Robinson would not hesitate to direct the jury to find a guilty verdict. On occasion, he would also direct the jury to find the accused guilty of a lesser offence. During the Kingston assizes of 1831, on two separate occasions Robinson reduced the charges against a prisoner: a murder charge was reduced to manslaughter, and a charge of 'riot' against two tempestuous Irishmen was changed to common assault.[20] In 1837, Robinson sat in judgment over one Patrick Welsh who had killed a friend by pushing him down a flight of stairs. In his summation to the jury, Robinson told them, 'I think clearly not murder – but manslaughter unless the act was justifiable or from accident in which prisoner was not culpable.' The jury apparently felt that there was no culpability, and Welsh was acquitted.[21]

King's Bench as the guardian of the rule of law in Upper Canada never shirked its supervisory duty. When a traveller was accused of stealing a cow that had been left in his care, the chief justice carefully drew a distinction between breaching a trust and committing larceny. Even though the jury convicted the traveller of larceny, the chief justice held that, in law, he could not have committed larceny because the cow had been given to him. At Robinson's insistence the traveller was set free.[22]

King's Bench was certainly no bloodthirsty court, but one that calmly and deliberately reviewed the circumstances of each case and, as was appropriate in criminal cases, gave the benefit of the doubt to the prisoner.

Most of the cases brought before the assizes involved riot or larceny. The tiresome litany of minor offences was enlivened by the occasional murder trial. The mandatory punishment for murder was death by hanging, and Robinson had the formula for passing sentence of death printed on the front of his notebook so that it would be available when needed. When the awful occasion arose, he would only have to insert the name of the unfortunate and the date of his execution. Cattle theft and rape also mandated the death penalty, but in those circumstances the punishment was usually commuted to banishment. Larceny, by far the most common crime, incurred a penitentiary term of three months. During the Kingston assizes of 1831, seven of twelve convictions were for larceny; in the 1834 assizes, seventeen of eighteen convictions were for that offence. In many cases, fines were added to the short jail terms; the chief justice undoubtedly recognized that district jails were usually over-crowded and that the government was always in need of money.

When a prisoner was found guilty of an offence, it was the duty of the chief justice to impose an appropriate sentence. During the Johnstown assizes of 1831, Robinson presided over the trial of the two Carey brothers, who were charged with the forgery of a deed. He cautioned the jury that the evidence did not appear to support the charge; nevertheless, Peter Carey was convicted. Robinson remained unconvinced of his guilt and used his authority to respite his sentence.[23] The case of Michael Dickson illustrated both Robinson's desire to see the law impartially applied and his conviction that moral offences should receive stern punishment. Dickson was charged in Brockville with an indecent assault on a female child.[24] Although the assault on the child was easily proved, the chief justice paid special regard to the surgeon's report. The child had sustained bruises and lacerations, but no penetration had taken place. Robinson told the jury that on the evidence Dickson could only be convicted of an attempted assault. Even though he was found guilty of this lesser offence, Dickson still received a severe punishment – thirty-nine lashes, eight months' imprisonment, and exposure in the pillory.

The chief justice regularly advised the lieutenant-governor on clemency appeals. It was a sign of his residual influence that his recommendations were invariably accepted. When he was forced to pass a death sentence on an arsonist, Robinson told Colborne that the convict was a man of 'partially deranged intellect' and deserved commutation.[25] Robinson was therefore called upon to act in two capacities – as judge and as the dispenser of royal mercy. In one bizarre case, the chief justice was asked whether clemency could be granted to a convicted sorcerer. A family in Baldoon, Kent County, had been subjected to supernatural manifestations, and a certain Robert Barker of Michigan had offered to drive out the spirit. The self-styled 'Wizard of Baldoon' posted a sign on the farmstead invoking the Holy Trinity and demanding that the alien spirit depart. This had no effect on the apparition, which continued to animate various objects and otherwise terrorize the family. Despite the fact that these proceedings were a source of considerable amusement in the township, the sheriff charged Barker under an ancient statute (9 Geo. ii) with practising witchcraft. Barker was convicted and sentenced to be pilloried and imprisoned in Sandwich jail for a year. He appealed to the lieutenant-governor, who referred the case to the chief justice. Robinson suggested that 'a month's imprisonment would not be misplaced and if he can't get out of Gaol in that time, I should think it must very much destroy the confidence of the wise people of Baldoon in his act, since many persons who never pretended to be conjurers have broken out of the Gaol of Sandwich in half that time.'[26]

Even though Robinson insisted on seeing that all defences were available to an accused, there was one group of offences that never failed to arouse his feelings of abhorrence: crimes against the moral code, which threatened the good order of society and deserved the harshest penalties. One such crime, which was not uncommon in the rural, isolated society of Upper Canada, was bestiality.[27] A young man, Moses Winter, was convicted during the Home assizes of 1831 of having carnal knowledge of a sheep, and the chief justice pronounced the mandatory death sentence.[28] In this case, as in most cases of taking liberties with livestock, the death sentence was commuted.

Another activity which brought down the condemnation of an indigant Christian community was the maintenance of brothels. One Sarah Hutchinson, who ran a bawdy house, initiated her own downfall by advising her neighbours that 'they might go & pay nothing if they went in Monday.'[29] The local sheriff learned of this good-neighbourliness and caught Mrs Hutchinson and her girls in bed one day at noon. The mere fact of being in bed at midday (rather than, for example, working in the fields) sufficed as proof of her activities and a conviction was entered. Mrs Hutchinson was pilloried and sent to prison for five months. At the same assizes, a person convicted of manslaughter received only a six-month imprisonment.

The chief justice's sensibilities were especially upset by the case of David Ellsworth, who was convicted of committing an unnatural act with another man. The enormity of this crime was beyond Robinson's comprehension; even though the jury recommended mercy, the chief justice commented that 'considering the horrid nature of the crime I thought it proper to pass sentence of death.'[30] Homosexuality was an offence that received the full condemnation of the courts and society. The mere allegation of homosexuality against one of Robinson's colleagues, George Markland, was sufficient to force him to resign in disgrace from his government offices. So concerned with the moral state of society was the chief justice that he told Macaulay he would like to see adultery and incest made into penitentiary offences:

The two later offences have on all occasions excited my moral energies for I am aware that a reproach rests upon us as a Court from the abominable state of morals in these particulars – but I have never found encouragement to propose the inflation of temporal punishment of these offences.[31]

Robinson's eagerness to prosecute moral offences was a common attitude in the nineteenth century. Criminal law has always concerned itself with the prevailing morality. Studies in the United States have indicated that during the early nineteenth century, there was a shift away from the punishment of crime as sin to the punishment of crime as an offence against property.[32] Others consider this to be an oversimplification, and maintain that throughout the nineteenth century morality remained an important consideration of the criminal jurist. The only change was in the 'type of morality proscribed and prosecuted.' It has been suggested that there was a shift in American prosecutions away from 'indoor' sins such as adultery and bastardy to 'outdoor' offences such as drunkenness and prostitution.[33] If so, Canadian law did not reflect that shift. Although Chief Justice Robinson's court was concerned about crimes against the public order, such as the keeping of Mrs Hutchinson's bawdy house and indecent assaults against children, it also remained uneasy about purely private matters such as sodomy and bestiality. Robinson thought that the courts should play an even greater role in reforming public morals. The zealous prosecution of minor criminal offences was a clear indication that Upper Canada's courts would not only maintain public order, but would act as a tool to attempt the reformation of the prevailing 'abominable state of morals.'

The chief justice's decisions reflected a growing Upper Canadian concern with morals in the ante-Victorian era. By the 1830s there was a pervasive fear of disorder,[34] a fear that was partially the result of the influx of immigrants, particularly the unruly Irish. In commenting on an 1822 act to stop overcrowding in jails, Robinson stated that 'the Gaols in this Province are at present so indifferent that a humane provision of this kind is the moe necessary.'[35] The district jails were not capable of handling the large number of prisoners or of providing any system of rehabilitation. A parliamentary committee visited modern institutions in the United States where rehabilitation was achieved by solitary confinement and hard labour. A penitentiary based on those principles opened in Kingston in 1835. A year later, a prison reformer, Dr Charles Duncombe, urged the prison to use a 'tranquillizing chair,' a medieval machine in which a prisoner sat restrained as his head was forcibly submerged in water, 'thereby [suspending] animation as long as may seem necessary to subdue his passions, and on allowing him to breathe he has invariably become a reformed man.'[36] Despite its harsh regimen, the penitentiary at Kingston was a utilitarian attempt to provide rehabilitation as well as punishment, and was a considerable improvement over the district jails.

The purpose of the criminal justice system was not only to safeguard life and property, but to enforce and uphold Christian morality. As chief justice, John Robinson had an ideal platform from which to propagate his views on the role of the law in society.

At every assize, before the presentation of criminal charges, the chief justice would deliver an address to the grand jury. The grand jury would then hear the evidence against the accused and decide whether to uphold or dismiss the charge. In the rural communities of Upper Canada the grand jury was an important institution; an erroneous decision could send an innocent man to trial and disgrace him forever. In one of his first sittings before a grand jury, Robinson felt compelled to caution the jurors that they should balance the protection of society against the injustice of defaming an innocent man.[37] Robinson used his addresses to the grand jury to expand on his view of the rights and duties of British subjects. The sittings were one of the few sources of public entertainment, and the chief justice was assured a large and usually receptive audience.

In one address he examined the basis of the judicial system. Rejecting out of hand the American emphasis on 'inalienable' individual rights, he argued instead that the order of society was a direct result of the duty owed by the subject to the sovereign:

But where a contemptible mankind in their social relations are readily deceived ... good civil institutions are required ... those we possess in concurrence with all subjects of the British Crown – To give stability to those institutions to prevent freedom of action from sinking into licentiousness and to preserve and improve that moral condition which is necessary to public and individual happiness, it is the duty of all to inculcate obedience to the laws – Reverence for them must be produced by the persistence of all good men & where that will not suffice, the restraints which the laws themselves impose must be Temperately but firmly enforced.

The chief justice reflected on the values that had made Upper Canada a prosperous, civilized community:

Order lies at the foundation of good government in the social state ... by all who are concerned in making or administering the laws for this rapidly increasing country, it should be felt that we, in this generation, are laying the foundations of a social system which is to extend its advantages or entail the consequences of its imperfections upon millions who will soon succeed.[38]

The chief justices' remarks were prophetic. He foresaw the establishment of a social order which already had firm roots in the Canadian frontier. More than Lower Canada or the neighbouring American states, Upper Canada welcomed British institutions and accepted the English rule of law as the basis for its freedom. Without this public order, temperately but firmly enforced, liberty and justice were impossible.

To men like John Beverley Robinson, civilized society consisted of a delicate balance of classes, a balance preserved by the application of the British constitution and adherence to the Church of England. It was the primary duty of the courts to preserve this balance rather than to preoccupy themselves with protecting individual liberties and freedoms. Robinson told a grand jury in the Western District that 'a love of Order is not only essential to the tranquillity but to the very being of any State – It becomes the foundation of mutual faith confidence and security.' This is not to say that men such as Robinson were unconcerned with personal liberties. As a lawyer and as attorney-general Robinson had fought to ensure that rules of law were respected by the government as well as by individuals. Before a Toronto grand jury, Robinson conceded that while 'popular institutions occasionally engender tumults ...' those institutions would be 'ill exchanged for the sickness of despotism.'[39] Yet it was through a 'love of order' that the individual would be free to exercise his rights. With a nod toward the Gourlays and Collinses of the province, Robinson speculated on the consequences of a breakdown in order:

When we behold an indifference to the observance of the Laws and a restless diligence to evade them – a want of reverence to Magistrates & Superiors a disrespect to stations, offices, ranks, and orders of persons ... we may consider these as symptoms fatal to the true liberty of that country – In such cases every little disappointment – every imaginary grievance – every wanton desire of change produces a ferment & threatens the public peace – Everyone carves out his own method of redress, and prosecutes his designs by the dictates of his own corrupt will – To prevent these evils a love of Order becomes necessary by which we are induced to conform to the laws and to promote the welfare of the community.[40]

Through his addresses to the grand juries, Robinson propagated his sense of Upper Canada as a society in which obedience was precious not because it led to servility but because it resulted in order, which in turn freed the individual to express his opinions, practise his religion, and expand his commerce. With the influx of British immigrants that began in the early 1830s, a greater percentage of the population was receptive to Robinson's appeal to order. The American infatuation with inalienable rights was foreign to them, and they agreed with Robinson's perception of order as the source of good government.

Chief Justice Robinson's court disproved the reformers' charges that justice in Upper Canada was partial or despotic. While no cases as infamous as the Forsyth or Willis affairs disrupted his court, it was clear from the decisions rendered by King's Bench that the courts would protect individual rights and that the meanest individual would have a fair hearing under the law. Throughout Upper Canada, surveyors were laying out new roads, and occasionally an incompetent surveyor would establish a road through private lands or fail to define the width of a road. When a farmer claimed that a new road infringed on and deprived him of some of his lands, the chief justice had to balance public against private rights:

It is true, on the one side, that the public convenience is involved in the question; from whence it may be argued, that the statute and everything done under it should receive a liberal interpretation. But, on the other hand, it trenches upon private rights of property, and the interference should go no further, nor be exercised in any other manner, than the legislature has expressly permitted. Statutes for all public works and objects of this kind, when they authorize depriving individuals of their property, are to be construed upon the principle last mentioned.[41]

While the public convenience could not justify depriving individuals of property, neither could public officials abuse their office by trampling on private rights. A settler built a cabin on land that had been expropriated for the Rideau Canal. Agents of the canal advised him not to build and later tore down his cabin. The chief justice began his inquiry into the question of liability by noting that the Rideau Canal was 'a public work of great importance' and that 'of necessity, private interests and convenience must, for the sake of such objects, be made to yield to the public welfare.' But the public welfare did not justify the agents' failure to inform the settler that they were acting under the authority of the Rideau Canal Act. By neglecting to invoke their authority, the agents had acted without any authority at all and therefore were liable for damages.[42] The powers of public officers were granted to them by Parliament, and acts in excess of those powers were quickly suppressed by King's Bench. In a case where a lock-keeper on the Rideau Canal had taken timber that was blocking one of the locks, the chief justice reminded him that he only had a statutory right to clear the timber, not to seize it.[43]

The test of the chief justice's impartiality was his conduct when political issues were presented to his court. When Sir John Colborne refused to pardon Francis Collins in 1829, a Hamilton mob burnt the lieutenant-governor in effigy. The assembly, suspecting that the tories had instigated the burning in order to discredit the reform movement, conducted an investigation. Allan MacNab, one of the rising stars of the tory faction, was called to the bar of the assembly to answer certain questions about the outrage. When he refused to co-operate, MacNab was cited for contempt and confined to the York jail for a few days. A martyr to the tory cause, MacNab kept the issue alive by maintaining that the assembly had exceeded its authority. He sued the Speaker, M.S. Bidwell, and Dr Baldwin for trespass and false imprisonment.[44] Since his case would be heard before the former tory leader, John Robinson, MacNab might have suspected that the reformers would be humiliated in court. However, the strict legal question before King's Bench was whether the assembly had the same authority as the British Parliament to cite for contempt. Even though the colonial legislature did not have the same powers as the imperial Parliament, Robinson held that if the assembly had the power to hold committees and call witnesses, that it must have the power to cite for contempt. To MacNab's chagrin, the tory court affirmed the validity of his imprisonment by the reform assembly.

MacNab's case gave the chief justice an opportunity to elaborate on his views of Upper Canada's government. There was no question that 'the legislature of this colony is subordinate to the imperial parliament.'[45] Although Upper Canada's government was, in Simcoe's words, 'the very image and transcript' of the British government, the assembly was not a 'body perfectly similar' to the House of Commons. Rather, in deference to the imperial system, colonial bodies were subservient to the British Crown. The assembly did not derive its authority from the people; legislative power flowed from the Crown to the colonial legislatures. Upper Canada's constitutional foundations were therefore very much in contrast with the notion of popular authority embedded in the American constitution.

American and Canadian jurisprudence also differed over the proper role of the courts. Ever since the United States Supreme Court declared an act of congress to be void in *Marbury* v *Madison* (1803), American courts had the potential not only to interpret the laws, but to add new dimensions to the constitution. In the United States, the written constitution, not the sovereign, was owed the superior obligation; any acts contrary to the constitution were illegal. Inevitably, with this immense power, 'the Supreme Court was thrust into the political arena and because of this fact was subjected to political influences and controls.'[46] This judicial activism was foreign to British courts, which were independent of politics and regarded themselves as mere interpreters of legislation; authority descended from the Crown and Parliament, and the courts had no business obstructing legislation. According to British tradition, legislative power resided in Parliament alone. Robinson consistently made it clear that he recognized the supremacy of Parliament:

The business of this Court is to administer justice, and we cannot too closely confine ourselves to it. His Majesty's subjects should all feel that they stand here upon an equal footing. We have to do with rights in this place, and with opinions only so far as they bear on these rights. To deviate to the debatable ground of politics would be departing from our proper sphere.[47]

The Court of King's Bench applied English legal procedures and the common law, and, under Robinson's direction, it fostered a respect for order in society as the basis for liberty and maintained the sovereignty of the British Crown as the source of that order.

12

Chief Justice, Speaker,
and Confidant

During the 1830s Upper Canada experienced significant demographic changes, changes that eventually altered the province's political complexion. Between 1830 and 1836 destitute British immigrants poured into the province. Lieutenant-Governor Colborne made every effort to encourage this influx and to steer the newcomers to counties settled by Americans so that republican sentiment could be diluted. The newcomers were awed by Upper Canada's vast spaces and puzzled by the egalitarian society of the frontier. One recent arrival, James Coleman, wrote to his sister in England: 'We are a strange mixture of nations here, English, Welsh, Scotch, Highland Scotch, Irish, Germans and Indians, free Negroes and Americans and a mixed progeny of the whole of them ...' and in this strange land 'every man is a gentleman if he neighter [sic] have shoe nor stocking to his feet.'[1]

The immigrants brought with them more than high hopes and a willingness to work. In 1832, cholera was introduced into the province by the new settlers. The towns were dirty and the sewage poorly drained, and the province was ill-prepared for any epidemic. When the disease appeared in June, healthy men and women found themselves attacked by an illness which within a few hours produced cramps, dehydration, and death. The disease was especially virulent in the towns, and in York the cholera car rushed the corpses away for mass burial.[2] Most people who had the means fled York for the relative security of the countryside. The chief justice was fortunate enough to be on circuit during the height of the outbreak. He instructed Emma to take the children to the Niagara peninsula until the cholera had passed. With paternal anxiety he ordered her to make sure the children drank only boiled water.[3] These precautions may have had some beneficial effects, for the Robinson family was spared the ravages of the disease.

The cholera outbreaks had a terrifying effect on Upper Canadian society, but they did not slow the rapid growth of population. Upper Canada was gaining in sophistication and prosperity, and those gains were to a large extent the result of improvements in the transportation system. The Welland Canal was finally ready for traffic in 1829. Robinson took part in the opening ceremonies, and in his congratulations to William Hamilton Merritt, he cited the canal as 'a proof against those who have maintained the opinion that the Welland Canal would never succeed'.[4] Even in the field of engineering, John Robinson saw the government's success as a vindication of its economic policies. As a tribute to the chief justice, the southern terminus of the first canal was named Port Robinson. Robinson's 'anticipating spirit' of the 1820s encouraged investment in Upper Canada's future, but it also left the province with an enormous debt. By 1837, public works had all but bankrupted the province. Despite its auspicious beginnings, the Welland Canal required constant repair and improvement and its debt eventually became so great that the government was forced to absorb the company. John Robinson, the visionary, correctly foresaw that the canal project would further the development of the interior. However, visionaries are not businessmen, and Robinson was unable to synchronize his vision of the province's future with the reality of its limited capabilities.

Upper Canada's political scene also was undergoing seasonal changes. In the election of 1830, the tories surprised the reformers and won a majority of seats in the assembly. This turn of events might have been explained by the public's goodwill toward the new lieutenant-governor or by the unpredictable personality contests and local rivalries that still decided most constituencies. Ironically, the tories failed to profit from their majority, for their leadership in the House had devolved upon two antagonistic men, Henry John Boulton and Christopher Hagerman. The government side floundered as the two openly disagreed with each other on the floor of the assembly. Even Francis Collins observed that Boulton and Hagerman 'cut a sorry figure in the shoes of John B. Robinson, who certainly was a man of singular cleverness in debate.'[5]

The tories also suffered from the existence of a whig government in England. Conciliation and appeasement were the prime policies of the new colonial secretary, Lord Goderich. He was disturbed when the tories used their majority to expel Mackenzie from the assembly. In his eagerness to accommodate the reformers, Goderich ordered that Mackenzie's prosecutors, Boulton and Hagerman, be dismissed from public office. This stance outraged Upper Canadian tories and demonstrated their lack of influence in London.

Even though the conservative faction had a solid grip on the legislature, the tories keenly felt their impotence in government. Most longed for the days of Sir Peregrine Maitland and lamented that Colborne was ineffectual and a reform sympathizer. Hagerman confronted the lieutenant-governor and bluntly told him that if he did not side with the 'friends of the government' he would 'soon leave the government without any friends and entirely destroy his own influence.'[6] Strachan was even more bitter. He was aware that Colborne had contemptuously referred to his favourite pupil as 'Jack Robinson' and that there was a movement afoot to dismiss the chief justice from his post as president of the executive council. According to Strachan, Colborne's 'plots & intrigues' had 'contributed to drive the Chief Justice out of the Executive Council.' Protest would have no effect, for 'popularity is [Colborne's] Idol & nothing else has influence.'[7]

While most tories felt disdain for the lieutenant-governor, Robinson's relations with Colborne were steadily improving. Colborne had no doubt formed his first impressions of Robinson from hearing tales of the dread 'Compact.' However, in a short time the lieutenant-governor was relying on and eventually seeking advice from the chief justice.[8]

Colborne referred more than routine legal matters to the chief justice for his consideration. While Robinson was himself ready to assist the lieutenant-governor with constitutional affairs, he was somewhat embarrassed by Colborne's tendency to refer administrative details to him for his opinion. As Robinson later explained,

Sir John Colborne did not always seem to bear in mind the distinction [between constitutional and civil matters]; and I was not surprised that he did not; for my long acquaintance with public business gave me of course a good deal of traditionary knowledge, which it was desirable the Government should have the advantage of.[9]

Robinson himself occasionally blurred the distinctions between legal advice and policy advice. When Colborne asked the chief justice whether it would be proper to remit the sentences of the Brockville rioters,

Robinson advised against doing so. In the first place, Robinson would not interfere with a sentence rendered by his brother judge. Second, it might be wise to let the punishment stand, for 'if before these months are over similar bodies of people at public meetings should exhibit the same violent conduct, it might convince the Government that it was not safe or proper to show mercy.'[10] The lieutenant-governor accepted this 'traditionary knowledge.' Sir John Colborne was a devout conservative, as were most general officers of his day, and he recognized in John Robinson a gentleman who shared his views and opinions. For the remainder of his term in office, and indeed long after that, Colborne sought John Robinson's counsel.

Even before the dismissal of John Walpole Willis, the reformers had begun to agitate for judicial reform. If the government was to be responsible to elected representatives, the first step was to remove appointed officials (such as judges) from government. The second demand, a consequence of the Willis incident, was that the judges be rendered 'independent of the Crown and people'; that is, that they serve on good behaviour, not at the Crown's pleasure. The Colonial Office was aware of these demands, yet when Colborne assumed office in 1828, the colonial secretary advised him that there was to be no change in policy. It was feared that the people of Upper Canada were so inclined to factionalism that a judge serving at the pleasure of the legislature would inevitably become a tool of that legislature.[11] After only a few months in the province, Colborne came to the conclusion that the chief justice was one of the few persons qualified to preside over the executive council. Yet even Colborne was willing to admit that 'occasionally [the Chief Justice] must, as a judge, be led too deeply into the political affairs of the colony.'[12]

When John Beverley Robinson became the chief justice presiding over the executive council, the reformers redoubled their efforts to have him removed from office. These intrigues were of little concern to Robinson, and his personal correspondence after 1830 shows few references to public affairs. By virtue of his offices, however, he was bound to play a role in political events. As president of the executive council, Robinson submitted the opinions of the lieutenant-governor's councillors to him. As Speaker of the legislative council, Robinson played an active part in formulating legislation. In 1830, rumours began to circulate in York that the chief justice was about to be removed from the executive council. Colborne, aroused by the rumours, wrote to the colonial secretary asking him to keep Robinson at his post. In Colborne's opinion, Robinson had performed creditably and 'the public will suffer considerably should the change take place.'[13] Nevertheless, the assembly's petitions had made an impression on Lord Goderich. In February 1831 he ordered that in the future no judge should be appointed to either the executive or the legislative council. Robinson was told to remain in the legislative council, but the dispatch also advised him to exhibit 'a cautious abstinence from all proceedings by which he might be involved in any political contention of a party nature.'[14] Robinson needed no further prompting, and shortly thereafter he resigned from the executive council. However, no whig administration could force Sir John Colborne to select his personal advisers. Robinson remained in fact, if not in law, the confidant of the lieutenant-governor. The chief justice understood the imperial system and bowed to the dictates of the Colonial Office. Goderich's instruction to the chief justice to abstain from 'political contention' was seen as an unwarranted accusation of partiality. The legislative council responded by sending an address to London reaffirming their confidence in the Speaker, and Robinson himself stated that he would be guided by 'my own judgment and discretion.'[15]

The proceedings of the legislative council are not extensively documented, but it appears that the Speaker took an active role in examining and in drafting the statutes presented to the council. This is not surprising given that, after more than a decade in public life, Robinson could not suddenly refuse to take sides in controversies. Speaker Robinson's intimacy with past disputes gave him a personal perspective on the questions before Parliament. In one instance, Attorney-General Boulton questioned the propriety of a bill passed by the legislative council to compensate a Mr Weekes. In Boulton's opinion it was improper for the legislature to offer redress, even though Weekes had lost all his land through a surveyor's error. Robinson admitted that private relief bills should be used sparingly. However, he drily reminded the lieutenant-governor that he had personally approved the measure and that Boulton failed to comprehend either the facts or the law relevant to the case.[16]

Weekes's case was but one example of the occasional leading role Robinson still assumed in government. Although the legislative council has never attracted much attention from scholars, it was a vital part of the Upper Canadian legislature. There was no question that the assembly had a more flamboyant membership, but the council equalled and occasionally surpassed the assembly in the production of legislation. In the session of 1831–2, the council enacted several reforms. Speaker Robinson introduced ten separate pieces of legislation. One of these was a reform bill directly related to the conviction and near-hanging of Mary Thompson in 1823. This incident had continued to haunt the chief justice, for in the first session of the Eleventh Parliament he presented a bill to remove the mandatory death penalty for the concealment of the death of bastard children. The bill was passed by the council, but the assembly showed no interest and it died on the order paper. In the second session, Robinson finally succeeded in having both houses abolish the harsh penalty.[17] Later he was to cite the assembly's indifference to this reform as a rebuttal of Mackenzie's charges that the assembly was the only body that had the good of the people at heart.

Two of the most important law reforms passed in Upper Canada, the Real Property Act of 1834 and the Capital Punishment Act of 1833,[18] were introduced into the legislature by the chief justice. The Real Property Act preserved the dower rights of widows and clarified the laws of conveyance and inheritance. Although it was based on an English reform bill, the Real Property Act was 'in several particulars carefully adopted to the circumstances of the province by the present Chief Justice.[19] Robinson was so closely connected with this reform that twenty years later the Real Property Act was still referred to as the 'Chief Justice's Act.'[20] Prior to 1833 it was difficult to define the terms of Upper Canada's criminal law. The Capital Punishment Act, introduced by Robinson into the legislative council and passed by the assembly with amendments, defined the penal laws and mitigated their severity.[21] The record of the legislative council stands as a refutation of reformer charges that it was a mere repository of tory relics and a hindrance to reform.

Although it was an active body, the council did not sympathize with reform aspirations and in 1831 rejected out of hand assembly bills to remove the chaplain's salary and abolish the right of primogeniture.[22] This rejection triggered an angry blast from the Colonial Advocate: 'From its very nature and composition [the legislative council] has scarce one feeling or sentiment in common with the country, being the mere breath of the executive.'[23] This criticism was not entirely unfounded, for most members had strong ties with the government. The council saw itself as the last bulwark against radical legislation. In the spring session of 1835, the legislative council considered eighty-three bills sent from the assembly and passed only twenty-three. Specifically rejected were assembly proposals to reform primogeniture and the clergy reserves. This intransigence worked both ways, however; in the same session, of eleven bills prepared by the council, only one received the assembly's approval.[24]

The council could also be a moribund body deserving of criticism. On occasion Robinson was hard-pressed to get a quorum to consider legislation. Incidents such as these lent some credence to Mackenzie's observation that the council was '7 or 8 men and sometimes not so many' whose only purpose was to 'reject the measures of the country almost as fast as they are sent to them.'[25] Still, the council was a useful addition to the legislative process. With the appointment of more moderate members, the council lost some of its intransigence. Sir John Colborne had ordered that the council's membership not be restricted to arch-tories, and several moderates, including Augustus Baldwin, the brother of Dr W.W. Baldwin, were elevated to the council. These new members undoubtedly had a tempering effect. In 1831, when the Colonial Office advised the council that the tenure of the judges was now going to depend on the judges' behaviour and not on the Crown's pleasure, the council acquiesced. When the assembly proposed a similar bill in 1834, the council advanced several amendments to permit the removal of a judge by the lieutenant-governor upon the address of Parliament and to permit an aggrieved judge to appeal to the privy council. By these directives, Goderich's administration was laying the groundwork for an independent colonial judiciary. The legislative council not only accepted these reforms but suggested amendments to facilitate their implementation.[26]

Although the council recognized the judges' independence from the political process, this did not stop the chief justice from exercising his prerogatives as Speaker. He introduced significant legislation and added his personal dissents to some of the bills passed by both houses. Ironically, during the 1830s Robinson's voice was raised against further borrowing for public works. In protesting a grant to improve navigation on the Trent River, Robinson cautioned the council to 'observe moderation' to avoid financial embarrassment.[27] The anticipating spirit had apparently given way to some measure of prudence.

Robinson proposed much of the legislation considered by the council, and was the only member in regular attendance. The council members acknowledged him as their leader and deplored the fact that because he was not on the permanent civil list the assembly could refuse to vote his Speaker's salary. In 1834, the council angrily noted that for the past three years Chief Justice Robinson had received no payment for performing his duties as Speaker. With understandable annoyance, Robinson wrote to Colborne that it was the assembly's policy toward 'the ordinary, indispensable public servants, however humble, [that] you shall not have the wages you have earned.'[28]

The *Colonial Advocate*, singularly lacking in sympathy, blasted the legislative council as being 'chiefly composed of persons dependent on the executive government for their salaries, pensions and fees of office, or who have been selected by that government, upon the principle on which the English tories have selected peers and bishops for the last forty years, absolute and unlimited servility.'[29] The government press responded that the council and especially its Speaker were the Crown's salvation in Upper Canada. Thomas Dalton's *Patriot* asked its readers to consider 'how regulated and temperate are the discussions of [the Legislative Council] as compared with those of the obstreperous Reformers in the Assembly.'[30] According to a tory correspondent, Robinson, his features 'regular pleasing and pointed with intelligence,' presided over this loyal legislature, and it was his burdensome duty to deal with the assembly's statutes:

The Bills as may be imagined when sent up from the lower House, are thickly studded with blunders, contradictions, imperfections numberless: those the Chief Justice corrects, expunges, reconciles and amends. The clumsy abortions the *lusus legis* of such men as Peter Perry, and that Psychological monstrosity Jos. Wilson, are thus hacked into shape.[31]

After the elections of 1834, the legislative council, even more than previously, became the final resting place for radical bills. In that year the electoral pendulum again swung in favour of the reformers. It was an ominous sign that the more moderate reformers such as Baldwin and Rolph abandoned the field to the radicals. While the new assembly contented itself with passing resolutions critical of the imperial system, Mackenzie devoted himself to producing an inflammatory report on grievances. To no one's surprise, the report concluded that Upper Canada's government was rife with corruption and overburdened with useless office-holders. The report was so honeycombed with errors that it was dismissed even by many reformers; yet its virulence stung the colonial secretary into a sudden awareness of Upper Canada. The Colonial Office determined to replace Sir John Colborne and essay a new approach in the turbulent colony.

Mackenzie's *Seventh Report on Grievances* cited the legislative council as a reactionary body that was insensitive to the public will and only served to obstruct necessary legislation. The chief justice leaped to the defence of the council, insisting that, with few exceptions, the two houses had worked well together. In fact, Robinson argued, more bills of a public nature originated in the council than were passed by the assembly.[32]

While the council was of significant benefit to the legislative process, it was an exaggeration on Robinson's part to maintain that the assembly and council co-operated; in fact, they remained strongly opposed to each other on vital issues. During the alien debates, the houses had had to abandon negotiations; the gulf between them was too wide to be bridged. After 1831, the assembly began to use its control of contingency supplies to deny the government's budget requests. The council consistently opposed this tactic and voted to pay the government the entirety of its budget. The council stood exposed as a bastion of toryism and a target of reformer rhetoric.

It required one final incident to sour Mackenzie and his radical colleagues on the colonial system. Just before Sir John Colborne left Upper Canada in early 1836, he ordered that fifty-seven Anglican rectories receive land endowments from the clergy reserves. The reformers pointed to the last-minute rectory endowments as a furtive attempt at Church domination. The concerns of the reformers were of no moment to Colborne, and in a farewell letter to Robinson he warned the chief justice that owing to the influence of the English radicals, the colonial reformers were given far too much authority. With considerable foresight, he added, 'I do think you will be properly *scalded* above and below, before the end of 1837.'[33]

By 1836, Robinson was preoccupied with the administration of justice, and his only foray into politics was as Speaker of the legislative council. The assembly of 1834 was committed to the principle of rendering the executive government responsible to the elected legislature, and the chief justice was entirely helpless to stop this movement. In the light of London's determination to exclude the judiciary from government, it must have seemed unlikely that Robinson would ever again play a significant role in political life. The unexpected now put in an appearance with the arrival in 1836 of Colborne's successor, that erratic and flamboyant individual, Sir Francis Bond Head.

13

Rebellion and Reaction

'He is a strange person, restless and bent upon some object or other to such a degree that he cannot control himself.'[1] John Robinson's portrait of Sir Francis Bond Head leaves us a vivid sketch of the turbulent individual who presided over the most severe civil strife ever to beset Upper Canada. The new lieutenant-governor had had an undistinguished military career, and was so apolitical that, as he readily admitted, he had never voted in his life. His knighthood and his notoriety he owed to his dexterity with the lasso, which peculiar talent had caught the admiration of William IV. In 1834, Head had become an assistant poor-law commissioner and had written an essay on the administration of the poor laws. Lord Glenelg, the whig colonial secretary, had chosen Head to be lieutenant-governor because of his reputed reform tendencies. In fact, Head's writings revealed a committed conservative and a tory somewhat to the right of John Robinson. It was this man who was welcomed to Toronto (as York was now called) in January 1836 as a 'Tried Reformer.'

By the mid-1830s, Upper Canada was becoming a more cosmopolitan society. The chief justice and his family were now able to spend Sunday afternoons relaxing on the garrison grounds, watching the Toronto Cricket Club face all comers. The prosperity and population growth of the early 1830s had greatly assisted the mercantile class. In 1837, the Upper Canada Club was founded as a haven for the province's harried élite. John Robinson was one of the founding members of the club, which quickly became a 'cultural and social island in the Upper Canadian wilderness.[2] It was a sign of the changing tory guard that many of the members, and indeed the club's founder, James Newbigging, were businessmen. This fraternal organization of the older gentry and the merchant class was an indication that the gentlemen had abandoned even the possibility of forming a landed aristocracy and were coming to see the business élite as a valuable urban addition to the conservative faction.

In 1836, a tragedy occurred that briefly threatened the fortunes of the entire Robinson clan. In June of that year, Peter Robinson suffered a stroke. John hurried to his bedside, and Peter confided in him that a balance stood against him in his accounts as commissioner of woods and forests. Peter was sure that the deficit, which stood at £6,000, was the result of accounting errors. John immediately involved himself in his brother's affairs, and discovered that the sum owing was more in the order of £11,000. Some years previously, the accounts for the Irish immigrations had been wound up; at that time Peter had had to pay £2,000 for discrepancies in the accounts. Fortunately, the value of Peter's lands (which he had acquired before entering government service) covered all his debts. It became a matter of honour to the Robinson family that the monies owed by Peter to the Crown be paid as soon as possible. The chief justice noted that he and four other men were to have guaranteed £5,000 security for Peter. It turned out that in addition to his lax accounting, Peter had never had those bonds executed. Honour was at stake, and John informed the government that he was prepared to sign the bond at any time.[3]

There was no hint that Peter had embezzled the government. He had not lived particularly lavishly, and his debts erased the sizeable fortune he had earned before entering public service. Perhaps the source of Peter's difficulties lay in his easy-going accounting and his over-reliance on subordinates. During the Irish immigrations, John had warned his brother to scrutinize the affairs of his clerks, but Peter had failed to act on the advice. However, there existed a deep bond between the brothers and John quickly came to Peter's aid during his illness. John Robinson's success was due in no small measure to the financial assistance given to him by his brother, and by clearing Peter's name, John was making a small repayment of the debt owed by him to his brother.

Before the onset of his illness, Peter had played a part in the opening confrontation between the 'tried reformer' Head and the real reformers. Head began his term with the conciliatory gesture of reading his instructions from the colonial secretary to the legislature. Lord Glenelg's instructions acknowledged the truth in Mackenzie's *Seventh Report on*

Grievances and ordered Head to resolve all outstanding complaints, without suggesting how this was to be done. The colonial secretary left no doubt that the imperial system was to remain intact: the assembly was reminded that the lieutenant-governor was responsible to the imperial Parliament, not to the colonials.

In an attempt to comply with his instructions, Head added several reformers to the executive council. Robert Baldwin and John Rolph agreed, after considerable persuasion, to join the executive. The addition of liberal politicians to his innermost council did not alter Sir Francis's conservative tendencies, however. He lumped the reformers together as a 'Republican Party' and dismissed them as inconsequential louts whose republican sentiments would be better expressed in the United States. Head was also slow to develop any rapport with the tories; much to Robinson's annoyance, an invitation to Government House did not arrive until March. Robinson found Head to be cold and lacking in tact. After dinner at Government House, the chief justice ruefully reported that he could not 'say that I felt perfectly at home – It must be confessed there is rather an air of desolation.'[4] Robinson also found Head's passion for publishing government correspondence most exasperating. No other government publicized its internal acts, and Robinson wondered why Head felt so compelled to give ammunition to demagogues like Mackenzie. Yet tory principles united the two men, and after their first meeting Head began to place substantial reliance on the chief justice. Sir Francis eventually concluded that Robinson possessed 'a combination of such strong religious and moral principles, modesty of mind, and such instinctive talent for speaking and writing, I have never before been acquainted with.'[5]

During their early meetings, Robinson cautioned the lieutenant-governor against meeting with the judges too frequently. Sir Francis 'had not experience in Government and therefore did not perhaps bear in mind distinctions of this kind which can nevertheless not be safely overlooked.'[6] On the crucial question of whether the executive council and lieutenant-governor should be responsible to the popular assembly, Head and Robinson agreed that such an idea was an affront to the British constitution. The chief justice had made it clear in his judgments that the Upper Canadian assembly was similar but inferior to the British House of Commons, publicly declaring that the assembly was by no means a 'body perfectly similar'[7] to the British House. It was therefore legally and practically impossible for the lieutenant-governor to be responsible to the assembly while at the same time serving the imperial Parliament. No man can serve two masters, and Sir Francis Bond Head had no intention of serving the likes of William Lyon Mackenzie.

The obvious reliance Head placed on Robinson infuriated the reformers, and Mackenzie thought he detected the clever hand of John Robinson behind the government's policies: 'It is evid[en]t to me that the Ch[ie]f Justice has been Head's mentor from first to last, altho the contrary may seem to be the case.'[8] He exaggerated Robinson's influence; in fact, the chief justice hesitated to counsel the lieutenant-governor on political matters. While his rejection of the concept of responsible government was undoubtedly known to Head, the chief justice did not comment publicly on the issue. Head's vigorous political campaign to crush his political opponents was entirely the result of his impulsive character. He was about to embark on a combative political course quite alien to the cautious nature of the chief justice. Robinson later remarked with some incredulity that Head never read or paused to reflect, but acted on observation and impulse.[9] Even so, the first sallies between the lieutenant-governor and the reformers concerned constitutional matters in which the chief justice probably played a limited role as éminence grise.

Robert Baldwin found it unconscionable that the lieutenant-governor did not see fit to consult regularly with either him or his colleagues in the executive council. Moreover, Head's policies were increasingly disliked by the assembly, and Baldwin became associated with a tory policy over which he had no real influence. He therefore presented a request signed by the entire council, including Peter Robinson and George Markland, that henceforth the lieutenant-governor should regularly consult with his executive.[10] John Robinson took a jaundiced view of the council's demands. This constitutional crisis was the result of Baldwin's sudden discovery that 'the Executive Council which they had been for years castigating as the source of all evil, had really but little to answer for.' Robinson was shocked to find his brother's and George Markland's names attached to such a document. Robinson knew that somehow Baldwin had hoodwinked them into joining his attempted coup. Head gave a copy of the executive council's demands to Robinson, who had no hesitation in telling the lieutenant-governor that the document was 'so very contemptible in itself – it desires what is inadmissable' and, even worse, 'it hints at revolution.'[11]

Sir Francis's reply to the council's petition is a thoughtful examination of the role of colonial bodies and contains detailed references to constitutional law; it is evident that Robinson had a significant impact on his thoughts. Indeed, the opening sentence of the reply – 'The constitution of a British colony resembles, but it is not identical with, the constitution of the mother country'[12] – is taken almost verbatim from the chief justice's decision in *McNab* v *Bidwell and Baldwin*.[13] The essential element of Head's argument was that the colonial government was inherently inferior to its imperial master and the lieutenant-governor therefore was answerable to the Crown, not the executive council.

As a result of this correspondence, the conflict between those favouring responsible government and the 'constitutionalists' who held to the existing imperial system was squarely before the province. The reformers either had to accept the colonial system as it existed or remain in opposition until their radical friends in London could effect a change within the Empire. In these circumstances, Baldwin and Rolph were eager to resign from the executive and, at Head's urging, the entire council, including Peter Robinson, left office. Head had won this first round by making an issue of responsible government.

While Head's publication of this correspondence defined the issues and showed that the reformers' real opposition was to the existing constitution, it also drew criticism. Robinson complained to Colborne that as a result of Head's impulsive act, 'everybody knows everything' and that important government matters were being discussed by 'all the shoemakers & tailors in town.'[14] Government remained, in the chief justice's opinion, a topic best left to gentlemen. Head's correspondence and the resulting resignation of the executive council was a polite affair and might have remained so had not the reformers in the assembly sought to discredit Head for dismissing his councillors. A select committee reported that Head had used the appointment of Baldwin and Rolph for deceitful purposes and that he was under the influence of 'secret and unsworn' advisers. When the assembly moved to stop government supplies, the lieutenant-governor's response was devastating. He refused assent to money bills already passed and prorogued the legislature. Upper Canada was thereby thrown into one of the most controversial campaigns in its history.

By 1836, the chasm between reformers and constitutionalists that had existed since the bitter years of the alien debates had widened. When Mackenzie dared to chair an investigation of the Welland Canal accounts, Robinson showed that he had lost none of his animosity toward the radical printer. Mackenzie remained 'that mean little creature who among honorable men and in an honorable age, would be *spurned* as a thing whose touch must calumniate.'[15] Colonel Talbot, in constant touch with the chief justice, gave a blow-by-blow description of the campaign. Head stumped the province on behalf of the constitutionalists, arousing the fears of the loyalists and British immigrants that the reformers were merely American republicans in disguise. The constitutionalists were well-organized, and under the banner of an effective leader they swept the reformers from the assembly. Talbot gleefully reported to the chief justice that

no exertions were wanting on the part of the Loyal to get wholesome members for Middlesex but the Rebels are too numerous and their bare faced audacity astonished me. They openly said that in less than two years, the same flag would be waving over St. Thomas and London as now in Buffaloe [sic], but my Boys with Twigs kept the scoundrels in order. It is indeed glorious news that Bidwell, Perry and Mackenzie are turned out ...[16]

William Robinson was handily elected in Simcoe and the tories, thanks to Sir Francis, were again in control of the assembly.

Following the 1836 election, there was an exhausted lull in Upper Canadian politics. The constitutionalist assembly worked well with the lieutenant-governor and a number of important bills were passed. However, the bitterness aroused by the 1836 campaign did not fade. Baldwin and Bidwell despaired of politics, while some, such as Mackenzie, began to contemplate violence. An economic crash at the end of 1836 threatened the very existence of most settlers. Money was flooding out of the province as British investors liquidated their holdings. Head aggravated the situation by refusing to suspend the payment of specie; oblivious to the pleas of the bankers and settlers to stop the outflow of capital, he deepened the anxiety caused by the crash.

The looming clouds of violence were darkest in Lower Canada. There the Colonial Office had abandoned conciliation and authorized the lieutenant-governor to obtain revenues without the assembly's consent. Mackenzie agreed with his Lower Canadian comrades that the time had come at last for a bold frontal assault on the imperial system in British North America. In July 1837 Mackenzie convened a group of like-minded dissidents and issued a declaration calling for a congress to remedy grievances. After this statement of purpose, Mackenzie toured the townships north of Toronto to raise troops. No one in the government took this activity seriously, and while Mackenzie preached rebellion, Head voluntarily sent all his regular troops to Lower Canada to assist in crushing the uprising there. During this uneasy time, the chief justice took his family on a prolonged vacation to New York State. Upper Canada had seen more than its share of agitation in the past, and no one suspected that Mackenzie's campaign would be anything more than rhetorical. Only a month before the outbreak of rebellion, Robinson blithely told Head that an insurrection was unthinkable.[17]

One Toronto resident, Colonel James FitzGibbon, suspected that Mackenzie was entirely serious and that an overthrow of the government was imminent. FitzGibbon, a former officer in the British Army, was one of the most reliable militiamen in the province. He drafted an emergency plan to call all loyal citizens to City Hall or the Parliament building in case of rebel attack. Trudging from house to house, FitzGibbon informed the residents of his mobilization plans. When he arrived at Beverley House, the chief justice admonished him to stop exciting the young bloods of Toronto. Robinson considered the talk of rebellion to be so much rubbish, and felt 'sorry to see [FitzGibbon] alarming the people in this way.'[18] Colonel FitzGibbon bowed to the chief justice's request and decided to notify only the heads of local families.

However, as more reports of seditious activity came in to the capital, an emergency meeting of the executive council was called. In view of the circumstances, constitutional niceties were dropped and the councillors were joined by all the judges and law officers. After a discussion of the reports, Head concluded that no rebellion was actually being planned and therefore no cause for alarm existed.

Soon enough, however, the rumours were confirmed by the news that an actual rebellion was in progress. Rebel forces assembled north of Toronto at Montgomery's Inn and set up pickets along the road in an attempt to isolate the city. By the evening of 4 December it was certain that the rebels intended to seize Toronto. On the morning of 5 December, alarm bells alerted the sleeping citizenry. The chief justice, his fellow judges, and the local bourgeoisie assembled on the market square, prepared to repel the rebel hordes. Sir Francis inspected his middle-aged guardians, noting that Robinson was armed with 'thirty rounds of ball cartridge in his cartouch.'[19] No doubt Robinson entertained hopes of exacting some measure of revenge on Mackenzie for previous insults. Emma Robinson and the younger Robinson children were placed on a steamer in Toronto harbour. The older boys, Lukin and John Beverley, were now ready to serve their sovereign: Lukin was assigned to the local militia, and John became an aide-de-camp to the lieutenant-governor.

After his bravado in sending away the remaining British regulars, Head seemed paralyzed now that rebel forces were actually near the city. FitzGibbon, against Head's orders, had posted a picket on the outskirts of Toronto which succeeded in repelling the first rebel assault. A day later, the rebel forces were dispersed after a brief skirmish at John Montgomery's tavern. Robinson was exultant after this victory over the republicans: 'The loyal feeling of her Majesty's true subjects has been nobly displayed today, and the result promises peace and happiness to Upper Canada for years to come.[20] The victory was complete when the reform leaders fled to the United States, leaving the province truly a tory bastion. Head had succeeded in convincing even those reformers who had taken no part in the rebellion, such as Bidwell, to leave the province for their own good. Surely now Britain would realize that those who advocated responsible government were republicans at heart and that the British connection could only be maintained by firmly supporting the loyal faction. All this was accomplished with no great thanks to Sir Francis Bond Head. In his report to the colonial secretary, he bragged that he had deliberately denuded the province of regular troops in order to encourage Mackenzie in his folly.[21] Robinson was probably speaking for most Upper Canadians when he said that 'any quiet Englishman will be apt to say that man would make a rebellion anywhere.'[22]

Although Mackenzie's farcical rebellion was easily snuffed out and the loyal feeling of Upper Canada convincingly displayed, Mackenzie himself escaped to the United States where he appealed to the Americans to help their Canadian brothers drive the red-coated rascals from North America. Thus the 'patriot' movement was born, organized almost exclusively by Americans and directed to liberate the Canadas from British rule. One of the patriots' first acts was to seize Navy Island, a Canadian outpost in the Niagara River. Soon, patriot organizations, or 'hunters' lodges,' were harassing the Canadian border and threatening an all-out invasion. Head hastened to the Niagara area to try to bolster the Canadian defences, leaving the chief justice in de facto control of the government. 'I am glad you are not bent to the ground by the weight of my chain,' Head joked; 'I am glad to get it off my neck.'[23] As provincial administrator, Robinson reported to the commander-in-chief, Sir John Colborne, that all the militias were loyal and eager to repel any invader. While this news was encouraging, the fact remained that the loyal forces were poorly armed and any attack on Navy Island was too risky. There were two things the province needed desperately: a competent military commander to succeed Sir Francis, and a new supply of weapons. Almost in desperation, he begged Colborne for help: 'Muskets & ball cartridges are our chief want – You would be delighted to see the fine forward spirit of the people – but there are not the means of arming one twentieth of those who are eager to turn out for duty.[24]

The province would prevail if the American government could be persuaded to discourage the hunters' lodges. Resuming his diplomatic role, Robinson wrote to H.S. Fox, the British minister in Washington, describing the tense situation on the frontier. He asked Fox to convince the American government that the patriot movement threatened the peace with Great Britain.[25] To his immense relief, Robinson received word in mid-January 1838 that Fox had succeeded. General Scott, Robinson's acquaintance from Queenston Heights, was being dispatched to the frontier to put an end to the patriot incursions. It was hoped that with the active co-operation of the American government the hunters' lodges would quickly be subdued. With remarkable ease the chief justice had left the courtroom and successfully assumed control of civil affairs in this crucial hour.[26]

The chief justice also tried to deter the hunters' lodges by drafting an act to control 'lawless aggression from subjects of foreign countries.' The act provided for the court-martial of any aliens or British subjects who invaded Upper Canada from the neighbouring states. The executive council was given the option to try such individuals in the regular courts. The Colonial Office doubted the legality of the measure, and advised its disallowance on the ground that aliens should be charged with treason and tried before civil courts. Robinson, furious at this response, told the lieutenant-governor that the Crown law officers themselves had committed an important error. The Americans who had invaded various territories of the Western District had never lived within 'the Queen's Peace' and therefore could not be traitors. The Colonial Office missed the point; aliens who had never lived in Upper Canada could not abjure an allegiance they had never acknowledged. In law they were pirates, and the act was correct to mandate their trial by courts-martial.[27]

In these times of crisis, Robinson looked upon the law not only as a system of justice but also as an effective means of influencing human activity. In 1814 he had insisted that in spite of war conditions traitors be given the full benefit of the law. Summary executions would never convince the populace that treason was being punished through 'the rational effects of justice.' Had Robinson, by his advocacy of the summary trial and execution of American raiders, become less tolerant in 1838? In fact, he had lost none of his respect for justice or his insistence on the rule of law in Upper Canada. Robinson sought to use the law to warn those who invaded Upper Canada they they faced the 'greater terror of immediate punishment,' and he cautioned them not to break the peace. The bill to try foreign aggressors was a terror tactic to frighten foreigners, not to cow the resident population. The act had another favourable result.

While it restrained foreign incursions, its existence meant that the government did not have to force the harshness of martial law on the entire province. Perhaps for those politically expedient reasons, the Crown law officers allowed the act.

In February 1838 came the news that Sir Francis Bond Head was to be recalled. The new lieutenant-governor, Sir George Arthur, arrived in the province in early March and relieved the chief justice of his unofficial executive duties. Unlike Head, Arthur had considerable experience both as a soldier and as a colonial administrator. He had served as governor of the convict settlement of Van Diemen's Land, and as superintendent of British Honduras he had suppressed a slave revolt. Arthur, accustomed to undertaking difficult tasks, would need all his resources to deal with a province whose jails teemed with captured rebels and whose borders were under imminent assault.

Mackenzie had barely fled across the border before a special commission was issued to the vice-chancellor to enable him to lay charges of high treason against the rebels. The Colonial Office feared that treason trials conducted so soon after the hysteria of a rebellion would be unnecessarily brutal. Lord Glenelg ordered General Arthur to ensure that 'no unnecessary severity will be sanctioned by you.'[28] Arthur read those instructions to the members of the executive council, who angrily replied that they, not Glenelg, had been subjected to Mackenzie's depredations and that the extreme penalty of the law should fall on all the rebel leaders.

For only the second time in Upper Canada's history trials for high treason were held. On the first occasion, the Ancaster assizes of 1814, John Robinson had prosecuted those traitors who had allied themselves with the American invaders. Now he sat in judgment over those of his fellow citizens who had tried to overthrow their legitimate government. The special commission gave the court the authority to try persons for crimes committed outside the district. Certain protections were granted to the prisoners; the court could hear only the charge of high treason, and a copy of the indictment and list of witnesses had to be given to the prisoner ten days before his trial. Robinson reminded the Toronto grand jury that considered the charges that they were under a heavy burden. Any attempt to overthrow the Crown was probably the most serious offence a subject could commit. Yet there were traces of whig sympathies in the chief justice, for he conceded that, on occasion, rebellion was justified. Rebellion was the prerogative of a free people; 'our laws indicate no doctrine so slavish, as the necessity of absolute submission to every degree of oppression and tyranny that a government can exercise.'[29]

The chief justice's conduct of the proceedings dispelled Lord Glenelg's fears that the rebels would not receive fair play. One rebel, John Anderson, admitted his crime, and his counsel advised him to plead guilty. Robinson told him that in view of the seriousness of the charge, he should ignore his attorney's advice and plead not guilty. Anderson vacillated, but eventually stood by his guilty plea. Two of the rebel leaders, Samuel Lount and Peter Mathews, did not receive the court's indulgence. Next to Mackenzie, they were the main organizers of the rebellion and evidence of their leading role was readily available to the Crown. The chief justice learned of Sam Lount's capture in January, and he commented at that time that Lount 'made many of the pikes & was an active leader.'[30] Robert Baldwin acted as Lount's and Mathew's counsel, and in view of the futility of a trial, he advised both men to plead guilty. On 29 March they appeared before the chief justice for sentencing.

That morning, the chief justice appeared to be uneasy as he was about to perform what should have been an automatic task. Mathews had fought in the local militia in the War of 1812 and Lount had been an Assemblyman. These were not mere felons who had maliciously harmed their fellows for personal gain, but idealists who had reacted against what they considered to be an arbitrary government. Robinson's address to the convicts[31] began by upholding the right of free men to revolt against autocracy. In the chief justice's opinion, however, the prevailing government was far from autocratic. Rather, it was a system in which men of the 'middle station of life' such as Lount and Mathews could obtain a comfortable and secure living. Instead of fostering this system, they had breached their public trust by trying to create a republican order. Borrowing from John Locke, Robinson told them, 'You lived in a country where every man who obeys the law is secure in the protection of life, liberty, and property; under a form of government, which has been the admiration of the world for ages.' Their crime was their attempt to overturn the prevailing order of society: 'You have, I fear, too long and unreservedly indulged in a feeling of envy and hatred towards your rulers.' The accused were condemned to death, and were cautioned not to expect pardons. Both judge and condemned appeared shaken at the end of the proceedings. That evening, Robinson confided to an old friend that the passing of sentence on Lount and Mathews had been one of the most painful acts of his career.[32]

Robinson's anxiety was not caused by the certainty that the sentence would stand without appeal or executive reversal, but by a nagging question: had Robinson fulfilled his duty to demonstrate publicly that these men were not being victimized for protesting their limited liberties? While still a young law clerk, Robinson had recognized the principle that the people must perceive their courts to be fair, disinterested tribunals. It must be understood by the public that Lount and Mathews would die not for any political beliefs, but because they had attempted to destroy the good order of society. The dissemination of this view was greatly aided when the *Christian Guardian* published the chief justice's address in its entirety. None the less, both condemned men were popular figures in Toronto and there was a great outcry of protest at their sentence. Sir George Arthur forwarded clemency petitions to the executive council, who in turn requested the opinion of the chief justice and the attorney-general. Robinson merely repeated that the convicts were not only rebels but the organizers of rebellion, and the law was quite clear as to their punishment. Amid great public sorrow, Lount and Mathews were hanged and buried in Potter's Field.

Not all the rebels were willing to plead guilty to the charges of treason. John Montgomery, the proprietor of the tavern where the rebels convened, put up a substantial defence. Although Montgomery had been a prominent reformer and a Mackenzie partisan, he had broken with Mackenzie a few months before the uprising and was apparently unaware of the planned rebellion. The Crown witnesses consisted of several loyalists who had been imprisoned at Montgomery's Tavern and who had seen but not heard the rebel operations. They testified that Montgomery had not been placed under any restraints and that he had conversed freely with Mackenzie and other leading rebels. The Crown brought forward non-partisan witnesses who testified that after his initial surprise at the outbreak Montgomery had willingly acted as commissary-general for the rebels. He had been observed sitting in a council of war and warning sleeping rebels of the advance of government troops. The Crown even summoned a reformer, William Ketchum, who swore that Montgomery had asked him what degree of assistance the rebels could expect within Toronto itself.

In his defence, Montgomery's lawyers presented twenty witnesses to cast doubt on the Crown's case. They pointed out that at the time of the outbreak, Montgomery had leased the inn and was there only to move his furniture. The fact that he stayed at the inn to protect his property was not in itself treasonous. One of Montgomery's servants testified that she heard Mackenzie threaten Montgomery if he did not join the rebellion. At the end of the case, the chief justice listed four points which, to him, indicated Montgomery's guilt:

1 As to his forebearing, that is not helping in everything as he could
2 As to his fear of his house being burnt, all who came here leaving rebels behind them might have had the same fear.
3 As to his being *averse* to the rebellion ... A man may be averse to murder or arson but if being present he does in any manner contribute to it, not being compelled, he must answer for it.
4 Why did not the prisoner come forward before the Sunday after the attack, having seen and known so much of the rebels and their proceedings.[33]

The jury found Montgomery guilty and recommended mercy.

In the opinion of one later commentator on Montgomery's case, 'It is clear that Robinson simply did not consider with an open mind the circumstances urged by the defense ...' and 'the extremely conflicting nature of the evidence presented and the complete lack of agreement among the witnesses as to the facts would seem to warrant dismissing the case on grounds of insufficient evidence.'[34] But it is expected in most criminal trials that there will be some measure of conflicting evidence. The question is not whether conflicting evidence exists, but whether the guilt of the accused is proven beyond a reasonable doubt. The fact remains that the only impartial testimony heard during the trial was to the effect that Montgomery had actively sought to procure supplies for the rebels. The jury had no hesitation in finding this evidence sufficient to enter a conviction. Montgomery did not accept the verdict with equanimity. In his address to the court, he condemned the Crown witnesses as perjurers and the judges and prosecutor as hopelessly biased. He further promised that when Chief Justice Robinson and his minions were broiling in hell, he, John Montgomery, would still be a publican on Yonge Street. The chief justice listened impassively and then ordered that he be hanged in two weeks' time.

Although Mackenzie remained out of the grasp of British justice, the trials of his associates continued on into April 1838. The chief justice tried 'General' Alexander Theller for having commanded the schooner *Anne* in its assault on Amherstburg.[35] Robinson, dismissing Theller's plea that he was a naturalized American, held that because he was British-born his act constituted treason. After Theller made a bumbling atempt to conduct his own defence, Robinson ordered two lawyers to assist him in presenting his case. While the court was circumspect in seeing that the accused obtained justice, in most cases guilt was manifest and defence futile. The only serious issue of doubt occurred in the case of young Charles Durand.

Durand, an active radical politician, was not part of Mackenzie's entourage at Montgomery's Inn. He was in Toronto on business when the rebellion broke out, and when the first alarms were sounded he boarded a stage for his home in Hamilton. The stage was stopped by none other than Mackenzie and a few of his men. All the passengers were searched, except for Durand, who spent a few minutes in conversation with Mackenzie. Rather than taking up with the rebels, Durand was left to walk home in the company of one of his fellow passengers, a Mr Schafer. Durand next turned up in Streetsville where he was questioned by some vigilant tories. His reputation as a radical had preceded him and made him an immediate object of suspicion. The only other evidence against Durand was two letters to an American gunsmith, Mills, ordering a supply of rifles, and a letter to Mackenzie in which Durand expressed the hope that Upper Canada would soon be free from 'the Colonial Office and downing-street oppression.' In his defence, Durand pointed out that he was in Toronto for legitimate business reasons and that he had called the rebellion a 'foolish crazy attempt.' He had known Mackenzie for years and it was therefore understandable that they should exchange words. The incriminating letters had been written months before the rebellion was even planned.

In his summation to the jury, Robinson was hesitant to accept the letters to Mills and Mackenzie as proof of treason: 'The letters not proved to be published will not prove any of the overt acts laid under the head of compassing.' On the other hand, the letters were hardly good character references. 'They are evidence of his opinions and motives and are material as arguing an assent to the rebellion in connection with his other conduct.'[36] The evidence the chief justice found to be the most persuasive (referred to only in his summation, not in his notes on the evidence) was that of Schafer, who accompanied Durand after their encounter with Mackenzie. Schafer testified that Durand had told Mackenzie to attack the defenceless capital as soon as possible. In fact this evidence was not particularly convincing, since it was unlikely that Durand would have made such incriminating statements in front of a total stranger. Robinson did not appear to be convinced that the totality of the evidence indicated Durand's guilt, and he left the decision entirely to the jury. 'I told the jury if they believed the evidence for the Crown and that the prisoner acted *obligingly* in what he did and said in furtherance of the rebellion then going on, it was sufficient to convict him of levying war.' After considerable deliberation, the jury found Durand guilty of treason. Many years later, Durand maintained his innocence and complained that 'the Chief Justice should have told the jury ... that circumstantial evidence would not do.'[37] Durand probably had a valid complaint; Robinson should have been more forthright in expressing any misgivings as to the sufficiency of the evidence.

Charles Durand's conviction in the face of meagre evidence was an exception among the cases tried under the special commission. After the leading rebels had been tried, the trials of the lesser figures rarely resulted in convictions since few overt acts of treason were proved. In the case of James Hunter, who was accused of inciting rebellion in the Whitby area, the jury did not find enough credible evidence to enter a conviction. Robinson's old political nemesis, Dr Morrison, was also acquitted of treason.[38] On 10 April John Montgomery, Charles Durand, and Alexander Theller were brought before the chief justice for sentencing. Even though all were sentenced to die, it was already known that the scaffold that had taken the lives of Lount and Mathews was being dismantled. The moderate British Colonist hoped that 'the examples that have been made ... are sufficient to vindicate the majesty of the law.'[39] The executive council had already discussed the matter of further executions; Arthur reported that they had concluded that while 'some of the most guilty offenders should be executed, I trust it will be found that the number may be reduced to a *very few*.'[40] In the event, only Lount and Mathews were executed under the auspices of the special commission.

The question now before the government was what to do with the hundreds of rebels awaiting trial in Upper Canada's jails. The justices of King's Bench advised the government that since the rebels no longer posed an internal threat it would be proper to pardon most of them. Indeed, the judges were of the opinion that if the hunters' lodges were not threatening the frontier, the rebels could be dealt with leniently.[41] The executive council decreed that the 'lesser' rebels could be released after entering into sureties to keep the peace. Altogether, fifty-five rebels presented themselves before the chief justice in May to apply for their discharge. Eventually eighty-three Upper Canadians suffered the harsh but not necessarily fatal punishment of exile to Van Diemen's Land. In later years, after the reformers had regained respectability, they condemned the treason trials as arbitrary acts of revenge and the chief justice as the 'Jeffries of Upper Canada.'[42] These charges were groundless; in fact, the treason trials showed that under the British constitution prosecution was sure and punishment restrained and usually lenient.

As a mark of approval of the conduct of the chief justice during and after the rebellion, Head recommended Robinson for a knighthood. But Robinson declined the honour, explaining that it was not customary in British America to confer knighthoods on judges. His real reasons for refusing were 'of a domestic nature.'[43] He had discussed the matter with Emma, and together they apparently concluded that the notoriety of a knighthood would do the family more harm than good.

With the tempestuous Head no longer in command of Upper Canada, the province responded positively to Lieutenant-Governor Arthur's able administration. He defused the threat of the hunters' lodges and laid the groundwork for an investigation of the causes of rebellion. Arthur was repeatedly warned to beware the advice of the tories, especially that of the chief justice. The issue of how much confidence the lieutenant-governor should place in his judges was raised at a meeting between Arthur and Robinson. Robinson denied any desire or intention to influence the government:

As Chief Justice I am, like my brother Judges liable to be called on for reports, and opinions and advice in those cases in which recourse would be had in England to the Judges, and in no others – I have no concern in the executive affairs of the Colony, and no claim or wish to be consulted in any of them, except where they have so direct a bearing upon the general administration of justice, as to make such a reference proper.[44]

Robinson explained that during the Colborne and Head administrations, he had been required to advise the government on matters of policy. That practice was irregular and a violation of colonial policy, but in the circumstances he was often the most experienced adviser available. Robinson was aware that in the 'hurry and anxiety of the moment Sir Francis did not consult appearances as much as was desirable.' The chief justice assured Arthur that he had no interest in taking any further part in public affairs. Arthur insisted that Robinson possessed 'extensive information upon every subject connected with the Province,'[45] and Arthur would have no hesitation in consulting him 'on any subject the political bearing of which might appear to me of more than ordinary importance to the interests of the Country.' The Robinson charm, which had seduced the Colonial Office and succeeding lieutenant-governors, also captured the confidence of Sir George Arthur. During the next two crucial years, Robinson and Arthur would have regular exchanges of ideas and suggestions on the course of Upper Canada's government. Lord Goderich's dispatch of 1831 mandating the separation of the judiciary from the

executive might never have been written. Robinson advised the lieutenant-governor on a variety of state matters, including appointments to the
militia and government posts.

In the aftermath of the rebellion the British began to doubt the wisdom of
traditional colonial policies and even to question whether it was worthwhile trying to retain their North American colonies. Lord Melbourne's
government concluded that some action was necessary to bind the
provinces to the Empire and at the same time relieve the grievances that
had precipitated the rebellion. Lord Durham, who had taken a leading
part in drafting the Reform Bill of 1832, was dispatched to British America
as governor-general with a special commission to examine the situation
and suggest remedies. Robinson doubted whether a radical peer would
stoop to consult the loyal faction:

I take it to be exceedingly unlikely that Lord Durham would consent to derive his
notions of remedies from any official authority in the Colonies – The principle most
consistently acted upon for ten years past – is to look upon residence in a Colony
as disqualifying a person from exercising a sound judgment upon any point
relating to its interests.[46]

Robinson's pessimism seemed justified when Durham allotted only five
days to study Upper Canada. After spending most of his time at Niagara
Falls, one day was set aside to consult with concerned individuals in
Toronto. On the quay to welcome the governor-general were the chief
justice, government officers, and even a few resident reformers. Robert
Baldwin actually managed to speak to Durham for twenty minutes, and
later sent him a letter outlining his vision of responsible government.
Durham also met with Robinson to hear the government's view of events.
After spending only twenty-four hours in the capital, Durham took a
coach to his official residence in Lower Canada. The chief justice
accompanied Durham as far as Prescott, and it was probably on this trip
that Durham gave Robinson a preliminary report on the reform of colonial
government.
    Astonished to be consulted on the reforms which he had feared would
be implemented before he ever saw them, Robinson resolved to influence
Durham's thinking. He made marginal notes along the length of the
manuscript, most of which were hardly flattering.[47] Robinson suggested
that the proposals were wholly inadequate and that Durham should turn
his attention to some alternative solution. Robinson's personal desire was

to see Montreal annexed to Upper Canada and to subject the remainder of French Canada to rule by a Crown-appointed council. Durham's proposals actually favoured a loosening of imperial ties, which would help the colonists attain self-government within the British Empire. His vision ran contrary to the prevailing wisdom, which held that the colonies would inevitably leave the Empire to join the United States. Durham's scheme would have abolished the legislative council; only an appointed executive council would stand between the people and the lieutenant-governor. Moreover, the executive council would confine its activity to accepting or suggesting amendments to legislation from the popular assembly. This scheme was far too radical for Robinson's liking. In his view the legislative council was a necessary counterweight to the assembly. Other radical proposals, such as fixing the government's civil list for six years and establishing regular dates for elections, took away from the Crown's prerogative. Durham's suggestions that the judiciary should be made 'open to impeachment by the Local Assemblies before the General Assembly' incurred Robinson's patriotic denunciation: 'Impeachment before an assembly elected by the popular voice is not English, & not proper.'[48]

He likewise took a dim view of Durham's proposals to create a federal legislature and judiciary for British America. Durham wished to grant this federal Parliament limited power over external affairs and trade. Robinson noted that these subjects were the sole domain of the imperial Parliament. In discussing a general government for the combined provinces, Durham described a division of powers between federal and provincial governments in a few paragraphs. Robinson, in a comment that future generations of Canadian constitutionalists would readily understand, remarked that 'this distribution of powers & duties will require long & careful consideration.'

Robinson must have been astounded when some of his suggestions were actually incorporated into Durham's report. The legislative council was not abolished, judges continued to be appointed by the Crown, and the recommendation to prorogue Parliament on a fixed day was dropped. Much to his relief, Robinson discovered that Durham was no ideologue and held no fixed ideas on how to reform Upper Canada's government. According to his biographer, 'Durham's remarkably open mind welcomed suggestions from all sources, Family Compact or Reform ... But these contributions of Robinson's came from a man who was not only one of the best political thinkers in the country, but who could probably win the Upper Canada Tories to any plan that satisfied him.'[49] So amenable was

Durham to suggestions that Robinson probably assumed that he had discovered a sympathetic friend, if not an ally. Durham wrote to Robinson, assuring him that 'I have sufficiently shown my desire not to force my own opinions against the settled conviction of those who from their position have a right to command respect and consideration.'[50] The chief justice was favourably impressed. Robinson cordially offered his services to Lord Durham and suggested that they meet again.

Suddenly, in August 1838, the chief justice was taken seriously ill with a stroke. At the same time he was seized by a deep depression. He later confided to his sister, Sarah Boulton, that after his first attack

my mind was constantly turning back to early scenes – & to those who had passed away with them – Those days seemed to me to have been the happiest – but only because we were then young & cheerful – & easily satisfied – When I looked back at the 20 or 30 years that had intervened I felt that I had been labouring & worrying myself in a great measure in vain – I believe I would have been well content to have had the chain then parted that bound me to earth.[51]

This melancholy was highly uncharacteristic of John Robinson and was not only the result of his illness. In July his brother, Peter, had died in Newmarket. Peter, who had not regained his health after his stoke, had never satisfied the debt owed to the Crown. Peter Robinson died loyal to the causes his family had supported, and in his will his UE Right, a farm lot of 190 acres originally granted to his father, was left to his son, Frederick, 'so that it may remain in the family and tend to strengthen his feelings of loyalty and attachment to his King.'[52] Most of Peter's estate went toward satisfying the sums owed to the government, and little remained for his family. After the estate was finally settled, John sent a memorial to the lieutenant-governor, testifying to Peter's devoted service in the cause of immigration and the fact that his defalcations had cost him the fortune he had acquired before entering government service.[53] Peter Robinson's death in disgrace and obscurity was an unfortunate ending for an Upper Canadian whose immigration projects had redeemed thousands of lives and brought needed settlers to the frontier.

Robinson's physical illness, the death of his brother, and the rebellion and its aftermath probably contributed to his depression. Lord Durham was but the first breeze in a tempest of change that was to end the gentle life in Upper Canada. John Robinson compared the lot of the Upper Canadian gentleman to that of an Irish Protestant landlord: both were islands of civilization struggling futilely against a rising tide of electoral politics.[54]

While Robinson despaired for Upper Canada's government, and almost for his own life, two factors kept him bound firmly to the earth. The first was his devotion to the Church. He possessed an unshakable belief that this life was a mere proving-ground for eternity and that diligent service to the Church on earth would be rewarded by eternal bliss. The second factor was his family and especially his relationship with Emma, whom he referred to as 'the sun of our little system.' Not only did she attend to the details of household life, she was the confidante, nurse, and prime supporter of Upper Canada's chief justice.

In September, Robinson suffered another relapse and decided that it was necessary to leave the province and to seek a slower pace of life in semi-retirement in England. He petitioned the lieutenant-governor for a leave of absence until such time as his health improved. At the same time, Lord Durham was taken seriously ill. His departure to England was hastened by the news that Lord Melbourne's government had refused to sanction his ordinance banishing eight rebels to Bermuda. Durham resigned, promising that he woud return to save British Americans from 'the evils to which you are now subjected.' Both Durham and Robinson would shortly leave British America, and with them the focus of the Canada debate would shift to England.

14

The Canada Debate

The ocean voyage took its toll on Robinson, and on his arrival in England he was forced to rest at Clifton before taking up residence in Cheltenham with his in-laws, the Merry family. Merely being in Engand seemed to work therapeutic wonders, for within a week the chief justice was 'almost free from pain, & early next week I hope to be in London.'[1] Wasting little time on doctors or medical treatment, he wrote to the colonial secretary, Lord Glenelg, advising him of his presence in the country. By then, it was common knowledge that Lord Durham would return to Britain shortly and submit a report aimed at repealing the old Canada Act and substituting a new colonial order.

Robinson was eager to take part in the upcoming debate and bring to bear the combined strength of his personality and his friends on behalf of those causes he cherished. He still hoped that Durham could be added to his list of allies and, recalling their meetings in Toronto, pledged that if 'he desires any help that I can give him, he shall certainly receive it.' Still, the tory in Robinson retained grave misgivings about Durham and his policies: 'He is unsound in important points – does not look temperately at difficulties – is rash in action – & is deeply committed to a destructive party & a destructive policy.'[2]

On his first venture into London, Robinson was disappointed to find Lord Glenelg away on an extended vacation. Nevertheless, he took the opportunity to meet with the new colonial under-secretaries, Sir George Grey and James Stephen. The last remnants of Lord Bathurst's regime had been swept aside with the appointment of James Stephen as permanent under-secretary in 1836. Under Stephen's direction, whig principles of conciliation and moral propriety dominated the Colonial Office. Stephen suspected that Mackenzie's claims of official corruption in Upper Canada were accurate and that what was needed in the colonies was the appointment of responsible colonists to the provincial executive. These views were so divergent from Robinson's that there was little hope of his influencing the present occupants of Downing Street. Still, he was too prominent an Upper Canadian to be ignored; he was advised to stay in touch with Westminister because Glenelg would presently desire his counsel. This waiting period freed Robinson to meet with old colleagues, to remember past campaigns, and to prepare for future ones.

Sir Francis Bond Head had written to Robinson soon after his arrival and requested the pleasure of his company. Robinson, Emma, and the smaller children were on their way to Head's residence at Atherstone when word arrived that Glenelg was ready to receive the chief justice. Leaving his family in Birmingham, Robinson immediately set out for London.

Although he did not arrive in good health, Robinson described the meeting with Glenelg as having been conducted with 'much cordiality & confidence.' The only disquieting aspect of the interview was Glenelg's refusal to reveal any elements of his Canadian policy.[3] In fact, Glenelg had no Canadian policy; the Colonial Office, along with the rest of the government, was waiting for Lord Durham's report to provide the definitive solutions for Canada's future.

On the day after his meeting with Glenelg, Robinson sought enlightenment from Durham himself. Unfortunately, he too proved to be uncommunicative. Robinson found the peer in ill health, and not 'inclined to enter into any account of what measures he intended to recommend.'[4] Further queries convinced Robinson that Durham had not yet decided on his final recommendations. Robinson yearned to influence him, but it was clear that the Upper Canadian tory would never 'be a fellow worker with any of the worthies who shone upon us last summer as the Satellites of "Durham".'[5] While Durham expressed the hope that Robinson would assist in refining details of the report, the chief justice knew that the 'gangs of radicals' who had Durham's attention would actually draft the document.

During the course of his career, John Robinson had tried to make himself an instrument of government, to rise above petty factionalism. He still hoped to identify with the imperial government, for he believed that 'the most desirable thing for the Colonies is that a firm & wise measure should proceed *from the Government*.'[6] If the Canadian administration was to be reformed, Robinson desperately wanted to play his part in curbing democratic excesses. If he was denied this opportunity, there was the possibility of striking out on his own: 'For my own part I have no ambition to be the originator of a scheme – though I would not shrink from it.'[7]

At Christmastime Robinson left London to rejoin his family at Atherstone. There he was greeted by the effervescent Head who, safely removed from power, could now devote his time to justifying his previous administration. Robinson later assisted Head in drafting *A Narrative*, Head's dramatized version of the Canadian rebellion. Robinson found in the draft manuscript a most 'unbecoming partisan spirit' and a 'deplorable want of tact'[8] which he feared would prejudice the Colonial Office against the government faction. Head accepted many of Robinson's comments and dropped some of the more inflammatory material from his book.

The parliamentary leader of the tories, Sir Robert Peel, was a neighbour of Head; he invited Robinson to dine with him at his mansion, Drayton House. Peel was vitally interested in Canadian affairs, and recognized Robinson as a reliable source of information on colonial developments. Their discussion of Mackenzie's ill-fated rebellion extended well into the night, and the chief justice was forced to stay over until morning. So intrigued was Peel that Robinson was again invited to Drayton House. His dinner companions, some of the most formidable tories in England, were also impressed by Robinson's astuteness. Once again, his personal charm had succeeded in creating an impressive coterie of allies, if not among the government, then certainly among the opposition. Peel appreciated Robinson's desires to steer clear of English politics, although he felt that 'nothing could be more natural than that you should adhere in this country to the intimacies and friendships, which the agreement in principle and the sense of common danger were so likely to cement in Upper Canada.'[9] With the reassurance that he still held the confidence of powerful individuals, Robinson returned to Cheltenham to await Lord Durham's report.

The text of the report was leaked to the *Times* on 8 February and published verbatim. Robinson was revolted at the radical nature of the document. 'It absolutely made me ill to read it,' he confided to Arthur. 'You said rightly to me once "Lord Durham is a bad man" – I should try in vain to find words to express the contempt I feel for him.'[10] To Emma he gave a more direct expression of his immediate reaction: 'That horrid report! Every sentence is a lie and a most mischievous lie.'[11] Robinson was shocked to discover in the report a condemnation of the Family Compact as the root of all evil in Upper Canada. The report found that the leading families of the Canadas exercised a monopoly of office and that this monopoly had generated the dissatisfaction that eventually led to rebellion. Durham's solution called for internal affairs to be conducted by the colonists themselves through their elected representatives. Harmony could be achieved in the Canadas by restricting the 'interference of the imperial authorities' and 'strengthening the influence of the people on its Government.' The executive should have the confidence of the people and should be responsible to the people, not to the Colonial Office. The imperial government should retain control only over certain aspects of external affairs.

According to Durham, the most immediate problem in the Canadas was the unsettled state of the lower province. The report suggested that this could be remedied by increased British immigration and by the forced anglicization of the French Canadians. Durham urged that the act of 1791 be repealed and that Upper and Lower Canada be reunited. Durham was sure that the French Canadians would eventually lose their nationalistic impulses under the pressure of an English administration.

Robinson appeared at the Colonial Office on the Monday morning following the release of the report, and found the usually sedate chambers in a state of bedlam. Not only had Durham's recommendations been a complete surprise to the officials, they had also come at the same time as the resignations of Lord Glenelg and his under-secretary, Sir George Grey. The permanent under-secretary, James Stephen, gave Robinson a copy of the report and asked for his comments. Stephen smugly added that he anticipated 'the *announcement* of the popular policy' to confirm the report as imperial doctrine. Robinson sardonically enquired, 'then what if Lord Durham had recommended the Governor to be elected by universal suffrage – or any other absurdity?'[12] Robinson left, saying that he very much doubted whether a character as low as 'Radical Jack' Durham could bring Britannia to her knees. Despite this bravado, Robinson was unsure what course the government might take. Robinson supposed that Lord Glenelg's resignation was motivated by his reluctance to put the report's recommendations into operation. He feared that the new colonial secretary, Lord Normanby, would unite with Durham to force this measure on the colonies.

In retrospect, these anxieties were unfounded. The report did not generate much newspaper comment, nor did it lead to a public debate on colonial issues. The liberal element in British politics did not actively defend the report or advance it as their solution to the Canada problem.[13] Nevertheless, the precarious government of Lord Melbourne was compelled by the radicals to do something about the Canadas. Robinson fearful that the government might use the report as a basis for remedial legislation, closeted himself in his room at the Spring Garden Hotel and devoured all 119 pages of Durham's text. Keeping an even temper while reading the report presented some difficulty; Robinson recalled 'I hardly found a passage I did not burn to expose.'[14] After two days of intensive study, he found that he was unable to compose a succinct criticism. A refreshing walk in St James Park cleared his mind, and he resolved to abandon the attempt to analyse the entire report; instead, he would write a criticism of Durham's specific proposals. The following day, in a single outburst of energy, Robinson wrote a detailed letter to Lord Normanby, giving his impressions of Durham's report and its likely consequences.[15]

Robinson's task was simplified by the many factual errors in the report, which made it an obvious target for criticisms. Moreover, Durham, contrary to his instructions, had not conducted a systematic investigation of conditions by calling witnesses and evidence. His conclusions, Robinson suggested, were drawn haphazardly from 'impressions of his Lordship's mind.' After discrediting the rationale of the report, Robinson went on to examine the individual recommendations. He referred to Durham's harsh evaluation of the French Canadians: 'It is not in that spirit that the dominion over half a million of free subjects should be exercised.' More repression would only drive the French Canadians farther from the British Crown. If a union was forced on French Canada, then the Catholic Church, heretofore a loyal influence, would side with the radical nationalists. Instead of solving the political ills of Lower Canada, the union of the two provinces would spread racial and religious animosities throughout Upper Canada. Under Durham's proposals there would be one legislature for all the Canadas, and in this legislature 'French and English, Catholic and Protestant will be almost equally balanced, and ... nothing could be looked forward to, but years of bitter, obstinate, dangerous contention.'

While most of the report's recommendations were merely unrealistic, Robinson saw a positive danger in the scheme for responsible government. Durham recommended that the government be conducted through department heads who held the confidence of the elected assembly. The lieutenant-governor would henceforth limit his authority to dealing with issues involving imperial interests. In Robinson's opinion, Durham was proposing to undertake the most radical experiment in direct democracy yet attempted. In Britain, the aristocracy exerted a counteracting pressure to public opinion. Even in the United States, the balance of power curbed the authority of the president, the congress, and the courts. Durham proposed to do away with all these constraints and make colonial government exclusively the unrestrained will of elected representatives. Robinson had no faith in democracy, and feared the passions of the unbridled mob. He recalled the rabble who stoned Castlereigh's house and understood democracy to mean that those folk would determine government policy. He dourly predicted that responsible government would lead to 'the decline of integrity and independence in public servants, of peace and contentment in society.'

Unlike Lord Glenelg, Normanby displayed considerable interest in Robinson's comments and twice recalled him for further discussions. These interviews reassured Robinson that Normanby had no intention of blindly adopting Durham's proposals. The Cabinet considered several options before announcing its Canada policy; one of the new proposals was put forward by a former Cabinet minister, Edward 'Bear' Ellice.

Ellice and Robinson made an interesting study in contrasts. Ellice, nicknamed 'Bear' because of his financial prowess, was the owner of several successful enterprises in Lower Canada and New York. He had not spent much time in British America; instead, he had worked his way into British politics, eventually becoming a leading whig. Because of his landholdings and participation in the union debate of 1822, Ellice was acknowledged as the Cabinet's expert on Canadian affairs. While Robinson was closeted in the Sprng Gardens Hotel writing a refutation of the report, Ellice presented yet another scheme for provincial union to the Cabinet. Under his plan, the Canadas would be governed by a bicameral congress seated in Montreal. Because of the influence of American institutions in Ellice's plan, Robinson immediately rejected it as an 'absurd scheme ... complicated [and] unpalatable from its *republican flavour.'*[16] Although the conflicting opinions of Ellice and Robinson both received consideration, Ellice's contacts in the Cabinet were far stronger than Robinson's, and the congressional plan was seriously advanced as a possible solution to the Canadian problem. Yet the colonial secretary listened patiently to Robinson's criticisms and even urged him to put forward his own proposals. Robinson, encouraged by Normanby's response, warned him that if the government attempted to implement Durham's or Ellice's dangerous schemes, he would be compelled to take independent action.

In fact, the chief justice had already been approached to initiate a unilateral campaign. Robinson found himself courted by none other than the Duke of Wellington. Over lunch at the duke's London mansion, Apsley House, the two men discussed defence measures to protect Upper Canada from further American incursions. The duke moved the conversation from the military to the political by reminding Robinson that Melbourne's ministry had no intention of strengthening Canadian defences. Robinson's non-partisan views were dangerously naive, warned the duke, and the only way to advance his program would be to support his natural allies. English politics were now 'miserable party warfare, in which all the grand interests of the nation are sunk.'[17] Other members of the 'ultras,' the high tories of British politics, courted Robinson; it was indicative of the company he chose to keep that Henry Phillpotts, Bishop of Exeter, became one of his correspondents. Phillpotts had fought the Reform Bill of 1831 and had been burned in effigy outside his cathedral by enraged Anglicans. The bishop feared that the 'revolutionary and Godless scheme' proposed for the Canadas would eventually be applied to Britain. It was only a short step from disestablishing the Church in the colonies, as Durham had proposed, to ending its prerogatives in the mother country. 'There is no crime,' Exeter urged Robinson, 'but decided resistance, to be followed by any who fear God.'[18] Despite this exhortation, Robinson did not commit himself to any faction.

Through the spring of 1839, John Robinson walked a political tightrope between the whigs and the tories. He was tempted to 'cut Normanby and bring the Duke of Wellington into fashion,' but he hesitated to align himself against the government. His old ally, Wilmot Horton, even acted as an intermediary between Robinson and Durham. The chief justice was surprised to find that Durham 'spoke in most handsome terms of me' and even talked of Robinson becoming a great figure in British politics, if only he would 'not oppose ... what was necessary.' 'The scoundrel,' retorted Robinson; 'I shall continue to work with all my heart on the right side.'[19] In a lengthy report to Lord Normanby, Robinson defined what he meant by the 'right side.'

If Durham's plans for French Canada were somewhat harsh, Robinson's were positively draconian.[20] The cornerstone of Robinson's plan was the incorporation of Montreal and the north bank of the Ottawa River into Upper Canada. The annexation of Montreal would give Upper Canada an ocean port, thereby guaranteeing the necessary taxes to support a public-works program in the interior. The chief justice explained his strategy to Strachan: 'If Upper Canada were to press strenuously for extending her limits to Montreal, & to shew no inclination to a Union, I should expect to find the Gov't come to that conclusion.'[21] The annexation idea had strong support in provincial conservative circles. In June 1838 Robert Baldwin Sullivan had written a critique of the union in which he proposed joining Montreal to the upper province. However strongly that idea might have appealed to Upper Canadians, it was lost without an influential British backer (such as Ellice) to present it to the Cabinet.

In addition to annexing Montreal to Upper Canada, Robinson also suggested that the Gaspé be annexed to new Brunswick. The truncated remains of Lower Canada were to be ruled by a non-elective council whose debates were to be conducted in English. French was to be phased out of the government and the courts, and English schools were to be established in every parish. The acts of the executive council were to be promulgated only in English and the French code civil was to be abolished. It was clear that any attempt to crush the French-Canadian nation would necessarily have entailed bloodshed and expense, something the Melbourne government was hoping to avoid.

If Robinson's plans for the annexation of Montreal gathered some support from the 'ultras' of British politics, there is no record of his scheme being seriously considered by the Cabinet. Instead, during March 1838, the Cabinet discussed Durham's report, Ellice's scheme, and Robinson's critique without making plans based on any of them. Two factions emerged in Cabinet: one, headed by Lord John Russell, favoured some kind of union; Lord Howick's faction wished to delay the question by establishing a commission to negotiate with the Canadians, a time-consuming undertaking. Eventually, the balance shifted in favour of Russell, who moved to the fore as the government's architect of provincial union. Russell's Canada Bill of 1839 was strongly influenced by Sir Charles Grey's scheme of 1836 to divide all the Canadas into five administrative units under one general assembly.[22]

Debate on Russell's Canada Bill was postponed while the government tried to gain approval for its Jamaica Bill. On 7 May Melbourne's government was defeated and, in an amazing turn of events, Sir Robert Peel hastened to form a government. Robinson's association with the tories would now bear fruit, and Durham's report and Russell's union bill could be consigned to the oblivion they merited. But Queen Victoria was not amused with the company of the tory ladies, and she asked Lord Melbourne to form another ministry. The notorious 'bedchamber crisis' defeated Peel's efforts, the Melbourne government was returned to office, and the Canada Bill was again put on the order paper.

With the Canada question left in suspense, it was not possible for Robinson to leave London. Emma and the children had remained in rural Cheltenham awaiting word that they were soon to return home. The prolonged separation dismayed Emma, and she chided her husband for abusing his health by remaining in the capital. He recognized the anxiety in Emma's query as to 'what gaities [engaged him] at night' and replied in mock anger that he had had enough of her spying on him with her 'thin nose and Argus eyes.' As long as there remained a chance that he might influence the government, he must tarry in London.[23]

With the British government on the verge of making drastic changes in the government of Upper Canada, conflicting resolutions were emanating from the provincial legislature. The assembly, led by mercantile interests, adopted a resolution calling for a union of the Canadas on terms favourable to the British province. Lieutenant-Governor Arthur, whose views coincided with Robinson's, had unsuccessfully opposed this resolution. Despite his known objections to the union, Robinson received a message from the legislative council in June instructing him to 'represent generally the interests of the province.' Robinson feared that the resolution of the popular assembly would assure the passage of Russell's Canada Bill, and he gloomily advised John Macaulay that

whatever shadow of hope there was, was destroyed when the resolutions of the U.C. Assembly came home approving the Union ... We should have been in a sad plight, depend upon it, if the glorious old Duke had not been still spared to us. Though in opposition he is all powerful.[24]

The government put forward the union proposal with little enthusiasm; it seemed the only way to salvage a bad situation. Few members of the Melbourne Cabinet thought that the union would solve the problems of the Canadas. However, as politicians before and since have known, in times of crisis the government must be seen to be doing something. Even this weak resolve was destroyed when Sir John Colborne convinced the Cabinet that any further subdivision of the Canadas was impractical. In a private letter to Robinson, Colborne angrily denounced Russell's plan. 'The Durham Republican Government' and the experiment in direct democracy, he insisted, would have a disastrous effect when applied to the French Canadians.[25] The Canada Bill was withdrawn pending further amendment. In the meantime an able whig statesman, Charles Poulett Thomson, was dispatched to the Canadas to convince the people of the necessity of union.

In April, Lord Normanby extended Robinson's leave of absence but showed no further interest in consulting him on Canadian affairs. The chief justice discussed with Arthur on the possibility of his remaining in England until the following spring. At that time, the Canada debate was sure to resume and, he reasoned,

with the Duke of Well[in]gton, Sir Robt. Peel, Ld. Stanley ... & many others, I can communicate freely on the most agreeable terms, & if the time is at hand when our destiny shall be in the hands of such men I believe I might be most useful – but I have no more to say on this point.[26]

Robinson realized that his future schemes would be based on a tory ascendancy, and he would just have to be patient until that ascendancy became a fact.

The chief justice passed a quiet English summer, interrupted only by the arrival of Archdeacon Strachan. At last the two men had something to celebrate: Upper Canada was finally to take its place among the other imperial dioceses of the Anglican world, and John Strachan was to be its first bishop. In August Strachan was consecrated at Lambeth Palace. John Robinson was deeply moved to be able to witness the ceremony, and in a wistful entry in his diary he noted, 'We thought little of this at Cornwall in 1806.'[27]

During this politically tranquil summer in the English highlands, the chief justice enjoyed two pleasures usually denied him in Upper Canada – rest and the company of his family. In the autumn, the Robinsons adjourned to Paris for six weeks and returned to England in the closing months of 1839. Although his health appeared to have improved, Robinson requested an extension of his leave of absence until the following spring, to ensure his recovery and because 'in the present very peculiar juncture as respects Canada I may not improbably be of greater service to the Colony by being in England than I could be otherwise.'[28] Normanby quickly assented to Robinson's continued presence, but James Stephen added certain conditions to the extension. The under-secretary stipulated that Robinson must be out of Britain by 1 March, before the resumption of the Canada debate. This cheap Yankee trick, Robinson angrily wrote to Arthur, was a whig device designed to 'remove me from England, before the fate of Canada is to be finally discussed & settled.'[29]

Four miles outside London, in a quiet cottage in Bridgefield, Wandsworth, the Robinson family passed the autumn of 1839. Away from the anxieties of political life, Robinson could reflect on the intrigues of the previous months. Lord Normanby had been replaced as colonial secretary by the architect of the latest union plan, Lord John Russell. Robinson considered Russell to be a 'superior man,' honest, firm in purpose, but unfortunately deeply committed to union. The erosion of official opposition to union depressed the chief justice. During that bleak English October he again lapsed into melancholy. He told his sister, Sarah Boulton, that he regretted that he had ever bothered to take part in public life.[30] Then his depression suddenly passed as he realized the course he must take: the time had arrived when he must strike out in defence of his principles.

At Bridgefield cottage, Robinson began a detailed examination of the new Canada Bill. His crusading, loyalist spirit was aroused: 'Nevertheless it is not the less our duty to struggle as hard as we can for whatever we think to be right.' Through November and December 1839 Robinson concentrated on writing a detailed attack on the government's colonial policy – an injudicious step, perhaps, for a chief justice to take, but in view of the government's obstinacy it was 'the only means by which anyone in these times can hope to act with effect.'[31] For John Robinson, who abhorred opposition and factionalism in politics, the time had come when revolt was justified. As he had been careful to note during the trial of Lount and Mathews, Englishmen are not slaves and they have the right to rise up against a real tyranny: 'I cannot otherwise satisfy my own feelings of duty to the Country I belong to.'[32]

The result of Robinson's efforts was *Canada and the Canada Bill*. A political broadside and far more, it embodied the loyalist principles on which Upper Canada was founded and which still motivated many of its leading men. The preface to the broadside was a letter to the colonial secretary in which Robinson explained that he was now appealing to the public in a final attempt to halt this disastrous union. Surely it had been obvious, he argued, that the self-reliant United States would break away from Britain, leaving her only a few colonies on the Atlantic and the St Lawrence. This separation was not a disaster but a blessing which left virgin territory to be settled for the Crown. There was no need to fear that the new colonies would ever wish to throw off the imperial yoke, since they were 'large enough to maintain a population sufficient, with the aid of Great Britain to defend them; ... they are not so situated as to admit of their combining to throw off the dominion of the mother country.'[33] Robinson's rosy perception of the past did bear some resemblance to reality. He hoped to prove to the English public that the separation of the colonies was not inevitable and that, given the proper conditions, the imperial connection could endure indefinitely.

One of those conditions was to put an end to the absurd notion of the rights of a French-Canadian nation in British America. Lower Canadians were content to be 'not greater men than their fathers' and were destined to be ruled by the more aggressive English.[34] Robinson proposed to assimilate the French Canadians by educating their children in English, by establishing English courts, and by gradually converting them to English ways, 'and then, when Lower Canada has been thus made an English colony, [restoring] to it the English constitution.' Robinson assumed that the metamorphosis of French Canadians into Protestant Englishmen coud be accomplished by way of legislative fiat. This assumption defied both logic and practicality. The French Canadians were a distinct national and cultural group within British America. They could only be made into an 'English colony' by way of genocide or mass deportation; neither of these alternatives was acceptable to the British government.

The union project was being consistently put forward as a solution to the intransigence of the French Canadians, without any hint as to how the union would make them more tractable. Robinson, in a lengthy critique of the proposed union, accurately noted its several major defects. Simple geography dictated that the enormous land mass of the Canadas should not be under one government. United, the Canadas would form one of the largest and least governable polities in the world. Robinson's alternative to union was to cede to Upper Canada the seaport of Montreal. If this was done, the upper province would be immeasurably strengthened, while the French Canadians would be limited to their rural hinterlands. Commercial traffic moving down the St Lawrence could come directly to Upper Canada. Montreal would serve the midwestern heartland and thereby become British America's New York.

It is fascinating to speculate on the possible outcome of Montreal's annexation. Without a great commercial centre, the French Canadian nation would have been left to an agricultural existence outside the mainstream of North American life. The loss of Montreal would have exacerbated the French Canadian hatred of Britain, and might have led to a determined separatist movement in the nineteenth century. But the annexation of Montreal was never considered by the British government, which had resolved to impose some form of union on the provinces. Robinson warned prophetically that union would only result in 'a long and jealous contest,' and keep alive 'feelings of animosity which might otherwise subside.'[35]

While Robinson devoted most of his efforts to warning of the perilous effects of union, other parts of the proposed bill also merited condemnation. Russell proposed to curb the legislative council by limiting the tenure of the members to eight years and by seeing that their appointments came from the local government and not from the Crown. To Robinson, these proposals threatened the fundamental rationale of the council as the only 'authority in the state which could dare do right, uninfluenced by the fear of offending any power or party.'[36] The council was the only body where men of family, education, and loyalty could influence the rude intrusions of the assembly. Only in the council could gentlemen place honour and duty ahead of their political fortunes.

Robinson's defence of the gentry went beyond the mere protection of their prerogatives. Espousing Blackstone's theory that 'a body of nobility' was essential to 'support the rights of both Crown and People, by forming a barrier to withstand the encroachments of both,'[37] he praised the council for protecting the province from a 'rash and unwise popular body.'[38] An elected council would mean the end of the gentry as an effective political force and would result in the government being subjected to the anarchic passions of the popular assembly.

Canada and the Canada Bill did not contain a defence of the established Church; Robinson only commented in passing that 'religion is the only secure basis on which civil authority can rest.'[39] The chief justice presumed that the British government understood the importance of the established Anglican church as the primary civilizing force in Upper Canada. It went without saying that such an institution must be fortified at every step.

Reactionary, anti-democratic, anti-French Canadian, *Canada and the Canada Bill* was also a testament to the loyalists' rejection of the American egalitarian society and a reversion to the whig principles of order and balance. In the loyalist tradition, all men were not created equal and authority did not flow from the sovereign people. The thoughts of Edmund Burke permeated *Canada and the Canada Bill*; Robinson, like Burke, was certain that 'there is no nation without an aristocracy.' Canada must be shielded from the levelling influences of the United States; this could only be done by fostering the élitist society, the established Church, and the balanced government of Crown, gentry, and people. Robinson's concept of good government was derived from the Glorious Revolution of 1688 and the limited monarchy that had emerged from it.[40] Why should Canada be denied the benefits of that form of government? After all, the limited monarchy persisted in Britain. George III had read Blackstone's *Commentaries*, and he believed it to be his prerogative to favour whichever party he chose. William IV chose Lord Melbourne to head the whig ministry when he was only one of several rivals.[41] As late as 1895, the British government was 'the last government in the Western world to possess all the attributes of aristocracy in working condition.'[42] If the government of Britain was still a balance between elected and hereditary rules, why should this balance be denied to the colonies?

Upper Canada was continually exposed to the democratic and egalitarian practices of the United States. In addition, the voting laws enabled small property owners to participate in elections. As a result, parties and leaders could compete to control the electorate. Very much in contrast to the autocratic governments in the Spanish and French empires and even in Britain itself, the Upper Canadian government reacted to the opinions of its electors, which included most of the adult male population.[43] *Canada and the Canada Bill*, a loyalist testament to the struggle to preserve the traditional form of British colonial government in North America, was a futile effort. John Robinson now found himself living in a world in which the principles of Edmund Burke were about to be discarded in favour of those of Thomas Jefferson.

Canada and the Canada Bill was published in January 1840, and was well received in tory circles. The *Times* felt that Robinson had assembled 'a larger stock of useful and authentic information in regard to the present position, wants, and prospects of [Upper Canada] than any other production on the same subject we have happened to meet with.'[44] By resorting to publication, Robinson acknowledged that he had no influence with the government. The book was an admission of failure; it came too late to assist those who sympathized with Robinson, and it convinced those who disliked him that he must be removed from the scene as soon as possible. In a private letter to Colborne, Sir George Arthur wrote that

[Robinson's] Pamphlet unfortunately came out too late – It was too pointedly against the Govt. measure from the Pen of an officer who was, by favour, enjoying a long leave of absence. I wish it had appeared earlier as an answer to Lord Durham's report – However I am very certain no man living intends better or is more honest in all his purposes.[45]

Arthur's immediate superior, Governor Poulett Thomson, was less charitable in his assessment. He considered the book to be 'wordy, inelegant, and very illogical.' Thomson was forewarned by Russell that Chief Justice Robinson was entirely 'in the hands of the Tories, Lyndhurst & Co.'[46]

While Robinson was writing his testament, events in Upper Canada had made union all but inevitable. In Upper Canada, Thomson, who had established a temporary residence at Beverley House, was entertaining local dignitaries and convincing them of the need for union. Beverley House took on an air of official elegance, with uniformed sentries and frequent state dinner parties. In order to cope with the entertainment, Thomson had another kitchen added; one pundit thought that it was this kitchen which was 'auxiliary, indirectly in getting the Union measure through the Upper Canadian Parliament.'[47] Robinson was not particularly pleased to have his 'radical tenant' using his beloved home as a base of operations in the campaign to coerce the provinces into agreeing to the union. Robinson wrote to his sister, 'You have abominable doings in Toronto all eminating [sic] from my *own* house. – I trust the pollution is over.'[48] Thomson used his three months in Toronto to effect substantial political changes in the province. Soon after his arrival, Thomson met with Attorney-General Hagerman, the leader of the government in the assembly. Thomson suggested to him that since the British government was determined to reunite the provinces, he should co-operate in having the plan approved in the assembly. During their conversation, Thomson mentioned that he would expect all Crown officers to support the union. Before leaving Britain Thomson had received instructions from Russell stating that henceforth all colonial department heads were to be discharged whenever 'public policy' deemed it expedient. Thomson's meaning was clear. If Hagerman did not choose to support the union project, his career as attorney-general was in serious jeopardy. Proudly, Hagerman reported to the chief justice that he had told Thomson of his opposition to the union and his determination to vote against it.[49]

Nevertheless, Thomson was an adroit politician; he began to swing the support of various factions behind the idea of union. Reformers were pleased with his hints that the government would work with and not against the assembly. His most telling argument was the promise that Britain would help the province out of its financial difficulties. The possibility of relief from the enormous public debt was leading a grudging majority of the assembly to accept the union. Robinson's distance from these events was now a liability, and he found himself helpless to influence opinions at home. While opposition to union was decreasing in Canada, Arthur lamented to Robinson that his absence was 'universally regretted by the Constitutional Party.'[50] In desperation Robinson wrote to his brother, William, giving him instructions on how to carry on the fight. He urged William to have the assembly debate the annexation of Montreal so that attention would be diverted from the union.[51] But on 19 December 1839 the assembly voted forty-seven to six in favour of union. So effective was Thomson's campaign – especially his promise to erase Upper Canada's debts – that even Hagerman voted with the government. A week later, the legislative council added its support to the measure. John Macaulay, now the inspector-general of Upper Canada and a councillor, agreed with the chief justice that union would be disastrous. But when the vote came in the council, Macaulay felt bound to support the proposal because 'the measure was one deliberately adopted by the Queen's Ministers.'[52]

While his support was crumbling at home, Robinson had earned the confidence of a formidable ally. At Christmastime he had been invited to the Duke of Wellington's country estate, Strathfield Saye. With boyish glee he reported to his sister that he was writing to her from the duke's very residence, using 'his illustrious pen and ink.' With tongue-in-cheek modesty he added, 'Don't talk [in Toronto] of my visit to my noble old host – for I don't like to appear what I really am – very vain of it.'[53] At the festivities Robinson again met with Sir John Colborne, now Lord Seaton, and an animated young writer called 'Boz' who was later to be better known by his proper name, Charles Dickens. The Duke of Wellington, who agreed with Robinson that the proposed union would be disastrous, pledged his support to halt the measure.

As the time for the debate of the new Canada Bill approached, the whigs marshalled their strength and looked for avenues of attack against their opponents. For one thing, they could certainly dispense with the unasked-for comments of a certain Canadian judge. The *Spectator* named Robinson and wondered why his continued presence was tolerated in London.[54] Questions were asked in Parliament as to why the chief justice remained away from his post for such a protracted period. Russell replied lamely that he had intimated to the chief justice that the time had indeed arrived when he should resume his official duties.[55] In March 1840 Russell told Robinson that he was thought to be in league with Lord Lyndhurst against the government. Robinson replied that Lyndhurst was one of his oldest English friends, and his own political stance was open to public scrutiny in *Canada and the Canada Bill*. After this, the conversation between the two men became more convivial and the colonial secretary discussed generally the measures the government intended to introduce. Robinson thanked Russell for consulting him and repeated his objections to the government's plans. The two men parted on terms of mutual respect.[56]

There was no need for the whigs to harry the chief justice from the mother country, for he had already made arrangements to return to Toronto in early April. Robinson was reconciled to the fact that the government would proceed with the union measure, but he still hoped that the duke's opposition might stall their plans in the House of Lords. On the day before he left England, Robinson paid a farewell call on the Iron Duke. In an attempt to reassure Robinson of his continued support, the duke told him, 'Whenever that question [of the union of the Canadas] comes on; you may depend upon this, I'll say what I think, if the Devil stands in the door.'[57]

The Duke's spirited arguments against the Canada Bill were among his final major addresses in the House of Lords. His exertions sapped his strength but failed to halt the union. The opposition cited Chief Justice Robinson as 'an authority whose opinions he was sure would be received with deference and respect on both sides of the House.'[58] Understandably enough, the government paid no heed to his opinions, and though William Gladstone lauded Robinson as 'a man of long experience, of resolute character,' *Canada and the Canada Bill* was dismissed as merely 'a long series of alternatives, out of which he was unable to choose any one as best.'[59]

The new Canada Bill survived in both the Commons and the Lords and became law. For the first time in his life, John Robinson failed to complete successfully a diplomatic mission. He had recognized 1839 as the watershed year that would see either the perpetuation of the old order or the beginning of a new system. Under Thomson's guidance the French and English nations were united, and a new political order was emerging in the Canadas. Events following the union were to prove the accuracy of Robinson's warnings. The governor would gradually place greater responsibility on elected officials at the expense of the gentry. A united legislature was a cumbersome and impractical vehicle for governing such vast and culturally distinct areas. A later historian wrote of the situation in Canada in 1856:

Behind the problem lay the divergent aims and desires of the two cultural communities bound within one structure of government; and aside from shared interest in material development, they seem to have found few common aims.[60]

Of immediate consequence to the chief justice was the emasculation of the legislative council. Although the chamber still existed, it was now a small, powerless addendum to the legislature. Prior to 1839, the gentry had used the council as their personal forum for defending their prerogatives. After the union, the Colonial Office came to rely on the opinions of the representative body, all but ignoring the former élites. Robinson's efforts in 1839 had failed, and his failure led to the end of the institutions he had cherished.

Robinson was bitter that his advice had not been heeded by the British government. The Cabinet had acted in so reckless a manner that Robinson began to question its ability to govern Canada. The colonial secretary was 'unable to bestow an hour – or a thought on Canadian matters'; this clearly proved 'the utter inadequacy of the system as applied to the colonies.'[61] The idealistic colonial of 1815, infatuated with all things English, had become a pragmatic Canadian statesman. But his disillusionment had more to do with the present occupants of Downing Street than with the essential form of government. John Beverley Robinson probably would have shared the imperial ardour of the late Victorians. But the erratic course being followed by Britain in 1840 finally instilled some doubts in Robinson as to the permanency of the colonial system.

The chief justice could hardly anticipate a hero's welcome on his return to Toronto. The reform press had already condemned his activities in the mother country and castigated him for being 'occupied in a manner by no means calculated to benefit the country.'[62] Robinson must have been surprised when, a few days after his return, a public reception was held in his honour. Hundreds of Torontonians attended the ceremony at which he was formally thanked for his efforts in 'calling the attention of the British government to some of the defective principles contained in that [union] measure.'[63] The chief justice was deeply affected by this patriotic welcome; however, he replied noncommittally that 'the best course is to strengthen, by all means, our connexion with that Great Empire.' To the *British Colonist*, Robinson's welcome was a 'staged affair' and his reply an injudicious attempt at political comment. Robinson's partisans defended him in the *Patriot*, stating that he had been right to oppose any surrender to 'democratic influences' and that his reply was completely non-partisan.[64]

This quick defence and his warm reception indicated the esteem in which Robinson was held by the community. He was the first Upper Canadian to play a significant role in imperial affairs, and his stature was far greater than that of a mere judge. To the loyalists and British immigrants, he was the embodiment of the loyalist tradition and their insurance that the British connection would be maintained in the new Province of Canada. Even to some reformers he was a symbol of simpler times and order in society. As one observer noted, 'Men no longer remember the ardent politician and skirmishes at elections. They only [recollect] the upright judge and his consistent, laborious life.'[65] The newspaper sniping proved that he could still generate controversy, and memories of the alien debates were not completely forgotten; but the rancour generated by the attorney-general was being replaced by reverence for the chief justice.

15

Lord Chief Justice

During the chief justice's prolonged absence from Upper Canada the spirit of reform underwent a remarkable revival. With the benevolent assistance of the governor, the reformers regained much of their respectability. An incident occurred shortly after Robinson's return that confirmed this turnabout.

Justice Jones resigned the speakership of the legislative council on the understanding that Robinson was to resume the office. Governor Thomson thought otherwise; in his opinion there was no need to appoint a new Speaker since the old legislative council of Upper Canada would cease to exist in a few months. Moreover, he was convinced that the chief justice had connived against his government and that he was 'the concentration and essence of the Family Compact in the Provinces.'[1] It was clear that Robinson would never receive any office or mark of favour from a whig administration.

Arthur briefed Robinson on the changed political complexion of the province. He informed Robinson that 'most injudiciously & improperly' the governor had refused to reappoint Robinson to the speakership. There was little to be done about this, for the colonial office supported Thomson; Robinson was warned that the denial of office was 'pretty good evidence of the party that is to be put down.'[2]

Relations between the governor and the chief justice were worsened by an incident that took place at the Queenston Banquet in July 1840. A monument to General Brock had recently been destroyed by vandals, and

Robinson had been called on to chair a banquet of government and commercial figures who had pledged to rebuild it. In proposing the health of the governor, Robinson was rumoured to have made slanderous comments on his character. Robinson denied saying anything improper, and the record of the proceedings gives no hint of untoward comments. But the rumour that Robinson had publicly insulted Thomson was easily believed, and Thomson acidly remarked to Arthur, 'your chief justice is reported to have had a cut at me at the Queenston dinner, but I will pay him off, he may depend upon it.'[3] To John Robinson there was no surer barometer of his loss of standing than to discover that not only did he have no influence with the governor but that he was actively disliked by the Crown's representative.

The issue of the speakership so strained relations between Robinson and the governor that they met only briefly in Kingston, the new capital of the united Canadas. The meeting was courteous but the conversation was trivial, and the closest the dinner talk came to politics was a discussion of Lower Canadian affairs. Still, this exchange of ideas was more agreeable than might have been expected, and Thomson – now Lord Sydenham – asked Robinson to call on him before leaving Kingston. They were never to meet again. In the autumn of 1841, Sydenham suffered a severe injury in a fall from a horse and died a few days later. Robinson was in Kingston during Sydenham's final moments and was called on to administer the oath of office to the new governor, Sir Charles Bagot.

In the post-Sydenham period many of Robinson's fears concerning the union became reality. Bagot hoped to govern through Sydenham's coalition ministry, but when confronted with a determined majority of English and French Canadian reformers he was compelled to rely on the reformers. Party politics – Robinson's dread 'factionalism' – had established itself as the natural outcome of the popular representative system. Even the new tory leader, William Henry Draper, supported these changes. In 1836 Robinson had persuaded Draper to leave his lucrative law practice and enter politics. The chief justice might have regretted this decision, for Draper trimmed his sails and proved himself to be a very pragmatic tory, receptive to any new scheme so long as it preserved the British connection. In that spirit (and to the disgust of his fellow tories) he had assisted Sydenham in having the union measure approved in Upper Canada. When the reformers gained control of the assembly, Draper did not cling to office but willingly surrendered the government to Baldwin and company. Under Draper's leadership, conservatives would be in office only when they were assured of popular support.

Draper was the forerunner of those moderate tories who would fight another day as a well organized and popularly based conservative party. The other faction, the true successors to Strachan and Robinson, consisted of ultras like Sir Allan MacNab and the 'high tories.' Their anti-democratic and anti-French policies had little support and eventually disappeared from the Canadian political spectrum. Even the prospect of the old tory John Robinson returning as an unofficial adviser to the governor sent a shudder through the political framework. A year after the arrival of a new governor, Sir Charles Metcalfe, it was rumoured that Chief Justice Robinson had dined with him on several occasions and had influenced his choices for the ministry. Under the heading 'Extraordinary Disclosure' the *Globe* revealed that Ogle R. Gowan, the provincial Orange leader, and the chief justice had dined with and sought to influence Metcalfe.[4] Robinson did send the governor a copy of *Canada and the Canada Bill* along with a statement of his opinion that union remained the greatest error in recent colonial policy.[5] Metcalfe sent a sympathetic reply and agreed that there was 'something rotten in the constitution.'[6] It is unlikely, however, that Robinson influenced Metcalfe's already arch-conservative views.

One result of the union was the end of Toronto's status as a capital city. Nevertheless, the city's position as a focus for trade from the Canadian interior was becoming apparent. A famous lakeboat captain, Hugh Richardson, had established a ship-building company in Niagara in 1831. Richardson had occasionally turned to the chief justice for advice and financial support, and in gratitude named one of his finest vessels, a four-hundred-ton ice-breaker, the *Chief Justice Robinson*. This steamer now made winter travel possible between Toronto and other provincial centres.

The city was growing more cosmopolitan. When Charles Dickens visited Toronto to deliver a series of readings, he was welcomed by the chief justice, who entertained the celebrated novelist at a society dinner at Beverley House. But Toronto's frontier past was still showing: the local Methodists, protesting Dickens' visit, decried the vice of novel reading. Dickens himself observed that 'the wild and rabid Toryism of Toronto is, I speak seriously *appalling*.'[7]

The chief justice's fortunes advanced along with the city's. In 1845 it was reported that his salary was the highest in the province next to that of the governor himself.[8] In 1846 the united assembly issued a new civil list to adjust government salaries, and the chief justice became a primary target. Robinson was denied the Speaker's salary, and his stipend as chief justice was reduced from £1,666 to £1,250. Although British colonial officials did not sanction the cuts, saying, 'it has always been admitted, that considering the onerous duties these judges have to perform, they were not over remunerated,'[9] the new civil list was given royal assent. The reduction in salary, while most unwelcome, did not cause Robinson any discomfort; he possessed considerable capital and lands, and donated portions of both to his many charities.

The chief justice's land investments were changing the face of Toronto. After selling six acres to the Law Society for Osgoode Hall and another strip along the west side of University Avenue, Robinson was left with a large area to the west of Bay Street. Immediately to the east of his holdings, the Macaulay family had developed a working-class residential district. In 1838 Robinson discharged the mortgage on his park lot; during the 1840s, he sold off individual lots with twenty-foot frontages. Even though Robinson's salary had been arbitrarily reduced, the income from his land sales must have made him one of the wealthiest of Torontonians.[10]

The chief justice's continuing joy was the pleasure of seeing his sons and daughters approach adulthood. Mornings at the Robinson household still began with prayers in which eight precocious adolescents were required to participate. The children were supervised by Emma Robinson, who retained 'much of the great beauty of her youth'[11] and whose charming personality still made Beverley House a social centre. The Robinsons held several balls to enliven Toronto's long winter nights, and at these parties the band of the local garrison could usually be prevailed on to provide the necessary quadrilles. Larratt Smith, an articling clerk, reported that at these soirées Emma Robinson acted as a matchmaker, introducing the young men to the daughters of the gentry.[12] With four unmarried daughters, Emma accepted these responsibilities with all requisite seriousness.

Lukin, the eldest son, followed his father's example and joined the legal profession. Although he established a modest practice, he never achieved renown as an advocate. John Beverley Robinson Jr was made of more spirited stuff. Delivering diplomatic messages to Washington during the Rebellion had given him a taste for the adventurous life. He too undertook a legal career, but was not content to remain in his father's household. One evening in 1845 he arrived home drunk; after an exchange of words with his father, he abandoned Toronto and joined his Uncle William in Simcoe, where William had founded a successful fur-trading business. Unlike his father, young Robinson enjoyed the rough-and-tumble of politics, and went on to become mayor of Toronto and eventually lieutenant-governor of Ontario.

The children were maturing and would soon be ready for marriage. It was inevitable that the patriarchs of Canada West should seek to solidify their own relationships through their sons and daughters. The young people did not necessarily object, for most of their lives had been spent around their fathers' associates and their families. Augusta Anne, the first Robinson girl to marry, was wed to James McGill Strachan in 1844; the families of the bishop and the chief justice were now joined by blood as well as by ambition. The happiest day in the Robinson household occurred in April 1846, when Louisa and Emily Robinson were both married in St James Cathedral – Emily to Capt. Henry Lefroi and Louisa to George W. Allan. The chief justice and his wife returned from the ceremony, and were surprised to find a portrait of their three married daughters hanging in the drawing room. Executed by the early Canadian painter George Berthon, this study of the Robinson girls with their rosy complexions and dangling curls is a classic portrayal of early Victorian femininity.

Many of John Robinson's old colleagues had long since decided, like him, to live out the remainder of their lives away from the political struggle. The 'enlightened' Christopher Hagerman who had for some years been a judge of King's Bench, died in May 1847. A few weeks later the two families were joined when John Beverley Robinson Jr married Mary Jane Hagerman. Colonel Talbot, another friend of the chief justice, was nearing the end of his career as lord of the Talbot settlement. The colonel appeared regularly at Beverley House, and when Robinson was on the southern circuit he often stopped at Port Talbot and stayed with the Lake Erie baron.

The struggles during the 1840s to preserve the Anglican establishment against the encroachments of secularism had drawn the chief justice and Bishop Strachan together. While they did not always agree on the most effective policies, each man used the other as an audience for his strategies to preserve the Church lands and the university. This dedication to purpose produced a warm familiarity. Writing to Robinson on the sabbath, Strachan remarked 'I believe one may write to a Wife or a Son and as I consider you the latter I am absolved.'[13]

Robinson's oldest and closest friend, John Macaulay, was still struggling to obtain a permanent position with the government. The success that had come so easily to John Robinson eluded his friend. When the reform party triumphed and seized control of patronage in 1842,

Macaulay was dismissed from the office of inspector-general. Robinson consoled his old friend, saying that 'there could scarcely be conceived a case of more direct & palpable & wanton injustice'; he assisted Macaulay in drafting a petition of protest to the Colonial Office.[14] Reform control of the government and patronage was a serious problem; the Crown's authority in Canada now rested upon a 'broken reed.' Robinson lamented that 'all scruples seem to have vanished in the conduct of public affairs ...' and 'character – services – pledges ...'[15] were no longer values treasured by the government.

Still, there was hope that the young generation could keep alive the dreams of New Albion. The Robinson sons were being prepared for university, and it was hoped that a proper Anglican education would later assist them in defending the British Crown. However, ever since Sir John Colborne steered the course of public education into the primary and secondary levels, the Anglicans of Upper Canada had been unable to put their Royal charter into effect by erecting a University. Finally, in 1843, the Anglican university, King's College, was opened and Chief Justice Robinson was called to speak at its dedication.

The Anglicans did not enjoy their victory for long. In 1849 the Baldwin-LaFontaine ministry amended the University Act to secularize King's College. All religious duties were abolished, and the name was changed to the University of Toronto. Robinson raged to Bishop Strachan, 'Can it be possible that the Government will insist upon it that the members of the Church of England shall have nothing but an accursed system of collegiate education even though they are willing to devote their own means to the establishment of a university!'[16] Strachan urged that they work together to create a privately funded Anglican college of divinity. Robinson disagreed; in his opinion, all education should be permeated with religious thought; Strachan's divinity college would not halt the disastrous momentum toward secularism.[17]

Nevertheless, Bishop Strachan determined to go to England to get the authority to erect a new religious college. Before setting up this institution, Strachan wished to have a royal charter. To that end, he asked Robinson to prepare a bill incorporating the college provincially.[18] Robinson had a petition in favour of the college circulated among the legislature's members and, to his astonishment, it gained considerable support, including the endorsement of Robert Baldwin. While Robinson succeeded in the province, Strachan encountered resistance in England. The colonial secretary, Lord Grey, feared that by granting Strachan his charter he would be antagonizing the Canadian government. The Canadian governor, Lord Elgin, suggested that Strachan be granted a limited charter which would restrict the power to grant divinity degrees to his own denomination. Robinson counselled the Bishop to accept the compromise. 'As to degrees,' Robinson advised Strachan, 'I am disposed to care but little for them & to trust to obtaining in better times an address to the Gov'n to grant a Royal Charter & in the meantime to go on without degrees.'[19] In 1851, the new Anglican university, Trinity College, was founded and John Robinson became its first chancellor.

Though Robinson never abandoned his support of the Church of England as the state church of Canada West, he did not doubt the legitimacy of other faiths. In 1842, Robinson came under criticism for having donated land at Holland Landing for a Methodist chapel. He replied that this land had belonged to his brother, Peter, and had been promised to the residents as a place for their church. The future strength of Canada could only be assured by supporting Christianity in whatever form it appeared:

In travelling through the rural portions of Lower Canada, the most agreeable objects in the landscape, to my eye, were the numerous parish Churches, although they were Roman Catholic; and if Providence had cast my lot among a French population, and the question whether they should have had a Church to worship in or not, had been addressed upon my giving a few feet of ground on which to place it, I believe I would have settled the question in the affirmative, not doubting it was serving the cause of religion.

While Robinson could not help but acknowledge the religious diversity of the Canadas, he did not concede that this was necessarily beneficial:

I have that confidence in what I believe to be true – that a dissemination of the rational doctrines, the pure worship, the incomparable liturgy, the just and tolerant spirit of our Church. I do sincerely believe the time will come when those who have separated themselves from her will gladly, and of their own accord return under her shelter.[20]

The chief justice could not bring himself to recognize fully the diverse religious nature of Canada West.

On one more occasion the chief justice attempted to use his influence on behalf of a cause that no longer aroused any popular support. The imperial statute of 1840 forbade the creation of any new clergy reserves and stipulated that most of the income from previous sales was to be divided between the Church of England and the Church of Scotland. This was a major concession to the Anglicans, who obtained 42 percent of the proceeds for a church to which only one-fifth of the population belonged. The major denominations of Upper Canada, the Baptists and Methodists, received only a fraction of the revenues.[21] Strangely, Strachan and Robinson rejected this highly favourable treatment and worked to undermine the act. Robinson wrote to the colonial secretary outlining various practical and moral objections to the compromise.[22] The Canadian Anglicans still had powerful support through the Society for the Propagation of the Gospel, and Bishop Strachan channelled this support through a new clergy corporation, to be called the Church Society.

The chief justice drafted the Church Society's prospectus, chaired its first meeting, and dedicated the society to obtaining a permanent source of funds for the future use of the Church of England. This bold attempt to reinstate an established church was doomed. The outcry of the dissenters against any ecclesiastical establishment made the united Parliament resolve to sell off the remaining clergy reserves as soon as possible. In 1855, the Secularization Act changed all reserves into Crown lands and formally repudiated the concept of government-supported religion. The long campaign to establish the Church of England in Upper Canada had finally ended in failure. Through the Church Society, the bishop and the chief justice had stirred up old animosities, and accomplished nothing for their church. Much to his dismay, the chief justice was forced to recognize that Canada would be a society with no established religion.

During the post-union period, Robinson remained very much in the background of public affairs. His personal correspondence with John Macaulay made it clear that he despaired of government: 'It is wonderful,' he wrote, 'how soon after their removal the Assembly numbers among its members a Papineau, Lesslie, Viger and Lafontaine.' Remembering the events of 1837, he remarked, 'It will be found that they soon will relapse into the old order of things.'[23] Robinson neither understood nor wished to be a part of this new political scene. He was content to remain a symbol of the British connection and devote himself almost entirely to the administration of his court. The courtroom, at least, was not subject to the liberalizing trends that distorted the familiar patterns of colonial government. On the bench, Robinson could apply the ageless principles of the English common law in the certainty that they would never be subject to radical change.

During his remarkable span of thirty-two years on the bench, Chief Justice Robinson involved himself in all major cases to come before the Court of Queen's Bench. In almost all cases, he delivered the judgment of the court. While he had the assistance of capable justices such as James Macaulay, Christopher Hagerman, and Jonas Jones, the chief justice almost invariably wrote the court's decisions. This task required him to perform prodigious amounts of work, and his friends complained that he had little time for anything but the law. Colonel Airey, a friend of Talbot, looked in vain 'for some period when His Honour the Chief Justice of the Province is not to be at some "Sitting" "Term" "Appeal", – either in Chancery-Court of Queen's Bench, King's College, et. cetera, ad infinitum.'[24]

Robinson's commitment to the law resulted in the production of hundreds of detailed judgments. His decisions constitute a formidable commentary on the state of the English common law as applied in Canada in the early nineteenth century. Although it is difficult to discern distinctive patterns in the individual decisions, one theme is constant:

Our adherence to the principles of the English common law is a duty imposed upon us by written law, and is therefore more strongly obligatory than it may be acknowledged to be in the courts of the United States. ... Whatever liberties therefore may have been assumed in foreign countries in departing from principles which are binding upon English courts, we are not allowed to exercise any such discretion.[25]

Even when American precedent was rational and instructive, loyalty, convenience, and, above all, duty made the chief justice defer to the English courts. At least in the law the Chief Justice would be able to preserve the British heritage in the new world.

The first act of Upper Canada's legislature had been to enact the English law in matters of property and civil rights.[26] As a result, centuries of English judicial decisions and statutes provided the early Canadians with a well-tried and comprehensive body of laws. In decision after decision, Robinson referred to English precedent to solve local problems. It was hoped that a complex procedural issue could be solved by an English decision expressly in point. For example, in *The Bank of Montreal v Grover* (1846) the chief justice balanced local custom, which permitted the owner of a promissory note to present the endorser with a notice of non-payment, against English precedent, which held that the notice of non-payment must be specifically stated in the pleadings by the holder. 'I think it is to be regretted that the law has been so settled,' Robinson lamented; however, he could not give a judgment for the holder of the note without 'going against many deliberate decisions of the several courts in England, by which we hold ourselves in general bound.'[27]

English rules were to be applied even when the rationales for the rules did not exist in Canada. The principle in *Flureau* v *Thornhill* that a vendor or property who was unaware of a defect in title was not liable for damages to the purchaser was a common-law rule which resulted from the chaos in English land-title registration. The chief justice accepted this exception to the rule of damages even though Canada had a comprehensive system of land registry that negated any need for it.[28] In Upper Canada, one of the commonest ways of enforcing an obligation was by way of assumpsit; this convoluted action had originally been a tort, but over time had evolved into an equitable way of enforcing contracts. Yet the courts still did not seem to know whether assumpsit was an action in tort or contract. When a question arose as to whether a plaintiff could simply state the amount of his losses in his pleadings rather than refer to a document that detailed the losses, Robinson was forced to rely on English decisions for an answer.[29]

English law at the time reflected the low status of women. In one case, a deserted wife had taken over her husband's farm and leased out part of the land to support herself. When she sued the tenant for trespass, she was forced to sue in her husband's name. Robinson recognized this as correct practice, for a wife in possession of her husband's land did not gain any estate in that land.[30] Even more degrading was the status of a seduced girl. Younger daughters were frequently hired out as serving help, and all too often their masters took sexual advantage of them. The common law looked upon this situation as primarily one of damage to goods. The parents of the ruined girl could sue for civil damages for the loss of their servant.[31] It was no defence to a charge of debauching to plead that one had the 'leave and license' of the woman, for 'the servant cannot give license.'[32] In such cases the law formally recognized the woman as her family's chattel, not as an independent person.[33]

In the early nineteenth century, fidelity to English precedent was especially important because so much of the court's activities centred on the interpretation of points of practice. Rules of pleading required parties to plead a specific issue of law, and if their pleading was defective their claim failed, regardless of its merits. The mere failure of a defendant to write 'by statute' in the margin precluded him from relying on the defence of official capacity.[34] Neither was a plea satisfactory if it made only an 'argumentative denial' of a claim.[35] Both the claim and the reply must cover all the points raised in the allegation. Queen's Bench was consistent in its strict application of the requirements of pleadings; when the governor-general sued as the assignor of a bond originally made to Sir John Colborne, Robinson held that 'although we know that the Governor-General of Canada is now in fact the only Governor of the country which once constituted Upper Canada, yet this should not the less have been stated, in order to make the right apparent.'[36]

In this restrictive atmosphere, it was no surprise that Chief Justice Robinson spent much of his time deciding complex issues of procedure. Inevitably, consistency overshadowed justice as an objective of the court. Even an attempt by Chancery Court to interpret corporate contracts in a manner 'intelligible and adapted to the age and country in which we live'[37] was rejected by Robinson in the Court of Error and Appeal. According to the chief justice, English principles prevailed; if a newer, more convenient rule appeared, it would be necessary to wait 'until we can see that the other courts in England take the same course, or until we find that the principle acted upon in that case is confirmed in the house of Lords ...'[38] Creative reasoning was not a trademark of Chief Justice Robinson's court. The strait-jacket of English precedent gave form and substance to Canadian law, but at the same time made it rigid and retrospective.

While Robinson considered it his duty to maintain English law in Upper Canada, he did not believe his judicial obligations required the blind application of precedent to every case. Even though the Upper Canadian legislature had adopted English law, certain exceptions were made; the English bankruptcy and poor laws would not be applied in the province. In the chief justice's opinion, those were not the only exceptions. Robinson felt that many of the adopted laws were meant to remedy stituations peculiar to England. It followed that they were 'either wholly or in a great degree foreign to this colony, have never been attempted to be enforced here, and have never been taken to apply to us.'[39] When asked to give effect to an English statute that had been intended to control the near-epidemic of gin-drinking among the English lower classes, Robinson observed that the act had been passed long before Upper Canada's creation and had no application to any social ills affecting the province. He refused to apply the act, saying, 'The main scope of the statute is for purposes wholly foreign to us.'[40] In another case, the chief justice refused to apply the Bubble Acts on the ground that Upper Canada had its own statutes to control fraudulent banking schemes.[41] Robinson made no attempt to define those classes of laws that were inapplicable to Upper Canada. In these few cases, however, he detailed those situations where the law of England was simply unsuited to British America.

Altering the laws to suit modern conditions was not a function of the courts, and Robinson advised the provincial Legislature to 'mould their own laws and proceedings so as to make the operation of the statute just and convenient.'[42] The united assembly was prepared to do just that. Colonial legislators were far less attached to British precedents than were colonial jurists, and laws could respond to local needs without regard to English procedure. The assembly was already producing a great deal of legislation, and by the 1850s, the chief justice could readily turn to a profusion of provincial statues to remedy disputes. Canadian ministries, for example, even more than American legislatures, participated in creating townships and laying out roads and canals. This type of legislative activity increasingly came to replace imperial statutes as a source of Canadian law. Thus, in 1831, King's Bench only referred to Canadian statutes in one-quarter of the reported cases; the remainder were decided by English statutes or precedents. By 1860, two-thirds of the cases decided by Queen's Bench cited Canadian statutes or precedents in support of judgment.[43]

In his study of the effect of the frontier on American life, Frederick Turner found that the frontiersmen's attitudes toward land and riparian rights created new legal principles. Turner discovered that 'we can study the process by which in a new land social customs form and crystallize into law.'[44] In the English tradition, property rights were granted indirectly from the monarch himself. But in North America, the vast amounts of land available on the prairies caused an alteration in the legal perception of property ownership; land and water rights became mere tradable commodities.

In the Province of Canada the legislature, not the courts, used its authority to pass laws to accommodate frontier conditions. On rare occasions, however, even the courts perceived regional needs that could only be satisfied by applying new principles of law. One such occasion arose in *Dean v McCarty* (1846).[45] A settler was clearing his land by burning a pile of logs when a sudden wind sprang up; the fire quickly ran out of control and destroyed part of a neighbour's fence. The neighbour, who admitted that the settler had acted prudently, sued him on the premise that he should have known that his act could harm the neighbour. Robinson decided that a finding of strict liability was not warranted in this case. Clearing the land was a necessary and normal part of life on the frontier:

It is not very long since this country was altogether a wilderness, as by far the greater part is still. Till the land is cleared, it can produce nothing, and the burning the wood upon the ground is a necessary part of the operation of clearing.[46]

The settler's act was only a part of the 'necessary business of mankind,' and he could not be held liable unless negligence was proven. The chief justice chose not to apply the prevailing doctrine of *sic utere tuo ut alienum non laedas* (use your own property so as not to injure that of another) to the case. That rule granted damages whenever a landowner did some act that resulted in losses to a neighbour. Robinson's decision seems to have run counter to the prevailing common-law precept that an occupier is always responsible for controlling fire on his premises. In North America, the common law served as a hindrance to development by restricting an owner's right to alter his lands. Robinson was (perhaps more than he realized) reflecting decisions of American courts where the *sic utere* rule was being discarded in favour of balancing competing land uses.

While the ruling in *Dean v McCarty* suited Upper Canada, English courts were devising different standards of occupier's liability. In *Rylands v Fletcher* (1868),[48] the House of Lords decided that it was not necessary for an owner to prove that his land had been damaged through his neighbour's negligence. If an owner brought or built something on his land that might injure his neighbour he was deemed to be liable for all the consequences of his act. Canadian lawyers were quick to seize the ruling as a basis for prosecutions on behalf of occupiers. However, when *Rylands v Fletcher* was first brought before Queen's Bench, the court rejected it in favour of *Dean v McCarty*. In *Gillson v The North Grey Railway Co.* (1872), workmen on a railroad burnt the brush they had cleared and in so doing damaged the plaintiff's land. The plaintiff based his case on *Rylands v Fletcher* and denied that he had to show negligence on the part of the railroad. Chief Justice Richards applied the frontier rationale that 'the contractor may use fire to burn log and brush heaps, which is the usual and oftentimes necessary course to pursue in clearing lands in this country. I do not think we are at liberty, sitting here, to overrule the very elaborate judgment of Sir John Robinson in *Dean v McCarthy* [sic].'[49]

Dean v McCarty continued to be applied in Ontario and in Alberta.[50] Yet two factors worked against the frontier rationale in *Dean v McCarty* becoming a unique addition to Canadian precedent. First, decisions of the

House of Lords carried great weight throughout the English-speaking world, and they tended to supersede decisions of local courts. Second, the rationale of *Dean* v *McCarty* became less acceptable as Upper Canada became a settled, cultivated area. The burning of brush was no longer an absolute necessity and there was no reason to exempt this activity from the normal laws of occupier's liability. In 1882 the Ontario Court of Appeal rejected *Dean* v *McCarty*, adopted *Rylands* v *Fletcher*, and reverted to the previous situation whereby 'the common law liability for all damage done exists.'[51]

Robinson's attempt in *Dean* v *McCarty* to erect a local rule suited to Upper Canada must be seen as an aberration by his court. For the most part, Queen's Bench made no adjustments in the law to suit North American conditions. Some scholars doubt whether the Turnerian thesis of frontier influence is even applicable to Canada.[52] Certainly the chief justice considered it to be his first duty to apply English law, not to recognize local customs. Far more representative of his approach to regional needs are his decisions on the question of waste. English precedent decreed that any alteration by a tenant of his estate, even if it increased the value of the property, constituted waste, for which the tenant had to pay damages. In the United States the doctrine meant that tenants could not clear virgin forests, and for the most part u.s. courts had long since dismissed it as inappropriate in North America.[53] Queen's Bench was not so audacious; fifty years after the Americans had repudiated the doctrine of waste, the chief justice upheld the general principle in Upper Canada.[54] Queen's Bench remained a bastion of the status quo.

In one area of the law there were few precedents to bind the court, and Queen's Bench could safely weigh local practice in making its decisions. The commercial law between producers and consumers was still in a state of development, and there was nothing to prevent the court from applying logic and local custom in solving problems. As lawyers, the justices of Queen's Bench had spent years acting for local businessmen. They recognized the uncertainties in the law that inhibited trade, and they acted to erase unreasonable difficulties. In addition to providing consistency, it was the intention of Queen's Bench to bestow legitimacy on prevailing business practices. In construing a contract for the sale of coal, the chief justice concluded that 'when we know what the general usage of trade is in regard to any branch of business, we are to look on the parties as intending to contract with reference to it ...'[56] The chief justice owned farmlands in Peel County and received considerable revenues from his tenants' wheat production.[57] Therefore, when he decided that a labelling of flour was also a warranty of the product, he was attempting to ensure the reliability of all business, including his own: '... the questions presented in such cases are so important to persons engaged in this branch of trade that the ground on which we decide them ought to be clearly understood.'[58]

Increased commercial activity resulted in the greater use of contracts. Consequently, the legal machinery to decide disputes involving these agreements was invoked more and more frequently. P.S. Atiyah found that nineteenth-century judges adopted a laissez-faire attitude toward contracts, and saw them as having essentially a negative function in assisting the parties to 'realize their wills.'[59] The courts did not examine contracts to see if they had been frustrated or if any inequality among the parties had resulted in an unfair contract; such concepts would have been entirely foreign to Robinson's Queen's Bench. The courts existed to regularize business proceedings, not to become involved in them:

It is of consequence that parties should be held to the terms of their contract, or no one would be able to proceed with confidence in executing the works which are now in progress, and which are so important to the community.[60]

Nineteenth-century courts have been condemned for their refusal to look beyond the contract itself, thereby 'ratify[ing] those forms of inequality that the market system produced.'[61] This presumes that courts have some innate ability to sense which contracts are unequal and how they should be rewritten. Robinson consistently refused to rewrite contracts when urged to do so.[62] Queen's Bench confined itself to determining what the parties had agreed to do and to enforcing the agreement for them. In *Reynolds* v *Shutes* (1847), the court limited its role to deciding what the parties had meant, saying that 'the plain intent of the covenant is to be regarded, and not barely its words.'[63] To facilitate commerce it was the duty of the court to give meaning to contracts, but it was outside their ambit to examine the fairness of the bargain.

Commerce in Upper Canada was still in a primitive state, and there was no extensive litigation between corporate bodies. The only significant commercial case of the period occurred when a foreign company sought to enforce an executory obligation in Upper Canada.[64] The chief justice held that the foreign company was not a legal person in the province and therefore could not enforce its claim. Although in the boom years before

1837 sixty corporations had been formed, the courts were not often called upon to make decisions about the relative authority of shareholders and directors.[65]

The use of seals by incorporated bodies was one of the key corporate questions faced by Robinson's court. Where he looked for guidance on this question reveals a great deal about his approach to legal reasoning. By the 1840s, companies were making dozens of contracts daily and it was absurd to think of using a corporate seal for all of these arrangements. American courts were beginning to recognize many contracts that were not under seal. Yet Queen's Bench steadfastly refused to make such an accommodation and instead applied the common-law requirement of seals in all corporate contracts. In *Hamilton* v *The Niagara Harbor and Dock Co.* (1842),[66] the defendant tried to evade its responsibility for the repair of a steam engine by explaining that the repairs were outside their corporate charter and, in any event, the agreement between the dock and the engine owners was not under seal. As a pro-commercialist, Robinson was willing to interpret the objects of the company in a broad fashion. The claim failed, however, because 'the affixing [of] the seal by the proper authority is the only evidence of the assent of the body to the contract.'[67] The plaintiff vainly argued that u.s. courts were no longer strict in requiring seals in such cases. That was all well and good for the United States, but the chief justice would not take any 'liberties' in departing from 'principles which are binding upon English courts.'[68]

The question of corporate seals was not so easily dismissed. In *Blue* v *Gas and Water Company* (1849),[69] Robinson again held that 'the authorities by which we are bound' would not permit the court to issue assumpsit against a company that had entered into a parol agreement not under seal. The seal could only be dispensed with if an actual conveyance of goods had occurred. Justice Macaulay and the majority of the court did not think that the law was settled in this matter. Macaulay looked at the circumstances of the case, which involved a customer who wished to purchase water from a private utility. Surely it would result in the 'utmost inconvenience' to require every customer to enter into a sealed contract; necessity obviated the need for seals in those cases. Finally, in *The Great Western Railway Company* v *The Preston and Berlin Railway Company* (1859),[70] even Robinson recognized that as a matter of practice it was necessary to enforce many executory contracts not under seal. It is interesting to note that Robinson's conversion to the majority's opinion in *Blue* was based on the fact that he could at last safely rely on English precedent in dispensing with seals.[71]

This enduring loyalty to English precedent was also apparent in Robinson's decisions on another matter of commercial law, the enforcement of promissory notes. On many occasions, the parties explained that they were mistaken as to the terms and asked the court to vary the requirements of the note. In one series of cases, Robinson forbade the use of parol evidence to vary existing terms.[72] The court would only hear parol evidence to clarify ambiguous wording. Robinson's strict application of the parol evidence rule has been thought to embody 'an important manifestation of a general unwillingness to make individualized adjustments to agreements that were unfair, or that had gone astray because of mistakes or unexpected circumstances.'[73] On the contrary, the application of the parol evidence rule was proof of the court's intention to ensure the security of notes. If the court was to become a party in adjusting notes, it considered to be unfair, the validity of all notes would be under continual question. In one case, a maker alleged that there was a verbal agreement that the note would not be enforced under certain circumstances. Robinson refused to hear this testimony, and instead concluded that 'such a verbal understanding is inadmissable, otherwise there would be no safety in taking the notes or bonds of parties.'[74]

In commercial matters such as the use of corporate seals and the admissibility of parol evidence, Robinson consistently relied on English precedent. Only where English rules were vague or nonexistent would the chief justice look to local custom. In one case, *The Bank of Montreal* v *De Latre*,[75] Robinson even complimented the u.s. courts for their interpretation of the law relating to bills of exchange. 'The American Courts have generally gone before those in England,' he observed, 'in moulding the principles of common law to suit supposed exigencies.'[76] Yet even in this case, where Robinson found u.s. decisions to be useful, his ultimate decision was based on English precedent. Even on commercial questions, Queen's Bench's authority came from English and not u.s. sources.[77]

From these early decisions emerged the principles that were to assist future judges in interpreting the law. For example, Robinson determined that the court could quash by-laws only where those by-laws were wholly or partially illegal.[78] This rule was applied eighty years later in Ontario, and it remains a principle of municipal law.

In a 1958 case, the Ontario Court of Appeal was faced with a question concerning a Quebec executor who had pleaded in Ontario to a civil suit concerning an estate.[79] The question arose as to whether the Quebec executor had become an executor in Ontario de son tort (literally, 'of his own wrong'; the term refers to a person who, without legal authority, intermeddles so as to make himself liable as an executor). Had he become liable to an Ontario court for the disposition of the estate? The solution was found by applying two of Robinson's decisions, *Haacke* v *Gordon*[80] and *Jessup* v *Simpson*.[81] The lawyer for one claimant argued that those cases stood for the proposition that an executor who pleads in defence of an action thereby becomes an executor de son tort. The executor's counsel maintained that despite Robinson's judgments, 'intermeddling' must be shown before the executor can become liable to a foreign court. In deciding the case, Justice Morden cited Robinson's decisions as an accurate summation of the law in Canada. *Haacke* stood for the proposition that by pleading to a case, an executor became part of it. However, *Jessup* established the fact that a foreign executor can safely deny that he is a party to an action without, by the mere act of denial, becoming joined to the action. Expressing gratitude to its predecessors, the Ontario court based its decision on the analysis supplied by Robinson's court of Queen's Bench.

In their totality, the decisions of Queen's Bench constitute a ready reference for Canadian jurists. By 1854, Chief Justice Robinson had seen the publication of fifteen volumes of Upper Canada Reports, and he observed that they formed the basis for 'estimating and examining the labours of the Court'[82] and were themselves tools to enable future lawyers to interpret Canadian common law.

Many of the decisions reached by Robinson's court continued to be applied long after his court had become a memory. The durability of his decisions reflects how firmly they were based in both logic and local practice. On the other hand, the law of civil litigation changed so dramatically after Robinson's death that the precedents he applied were of little use to succeeding courts. With these early decisions of Queen's Bench, the great continuum of experience dating back to Coke and Blackstone found root in Upper Canada. Through the medium of John Robinson, the common law was and is applied and refined by generations of Canadian judges.

In contrast to Canadian practice, it has been suggested, u.s. courts in the early nineteenth century were engaging in critical re-examinations of the common law. Functional analysis of the rationales behind common-law principles resulted in many precepts being cast aside and newer, more appropriate rules being substituted, and the common law became an instrument for effecting social policies. As Morton Horwitz has observed, 'Especially during the period before the Civil War, the common law performed at least as great a role as legislation in underwriting and channeling economic development.'[83] Important elements of the common law were altered or repudiated in order to facilitate the transition to industrial capitalism, and 'commercial and entrepreneurial interests thus saw the private law shaped to their own interest.'[84]

Competition was the essence of emerging industrial capitalism and, according to Horwitz, the courts played a role in encouraging competition. By denigrating exclusive franchises, encouraging diverse water uses, and discouraging enforcement of the usury laws the courts subsidized this new economic development. Canada likewise wanted to foster its emerging industries, but the approach of Queen's Bench to exclusive franchises, riparian rights, and the usury laws was significantly different from that of the U.S. courts.

In both countries there was extensive construction of dams and mills to irrigate and process crops. Whether water could be penned back for mill use or must be allowed to flow downstream to other users was a vital question. In order to encourage new industries in the United States, watercourse rights were no longer based on 'natural flow' but rather on reasonable use.[85] The premise behind this statement – that before the nineteenth century an idyllic right to natural flow prevailed – is questionable.[86] In an early Upper Canadian case, Justice Sherwood observed that 'a prior occupancy does give a right and property in a current of water to the first occupant.'[87] This was hardly a 'fundamentally new outlook on the question of conflicting rights to property,'[88] but rather a reiteration of existing common law that a sanctioned user of a watercourse could continue to pen back or otherwise use waters to the detriment of his neighbours. On this issue, there does not appear to be a great conflict between Canadian and American decisions, for jurists in both countries looked to the common law for their authority. Even while Robinson admitted that a riparian owner had a 'natural right, of having the water flow in its usual and proper course,'[89] that right could be limited by a pre-existing grant or use.[90] The basis for this reasoning owed more to Blackstone than to any desire to accommodate industry.

American courts chafed under the restrictions on competition inherent in the common law. According to Blackstone, damages could result merely from setting up a new business in competition with an existing firm. One of the earlier forms of American enterprise was the private ferry or highway, established under a government licence. In the landmark *Charles River Bridge* case, the United States Supreme Court held that any bridge of ferry company could compete with an existing licensed servce.[91]

Upper Canadian courts, however, did not see fit to encourage open competition by denigrating Crown franchises. The chief justice agreed with Blackstone that any Crown franchise that permitted ferries was made 'not for the benefit of the Crown, as distinct from the benefit of the public.'[92] Therefore, because the ferry service was quasi-public in nature, an exclusive franchise was presumed,[93] and it would not be proper to permit a competitor to interfere with the grantee's exclusive rights.

On both sides of the St Lawrence usury laws restricted the amount of interest a lender could charge. These laws inhibited the free flow of capital and constituted an interference with competition. In 1808 the Massachusetts Supreme Court effectively negated the usury laws by applying the rule that the original endorser of the note could not testify that the transaction was usurious. Chief Justice Parsons added that 'any rule of law, tending unnecessarily to repress this circulation is therefore against public policy.'[94] Robinson would not apply any rules of evidence to nullify the will of Parliament: 'In determining upon the propriety of granting this amendment, I reject all arguments upon the supposed policy or impolicy of the usury laws; while they are in force, they are to be carried fairly into effect.'[95] Neither did he consider himself at liberty to comment on the public policy of usury laws. Such an expression of judicial restraint would have been looked upon as a quaint anachronism by contemporary American courts, which were busily expanding their function to include the creation as well as the interpretation of legal rules.

In many areas of traditional law, such as riparian rights, Queen's Bench and the American courts both applied the inherited common law. In other areas (usually those related to commercial activities) the Americans led the way in changing the law to suit an expanding economy. John Robinson was content to leave changes in those areas to the duly elected legislatures. Even when he considered statutes to be harsh or unjust, they were to be applied nevertheless.[96] Robinson's fidelity to common-law principles was almost as great. Consistency was the great objective of the law, greater than Robinson's personal view of equity:

If I were thus to set entirely aside one principle so well known, and so long and so constantly acted upon, I know not why I might not as well feel at liberty to disregard every other principle of which I do not approve, and deliver the law, not as I find it to be, but as I think it ought to be.[97]

Such deference to authority is a striking characteristic of Canadian law and in stark contrast to American practice. Under Robinson's influence, the Canadian judiciary, in strict compliance with the British constitution, denied any active role to the courts in effecting social policy. Professor R.C.B. Risk, after an examination of Robinson's judicial career, concluded that

Robinson led the common law courts throughout a long and important period and he was one of the early makers of a tradition that has become dominant among Canadian judges: deference to authority, denial of any significant creative power, and denial of any general attitudes beyond fidelity to statutes and the accumulation of precedent.[98]

While this is an accurate assessment of Robinson's impact on the Canadian judiciary, it should be noted that his 'denial of any significant creative power' was itself derived from his adherence to the loyalist principles of supremacy of Crown and Parliament. If Robinson had only a passing effect on Canadian political life, his judicial career made a significant contribution to the 'deference of authority' apparent in the judiciary. His constant repetition of the duty of judges to apply the law assured the supremacy of the lawmakers and fostered the ideal of Parliament as the only legitimate source of legal change.

A discussion of the effect of Robinson's decisions may tend to obscure the fact that his role as judge was essentially to decide individual disputes between aggrieved parties. He did not expect to create great legal trends out of these distinct cases, and merely fulfilled his duty in interpreting the law. Especially by the late nineteenth century, American jurists were examining scientific theories to arrive at the 'correct' application of the law.[99] Robinson held no such illusions. Law consisted of the rules that the farmer, railroad engineer, and banker applied to their transactions. Just as religion was a part of his daily existence, the law was a facet of life, not a collection of abstract principles.

It is not surprising that after so controversial a career in public life, John Robinson had acquired his share of enemies. Charles Durand, one of the men convicted in the rebellion of 1837, returned to the province in 1844 after being pardoned. Whenever Durand appeared in the courtroom, the chief justice could not forget, even in the interests of justice, that he was facing a convicted traitor. Shortly after his pardon, Durand met the chief justice in the parliamentary library. Robinson looked up, recognized Durand, and spat out, 'are you back again?'[100] According to his detractors, Robinson's political prejudices affected his judicial decisions.

John Rolph was reported to have said that after 1830 'he could not get justice in the court in which this man presided.'[101]

Durand and Rolph were hardly objective observers, and the reported cases reveal a judge who was neither dogmatic nor dictatorial. It was not uncommon for him to remark, for example, 'I cannot say I have not felt difficulty in this case, or that I am wholly free from doubt now.'[102] Humility and a willingness to question one's own judgment are admirable characteristics in any judge. Robinson recognized the human element in law, knew that it was not an exact science, and acknowledged that his judgments reflected his own biases and opinions.

In 1850, Robinson's long years of service on behalf of the Crown were recognized. The statutes of the Order of the Bath were altered to allow its presentation for meritorious civil as well as military service. The governor, Lord Elgin, was eager to present this honour to some worthy Canadian. Although Elgin, the son-in-law of Lord Durham, sympathized with the reform movement, he realized that Robinson's years on the bench could not be overlooked. Besides, Elgin reasoned, '[Robinson] is the head of the old Compact, but a clever man and a perfect Idol with a certain set.'[103] With this less than enthusiastic recommendation, the offer of a knight-hood was made to the chief justice. Robinson replied that his public service 'has in truth been neither very short nor very light,'[104] and that he would accept the honour. Elgin thought that although Robinson's acceptance was 'not remarkable for good taste or modesty'[105] in the circumstances he should certainly receive the knighthood. While he was no longer an active standard-bearer, Robinson remained the symbol of British tradition in Canada, and that 'certain set' would applaud any government that honoured its hero.

Further honours soon followed. Lord Seaton, Robinson's friend and constant correspondent, used his influence to have Robinson admitted as a baronet of the United Kingdom.[106] This imperial honour accorded to Robinson and his family a degree of pretension to aristocracy that, in the chief justice's opinion, the province badly required.

Sir John Beverley Robinson, Bart, was now more than a colonial jurist. To many Canadians he represented their enduring British heritage. To his allies in the mother country he was proof that their beliefs and way of life flourished in far-off Canada. An incident in 1849 indicated that the popular perception of the chief justice was changing. Robinson never bothered to hide his disdain for reform politicians, and when Lord Elgin visited the province, the chief justice made no effort to call on him. Robert

Baldwin was warned that 'when the Chief Justice neglects to do honour to a Governor!! *war is not over* that is clear.' Although Robinson had lost none of his intransigence, a few reformers were finding something admirable in his enduring toryism. A friend of Baldwin's wrote, 'I have just seen the chief justice Robinson charge to the grand jury. I think it is the best thing he has ever written ... [he is] the bone and sinew of the former compact.'[108]

16

'If I Am Right,
Thy Grace Impart'

'This is a strange state now,' Robinson mused to Lord Seaton in 1850; 'Canada has never since 1827 been an easy or a satisfactory colony to govern ... but its natural advantages are rapidly raising it to prosperity.'[1] Robinson dated the beginning of political decline from the Colonial Office's betrayal of the government during the alien debates. Despite this decline, the chief justice had lived to witness Canada's development into one of the most prosperous nations within the British Empire. The vision of New Albion had long since faded, however. Although the population of Canada West was now almost a million, less than 20 percent of the population was of English origin.[2] Pockets of toryism remained, but the reformers dominated most areas of the province. Moreover, radicalism was on the rise and the new Clear Grit party was pressing for elective democratic institutions. The upsurge in radicalism led the chief justice to conjecture in 1850 that the union would soon be dissolved, since 'the radicals are now becoming impatient of the phalanx of Frenchmen that enables the Government to carry what they please – liberal or illiberal.'[3] Even when a liberal–conservative coalition assumed power in 1854, the old Family Compact would have been hard-pressed to identify many true tories in the government. The leader of the new, pragmatic conservatives was John A. Macdonald, attorney-general for Canada West. Macdonald, a follower of William Henry Draper, went so far as to sponsor a bill to secularize the clergy reserves. The protracted struggle to preserve a state endowment for religion had finally ended in the allocation of reserve funds to the municipalities. Canada was indeed in a 'strange state' if a tory leader acknowledged the secular nature of Canadian society.

Robinson had contact with the new tories through his official duties with Macdonald. The attorney-general often queried the chief justice on the propriety of criminal sentences, and even had the temerity to upbraid Robinson for indecisive sentencing reports he received.[4] But Macdonald was thoroughly British, and when he questioned the chief justice on the desirability of second commutations of capital offences, Macdonald rejected the proposal 'lest we might drift by degrees into the American system.'[5]

Perhaps to understand his family's American origins, John Robinson embarked on a tour of the United States in May 1851. On his way through Virginia, he visited William and Mary College and Yorktown, both of which had been part of his father's early life. While on a steamer travelling between Washington and Fredericksburg, he met Conway Robinson, a leading member of the Virginia bar and a distant relation. Through him John Robinson was introduced to the other branches of the Robinson family who still lived in Virginia. 'I found myself at once among friends and connections,' he observed.[6] Robinson returned from Virginia reconciled with his American cousins, even though he continued to abhor their political institutions.

By the 1850s the chief justice had attained the honour and wealth for which he had always striven. It was especially gratifying to him that his third son, Christopher, seemed eager to follow his father's path. In 1850 Christopher made a pilgrimage to England and the Continent before beginning his legal career. Nevertheless, life still had its moments of pain. His daughter Louisa died in 1852 while travelling in Italy. Robinson's religion appears to have comforted him, and the chief justice reminded John Macaulay, who had also lost a daughter, 'God's will must prevail.'[7]

The chief justice himself was beginning to feel the approach of old age. By the mid-1850s he was no longer able to ride, a pastime he had always treasured. He now had to restrict his leisure activities to the reading of history, biography, and, of course, the Bible. Always the consummate advocate, Robinson made notes on the gospels and contrasted the verses on justification by faith. If given the opportunity, he would probably have written a detailed legal analysis of the New Testament. However, time was one commodity no longer in great supply for the old tory. The intense concentration on the cases before him drained his strength. Despite his failing health he was still the most sought-after public orator in Canada West. His address at the foundation of the provincial lunatic asylum in

1846 was one of the most moving speeches ever made in Toronto. Even his portrait, executed by Berthon in 1846 at the request of the Law Society, seemed to embody the eminence of a great man. The portrait, with symbols of the Crown dominating the background, captured Robinson's aristocratic bearing; even the ermine trim on his gown was a tangible sign that British nobility survived in Canada.

Robinson's pretensions already seemed sadly anachronistic, however. How long could an 'age of simplicity' last in a world where 'steamers and railroads are flourishing'?[8] During the Robinson family's vacation in Buffalo in 1837, the chief justice had taken his first train trip from that city to Manchester. The distance of twenty-two miles was crossed in the astounding time of an hour and a half. Robinson reported, 'I liked the whole concern better than I expected after the accounts I had heard of it – but it is a humble specimen of a railroad.'[9] During the 1840s, Upper Canadians still relied on and invested in the canal system; as a result, railroad development lagged far behind that of the United States. When the first extensive railroads were built in the 1850s, the effect on Canada West was dramatic. Iron rails bound the farmlands to seaports, ended the isolation of the interior, and introduced new industries. It was expected that the workers of the province would 'screw up their energies to railroad speed.'[10] Yet railroads could also destroy: crops were set afire by flying cinders, and livestock and, sometimes, people were struck by trains. John Robinson, a man of the eighteenth century, was called on to adjudicate questions involving nineteenth-century technology.

The law's unfamiliarity with the new technology was evident in one of the first reported cases dealing with a railway. The pleadings alleged that the defendant's 'steam carriage' containing 'igneous matter' had ignited some of the plantiff's timber. The plaintiff received damages at trial, but on appeal Robinson quashed the decision. While railroads were obliged to act with due caution, progress required that they not be held responsible for every chance spark flying from their engines:

In actions of this nature it is always necessary to be borne in mind, that it is more than railway companies can be expected to undertake, that the business which they are conducting should be always so managed as to prevent accidents ...[11]

Because railroads were constructed for the public benefit (the chief justice ignored any profit motive) they should not be held to a strict standard of liability. In a case where a railroad company neglected to put up a fence around its tracks, the Chief Justice noted that these occurrences are unfortunate in their effect upon the interests of a company whose exertions have conferred great benefit upon the community; and perhaps with the greatest care accidents will occasionally take place.[12]

Where the legislation was not specific, Robinson usually ruled in favour of the railroads, the servants of the public good. Even though Parliament had approved the line of a railroad, the chief justice held that the company could make minor alterations to the course without having to obtain parliamentary approval.[13] When an obstreperous passenger refused to pay his fare, Robinson upheld the right of the conductor to put him off. Thanks to the railroad, the speed and efficiency of travel within the province had been greatly increased, and the operation of the railways should not be jeopardized by malcontents: 'It is a matter in which the public are interested, that there should be no such impediment in the way to obstruct the prompt and regular progress of the train.'[14] Robinson made his own contribution to the public weal when a railroad was built across his property at Innisfil.[15]

Throughout the 1850s Queen's Bench was confronted by novel damage claims resulting from the operation of the railroads. The legislature was anxious to encourage railway construction, and enabling statutes often contained clauses that released the companies from tortious liability. In his application of these statutes, Robinson usually revealed his bias in favour of the 'anticipating spirit.' In *Hill v The Ontario, Simcoe and Huron Railroad Union Company* (1856), a discharge of steam from a passing train burnt down the plantiff's barn. Robinson, as trial judge, balanced the competing rights of the two parties:

The plaintiff had a right to use his barn and barnyard as farmers generally use them, and ... if he chose to allow it to remain near the track he must submit to the risk which would exist as a consequence of the Legislature having entrusted the defendants with an agent of a dangerous character, provided they used all the appliances and precautions which could be expected reasonably from them.[16]

In defining liability in railroad cases, the chief justice chose not to look beyond the directions given by the legislature. Railroads could even block a person's right-of-way because 'it is necessary for the railway, and the law allows it.'[17]

In one case, the legislature and courts joined to grant the railroads considerable freedom from liability. The Railway Clauses Act established a six-month limitation period on actions for 'injuries sustained by reason of the railway.'[18] In *Browne* v *The Brockville and Ottawa Railway Company* (1860),[19] the plaintiff sustained damages as a result of a collision in which the train's engineer was at fault for not blowing the required signal. Did 'by reason of the railway' refer to this kind of negligence or only to the faulty construction of the railway itself? The six-month limitation period obviously applied to construction defects; if the limitation was extended to simple negligence, then the public was at a severe disadvantage. Injury claims would have to be processed almost as soon as they were incurred. Robinson held that '"by reason of the railway" is a very comprehensive expression, and we think extends to an injury on the railway by reason of the use made of it.'[20] If the statute was worded in a general manner, then it was the court's duty to give it a general interpretation. If the public was to be protected, it was the prerogative of the legislature to so direct the courts.

It has been suggested that similar attitudes existed in nineteenth-century American courts; 'absolute liability might have strangled the economy altogether,'[21] and the courts would only find liability if negligence could be shown. But u.s. judges tended to regard the mechanical monsters with great suspicion. Courts in California and New Hampshire, for example, almost invariably awarded damages against railroads for causing fire damage to property.[22] In those courts, the storing of crops near a railway was not considered a submission to the risk, and the railroad was held strictly liable for any damage it caused.[23] Robinson, much more than u.s. judges, considered railroads to be agents of the public good, and he was unwilling to hold them to exacting standards of care.

There were occasions when even Robinson felt obliged to apply the liability provisions in the railroad statutes to protect the public, however. When railroad construction resulted in flooding, the chief justice found that the company had breached a duty placed upon it by statute.[24] Despite a statute that removed liability from a railroad whose trains had struck cattle running at large, Robinson still imposed liability on the railroad on the ground that it had not used care and caution to avoid the collision.[25] Queen's Bench rarely extended the requirements of the statute to protect the public; however, when Robinson reviewed the act incorporating the Great Western Railway,[26] it was clear that the legislature had not gone far enough. The act only required the railroad to fence highway crossings to the east of London. By applying a 'reasonable construction,' Robinson held that the same clause applied to all highways to the west of London.[27]

Moreover, the conductor was under a common-law duty to try to avoid hitting cattle or persons on the highway crossings.[28] In the era before the invention of the air-brake, this placed heavy responsibility on the proprietors of the railroads. Despite these decisions in favour of the public, Queen's Bench usually placed the burden of economic loss on the victims, thereby encouraging the growth of the railroad system.

Questions concerning the railroads were not the only novel problem confronting Queen's Bench. The 'strange state' of Upper Canada was made even stranger by the introduction of district councils in 1841. This innovation more than any other put an end to the reign of the gentry magistrates and signalled the beginning of popular government on the local level. Then in 1849 Robert Baldwin's Municipal Act[29] provided for the incorporation of municipalities and established a full system of popularly elected local governments. In one of his Cassandra-like prophecies in *Canada and the Canada Bill*, Robinson had warned against precisely this devolution of power. District councils, he had insisted, would not only detract from the sovereign power of Parliament, they would result in 'a perpetual state of agitation and excitement.'[30] Nevertheless, local self-rule came into being as a necessary corollary of responsible government, and, as chief justice, Robinson was called on to define the jurisdiction of the new system of municipal government.

One question concerning the authority of the new councils bedevilled Robinson's court. A long-established rule held that the court could quash a municipal by-law on the ground that it was 'unreasonable' – that is, that it was oppressive or passed in bad faith. This power was derived from the maxim that 'Parliament never intended to give authority to make such rules; they are unreasonable and *ultra vires*.'[31] Yet Queen's Bench hesitated to use this authority. In 1838 Justice McLean found that a by-law was acceptable because 'the passing of such a by-law or regulation by the board is sufficient evidence that it was thought reasonable.'[32] Robinson took a bolder approach. In 1853, a local council in Darlington attempted to pass a by-law closing all public houses.[33] When put to a vote, the by-law was defeated by a thirsty electorate. The council then passed a by-law limiting the number of taverns to one (in a remote corner of the township) and restricting the types of persons it could serve on the sabbath. When the case came before him, the chief justice conceded that the enabling statute gave the municipality the power to limit the number of public houses. However, the statute specifically required any prohibition by-law to be put to a vote. Robinson concluded that the by-law was 'intended to give the go-by to a legislative enactment.'[34] McLean's cautious approach was rejected; the mere passing of a by-law did not make it 'reasonable.' If the facts showed that the council had abused its delegated powers or had acted in an oppressive or discriminatory way, the courts could strike down the by-law.

In subsequent cases, Robinson defined 'unreasonableness.' It was not unreasonable for a council to pass a by-law that was restrictive but that still accommodated local customs.[35] Nor was it unreasonable for a council to grant only two tavern licences.[36] The power of judicial review was used sparingly, and succeeding courts applied the principle in *Darlington* only in instances of 'manifest oppression.'[37]

To some, the court's power of review seemed to be an interference with the powers of local boards. A 1913 amendment to the Municipal Act excluded 'unreasonableness' as a ground of review.[38] Eventually, unreasonableness as a ground for dismissing improper by-laws was again granted limited recognition by the courts. In *Bell* v *The Queen* (1979),[39] the Canadian Supreme Court struck down a by-law on the ground that it was a violation of private rights. (Ironically, in applying the doctrine of unreasonableness, the court ignored the early decisions of Queen's Bench and instead relied on English cases.[40] In the same self-denigrating style that led to the rejection of *Dean* v *McCarty*, Canadian courts ignored their own precedents and instead sought guidance from the more prestigious law courts of England.)

The Courts may have been having difficulty in establishing rules to deal with the changes occurring in the 1850s, but the Parliament of the United Canadas was not. Public dissatisfaction with lengthy and costly court procedures was bringing the judicial system into question, and some reformers were beginning to challenge the existing court structure. One area that desperately required legislative reform was the law of court procedures. The latest generation of U.S. jurists had little respect for ancient procedures and conducted a comprehensive reevaluation of their own judicial system. The resulting Field Code was studied in England, and in 1852 a Common Law Procedue Act consolidated and simplified English court proceedings. The Canadas enacted a similar statute in 1856.[41] This remarkable act consolidated or repealed twenty-four other acts, clarified the procedures for the ejectment of tenants and the filing of pleadings, and, most significantly, section 291 permitted a superior court judge to make such amendments to pleadings 'as may be necessary for the purpose of determining in the existing suit the real question in controversy between the parties.' This act showed the legislature's intention that henceforth the courts should not engage in technical debates but should adjudicate on the merits of the disputes before them. In 1862, as he was about to leave the bench, Robinson lamented that these reforms had not been introduced earlier. He remarked that so many of his cases had concerned *vexatio de lana capricia*, or disputes about nothing, that 'I think we all used to feel with somewhat of shame, while we were unwillingly engaged in them.'[42]

Robinson had been especially critical of the pre-existing law in regard to landlord and tenant, or ejectment. Any error in the landlord's pleadings could result in a verdict for the tenant. Robinson's arch-conservative views showed in his observation that juries were inclined 'to favour any available weakness which disposes necessary to believe that the poor are always in the right – at least when they find themselves engaged in a contest with the rich.'[43] With satisfaction, Robinson noted that 'great changes have been made in the action for ejectment' and that the caprice of a jury could no longer deprive a landlord of his property.'[44]

The Common Law Procedure Act contained innovations not included in the English statute. Section 156 empowered a judge to appoint an arbitrator to investigate a claimant's accounts in order to determine the amounts payable. Robinson, interpreting this section without the guidance of English courts, noted somewhat caustically that 'the power to refer under that clause is very extensive – more extensive perhaps than was certainly intended.[45] In another case, Robinson pointed out the act's failure to provide for the release of a judgment debtor once the debt had been paid.[46] Although he was nearing his seventieth year, the chief justice had no difficulty in apprehending defects in the legislation, and his comments betray a wistful desire to redraft the act to his own specifications.

While the Common Law Procedure Act was a major advance in the modernization of Canadian law, an even greater step occurred in reforming the court system itself. Public dissatisfaction with the operation of Queen's Bench and Chancery were becoming apparent during the 1840s. Court proceedings were expensive and time-consuming, and it was widely suspected that the legal profession profited from this inefficiency. During the 1840s, the Baldwin–LaFontaine government determined to investigate and, if possible, reform the courts. The final impetus for change came from an unlikely source – an immigrant lawyer, William Hume Blake.

Blake had come to Canada from Ireland in 1832 and had eventually gravitated to Toronto and entered the legal profession. Despite his gentle origins, Blake's political leanings were the opposite of John Robinson's. His family had not lost their estate to the American republic, and they had not been required to defend their new home from 'vulgar democracy.' Blake did not share Robinson's unquestioning devotion to British institutions, and he strongly favoured reform. In 1844 Blake had stood as a reform candidate against William Robinson; after being defeated he had alleged, without any proof, that the chief justice had intimidated the local bar into supporting his brother.[47]

If there were to be court reforms, it was essential that they have the support of the sitting judges. Blake later proclaimed that there was 'no man in the Province whom he more unfeignedly respected' and who was more 'an honour and an ornament to his country'[48] than Chief Justice Robinson. The first commission empowered to investigate Chancery in 1843 included Justice Macaulay, three equity lawyers, and the chief justice.

In addition to the discontent over Chancery there were complaints from reformers about the lack of an adequate appellate jurisdiction in the courts. Upper Canada's original Judicature Act of 1794 made the lieutenant-governor, the chief justice, and two or more members of the executive council a court of appeal. However, appeals to the executive council were rare and usually futile. In January 1845 Blake wrote Baldwin a letter outlining his plans for judicial reform. The enlargement of Chancery was but one small part of his grand design. Blake found 'the position of our common law court from which there is no appeal ... truly alarming.' With considerable bitterness toward the chief justice and Queen's Bench, he reported that 'the danger to liberty from this despotic tribunal is most imminent.'[49] One critic, Robert Sullivan, warned Baldwin that

the state of the Court of Queen's Bench without any Court of equal jurisdiction & with no effectual appeal ... has given an oracular character to the decisions of the Chief Justice, whether right or wrong they are law and adjudication is legislation. This is a dangerous and hurtful power to be placed in the hands of one Court and consequently of the leader of that Court.[50]

Despite this discontent, there was no resolve on the part of the government to reform Chancery and still less to overhaul the entire judicial system. This lethargy dissipated with Blake's election to Parliament in 1847 and his appointment as solicitor-general of Canada West.[51]

Blake realized that the opinion of the judges was all-important. If his plans for judicial reform could be demonstrated to be the result of a consensus between the court and the government, then the measure would be accepted without question by Parliament. Fortunately for the solicitor-general, the judges' thoughts on reform approximated his own. Robinson was against the enlargement of Chancery, at least until another judge had tried to make a success of the office. Justice McLean suggested creating one new court of common pleas and giving it an equity jurisdiction. Robinson disagreed. Ironically, Blake found himself siding with Robinson; he concluded, 'I would rather countenance one court of equity with one judge and erect a separate court of appeal as mentioned by the Chief.'[52] Blake was especially pleased with Robinson's suggestions for a new appellate court. The chief justice proposed keeping the existing Queen's Bench and Chancery as they were and selecting an appeal court from among the best superior court judges. After the meeting Blake referred to the plan for an appeal court as the 'proposal of the Chief.'[53]

When Blake's reform bills were finally introduced, they called for an enlargement of Chancery, the creation of another common-law court, and the establishment of a court of error and appeal. Another bill provided for a reform of the law of evidence by requiring disclosure of the facts in civil and criminal matters. Blake's Judicature Act was an adroit piece of legislation that not only rationalized the administration of justice but also satisfied the opposition by preserving the essential elements of the English courts. In a cordial letter to Baldwin, the chief justice wrote that the proposed amendments to the Judicature Act 'are not *radical* changes.'[54]

If one can judge by the reported cases, Blake's reforms were readily accepted by the chief justice. In one case where a defendant was served with notice under the new Evidence Act, Robinson was not inclined to dismiss a verdict against him. The new rules were quite clear and were to be obeyed both by attorneys and by their clients.[55] The judicial reforms also resulted in the chief justice becoming ex officio head of the new appeals court. The 'oracular character' of Robinson's decisions was, if anything, enhanced by his elevation to the highest court. The appointment also resulted in Robinson, a man who had spent a lifetime in the common law, becoming a judge in an unfamiliar equity court.

As head of the Court of Error and Appeal, Robinson frequently came into conflict with the new chancellor of Upper Canada, William Blake. One question that divided the two men concerned the property rights of squatters. In the early days of Upper Canada many settlers had farmed

Crown or clergy reserves under a lease. These were usually long leases with options to purchase, and, because land was plentiful and sheriffs few, the settlers tended to remain on the lands long after their leases had expired. The chief justice's approach to the problem was that of an unyielding English judge. Squatters had no legal claim to the land they farmed and therefore they should be evicted. To John Macaulay he wrote, 'I have no sympathy for the genus *squatter* ... If I were Louis Napoleon legislating for a country I would allow no presumptive right to be given those who have gone upon land which they well knew they had no claim.'[56] Fortunately, John Robinson was not the Emperor of Canada West. Many of the squatter cases came before Blake's Chancery Court, and equity proved itself to be more flexible than the common law in dealing with squatters. Equity reasoned that the government was mistaken to grant land upon which a squatter held a limited estate.[57] Robinson was not so forgiving; to him the land patent was the superior sign of possession and should not be limited by any equitable rights.[58]

In *Holmes* v *Mathews*,[59] equity and common law came into a direct collision. Blake held that after parties had transferred property unconditionally, the Chancery Court could still look at parol evidence to discover some fact that would indicate that the parties did not wish to make an unconditional transfer but had intended to create a mortgage. On appeal, the chief justice struck down this decision. He felt that the Statute of Frauds dictated that when a land conveyance was put into writing, both parties were obligated by it and could not later alter its terms on parol evidence: 'every man ought to be able to rest secure in the enjoyment of what his deeds assure to him.'[60] As a result of the railway boom, land prices were soaring in some parts of the province; Robinson felt that entrepreneurs should not be subjected to the additional risk of seeing their contracts negated:

I allude to the many great railway projects which are at present being actively proceeded in, and in the way of being certainly accomplished by the aid of English capital, which has been freely embarked in them to the amount of some millions sterling. ... What a temptation such a state of things affords to just such fraud and perjury as the Statute of Frauds was meant to protect people against![61]

Although Robinson played a lesser role than Blake in revitalizing the judiciary, his decisions set the tone for his own and future courts. His judgments established the courts as interpretive bodies that settled disputes by applying existing laws. As a result, the law was predictable;

the businessman could safely expect his deed to be honoured, his contract enforced. If there was to be law reform, it must come from the Crown and its elected Parliament.

Robinson's years on the bench slipped by, and it began to appear as if he would never see England again. Then, in the spring of 1855, Emma and John received an invitation from their married daughters, Emily and Mary, to visit them in London. The voyage was an uncommonly rough one, and when the chief justice's ship rounded the Head of Kinsale he noted in his diary that this was the place where the *Albion* was lost in 1822. Did Providence mean him to share the same fate as Anne Powell? Apparently fate had no immediate plans for him; Robinson's ship, the *Asia*, passed safely into Liverpool.

Fifteen years had passed since Robinson had seen the mother country, and many of his old friends and colleagues had passed away. But enough of Robinson's fellow-intriguers remained to give him an enthusiastic welcome. The irrepressible Sir Francis Bond Head ushered the chief justice back to England, telling him, 'whether you arrive here by night or by day "in thunder lightening or in hail" you will meet with a hearty welcome.' Head counselled Robinson to enjoy his vacation and 'let your moustachios grow.'[62] (This allusion to the current style of cultivating facial hair was lost on the chief justice, who maintained his clean-shaven appearance.)

A few days after his arrival in London Robinson dined with Sir Robert Inglis, an acquaintance from the days of the Canada debate. Inglis entertained the Robinsons frequently during April, until the chief justice was again familiar with his old London haunts. Early in May, Robinson began a tour of England in order to observe the English judiciary in action.

He travelled north to York where Baron Parke, one of the foremost common-law jurists, presided over the assizes. Like John Robinson, Parke was a black-letter lawyer who strictly upheld the technical requirements of the law. However, his 'good-humoured way of getting through the business' both amused and instructed Robinson. In contrast to the chief justice, who was 'prompt to suppress any indecorum,'[63] Baron Parke 'laughed at all jokes, whether good or bad' and even cut short a barrister's rather eccentric argument by chuckling 'non*sense*, non*sense*.'[64] Robinson was impressed by the high degree of ability exhibited by the English jurists; even Parke's informality disguised a disciplined legal mind. His observations led him to conclude that 'on the whole, I saw nothing very peculiar in the system here. Like circumstances seem to produce like

courses and consequences, here and there.' Of course, Robinson had
done all he could to insure that the Canadian and British courts would be
substantially similar and would therefore inevitably share 'like courses
and consequences.' Robinson thoroughly enjoyed the York assizes, and
was even invited by Justice Carswell to sit beside him on the bench.
'Now,' quipped Carswell, 'I shall be very nervous having a Chief Justice
watching me.'

The highlight of Robinson's tour was a royal levee at St James Palace.
The chief justice, resplendent in his court dress and wearing his Detroit
medal and his Order of the Bath, was presented to Queen Victoria. As he
finished making his salutations, the Queen made a comment to him.
Robinson did not catch her remark, but he assumed that 'it was some form
of congratulations.' He gloried in his brush with royalty, but he was most
comfortable in the company of his legal colleagues. Although he had not
met many of the justices of the English courts, they were familiar with
Robinson's appeal judgments, and they felt a kinship with their Canadian
colleague. Sir Edward Ryan complimented Robinson on his judgment in
Holmes v *Mathews*. Pemberton Leigh, a judge of the judicial committee of
the privy council, had reviewed several of Robinson's decisions and,
upon being introduced, dismissed all pleasantries with the comment, 'I
know Chief Justice Robinson well and he is well known in England.' In
London, Robinson was invited to dine with Baron Parke; the chief justice
recorded that the dinner conversation invariably revolved around points
of law.

Robinson's continuing interest in commercial activity led him to
examine the work in progress on the *Great Eastern* and meet the eminent
British scientists, Faraday and Babbage. He was also drawn to visit the
Yorkshire countryside. At Cleasby, the somnolent village from which
Christopher Robinson first made his way to America, Robinson attended
the Sunday service. The farming folk were surprised to have any stranger,
especially a Canadian member of the Order of the Bath, attend their divine
worship. After a perusal of the church records, Robinson confirmed that
his family had indeed originated in the area and he hoped that eventually
one of the Robinsons would buy a plot 'in the parish to which, in England,
they belong.'

The chief justice himself showed no inclination to retire into rural
oblivion. In June, Robinson and his friend, Jonas Jones, took ship for
Ireland. The chief justice could not escape the notoriety of being the
foremost British American ever to visit the British Isles. Although he had
no official status and represented no political cause, Robinson was

universally recognized as Canada's state representative. After only two days in Dublin, he was invited to dine with the lord-lieutenant and was given an official tour of the city. After a few days of relaxation near the Lakes of Killarney, the Irish excursion was cut short so he could return to England to receive yet another honour.

Oxford had determined to recognize this distinguished Canadian by granting him the honourary degree of Doctor of Civil Laws. At the ceremony, one of Robinson's fellow laureates was Alfred Tennyson. As was thought to befit a poet, Tennyson appeared 'an uncombed slovenly looking person.' Robinson was fastidious about his own appearance, and his diary indicates that he took careful note of the dress of the men and women around him. Unfortunately, he associated casualness in dress with moral or intellectual inferiority.

He met for what he knew to be the last time with Lord Seaton and Sir Francis Bond Head. They reminisced about the days when both they and Upper Canada were young and hopeful. Now all that remained to them was to fulfil the remaining duties of their years, Seaton as a soldier in Ireland, Head as the terror of the small game of Northhamptonshire, and Robinson as chief justice of Upper Canada. In August 1855 Robinson left the nation whose institutions he cherished and returned to the country where he had done so much to implant those institutions.

Robinson's advancing age was causing him difficulty in performing his duties on the bench and the assize circuit. He confined his public activities to assisting his favourite charities, notably the Church of England and the committee to reconstruct General Brock's monument.

In late 1859 Canadians began to prepare for a monumental event. It was announced that to confirm and strengthen Canada's attachment to the Crown, the Prince of Wales would make a tour of the Canadas and parts of the United States in 1860. Though most Canadians, conservative and liberal, remained strong monarchists, the prince's trip was not consistently smooth. In Kingston he was confronted by a mob of Orangemen who refused to allow him to land without his passing under an orange arch. While the prince's Toronto welcome was somewhat more cordial, the Orangemen, who were out in force, harassed the royal party.

Perhaps with some relief, the prince abandoned government ceremonies to attend a reception in his honour at Osgoode Hall. Since its erection in 1829, the building had undergone significant changes. In 1844, an east wing was built; in 1857 the structure was completely renovated and expanded, and a library added. The Law Society entertained the prince in the new Great Library, and the chief justice presided over the reception both literally and figuratively. His portrait hung above the fireplace in the library, from which position his stern visage looked down on the festivities. While it is unlikely that Robinson danced the quadrilles that evening, advancing age and gout having halted his more strenuous activities, the very presence of the Prince of Wales in Canada gladdened him and reaffirmed his faith in the enduring connection between Canada and Britain.

A few days after the reception, the chief justice headed a small band of survivors of the Battle of Queenston Heights in the ceremonies inaugurating the monument to General Brock. Robinson presented the loyal address to the prince and expressed the veterans' joy at seeing a member of the royal family in the province they had fought to preserve for the Crown. The prince replied that the monument at Queenston Heights gave him 'pride in the gallant deeds of my countrymen.' Because the royal tour was also a diplomatic mission to reconcile Britain with the United States, the Prince observed that 'we readily acknowledge the bravery and chivalry of that people by whose act [Brock] fell.'[65] Britain's relations with the American republic were becoming more important than the old imperial connection with Canada.

Ever since the Webster-Ashburton Treaty of 1842, dealings between Britain and the United States had been on an amicable and formal basis. It was hoped that the state visit of the Prince of Wales would strengthen the ties of friendship. But the slavery issue threatened to destroy this fragile goodwill. After the passing of the Fugitive Slave Act in 1850, escaped slaves from the southern states fled to British America and particularly Canada West. The people of the Canadas were strong supporters of abolition, and they sheltered even those fugitives who had committed crimes. The abolitionists were in constant fear that article x, the extradition provision of the Webster-Ashburton Treaty, would be used to recapture slaves who thought they had gained freedom under the British flag.

The prince had hardly left Canada when just such an incident occurred. John Anderson, a fugitive slave living in Brantford, admitted to having stabbed a white man while escaping from slavery in Missouri. Missouri indicted Anderson for murder, and in October 1860, the United States formally requested his extradition. The abolitionist press championed Anderson's cause and demanded that Attorney-General Macdonald immediately release the fugitive, who had been arrested as soon as the American warrant arrived. Macdonald, however, was conscious of the serious diplomatic implications of the case; he insisted that the matter be turned over to Queen's Bench where Anderson's counsel, Samuel B. Freeman, could request a writ of habeas corpus.[66]

During the course of the hearing in November, Freeman stressed that Anderson's act of turning on and stabbing a white planter who was pursuing him with the intention of returning him to slavery was not an act that constituted murder. In Canada, no man had the authority to enslave another, and therefore it was the planter's act that was illegal. Anderson's assault was necessary to preserve his own freedom and was therefore justified. The Crown prosecutor, however, argued that the fatal blow was struck after the planter fell. Moreover, under Missouri law, the planter had full legal authority to pursue escaped slaves. The justices of Queen's Bench listened impassively to the evidence and only rarely interrupted counsel with questions.

Robinson's opinion of blacks was not as liberal as that of the abolitionists, but was probably a commonly held one for that period. Many escaped slaves were settled around Amherstburg. When one of them was convicted of cattle theft, the chief justice reported to the lieutenant-governor that the convict had fled the province. He added, 'I think I would have him where he is. They have too many such people about Amherstburg already. He was convicted in killing a cow on the common with intent of stealing the carcase, a very common offence among the blacks.'[67]

Black or white, the law was to be applied as Parliament had written it. But legal niceties were lost on the vocal and unruly crowd of black and white Torontonians who packed the courtroom in Osgoode Hall to hear the decision. Armed police patrolled the courtroom and a company of militia was stationed on the grounds. The chief justice began his judgment by stating that there were defects in the magistrate's warrant, but they did not make it invalid.[68] As Robinson understood the issue, the question before the court was whether the law of the state where the act was committed or the law of the state where the fugitive was being held should be used to determine the nature of the offence. Article x only stipulated that the act must be a crime in the requesting state. Robinson concluded that the court had to look at the *lex loci*, the law of the place where the crime was committed, and use that as a measuring stick to determine whether the act constituted a crime. Thus, Missouri law, which permitted any white man to pursue an escaped slave, had to be recognized. The planter was acting under 'legal authority as much as if he had been armed with process,' and therefore Anderson had committed a criminal act subject to extradition. Rejecting Freeman's argument that the act must be a crime in the province before extradition could be granted, Robinson noted that the statute only stipulated that the 'evidence of his criminality' must be in accordance with provincial laws. The chief justice was well aware that his decision could lead to Anderson's re-enslavement, or even to his lynching, and saw that outcome as a harsh but inescapable result of the Webster-Ashburton Treaty. While at the end of his judgment Robinson expressed the hope that the political authorities would exercise their merciful prerogatives, as far as the court was concerned the judges 'must conform to what the law requires, and are not at liberty to act upon considerations of policy or even of compassion, where a duty is prescribed.'[69]

The next justice to speak, Archibald McLean, a former comrade of Robinson's at Queenston Heights, rejected the chief justice's reasoning. A fervent abolitionist, he agreed with Freeman that the oppressive slave laws of Missouri should never be cited in Canada in order to return a man to bondage. McLean passionately argued that Anderson's act was justified by 'the desire to be free which nature has implanted in his breast.'[70] The third justice, Robert Burns, agreed with the chief justice, and Anderson was remanded to prison to await a warrant from the United States.

Public reaction to this decision was immediate and violent. Osgoode Hall was cleared of spectators, and a menacing crowd formed just outside the Hall. Only Samuel Freeman's intervention prevented the mob from making an attempt to free Anderson by force.[71] Indignation was expressed at mass meetings held throughout the Canadas, and resolutions condemning the verdict were passed. At one rally held in the St Lawrence Hall, a prominent American abolitionist rhetorically asked, 'Does not your Chief Justice know that Anderson will scarcely have set foot within Missouri ere he will be seized by a mob, and amidst fiendish exultations be burnt at the stake?'[72] The abolitionist press condemned Robinson's judgment and found that it lacked 'great research ... even of tolerably fair *nisi prius* law.'[73] Many Canadians interpreted the court's decision as upholding slavery, and there were dark hints among the abolitionists that Robinson's Virginian slave-owning origins had motivated his decision.[74]

Interest in the Anderson case soon extended beyond the Canadas. Although Robinson's judgment was highly unpopular with the British public,[75] one of the most respected legal journals, the *Law Times*, felt that the decision was technically correct and even complimented Robinson for having the courage to make an unpopular decision in the face of 'the caprices of popular sentiment or passion.'[76] Undaunted, the British abolitionists brought a motion for habeas corpus before the English Court of Queen's Bench. After justifying their position with references to centuries-old precedent, the court instructed the sheriff of Toronto to release Anderson. This decision, while it may have pleased abolitionists, outraged Canadians who saw it as a threat to responsible government. Of what use were colonial courts and legislatures if an English court could issue an order in the colony?

In addition to the nationalist furor created by the Anderson case, anti-slavery sentiments were unleashed. The chief justice's judgment refusing habeas corpus was condemned by a citizenry only vaguely aware of the issues involved. In fact, Robinson's rationale constitutes the basis for the modern interpretation of the criteria for extradition.[77] If the requesting state alleges the facts of a crime that is also a crime in the holding state, then extradition is to follow. Robinson's decision was legally sound, but even modern writers describe his judgment as a 'myopic and astigmatic view of the human rights aspect of the case.'[78] The chief justice's reward for the painstaking effort required to produce his definitive judgment was public condemnation. As a contemporary journal noted, 'so strongly prejudiced was public opinion that the popularity of the Bench seemed to suffer.'[79] Perhaps the time had come for younger men to administer the law for the benefit of the ungrateful public.

In March 1861 Robinson asked the governor, Sir Edmund Head, to relieve him of his duties in the Court of Queen's Bench.[80] Deteriorating health made it impossible for Robinson to travel on circuit, and this led to delays in processing the work of the court. But complete retirement from the legal world was not what the chief had in mind, and he asked the governor to make some arrangement so that he might continue to sit on the Court of Error and Appeal. Sir Edmund immediately replied that Robinson's resignation would be 'embarrassing and inexpedient,' and in any event no replacement was immediately available.[81] In the meantime, Attorney-General Macdonald set about drafting a statute that would enable Robinson to remain on the Court of Error and Appeal. Macdonald's efforts on behalf of the chief justice indicated his respect for one of the province's surviving founders. So accommodating was the attorney-general that by May 1861 an act was passed which authorized any retired justice of the superior courts to continue to preside as a judge in the Court of Error and Appeal.[82]

The chief justice's health was obviously failing, and in May he was seized by a severe cold and fell into a shivering fit while presiding on the bench. In January 1862 he renewed his application to retire and expressed his dread of having to go on circuit once more.[83] This time Macdonald accepted his resignation. In fulfilment of Robinson's wish to remain on the bench in an auxiliary capacity, a statute creating the new office of president of the court was drafted by Macdonald and presented to the chief justice for his approval. The jurisdiction and oath of office of the new position were only vaguely defined. 'Will you be good enough to give me your opinion on this legislation?'[84] the ever-solicitous Macdonald asked Robinson. For perhaps the only time in Canadian history, a judge was asked to write the terms of his own office.

In March 1862, after almost thirty-three years of service, John Robinson retired from Queen's Bench and was formally sworn in as president of the Court of Error and Appeal. It was deemed appropriate that the Law Society hold a banquet to mark the end of Robinson's distinguished career. The commanders of the Toronto garrison, the local clergy (headed by Bishop Strachan), and the leading members of the bar attended a June banquet in Osgoode Hall's Great Library. The library, normally a place of research and contemplation, was decorated with flowers, and an orchestra was hired for the occasion. Testimonials were presented to the former chief justice from several members of the bar. As he acknowledged their speeches, Robinson looked back over the years and remembered the one man who more than any other had given him the affection and self-confidence which had inspired his career. He spoke of the Reverend John Stuart, his teacher and foster-father. John Robinson had never known his real father, and fate had stolen his doting foster-father from him at an early age. Robinson noted that he was leaving the bench with some regret and that the court 'has constituted my home.' While he was pleased to remain on the bench to hear appellate cases, the time was drawing near when he must render his final account. With this sobering thought, the baronet retired for the evening, leaving Osgoode Hall echoing with 'music and merry jest,' a memorable farewell on a pleasant summer evening.[85]

In describing the tribute to the former chief justice, the *Globe* admitted that its reform sentiments were in opposition to Robinson's views. Still, even the reformers had to concede the influence of one of the last standard-bearers of the Family Compact: 'In Reference to one part of his public career no limit need be placed on our praises. He was a strong friend of the British connection, and defended this outpost of England with a courage which knew no difficulty.'[86] The old tory need have no fear that the province was falling into alien hands. His son, John Beverley, after making a fortune in land speculation, had become an important figure in municipal and provincial politics. Christopher was already a Queen's Counsel and well on his way toward establishing a prominent legal career. Charles Walker was commissioned a regular officer in the Prince Consort's Regiment. Robinson's sons were beginning to achieve fame in imperial as well as Canadian affairs; John Beverley eventually became lieutenant-governor of Ontario, Christopher was offered a knighthood for his services to the Crown during the Bering Sea negotiations, and Charles Walker was made a major-general in the British Army. Robinson's sons kept the British connection intact in Canada.

In the fall of 1862, Robinson again suffered an attack of gout. This time he recovered slowly. Nevertheless, in January 1863, he attempted to take part in some of the proceedings of the Court of Error and Appeal. After working for only a few days he suffered a seizure. He was sitting at his desk working on his judgments when the final attack came. By the end of January his strength was fading, and Bishop Strachan was called to administer the last sacrament. With his beloved Emma at his side, Robinson intermittently recited verses from Pope's Universal Prayer. He died in the early morning of 31 January 1863.

At the request of the Law Society, the chief justice was given a state funeral. On the day of the funeral, Robinson's body was taken to lie in Osgoode Hall, whose white marble pillars had been draped with black crêpe. From the Hall, Robinson's casket was escorted by his brother judges of law and equity to St James Cathedral. Despite the freezing weather, much of the city turned out to watch the procession. The aged Bishop Strachan was visibly shaken as he attended the services for his former student and friend. The bishop, who had attempted to supervise so much of his student's life, had already made provision for him in death. Robinson was to be buried in Strachan's own vault in St James Cemetery.

Sir John Beverley Robinson, born in the year of Upper Canada's creation, died less than five years before the confederation of the British North American colonies, a confederation he considered to be essential to the survival of British America as a separate nation under the Crown. He would never see the fruition of his dream of 'the *British North American Provinces* [united] into one grand confederacy ... and connect[ed] ... more closely with the empire.'[87]

Epilogue

When John Beverley Robinson first travelled to England in 1815, he amused the children of the Merry family by showing them the old and curious coins that were in circulation in Upper Canada. English coinage had been updated and no longer resembled the currency of that isolated colony. Similarly, the political views of the loyalists were, in the early nineteenth century, cut off from the changes occurring in Britain and the American republic. Just as the coins of former monarchs disappeared, the pillars of loyalist society – a frontier oligarchy, an established Church, and a docile yeomanry – eventually succumbed to the impact of British liberalism and American democracy.

During this formative period, John Robinson was the pre-eminent figure in Upper Canadian public life. Between 1820 and 1829, he led the government in the assembly and to an almost equal extent in the lieutenant-governor's mansion. His prominence among provincial leaders justified Strachan's comment: 'to him I give up in most things, but to no other.'[1] Even after his appointment to the bench, he retained considerable influence in the lieutenant-governor's circle; as late as 1838, the Crown's representative referred to Robinson as his 'good Pilot.'[2] Throughout this period, Robinson was the dominant figure; whether in the formulation of emigration projects, loans to canals, or response to the alien question, he shaped the policies and the very face of Upper Canada's government.

The one pillar of loyalist society that survived and was strengthened after Robinson's passing was devotion to the Crown. John Robinson, the colonial Englishman who trembled as he stood on the site of Charles i's execution, would have relished the imperial fervour of the late Victorian Canadians. Yet there was a subtle distinction between Robinson's hopes for the Empire and the manner in which it eventually evolved. He did not expect that the colonies would remain subservient, and he anticipated the day when confederations of colonies would be granted the 'opportunity of making known their wants, their interests, and their dangers in the great Council of the Nation, [which] would make them feel themselves as *parts* rather than dependencies of the Empire.'[3] Integration of the colonies within the British imperium was never seriously considered by London, and even when the Empire was hard-pressed by war, the Imperial War Cabinet was a pale reflection of a great 'Council of the Nation.'[4]

The other pillars of loyalist society, the tory values that Robinson espoused, were rooted in the thought of the eighteenth century and were embodied in adherence to the established Church, a hierarchical society, a disdain of democracy, and support of the balanced constitution of King, Lords, and Commons. Central to Robinson's concept of society was the right of the 'gentleman of high character, of large property, and of superior information' to govern lesser men.[6] The gentleman would exercise this authority from the legislative council, and Robinson devoted himself to preserving the independence of that institution. In the quality of its membership and in the public-spirited nature of its acts, Robinson considered an appointed council an essential element of good government.

Perhaps even more important to the 'social mortar' was the established Church. In 1824, Robinson warned darkly against the 'progress of sectarian ascendancy, and its potential effects.'[7] Time and again, Robinson campaigned on behalf of the Church and defied the Colonial Office itself in order to preserve Anglican prerogatives, all in the belief that the 'rational doctrines'[8] of the Church of England would eventually pervade Canadian life.

Overlaying Robinson's support for the established Church and his hope that Upper Canada's rude society would develop 'distinctions of hereditary rank'[9] was a simple political philosophy: 'the principle of a Monarchy is honour' and 'the principle of democracy is mere unmitigated selfishness.' It was unthinkable to permit elected officials to have absolute control of the executive, for inevitably 'all considerations of what is just & becoming seem to be disregarded.'[10]

It has been suggested that these cardinal points of early tory doctrine survived, albeit in a modified form, and that 'their fundamental attitudes remained, and these they succeeded in imparting to the bulk of the electorate.'[11] Yet by the late nineteenth century the possibility of dispensing with democracy had become a remote one even to the most avid tory. The idea of erecting 'distinctions of hereditary rank' was as anachronistic as a tricorn hat. In a religiously diverse society, secularism went without serious challenge, and the individual struggle for personal gain became the new religion of the industrializing society. The tory emphasis on 'the primacy of the community over individual selfishness' and 'religion as a mortar of the social order'[12] gave way to popular government and sectarianism just as surely as horsepower surrendered to steam. Robinson did not think that he had imparted tory values to succeeding generations; looking back in 1839, he remarked ruefully, 'I had been laboring & worrying myself in great measure in vain.'[13]

The most discomfiting aspect of this failure was the role of the mother country in defeating Robinson's plans. Before 1827, Robinson had dreamt of a 'new Albion,' of a permanent bond between Upper Canada and England. The base treason committed by the Colonial Office during the alien debates ended this dream forever and left the province at the mercy of reformers. In 1839, lamenting for the Empire, he wrote,

we must submit like good subjects, and see our Colonies transmuted into republics, because a visionary, or something worse, has wormed his way into a peculiar position in the Colonial Department.[14]

Robinson's desperate desire to marry his pride in Canada with imperial union was blocked by the actions of the Empire itself. He simply would not condone actions of the imperial government that weakened both the Canadas and the Empire, and it was not unusual for him to bemoan the 'detestable state [in which] His Majesty's ministers have at length succeeded in placing these Colonies.'[15]

The Colonial Office was responding to liberal changes only vaguely understood by Robinson. By his own admission he was no politician, and his career showed a marked inability to gauge or even take into account public feeling. Even though his approach to the alien question was a rational response to an irrational situation, Robinson could not recognize that public discontent over the pretensions of the Church of England and the power of local oligarchs required a change in attitude. So oblivious was Robinson to those changes that he never reconciled himself to a secular Upper Canada or to responsible government. He presumed that eventually the province would come to its senses and revert to the genteel autocracy of former days. It is a startling revelation to discover that, as late as 1851 he considered that

we shall have some years of coarse, vulgar democracy, enough to worry us in our time, our sons, or at least our grandsons will see the beginnings of a reconstruction of the social edifice – more worthy of the human race – after the Church of England shall have obtained an undisputed ascendancy which in the progress of time I take to be inevitable – and after men have seen one fallacy after another in the democratic system exposed and have suffered enough from their mistake ... before people can be satisfied what is for their own good.[16]

As a politician, John Beverley Robinson failed to achieve his objective, the preservation of the gentry society. Because of his failure he made a far less enduring impact on Ontario's political myth than he might have hoped; yet Robinson perhaps achieved more than he himself understood. While his political ideals were not implanted in Canada, his career as a judge left an indelible imprint not only on judicial practice but also on Canadian concepts of law and government. Through the chief justice, British values as reflected in the English common law were upheld and applied. Moreover, the independence of the judiciary from the legislative process was encouraged by Robinson's court. He made it clear in case after case that the duty of the court was to administer the law, not to pass on the merits of legislation. Unlike u.s. courts, which became free to speculate on the effects of statutes, Robinson's Queen's Bench scrupulously ceded the law-making power to the elected legislature. In the absence of judicial intervention, it was possible for community social pressures to focus entirely on Parliament as the legal body ultimately responsible to the people.

The denial of any significant creative powers to the courts and the restriction of judicial activity to the interpretation of statutes is a tradition that has survived in the Canadian judicial myth. To some extent the tradition endured because, for almost a century after Robinson's death, the final appellate court for Canadians was a British tribunal – the judicial committee of the privy council. Therefore the method of judicial subservience as well as the doctrine of the common law survived in Canada. Canadian courts unquestioningly accepted the decisions of superior courts. This attitude is lamented by some who regard the less inhibited u.s. judiciary as a dynamic addition to the process of legal change. Academics are especially disappointed with the passive role of Canadian courts. In their view, the courts have 'elevated a concept that only the legislature has lawmaking power into a formidable barrier to improvement and adaptation of law through the judicial process.'[17] However formidable that barrier may be, it results in social change being given effect by the representative institution of government, Parliament. When, in 1837, Robinson advised a grand jury that 'the business of this Court is to administer justice, and we cannot too closely confine ourselves to it ... To deviate to the debatable ground of politics would be departing from our sphere,'[18] he was articulating a philosophy that would become entrenched in the Canadian judiciary. The same reasoning was repeated by Chief Justice Bora Laskin in 1975:

Parliament, in fastening upon certain behaviour or conduct or activity as criminal by proscribing it with penal sanctions, exercises a judgment which is not constitutionally impeachable simply because it may attract the opposition of a section of the population. The remedy or relief, as the case may be, lies with Parliament and not with this Court.[19]

In addition to advocating the supremacy of Parliament, Robinson's decisions also reflected the growth of a typically Canadian aversion to radical social change. Freedom did not, as in the United States, make its citizens solely the beneficiaries of liberties; rather, it imposed a duty on the individual to support and defend his government. The greatest crime of Lount and Mathews was their attempt to overthrow a just and benevolent government. The two traitors died for their violent indulgence in a 'feeling of envy and hatred towards [their] rulers.' Proof of the survival of this attitude was provided by the massive show of public support for the imposition of the War Measures Act in 1970. As a result, some social scientists believe that 'Canadian society is deficient, not in respect for law but in respect for liberty.'[20] If it is true that Canadian society exhibits an undue deference to authority, there has been little attempt made to determine the source or even the nature of this sentiment. Perhaps the Canadian reverence for peace, order, and good government can be traced to the years in which Canadian institutions were being given form.

At the time of the Ancaster assizes, John Robinson conceded that treason trials were necessary to awe the disaffected. His insistence on the preservation of order was repeated many times in Canada. Yet even in the midst of war Robinson also insisted that the rule of law be applied and that 'military power' be subordinated to the 'rational effects of justice.' When faced with a riot among Irish canal workers, Robinson strongly argued against sending in the militia: 'Of all things it is the least desirable to resort to military force except upon a necessity that no one can dispute.'[21] The civil power was not to be used to overawe the country but to protect it from anarchy.

The rule of law was the source of freedom in Canada, and it did not require (as in the United States) entrenchment in a formal code. The freedom of the individual was guaranteed not by a bill of rights, but by the existence of an independent and objective judiciary. In his charges to the grand juries, Robinson emphasized that the law was not a blunt instrument but a rational code that enabled the individual to exercise his liberties. From the time of the Ancaster assizes to the trial of John Anderson, Robinson consistently upheld the right of the individual to a fair trial. At the same time, he maintained that it was the duty of the subject to support the government that guaranteed him these liberties. In effect, he saw the need for order and the guarantee of the rule of law as mutually supportive concepts.

John Beverley Robinson's major contribution to the prevailing myth lies in his advocacy of the concept of life, liberty, and property not only as the source of public order but also as the guarantee of individual freedom.

Abbreviations

AGP	Attorney-General's Papers
AJLH	*American Journal of Legal History*
Alta. L.R.	Alberta Law Reports
B. & C.	Barnewall and Cresswell's English King's Bench Reports
BP	Baldwin Papers
BPP	British Parliamentary Papers (Shannon 1971)
Ch.	Chancery Court Reports
CHR	*Canadian Historical Review*
COP	Colonial Office Papers
D. & R.	Dowling and Ryland's English King's Bench Reports
DLR	Dominion Law Reports
E. & A.	Court of Error and Appeal
JBRJB	J.B. Robinson Judge's Book
JLC	Journals of the Legislative Council
JPP	Jarvis–Powell Papers
JSP	John Strachan Papers
LJ Ex.	Law Journal, New Series, Exchequer Division
LR 1 Ex.	English Law Reports, Exchequer
LR 3 HL	English and Irish Appeal Cases
LS Gaz.	*Law Society of Upper Canada Gazette*
Mass.	Massachusetts Reports
MP	Macaulay Papers
MTL	Metropolitan Toronto Library

OAR	Ontario Appeal Reports
OH	*Ontario History*
OHSPR	*Ontario Historical Society Proceedings and Transactions*
OR	Ontario Reports
OWN	Ontario Weekly Notes
PACR	Public Archives of Canada Reports
PAO	Public Archives of Ontario Reports
PP	Powell Papers (Metropolitan Toronto Library)
RL	J.B. Robinson Letterbook
RP	J.B. Robinson Papers
Salk.	Salkela's English King's Bench Reports
SCR	Supreme Court Reports
SP	Selkirk Papers
UCKB (OS)	Upper Canada King's Bench (Old Series)
UCLJ	*Upper Canada Law Journal*
UCQB	Upper Canada Queen's Bench
UTLJ	*University of Toronto Law Journal*

Notes

The main source of information on the life of Sir John Beverley Robinson is the Robinson Papers held by the Ontario Archives. These are contained on eight reels of microfilm and include the catalogued papers and diaries. John Robinson's personal letterbook is a part of this collection. The Ontario Archives also hold other manuscript collections cited in this book, including the Macaulay Papers, Upper Canada Sundries, Jarvis–Powell Papers, John Strachan Papers, Attorney-General's Papers, and part of volume 42 of the Colonial Office Papers. Reference is also made to the Powell and Baldwin Papers held by the Metropolitan Toronto Library. The Public Archives of Canada hold the Selkirk Papers, Colborne Papers, and the Colonial Office Papers. The Supreme Court of Ontario gave me access to the J.B. Robinson Judge's Book.

CHAPTER 1 THE LOYALIST TRADITION

1 Julia Jarvis *Three Centuries of Robinsons* (Toronto 1953)
2 RL, C. Robinson to R. Robinson, 6 July 1793
3 RL, C. Robinson to Simcoe, 1795
4 31 Geo. III (1791) (UK)
5 E.A. Cruikshank *The Correspondence of Lieutenant Governor John Graves Simcoe with Allied Documents Relating to his Administration of the Government of Upper Canada* I (Toronto 1923–31) 53
6 32 Geo. III (1792), c.1 (UC)

7 34 Geo. III (1794), c.2 (UC)

8 33 Geo. III (1793), c.7 (UC)

9 W.R. Riddell 'An Official Record of Slavery in Upper Canada' *OHSPR* xxv (1929) 393 Despite the passage of this bill in the assembly, it was not approved by the legislative council.

10 C.W. Robinson *Life of Sir John Beverley Robinson* (Toronto 1904) 9

11 RL, Stuart to Strachan, 25 November 1803

12 *Upper Canada Gazette* 24 August 1805

13 MP, J.B. Robinson to Macaulay, 25 November 1808

14 RP, Strachan to J.B. Robinson, 15 October 1807

15 Ibid. same to same, 7 July 1808

16 Edith G. Firth *The Town of York 1793–1815* (Toronto 1962) lxxix

17 MP J.B. Robinson to Macaulay, 31 May 1808

18 Ibid. same to same, 13 September 1810

19 Ibid. same to same, 24 July 1810

20 RP, Strachan to J.B. Robinson, 16 November 1807

21 MP, J.B. Robinson to Macaulay, 31 May 1808

22 S.F. Wise 'The Rise of Christopher Hagerman' *Historic Kingston* xiv (1965) 12

23 MP, J.B. Robinson to Macaulay, 25 November 1810

24 Firth *Town of York* 233

25 MP, J.B. Robinson to Macaulay, 1 February 1809

26 Ibid. same to same, 13 September 1810

27 Ibid. same to same, 25 November 1810

28 RP, Strachan to J.B. Robinson, 30 September 1809

29 Ibid. same to same, 25 January 1809

30 MP, J.B. Robinson to Macaulay, 13 September 1810

31 Matilda Edgar *Ten Years in Upper Canada in Peace and War 1805–1815* (Toronto 1890): T.G. Ridout to T. Ridout, 11 October 1811 (at 63)

32 JSP, J.B. Robinson to Strachan, 18 September 1811

CHAPTER 2   THIS OUTPOST OF ENGLAND

1 J.B. Robinson *Canada and the Canada Bill* (London) 1840; Johnson Reprint 1967) 36

2 RP, narrative (in the form of a letter probably intended for Dr Strachan), 14 October 1812

3 D.B. Read, *Life and Times of Major General Isaac Brock, KB* (Toronto 1894) 229. John Richardson in *Richardson's War of 1812* (Toronto 1902) states on page 115 that Robinson assumed the command during Captain Heward's absence. This is not surprising given that Heward was Robinson's brother-in-law. How-

ever C.W. Robinson's reference in his *Life of Sir John Beverley Robinson* to his father's being mentioned in Sheaffe's report of the battle appears to be false. This report, Sheaffe to Prevost, 13 October 1812, (see footnote 7, page 281) refers to a Lieutenant Richardson, not Robinson. It is apparently a reference to Lieutenant Reuben Richardson who commanded the flank company of the First York Regiment.

4 RP, Strachan to J.B. Robinson, 9 November 1812
5 W.R. Riddell *The Life of William Dummer Powell, First Judge at Detroit, and Fifth Chief Justice of Upper Canada* (Lansing 1924) 112–213, quoting Powell: 'The admirable success of the first attempt [Macdonell's appointment] encouraged one to urge almost an inconsistency upon Major General Sheaffe in the appointment of Mr. J.B. Robinson to succeed Mr. McDonell [sic].' See also RP *J.B. Robinson Memorandum*: 'I [Robinson] had only seen him [Sheaffe] once as he passed our station on the river, and again during the action at Queenston, and had no acquaintance with him. When I waited upon him, which I did the day I landed, he told me that he had placed me in the office at the suggestions of Mr. Justice Powell, who was an old and intimate friend of his.'
6 COP, H.J. Boulton to Bathurst, 8 March 1813
7 William Wood, ed. *British Documents of the Canadian War of 1812* I (New York 1968) 487
8 RP, J.B. Robinson to MacMahon, 22 December 1812
9 UC Sundries, de Rottenburg to Brenton, 7 July 1813
10 RP, *J.B. Robinson Memorandum*
11 A.G. Doughty and D.A. McArthur, eds. *Documents relating to the Constitutional History of Canada, 1791–1818* (Ottawa 1914) 435
12 William M. Weekes 'The War of 1812: Civil Authority and Martial Law in Upper Canada' *OH* XLVIII (1956) 147, at 158
13 RP, R. Loring to J.B. Robinson, 21 May 1814
14 J.B. Robinson to R. Loring, 2 June 1814, cited in Doughty and McArthur *Documents ... 1791–1818* 437.
15 Ibid. at 438
16 RP, J.B. Robinson to R. Loring, 28 June 1814
17 UC Sundries, Scott and Powell to Prevost, 25 September 1813
18 Memorandum of Justice W.D. Powell, quoted in E.A. Cruikshank 'John Beverley Robinson and the Trials for Treason in 1814' *OHSPR* XXV (1929) 191
19 OA *Minutes of the Executive Council of Upper Canada* 14 August 1813
20 UC Sundries, Powell to de Rottenburg, 14 August 1813
21 RP, de Rottenburg to J.B. Robinson, 13 August 1813
22 UC Sundries, J.B. Robinson to de Rottenburg, 20 August 1813
23 Ibid.

24 AGP, draft, J.B. Robinson to R. Loring, 22 April 1814

25 UC Sundries, J.B. Robinson to de Rottenburg, 20 August 1813

26 AGP, draft, J.B. Robinson to R. Loring, 20 April 1814

27 RP, MacMahon to J.B. Robinson, 26 November 1813

28 An Act to empower His Majesty, for a limited time, to secure and detain such persons as His Majesty shall suspect of a treasonable adherence to the enemy 54 Geo. III (1814), c.5

29 RP, J.B. Robinson to R. Loring, 25 March 1814

30 Blackstone *Commentaries on the Laws of England* (London 1758) I 44

31 W.R. Riddell, 'The Ancaster "Bloody Assize" of 1814' *OHSPR* xx (1923) 107

32 RP, J.B. Robinson to R. Loring, 22 April 1814

33 Ibid. R. Loring to J.B. Robinson, 8 May 1814

34 Ibid. J.B. Robinson to R. Loring, 20 April 1814

35 Ibid. same to same, 12 May 1814

36 AGP, draft, Scott, Powell, and Campbell to Drummond, 13 May 1814

37 RP, J.B. Robinson to R. Loring, 18 June 1814

38 COP, Drummond to Bathurst, 10 July 1814

39 A.L. Burt *The Evolution of the British Empire and Commonwealth from the American Revolution* (Boston 1956) 139

40 Robinson *Canada and the Canada Bill* 15

41 AGP, draft, J.B. Robinson to Lorng, 30 March 1814

42 An Act to afford relief to Barristers and Attornies and to provide for the admission of Law Students within this Province 55 Geo. III (1814), c.3

43 The situation deteriorated further in November 1814. Robinson had prepared commissions to confiscate traitor's lands under the Alien Act, and in order for him to bill the government for his services the confiscations had to be put into effect. Boulton showed no inclination to co-operate, and Robinson enquired angrily whether Boulton intended to issue new commissions: RP, J.B. Robinson to Boulton, 5 April 1815. See also Robert E. Saunders *John Beverley Robinson: His Political Career, 1812–1840* (MA thesis, University of Toronto 1960): 'The very manner in which they [Boulton and Robinson] exchanged offices – the one demoted, the other promoted – would hardly make for amicable relations' (at 61).

44 RP, memorial to Sir Gordon Drummond (n.d.)

45 Ibid. J.B. Robinson to Drummond, 14 April 1815

CHAPTER 3 GENTLEMAN OF LINCOLN'S INN

1 RP, diary entries 1815–17

2 Walter Bagehot *Literary Studies* III (New York 1938) 252–3. It was not until 1833 that the Law Society established a course of lectures for students.

3 RP, diary, 15 November 1815: 'I dined again at the Hall on boiled chicken and roast mutton.'

4 Ibid. 5 November 1815

5 Ibid. 6 November 1815

6 Ibid. 5 December 1815

7 Ibid. 19 October 1815

8 Ibid. 5 January 1816

9 Ibid. 16 April 1816

10 Ibid. 19 February 1816

11 Ibid. 16 November 1815

12 RP, Strachan to J.B. Robinson, 30 September 1816

13 RL, Strachan to J.B. Robinson, 20 November 1815

14 Ibid. same to same, 25 January 1816

15 Ibid. same to same, 7 May 1816

16 Boulton Papers, H.J. Boulton to D'Arcy Boulton, 3 April 1816

17 RL, Strachan to J.B. Robinson, 25 January 1816

18app, J.B. Robinson to W.D. Powell, 12 September 1815

19 COP, Bathurst to Drummond, 10 January 1815

20 Helen Taft Manning *British Colonial Government after the American Revolution 1782–1820* (Hamden 1966) 483–4

21 RP, diary, 28 December 1815

22 Ibid. 19 February 1816

23 Ibid. 5 November 1815

24 Ibid. 15 November 1815

25 Ibid. 15 November 1816

26 George W. Spragge, ed. *John Strachan Letter Book* (Toronto 1964), Strachan to J.B. Robinson, 20 November 1815 (at 103).

27 COP, J.B. Robinson to Bathurst, 15 February 1816

28 RP, Emma Robinson to J.B. Robinson, May 1816

29 Ibid. J.B. Robinson to Emma Robinson, 4 July 1816

30 Ibid. Emma Robinson to J.B. Robinson, July 1816

31 Ibid. diary, 21 November 1816

32 PP, J.B. Robinson to W.D. Powell, 7 February 1817

33 RP, diary, April 1816

34 Ibid. 26 April 1817

35 Croker Papers, Walter Scott to J.W. Croker, March 1817: 'We are all shocked at your giving your mob so much head.'

36 RP, Strachan to J.B. Robinson, 30 September 1816

37 PP, J.B. Robinson to W.D. Powell, 6 December 1816

38 Ibid. Mrs W.D. Powell to G.W. Murray, 2 November 1817

CHAPTER 4 PUBLIC LIFE

1 Lucy Booth Martin *Toronto, 100 Years of Grandeur* (Toronto 1978) 46
2 Law Society of Upper Canada 'Minutes of Convocation' November 1817
3 RP, W. Merry to J.B. Robinson, 6 September 1817
4 COP, Gore to Bathurst, 25 November 1816
5 Ibid. Bathurst to Gore, 14 April 1817
6 RP, W. Merry to J.B. Robinson, 5 September 1817
7 Ibid. same to same, 6 September 1817
8 Spragge, *John Strachan Letter Book*, Strachan to Gore, 16 July 1817, (at 136)
9 UC Sundries, J.B. Robinson to Hillier, 14 August 1820, land titles; J.B. Robinson to Hillier, 17 July 1820, criminal law
10 W.R. Riddell 'The First Attorney General of Upper Canada – John White (1792–1800)' *OHSPR* XXIII (1926) 413
11 Lillian F. Gates *Land Policies of Upper Canada* (Toronto 1968) 100–2
12 A.G. Doughty and N. Story, eds *Documents Relating to the Constitutional History of Canada, 1819–1828* (Ottawa 1935), Gore to Bathurst, 7 April 1817 (at 3)
13 Ibid. Bathurst to Smith, 30 November 1817 (at 5–6).
14 Ibid., opinion of the attorney-general, April 1818 (at 6–9), and report of the executive council, 16 April 1818 (at 9)
15 J.M. Gray *Lord Selkirk of Red River* (Toronto 1963) and M.W. Campbell *The North West Company* (Toronto 1957)
16 RP, diary, 17 December 1816
17 J.L. Henderson, ed. *John Strachan: Documents and Opinions* (Toronto 1969): Strachan to William McGillivray, 2 May 1813 (at 55–6)
18 Spragge, *John Strachan Letter Book*, Strachan to J.B. Robinson, 7 September 1816 (at 4)
19 Henderson *Documents and Opinions* 'A Letter to the Right Honorable the Earl of Selkirk ...': 'to encourage emigration to the Red River, is to sacrifice the superfluous population of Great Britain, and to injure her American colonies ...' (at 62).
20 BPP V, J.B. Robinson to Selkirk, 19 April 1818 (at 456)
21 Ibid. J.B. Robinson to Maitland, 5 December 1818 (at 455)
22 SP, J. Woods to Selkirk, 28 February 1818
23 BPP V, Bathurst to Sherbrooke, 11 February 1817 (at 256)
24 PACR 1896, Powell to Maitand, n.d. (at 88)
25 BPP V, J.B. Robinson to J. Allan, 12 September 1818 (at 443)
26 Ibid., J. Allan to J.B. Robinson, 16 September 1818 (at 443–4)
27 Ibid., J.B. Robinson to Maitland, 5 December 1818 (at 448)
28 Ibid. at 453

29 Ibid. at 454: 'I considered myself fortunate in thus having the benefit of Mr. Gale's talents, and knowledge of facts and evidence ...'

30 W.H. Pearson *Recollections and Records of Toronto of Old* (Toronto 1914) 77

31 J.C. Dent *The Story of the Upper Canadian Rebellion* I (Toronto 1885) 13

32 Amos *Report of the Trials in the Court of Canada Relative to the Destruction of the Earl of Selkirk's Settlement at Red River* (London 1820). See also Gray *Lord Selkirk of Red River* 291–301.

33 SP, J. Gale to Lady Selkirk, 30 October 1818

34 BPP V, Selkirk to Maitland, 21 October 1818 (at 439): 'My conduct has been misrepresented, and my character traduced in the most infamous manner' (at 440).

35 Ibid. J.B. Robinson to Maitland, 15 March 1819, 466

36 RP, memorandum

37 BPP V, J.B. Robinson to Maitland, 5 December 1818 (at 454)

38 PP, W.D. Powell to wife, 11 September 1818

39 *UCLJ* (March 1863) 62

40 COP, Bathurst to Maitland, 11 May 1819

41 Henry Scadding *Toronto of Old* (Toronto 1878) 122

42 F.M. Quealey 'The Administration of Sir Peregrine Maitland, Lieutenant Governor of Upper Canada, 1818–1828' (PHD thesis, University of Toronto 1968): 'He [Maitland] was quite prepared to delegate as much of his authority as possible to his chief lieutenants, especially to his private secretary, Major Hillier' (at 109).

43 PP, J.B. Robinson to W.D. Powell, 6 November 1816

44 E.A. Cruikshank 'The Government of Upper Canada and Robert Gourlay' *OHSPR* XXIII (1926) 65, at 124

45 Ibid. at 134

46 Ibid. J.B. Robinson to S.P. Jarvis, 13 June 1818 (at 145)

47 Ibid. same to same, 13 June 1818 (at 146)

48 Ibid. J.B. Robinson to Colonel Smith, 29 June 1818 (at 152)

49 Ibid. Maitland to Bathurst, 19 August 1818 (at 156–7)

50 Robert Gourlay *Statistical Account of Upper Canada* I (London 1822) 575–6

51 Cruikshank *The Government of Upper Canada* Richmond to Bathurst, 11 August 1818 (at 156)

52 PAO, 1913 *Journals of the Assembly* 28 October 1818 (at 38)

53 Cruikshank *The Government of Upper Canada* Judges Powell, Campbell, and Boulton to Maitland, 10 November 1818 (at 164)

54 Ibid. Swayzie to Hillier, 16 December 1818

55 Ibid. Maitland to Goulburn, 22 July 1819 (at 171)

56 Ibid. J.B. Robinson to Colonel Smith, 29 June 818 at 152

57 Gates *Land Policies of Upper Canada* 113
58 Cruikshank *The Government of Upper Canada* William Dickson to Hillier, 23 August 1819 (at 172)
59 Doughty and Story *Documents ... 1819–1828* Maitland to Bathurst, 19 July 1819 (at 24–5)
60 Ibid. J.B. Robinson to Hillier, 10 June 1819 (at 26)
61 S.F. Wise 'John Macaulay: Tory for all Seasons' in Gerald Tulchinsky, ed. *To Preserve and Defend: Essays on Kingston in the Nineteenth Century* (Montreal 1976) 188
62 MP, Strachan to Macaulay, 9 October 1820
63 COP, Hillier to Goulburn, 26 September 1819. The 'secret service fund' was a slush fund; Hiller placed government advertising in Macaulay's paper to keep it solvent and to encourage it to support the government.
64 Ibid. J.B. Robinson to Bathurst, 15 February 1816; see also R.L. Fraser 'Like Eden in Her Summer Dress: Gentry, Economy, and Society, Upper Canada, 1812–1840,' (PHD thesis, University of Toronto 1979) at 17.
65 *Kingston Chronicle* 26 March 1819
66 Ibid.27 August 1819
67 *Upper Canada Gazette* 29 June 1820
68 W.R. Riddell 'The First Canadian War-Time Prohibition Measure' *CHR* I (1920) 189
69 MTL, broadside collection, 1820
70 *Kingston Chronicle* 30 June 1820

CHAPTER 5   PARLIAMENTARY LIFE

 1 MP, J.B. Robinson to Macaulay, 22 January 1821
 2 PAO 1913, 2 February 1821 (at 268)
 3 Ibid. 3 February 1821 (at 271)
 4 Ibid. 10 February 1821 (at 320)
 5 MP, Hagerman to Macaulay, February 1821: 'We [Robinson and Hagerman] are the only two who take any decidedly active part in opposition to the little gentleman [Nichol].'
 6 *Upper Canada Gazette* 8 February 1821, reporting debate of 5 February 1821
 7 MP, J.B. Robinson to Macaulay, 19 February 1821
 8 Ibid.
 9 MP, Hagerman to Macaulay, February 1821
10 UC Sundries, J.B. Robinson to Hillier, 10 September 1820
11 *York Weekly Post* 22 February 1821, reporting debate of 8 February 1821
12 MP, Hagerman to Macaulay, 17 February 1821

13 UC Sundries, J.B. Robinson to Maitland, 21 April 1819
14 Alan Wilson *The Clergy Reserves of Upper Canada: A Canadian Mortmain* (Toronto 1968) 44–5
15 Doughty and Story *Documents ... 1819–1828* opinion of the Law Officers of the Crown, 15 November 1819 (at 27–8)
16 An Act to establish an uniform Currency throughout this Province 2 Geo. IV (1821), c.13
17 UC Sundries, J.B. Robinson to Hillier, 18 November 1818
18 MP, J.B. Robinson to Macaulay, 19 February 1821
19 PAO 1913, 5 February 1821 (at 272)
20 Ibid. 31 March 1821 (at 428–35)
21 Fraser 'Like Eden in Her Summer Dress' 105
22 MP, J.B. Robinson to Macaulay, 1 April 1821
23 PAO 1913, 31 March 1821 (at 433)
24 MP, Hagerman to J.B. Robinson, 3 March 1821: 'We are far from being in the deplorable state he [Nichol] has constantly asserted.'
25 Fraser 'Like Eden in Her Summer Dress' 113
26 PAO 1913, 28 March 1821 (at 420–1)
27 RL, J.B. Robinson to Seaton, 13 June 1854
28 PAO 1913, 14 April 1821 (at 512)
29 MP, J.B. Robinson to Macaulay, 11 March 1821
30 PAO 1913, 9 February 1821, and M.P., Hagerman to Macaulay, 28 February 1821: 'The extraordinary manner in which Horne conducts his paper compels Robinson and myself to depend on you [Macaulay] for a faithful representation of our sentiments.'
31 PP, J.B. Robinson to Powell, 19 January 1819
32 MP, Strachan to Macaulay, 13 June 1820
33 Ibid. J.B. Robinson to Macaulay, 18 November 1821
34 RP, charge to the grand jury, Picton, 28 September 1825
35 Fraser 'Like Eden in Her Summer Dress': 'The gentry were faced with a major contradiction in their self-image – the absence of landed estates to support the traditional political language of their assumed rank' (at 208).
36 Firth *The Town of York*: The chief justice's wife, the personification of Upper Canadian snobbery, once described a dinner invitation as 'a piece of insolence & rejected it accordingly, accustom'd to proper respect from those who are consider'd by me as far their superiors' (Mrs. W.D. Powell to George Murray, 25 November 1805, at 256–7).
37 S.D. Clark *The Developing Canadian Community* 2d ed. (Toronto 1962): 'Distinctions of social class found little recognition in poneer communities where the demands of neighbourhood association pressed so heavily upon the inhabitants' (at 65).

38 RP, diary, 23 September 1815
39 J. Phean 'A Duel on the Island' *OH* LXIX (1977), W.W. Baldwin to his wife Phebe, 2 April 1812 (at 237)
40 W.R. Riddell 'The Solicitor General Tried for Murder' *Canadian Law Times* XL (1920) 636
41 JBRJB, Brockville assizes, *R.* v *John Wilson*
42 Doughty and Story *Documents ... 1819–1828* petition of the freeholders of Lennox and Addington, 82–3
43 MP, J.B. Robinson to Macaulay, 18 November 1821
44 Wise 'John Macaulay' 192–3
45 PAO 1914, 29 November 1821 (at 37)
46 Ibid.
47 MP, J.B. Robinson to Macaulay, 13 December 1821
48 PAO 1914, 11 December 1821 (at 66). The bill would have guaranteed the equal distribution of the property of a person who died intestate, thereby abolishing the ancient rule of inheritance whereby the eldest male in the same degree succeeded to the ancestor's lands to the exclusion of all others.
49 Ibid. 29 December 1821 to 4 January 1822 (at 125–52)
50 *Kingston Chronicle* 22 February 1822
51 Ibid.
52 Dent *Story of the Upper Canadian Rebellion* 101
53 PAO 1914, 4 January 1822 (at 152), vote seventeen to sixteen in favour of motion
54 Doughty and Story *Documents ... 1819–1828*; *Quebec Gazette* 4 April 1822, reprinted from *Upper Canada Herald* (at 87)
55 *Kingston Chronicle* 11 January 1822
56 PAO 1914, 4 December 1821 (at 44)
57 *Kingston Chronicle* 14 December 1821, reporting debate of 28 November 1821
58 PAO 1914, 21 November 1821 (at 3)
59 MP, J.B. Robinson to S, 19 December 1821
60 PAO 1914, 22 December 1821 (at 96–112)
61 UC Sundries, Strachan to Hillier, 21 March 1822
62 Ibid.
63 PP, J.B. Robinson to Powell, 15 January 1822
64 UC Sundries, Powell to Maitland, 19 January 1822: 'The morning in your presence softened by the appearance of sympathy. I lost all command and betrayed a weakness which I implore your Excellency to forget.'
65 PAO 1914, J.B. Robinson to Maitland, 14 January 1822 (at 181)

CHAPTER 6 AN ADVOCATE IN ENGLAND

1 JPP, Anne Powell to Mrs W.D. Powell, 6 September 1818
2 Ibid. W.B. Robinson to S.P. Jarvis, 28 January 1822
3 Sir Henry Lefroy *Autobiography.*
4 PP, Mrs W.D. Powell to Eliza Powell, 3 February 1822
5 UC Sundries, J.B. Robinson to Hillier, 24 February 1822
6 JPP, Eliza Powell to Mrs Samuel Peters Jarvis, 12 June 1822
7 Ibid. S.P. Jarvis to wife, 21 November 1823
8 RL, J.B. Robinson to Strachan, 29 June 1822
9 Ibid. same to same, 29 June 1822. Powell seemed to suspect that Robinson
  was going to use the question of the union of Upper and Lower Canada to
  take away some of his family's sinecures. According to Robinson, 'I dare say
  he thought I was urging a union of the Legislature in some measure for the
  satisfaction of taking their salaries away.'
10 UC Sundries, J.B. Robinson to Hillier, 9 April 1822
11 Ibid. same to same, 20 March 1822
12 Ibid. J.B. Robinson to Maitland, 16 July 1822
13 E.G. Jones *Sir R.J. Wilmot Horton, Bart, Politician and Pamphleteer* (MA thesis,
   Bristol 1936): Greville to Wilmot, 4 December 1821 (at 39)
14 UC Sundries, J.B. Robinson to Hillier, 9 April 1822
15 J.C. Beaglehole 'The Colonial Office, 1782–1854' *Historical Studies Australia
   and New Zealand* I (1940–1) 181
16 UC Sundries, J.B. Robinson to Hillier, 9 April 1822
17 RL, J.B. Robinson to Strachan, 29 June 1822
18 Beaglehole 'The Colonial Office' 177
19 J.E. Cookson *Lord Liverpool's Administration – The Crucial Years, 1815–1822*
   (Edinburgh 1975)
20 UC Sundries, J.B. Robinson to Hillier, 9 April 1822.
21 Actually, *reunite,* for the act of 1791 had divided the former province of
   Quebec.
22 Helen Taft Manning *The Revolt of French Canada 1800–1835* (Toronto 1962)
   248–9
23 UC Sundries, J.B. Robinson to Hillier, 22 April 1822
24 PAO 1914, J.B. Robinson to Wilmot, 23 April 1822 (at 251–6)
25 Ibid. at 254
26 UC Sundries, J.B. Robinson to Hillier, 23 July 1822
27 *Parliamentary Debates* (new series VII) 20 June 1822 (at 1199)
28 UC Sundries, J.B. Robinson to Hillier, 19 July 1822: 'This private history of
   these measures of which of course Canadian will feel keenly or may be

excited to do so, I have written to no one else, nor shall I. It will of course find its way out but not thro' me. You had better I think select the best report and send it at once to Macaulay ...'

29 RL, J.B. Robinson to Strachan, 29 June 1822
30 Ibid.
31 UC Sundries, J.B. Robinson to Hillier, 19 July 1822
32 RL, Strachan to J.B. Robinson, 13 June 1822
33 Ibid. J.B. Robinson to Strachan, 29 June 1822
34 Ibid. Strachan to J.B. Robinson, 1 September 1822
35 Ibid.
36 UC Sundries, J.B. Robinson to Maitland, 16 July 1822
37 Ibid. J.B. Robinson to Hillier, 17 July 1822
38 3 Geo. IV (1822), c.119
39 R.W. Horton *Exposition and Defence of Earl Bathurst's Administration of the Affairs of Canada* (London 1838) 9
40 PAO 1914, J.B. Robinson to Hillier, 27 August 1822 (at 275–62)
41 Ibid. at 259
42 RL, Strachan to J.B. Robinson, 1 September 1822
43 *Kingston Chronicle* 21 June 1822
44 *Kingston Chronicle* 1 November 1822
45 MP, Strachan to Macaulay, 13 November 1822
46 UC Sundries, J.B. Robinson to Hillier, 18 December 1822
47 Ibid.
48 Donald Creighton *The Empire of the St. Lawrence* (Toronto 1956) 217
49 UC Sundries, J.B. Robinson to Hillier, 23 August 1822
50 Ibid. same to same, 11 November 1822
51 Ibid. same to same, 26 November 1822
52 PAO 1914, J.B. Robinson to Hillier, 28 December 1822, and Wilmot to Hillier, 27 December 1822 (at 345–6)
53 UC Sundries, J.B. Robinson to Hillier, 26 November 1822
54 RP, J.B. Robinson memorandum
55 'Plan for a General Legislative Union of the British Provinces in North America' pamphlet printed in London in 1824, taken from a letter from J.B. Robinson to Lord Bathurst. Reprinted in *Four Early Pamphlets on the Subject of Confederation and Union of the Canadas* (Toronto 1967)
56 Ibid. at 29
57 Ibid. at 31–2
58 Ibid. at 40
59 *Review of a Plan for Uniting the Provinces of North America under a Congress or General Legislature*: this report is initialled by either S.S. or J.S. If it was pre-

pared by J.S., it is possibly the work of James Stephen, as quoted in K.L.P. Martin 'The Union Bill of 1822,' *CHR* v (1924) 43, at 50

60 Ibid. 52.
61 UC Sundries, J.B. Robinson to Hillier, 18 December 1822
62 Ibid.
63 Ibid. same to same, 26 January 1823
64 RP, J.B. Robinson to George Arthur, 9 March 1841
65 Gates *Land Policies of Upper Canada* 123–4
66 UC Sundries, J.B. Robinson memorandum dated 14 January 1823: also in RP, copy of paper submitted by J.B. Robinson to Wilmot, 10 January 1823
67 Gerald M. Craig *Upper Canada: The Formative Years 1784–1841* (Toronto 1977) 165–8
68 Wilson *Clergy Reserves of Upper Canada* 72
69 UC Sundries, W. Hill to Wilmot, 11 February 1823
70 *Kingston Chronicle* 31 January 1823
71 Ibid. 14 March 1823
72 UC Sundries, J.B. Robinson to Hillier, 18 December 1822
73 *Kingston Chronicle* 11 July 1823
74 Ibid.
75 Ibid. 21 February 1823
76 UC Sundries, J.B. Robinson to Hillier, 18 December 1822
77 RP, J.B. Robinson to Wilmot Horton, 6 March 1827
78 MP, J.B. Robinson to Macaulay, 25 March 1823
79 UC Sundries, J.B. Robinson to Hillier, 10 June 1822
80 RL, J.B. Robinson to Wilmot Horton, April 1823
81 John and Robert Cartwright Papers, Strachan to J.S. Cartwright, 10 January 1842. I am indebted to Dr R.L. Fraser for bringing this passage to my attention.
82 MP, J.B. Robinson to Macaulay, 25 March 1823

CHAPTER 7 'HE SERVES THE KING, SIR'

1 Sir Peregrine Maitland's mansion was destroyed by fire in 1842. A sand deposit was discovered at Stamford and the estate was eventually criss-crossed by railroads and disfigured by quarries. Nothing remains of the original estate: see Quealey 'Administration of Sir Peregrine Maitland.'
2 RL, J.B. Robinson to Peter Robinson, 20 July 1823
3 Ibid.
4 MP, J.B. Robinson to Macaulay, 25 July 1826
5 'An Act to repeal part of and amend an Act passed in the thirty seventh year

of His Late Majesty's reign, intitled An Act for the better regulating the practice of Law ...' 2 Geo. IV, (1822), c.5; *Kingston Chronicle* 28 December 1821, reporting debate of 3 December 1821.

6 *Kingston Chronicle* 28 December 1821, reporting debate of 4 December 1821

7 Ibid.

8 'An Act to repeal part of and amend the Laws in force respecting the practice of His Majesty's Court of King's Bench' 2 Geo. IV (1822) c.1, s.45

9 AGP, Leonard to J.B. Robinson, 30 October 1826, and J.B. Robinson to Leonard, 3 November 1826

10 J.B. Robinson Docket Book 1817–21, *Wm. Dickson* v *Daniel Penfield* (Hilary Term 1818)

11 Ibid. *Wm. Murray* v *S.P. Jarvis* (1819)

12 (1824) Taylor UCKB 70

13 Ibid. at 74–5

14 *McIver et al.* v *McFarlane* (1824) Taylor UCKB 113

15 *Colonial Advocate* 5 August 1824

16 *Brown* v *Hudson* (1826) Taylor UCKB 390

17 *UCLJ* (March 1862) 62

18 RL, M.S. Bidwell to W.B. Robinson, 24 February 1863

19 (1826) Taylor UCKB 336

20 Ibid. at 339

21 *Weekly Register* 6 November 1823

22 UC Sundries, W.D. Powell to lieutenant-governor, 22 September 1820

23 *UE Loyalist* 30 September 1826

24 See UC Sundries, J.B. Robinson to Hillier, 2 December 1820. As a result of the numerous mandatory death sentences, petitions for clemency were a regular feature of criminal procedures. Robinson complained that the government was forced to consider as many pleas for clemency as charges of misconduct. The government therefore incurred 'an expense in granting its pardon at least equal to that incurred by the prosecution.'

25 *Weekly Register* 21 August 1823

26 AGP, King's Bench Criminal Assizes Minute Book, Home District, October 1823; see also Robert L. Fraser 'Mary Thompson' in *Dictionary of Canadian Biography* VI.

27 UC Sundries, W.D. Powell to Hillier, 25 October 1823

28 UC Sundries, W.D. Powell to Hillier, 29 October 1823

29 Ibid. same to same, 28 November 1823

30 This bill was eventually disallowed in England.

31 According to his father-in-law's will, Wilmot was obliged to add his wife's name, Horton, to his own if he wished to benefit from her substantial inheritance.

32 An Act to repeal several Statutes of this Province respecting the election of Members of the House of Assembly ... 4 Geo. IV (1824), c.3

33 *Weekly Register* 4 December 1823

34 PAO 1914, 6 December 1823 (at 537); also *Weekly Register* 18 December 1823

35 Fraser 'Like Eden in Her Summer Dress' 92

36 Gates *Land Policies of Upper Canada* 145–6

37 Merritt Papers, J.B. Robinson to Merritt, 6 June 1850

38 Ibid.

39 Ibid.

40 PAO 1914, 12 December 1823 (at 546)

41 Ibid. 5 January 1824 (at 607)

42 Robinson *Canada and the Canada Bill* 42–3

43 Quealey 'Administration of Sir Peregrine Maitland.' While commanding troops in South India, Maitland became incensed when he was instructed to observe some of the 'heathen customs' of his native troops.

44 Catton Papers, J.B. Robinson to Wilmot Horton, 25 September 1824

45 COP, J.B. Robinson to Wilmot Horton, 16 February 1825; same to same, 30 January 1825; same to same, 8 January 1824

46 Allan J. Coheo 'Early Banking in Upper Canada' *Historic Kingston* xxx (1982) 47

47 *Kingston Chronicle* 7 March 1823

48 MP, J.B. Robinson to Macaulay, 2 March 1824

49 RL, J.B. Robinson to Peter Robinson, 29 March 1824

50 *Hon. G.H. Markland et al. (Commissioners for Settling the Affairs of the Pretended Bank of Upper Canada) v Bartlet* (1824) Taylor UCKB 146, at 152

51 MP, J.B. Robinson to Macaulay, 2 March 1824

52 *Colonial Advocate* 18 May 1826

53 Lillian F. Gates 'The Decided Policy of William Lyon Mackenzie' *CHR* (1959) 198

54 *Colonial Advocate* 27 May 1824

55 Ibid. 28 October 1824

56 UC Sundries, J.B. Robinson to Hillier, 19 May 1824

57 MP, J.B. Robinson to Macaulay, 12 June 1824

58 RL, Strachan to J.B. Robinson, 10 June 1822

59 MP, J.B. Robinson to Macaulay, 12 June 1824

60 *Weekly Register* 15 July 1824

61 MTL broadside collection, broadside attacking George Duggan, 1824

62 MP, J.B. Robinson to Macaulay, 12 June 1824

63 *Weekly Register* 7 July 1824

64 Lindsey-Mackenzie Papers, William Bergin to Mackenzie, 31 August 1824, in Firth *The Town of York* 95–6

65 amp, J.B. Robinson to Macaulay, 12 June 1824
66 G.H. Patterson 'Studies in Elections and Public Opinion in Upper Canada (PHD thesis, University of Toronto 1969)
67 RL, Merry to J.B. Robinson, November 1824
68 Ibid. Wilmot Horton to J.B. Robinson, 14 January 1825
69 Ibid. J.B. Robinson to Peter Robinson, 26 November 1824

CHAPTER 8   THE ALIEN DEBATES

1 W.D. Lesueur *William Lyon Mackenzie* (Toronto 1979): Mackenzie to Earl Dalhousie, 1824, at 107
2 *Colonial Advocate* 27 January 1825, reporting debate of 22 January 1825
3 Ibid. 14 February 1825, reporting debate of 4 February 1825
4 *Upper Canada Herald* 22 February 1825
5 *Kingston Chronicle* 25 February 1825
6 *Colonial Advocate* 21 February 1825, reporting debate of 19 February 1825
7 Ibid. 28 February 1825
8 Ibid. 3 March 1825, reporting debate of 18 February 1825
9 Hugh G.J. Aitken *The Welland Canal Company – A Study in Canadian Entrprse* (Cambridge 1954)
10 *St Catharines Journal* 25 February 1836: J.B. Robinson to Merritt, 13 December 1833
11 *Journal of the House of Assembly* 1825; 'Report of the Joint Committee on Internal Navigation' 6 April 1825
12 *Colonial Advocate* 21 February 1825
13 Ibid. 18 April 1825
14 Ibid.
15 2 B. & C. 779; 4 D. & R. 394
16 Doughty and Story *Documents ... 1819–1828* opinion of the law officers, 13 November 1824 (at 234–5)
17 *Colonial Advocate* 7 April 1825
18 COP, Maitland to Bathurst, 22 April 1825
19 Ibid.
20 *Colonial Advocate* 28 April 1825
21 The Canada Company was the idea of a Scottish novelist, John Galt, who intended to use a private company to sell large tracts of government land, including clergy and Crown reserves, to settlers.
22 UC Sundries, J.B. Robinson to Maitland, 7 July 1825
23 COP, J.B. Robinson to Hillier, 31 May 1825
24 UC Sundries, J.B. Robinson to Hillier, 6 June 1825

25 Ibid. same to same, 7 July 1825
26 Wilson *Clergy Reserves of Upper Canada* 82
27 UC Sundries, J.B. Robinson to Hillier, 6 July 1825
28 COP, J.B. Robinson to G. Wilson, 28 July 1825
29 RP, J.B. Robinson to Wilmot Horton, 6 March 1827
30 COP, Bathurst to Maitland, 22 July 1825
31 RP, J.B. Robinson to Wilmot Horton, 6 March 1827
32 Charles R. Sanderson, ed. *The Arthur Papers* III (Toronto 1959), J.B. Robinson to Arthur, 28 September 1841 (at 461)
33 RP, *Report of the Lieutenant-Governor to the House of Assembly*, 15 November 1825
34 J.B. Robinson, *Speech in Committee on the Bill for conferring Civil Rights on certain Inhabitants of this Province* (York 1825)
35 *Colonial Advocate* 15 December 1825
36 *UE Loyalist*, 27 January 1826, reporting debate of 18 January 1826
37 *Colonial Advocate* 12 January 1826
38 Ibid. 2 February 1826, reporting debate of 6 January 1826
39 *Canadian Freeman* 19 January 1826
40 *Colonial Advocate* 2 February 1826
41 Craig *Upper Canada: The Formative Years* 117
42 *Kingston Chronicle* 21 December 1825, quoted in *Colonial Advocate* 5 January 1826
43 MP, Stanton to Macaulay, 29 January 1826
44 Ibid. J.B. Robinson to Macaulay, 29 March 1826
45 Ibid. same to same, 11 April 1826
46 RP, J.B. Robinson to Strachan, 29 January 1827
47 COP, Maitland to Bathurst, 6 April 1826
48 RL, J.B. Robinson to Peter Robinson, 9 May 1824
49 Jean S. McGill *A Pioneer History of the County of Lanark* (Toronto 1979) 100
50 Paul Knapland *James Stephen and the British Colonial Sysem 1813–1847* (Madison 1953) 67
51 *Colonial Advocate* 18 May 1826
52 MP, Hillier to Macaulay, 29 June 1826
53 UC Sundries, Boulton to Hillier, 4 November 1826
54 7 Geo. IV (1826), c.68 (UK)
55 RP, Bathurst to Maitland, 31 August 1826
56 *Colonial Advocate* 18 January 1827
57 *UE Loyalist* 3 February 1827, reporting debate of 11 January 1827
58 Ibid. 10 February 1827, reporting debate of 29 January 1827
59 Ibid. 16 February 1828, reporting debate of 6 February 1828
60 Doughty and Story *Documents … 1819–1828* Maitland to Bathurst, 3 March 1827 (at 356–62)

61 Francis Collins *An Abridged View of the Alien Question Unmasked* (York 1827)
62 *Colonial Advocate* 22 February 1827
63 COP, J.B. Robinson to Peter Robinson, 10 May 1827
64 JSP, Strachan to J.B. Robinson, 23 April 1827
65 Doughty and Story *Documents ... 1818–1828* Wilmot Horton to Maitland, 6 July 1827 (at 362–3)
66 Ibid. Goderich to Maitland, 10 July 1827 (at 363–6)
67 COP, Maitland to Goderich, 2 October 1827
68 MP, Stanton to Macaulay, 10 February 1828
69 Ibid.
70 John Garner *The Franchise and Politics in British North America 1755–1867* (Toronto 1969) (at 169)
71 RL, Peter Robinson to J.B. Robinson, 29 October 1827
72 Ibid. Stephen to J.B. Robinson, 19 July 1828

CHAPTER 9   'POLITICS I AM NOT FOND OF'

1 Thomas Dalton *Letter to C.A. Hagerman* (Kingston 1824) in S.F. Wise 'Kingston Election and Upper Canadian Politics, 1820–1826' *OH* LVII (1965) 214
2 W.S. Wallace *The Family Compact* (Toronto 1915) 3–4
3 Graeme Patterson 'An Enduring Canadian Myth: Responsible Government and the Family Compact' *JCS* XII (1977) 3, at 6
4 W.L. Mackenzie *Sketches of Canada and the United States* (New York 1833) 409
5 Aileen Dunham *Political Unrest in Upper Canada, 1815–1836* (Toronto 1963; first prited 1927) 44
6 Craig *Upper Canada: The Formative Years* 107
7 COP, Maitland to Goulburn, 19 August 1819
8 Quenley 'Administration of Sir Peregrine Maitland' 109
9 MP, J.B. Robinson to Macaulay, 21 December 1829
10 F.H. Armstrong 'The Oligarchy of the Western District of Upper Canada, 1788–1841' *Canadian Historical Association Report* (1977) 86
11 Michael S. Cross 'The Age of Gentility: The Formation of an Aristocracy in the Ottawa Valley' ibid. (1967) 105
12 J.E. Rea *Bishop Alexander Macdonell and the Politics of Upper Canada* (Toronto 1974) 216
13 See correspondence in AGP 1821. W.M. Berczy protested to Robinson that magistrates on the Thames River had made a biased decision that was not justified by any evidence. Robinson agreed, and ordered the magistrates to amend their decision to conform to the evidence. They refused to do so, and Berczy reported that 'that Gentleman [the attorney-general] was at a loss in

what way to bring an action in a case so unforseen': Berczy to Hillier, 26
September 1822

14 S.F. Wise 'Upper Canada and the Conservative Tradition' in Edith Firth, ed.
   Profiles of a Province (Toronto 1967) 20 at 26
15 Patterson 'Studies in Elections' 407
16 Wise 'Upper Canada and the Conservative Tradtion' 21
17 Wise 'John Macaulay' 200–1. Hagerman's appointment to the bench was not
   confirmed and on this occasion he served for only a few months.
18 MP, J.B. Robinson to Macaulay, 19 July 1828
19 UC Sundries, J.B. Robinson to Colborne, 21 October 1829
20 Ibid. J.B. Robinson to ——— 31 May 1833
21 Ibid. J.B. Robinson to Hillier, 26 November 1822
22 AGP, J. Strobridge to J.B. Robinson, 30 March 1827
23 Quealey 'Administration of Sir Peregrine Maitland' chap. 15
24 *Journal of the House of Assembly* 1828 'Report of the Select Committee on the
   Petition of William Forsyth'
25 Josephine Phelan 'The Tar and Feather Case: The Gore Assizes August 1827'
   OH LXVII (1976) 17
26 UC Sundries, J.B. Robinson to Hillier, 1 December 1826
27 JSP, Strachan to J.B. Robinson, 23 April 1827
28 COP, J.B. Robinson to Hillier, 12 May 1828
29 Ibid. Willis to Colonial Secretary, 21 April 1828
30 Ibid. Maitland to Huskisson, 14 May 1828
31 PP, S.P. Jarvis to W.D. Powell, 24 April 1828
32 *Canadian Freeman* 17 April 1828
33 COP, Stephen to colonial secretary, 5 June 1828
34 Robert Hett 'Judge Willis and the Court of King's Bench in Upper Canada'
   OH LXV (1973) 19, at 26

CHAPTER 10   TORY TWILIGHT

1 *UE Loyalist* 2 February 1828, reporting debate of 23 January 1828
2 Ibid. 1 March 1828, reporting debate of 22 February 1828
3 MP, J.B. Robinson to Macaulay, 24 January 1828
4 Ibid. Stanton to Macaulay, 10 February 1828
5 RP, M.S. Bidwell to W.B. Robinson, 24 February 1863
6 Ontario Archives, Mary O'Brien's journal, 21 February 1829
7 *Canadian Freeman* 25 October 1827
8 Ibid. 5 June 1828
9 Ibid. 25 October 1827

10 *Colonial Advocate* 5 November 1827

11 Ibid. 15 November 1827

12 Mackenzie's gloating was not mere speculation. The Roman Catholic bishop and leader of the Highland Scots, Alexander Macdonell, has asked Robinson to contest the Glengarry seat: 'I am convinced and so is every elector in the County that of all the Candidates that could present themselves you are the one that has it in his power to do the most good to the County with the least trouble to himself' (Alexander Macdonell Papers, Macdonell to J.B. Robinson, 27 December 1827). There is no record of Robinson's reply.

13 COP, Maitland to Sir George Murray, 18 September 1828: 'Dr. Morrison was a few years ago admitted as a Copying Clerk in the Surveyor General's Office, and was removed from thence on the representation of the Surveyor General for misconduct': in Firth *Town of York* 118.

14 MP, J.B. Robinson to Macaulay, 24 January 1828

15 *Canadian Freeman* 17 July 1828

16 COP, Maitland to Murray, 12 August 1828

17 Hartwell Bowsfield 'Upper Canada in the 1820s – The Development of a Political Consciousness' (PH D thesis, University of Toronto 1976): 'Upper Canadians had shaped an embryonic party system which would be the vehicle for later and more systematic organizations of political sentiment' (at 374).

18 Patterson 'Studies in Elections' 499

19 *Gore Gazette* 14 June 1828

20 COP, Maitland to Murray, 18 September 1828

21 MP, J.B. Robinson to Macaulay, 28 November 1828

22 *Canadian Freeman* 16 October 1828

23 Ibid. 30 October 1828

24 PP, S.P. Jarvis to W.D. Powell, 24 December 1828

25 Quealey 'Administration of Sir Peregrine Maitland': '... still when all this has been said, it seems that Robinson was unduly vindictive in his pursuit of this conviction ... it should probably remain a blot on Robinson's record' (at 203).

26 Firth *Town of York* S.P. Jarvis to W.D. Powell, 24 December 1828 (at 159–60)

27 MP, J.B. Robinson to Macaulay, 28 November 1828

28 RP, J.B. Robinson to Wilmot Horton, 24 December 1828

29 *Kingston Chronicle* 24 January 1829

30 *Colonial Advocate* 12 February 1829

31 Ibid.

32 Firth *Town of York* quoting the *U.E. Loyalist* of 7 March 1829 (at 121–2)

33 This bill was never granted royal assent.

34 UC Sundries, J.B. Robinson to Mudge, 19 March 1829

35 Spragge *John Strachan Letter Book* 122

36 *Journal of the House of Assembly* 1828 'Report on the Petition of Bulkeley Waters'
37 JSP, Maitland to J.B. Robinson, 27 April 1829
38 Ibid. Macaulay to J.B. Robinson, 22 February 1850
39 MP, J.B. Robinson to Macaulay, 21 August 1828
40 RP, memorandum

CHAPTER 11   A LOVE OF ORDER

1 Ontario Archives, Mary O'Brien's Journal, 10 April 1830.
2 Law Society of Upper Canada 'Minutes of Convocation' 9 January 1827 (at 119)
3 Only a year after this sale to the Law Society, Robinson sold 5.1 acres of the same park lot to King's College for only £127. Also in 1829, another sale of 50 acres to King's College was made at a price of £1,350: abstract to Park Lot 11, Toronto Land Registry Office.
4 Law Society of Upper Canada 'Minutes of Convocation' 21 November 1824 90
5 D.B. Read *Lives of the Judges of Upper Canada and Ontario* (Toronto 1888) 137
6 *Evans et al.* v *Shaw* (1829) Draper UCKB 14: 'my brothers and myself have anxiously endeavoured to bring our minds to the same conclusion upon it, but I regret to say we have not succeeded in that attempt, and it therefore only remains that we declare the opinions which we have severally formed' (at 18).
7 *Holt* v *Jarvis* (1830) Draper UCKB 170
8 *Baker* v *Booth* (1830) Draper UCKB 65
9 *Phillips* v *Redpath and McKay* (1830) Draper UCKB 68
10 *Robinet* v *Lewis* (1830) Draper UCKB 164
11 *Grant* v *McLean* (1834) 3 UCKB (OS) 443
12 *Rex* v *Justices of Newcastle* (1830) Draper UCKB 204
13 *Evans et al.* v *Shaw* (1829) Draper UCKB 14 at 18
14 *Doe ex dem. Jackson* v *Wilkes* (1835) 4 UCKB (OS) 142
15 H. Pearson Gundy 'The Family Compact at Work: The Second Heir and Devisee Commission of Upper Canada, 1805–1841' *OH* LXVI (1974) 129
16 JBRJB (1830) *Elmsley* v *Guouette* Home Assizes (SCO)
17 Ibid. (1834) *Allan* v *Wallbridge* Kingston Assizes (SCO)
18 Ibid. (1838) *Tuck* v *Reaman* Home Assizes (SCO)
19 Ibid. (1831) *R.* v *McMahon* Cornwall Assizes (SCO)
20 Ibid. (1831) *R.* v *Lee* and (1831) *R.* v *Mulgrew and Mulgrave* Kingston Assizes (SCO)
21 Ibid. (1837) *R.* v *Welsh* Cornwall Assizes (SCO)

22 UC Sundries, J.B. Robinson to Rowan, 27 August 1833
23 JBRJB (1831) *R. v Carey and Carey* Brockville Assizes (SCO)
24 Ibid. (1831) *R. v Dickson* Brockville Assizes (SCO)
25 UC Sundries, J.B. Robinson to Rowan, 25 October 1833
26 Ibid. J.B. Robinson to —— n.d.; also see Fred Hamil *The Valley of the Lower Thames, 1640 to 1850* (Toronto 1951) 182–6.
27 Convictions for bestiality are noted in the *Colonial Advocate* 15 September 1831.
28 JBRJB (1831) *R. v Winter* Home Assizes (SCO)
29 Ibid. (1830) *R. v Hutchinson* Home Assizes (SCO)
30 UC Sundries, J.B. Robinson to Colborne, October 1829. Ellsworth eventually received a lesser penalty.
31 MP, J.B. Robinson to Macaulay, 8 December 1835. Robinson did not take the moral state of society entirely seriously. He wryly advised Macaulay that the penalty for bigamy should if anything be reduced, for 'should you not consider that an Irishman, or any other man who has two or three wives has already the penalty of hard labour.'
32 William E. Nelson *The Americanization of the Common Law: The Impact of Legal Change on Massachusetts Society, 1760–1830* (New York 1975)
33 M.S. Hindus 'The Contours of Crime and Justice in Massachusetts and South Carolina, 1767–1878' *AJLH* XXI (1977) 217
34 J.J. Bellomo 'Upper Canadian Attitudes Towards Crime and Punishment' *OH*, LXIV (1972) 11
35 UC Sundries, J.B. Robinson to Hillier, 14 January 1822
36 *Report of the Commissioners on the Subject of Prison, Penitentiaries, etc.* (1836) as quoted in Rainer Baehre 'Origins of the Penitentiary System in Upper Canada' *OH* LXIX (1977) 185, at 196
37 *Upper Canada Herald* 7 October 1829
38 RP, charge to the grand jury, 4 August 1830
39 Ibid. charge to the grand jury, Toronto, 25 May 1841
40 Ibid. charge to the grand jury, Western District, 1836
41 *R. v Sanderson* (1833) 3 UCKB (OS) 103, at 109
42 *Phillips v Redpath and McKay* (1830) Draper UCKB 68
43 *Gould v Jones* (1833) Draper UCKB 144, at 152
44 *MacNab v Bidwell and Baldwin* (1830) Draper UCKB 14
45 Ibid. at 152
46 C.G. Haines *The Role of the Supreme Court in American Government and Politics, 1789–1835* (Berkeley 1944) 613
47 RP, charge to the grand jury, 1837

CHAPTER 12   CHIEF JUSTICE, SPEAKER, AND CONFIDANT

1 UC Miscellaneous, J. Coleman to sister, 10 June 1833
2 Geoffrey Bilson *A Darkened House – Cholera in Nineteenth Century Canada* (Toronto 1980)
3 RL, J.B. Robinson to Emma Robinson, 20 August 1832
4 Merritt Papers, J.B. Robinson to Merritt, 11 December 1829
5 *Canadian Freeman* 20 January 1831
6 MP., Christopher Hagerman to Macaulay, 17 April 1832
7 Ibid. Strachan to Macaulay, 31 January 1831
8 For example, in 1833 Colborne asked Robinson who should serve as Presidet for the Executive Council: M.P., J.B. Robinson to Macaulay, 25 March 1833.
9 Sanderson *The Arthur Papers* I J.B. Robinson to Arthur, 16 April 1838 (at 78)
10 Colborne Papers, J.B. Robinson to Colborne, 23 September 1833
11 BPP VI Murray to Colborne, 29 September 1828 (at 221–3)
12 Ibid. Colborne to Murray, 16 February 1829 (at 301)
13 PACR 1899, Colborne to Hay, 17 September 1830 (at 359)
14 COP, Goderich to Colborne, 8 February 1831
15 *Journal of the Legislative Council* 2 December 1831 at 17
16 UC Sundries, J.B. Robinson to Colborne, 25 February 1830. At the end of this scathing attack on Attorney-General Boulton's report, the Chief Justice added, 'I have felt it proper to take the trouble of giving this statement, in order that a very unconscientious proceeding, as it strikes me, may at least not be confirmed through misapprehension. Pray excuse this long answer to your note and having done so, I have not the slightest desire to interfere.'
17 *Journal of the Legislative Council* 1 December 1831 at 15
18 *An Act to amend the Law respecting Real Property* ... 4 Wm. V (1834), c.1; An Act to Reduce the Number of Cases in which Capital Punishment may be inflicted ... 3 Wm. IV (1833), c.3
19 *Upper Canada Jurist* (1844) 19–20
20 *Debates of the Legislative Assembly of United Canada* XI Part 4; Col. Prince's speech of 29 March 1853 at 2137.
21 *Journal of the Legislative Council* 1832 at 26, 28, 29, 31, 32: see also John D. Blackwell 'Crime in the London District, 1828–1837: A Case Study of the Effect of the 1833 Reform in Upper Canadian Penal Law' *Queen's Law Journal* VI (1981) 528.
22 *Journal of the Legislative Council* 16 December 1831 32
23 *Colonial Advocate* 5 January 1832
24 *Patriot* 28 April 1835
25 *Colonial Advocate* 18 February 1830

26 *Journal of the Legislative Council* 31 December 1833 at 39–40 and 9 January 1834 at 46

27 *Journal of the Legislative Council* 13 February 1837 at 126

28 *Colborne Papers J.B. Robinson to provincial secretary, 26 April 1830*

29 *Colonial Advocate* 5 January 1832

30 *Patriot* 8 March 1836

31 *The Courier* 21 March 1835

32 COP, J.B. Robinson to Colborne, 16 May 1835

33 RL, Colborne to J.B. Robinson, 12 July 1836

CHAPTER 13   REBELLION AND REACTION

1 RL, J.B. Robinson to Emma Robinson, 12 February 1839

2 J.K. Johnson 'The Upper Canada Club and the Upper Canadian Elite, 1837–1840' *OH* LXIX (1977) 151, at 154

3 Sanderson *The Arthur Papers* I, J.B. Robinson to Head, 9 July 1836 (at 10–12)

4 Colborne Papers, J.B. Robinson to Colborne, 20 March 1836

5 F. Head *The Emigrant* (New York 1849) 227

6 Sanderson *The Arthur Papers* I, J.B. Robinson to Arthur, 16 April 1838 (at 78)

7 *MacNab* v *Bidwell and Baldwin* (1830) Draper UCKB 144

8 Mackenzie-Lindsey Papers, entry under 'Sir Francis Bond Head.'

9 RL, J.B. Robinson to Strachan, 24 January 1839

10 BPP IX, executive council to lieutenant-governor, 4 March 1836 (at 474–5

11 Colborne Papers, J.B. Robinson to Colborne, 20 March 1836

12 BPP IX Head to executive council, 5 March 1836, 475–8

13 above, note 7

14 Colborne Papers, J.B. Robinson to Colborne, 20 March 1836

15 MP, J.B. Robinson to Macaulay, 22 January 1836

16 RL, Talbot to J.B. Robinson, 10 July 1836

17 Colborne Papers, J.B. Robinson to Head, 1 November 1837

18 J. FitzGibbon *Appeal to the People of the Late Province of Upper Canada* 10

19 Head *The Emigrant* 209

20 RP, 'Notes on the Rebellion of 1837,' 7 December 1837

21 BPP IX Head to Glenelg, 19 December 1837, at 155–9

22 RL, J.B. Robinson to Emma Robinson, 12 February 1839

23 Ibid. Head to J.B. Robinson, 4 February 1838

24 Colborne Papers, J.B. Robinson to Colborne, 13 January 1838

25 Ibid.

26 See RL, military secretary to J.B. Robinson, 25 October 1838: 'In all of which

arrangements [formation of militia regiments] I have often written for your experience and friendly advice for I have found no one to take your place.'

27 UC Sundries, J.B. Robinson to Arthur, 28 June 1838
28 BPP IX, Glenelg to Arthur, 30 January 1838, at 527
29 *British Colonist* 15 March 1838
30 Colborne Papers, J.B. Robinson to Colborne, 18 January 1838
31 *Christian Guardian* 4 April 1838
32 Read *Lives of the Judges* 240. See also R.D. Edwards *Patrick Pearse and the Triumph of Failure* (New York 1977). General Blackadder, after passing sentence of death on Irish rebel leader Patrick Pearse remarked to some friends, 'I have just done one of the hardest tasks I have ever had to do. I have had to condemn to death one of the finest characters I have ever come across' (at 319)
33 RP, J.B. Robinson notes on the Treason Commission of 1838; *R. v Montgomery* 2 April 1838
34 E.A. Lacey 'The Trials of John Montgomery' *OH* LII (1960) 141, at 154
35 RP, J.B. Robinson notes on the Treason Commission of 1838; *R. v Theller*, 4 April 1838
36 Ibid. *R. v Durand* 7 May 1838
37 C. Durand *Reminiscences of Charles Durand of Toronto, Barrister* (Toronto 1897) 356
38 Because of a possible conflict of interest Robinson declined to preside over his case.
39 26 April 1838
40 BPP IX Arthur to Glenelg, 14 April 1838, (at 530)
41 UC Sundries, Report of Robinson CJ and Jones J, 2 May 1838
42 C. Lindsey *Life of Mackenzie* 40
43 Sanderson *The Arthur Papers* I J.B. Robinson to Arthur, 3 May 1838 (at 101)
44 Ibid. same to same, 16 April 1838 (at 78)
45 Ibid. Arthur to J.B. Robinson, 17 April 1838 (at 80)
46 Ibid. J.B. Robinson to Arthur, 4 July 1838 (at 219)
47 Ibid. same to same, 27 July 1838 (at 248)
48 Ibid. at 248
49 Chester New *Lord Durham – A Biography of John George Lambton First Earl of Durham* (London 1968) 464
50 Sanderson *The Arthur Papers* I, Durham to J.B. Robinson, 16 September 1838 (at 274)
51 RL, J.B. Robinson to Sarah Boulton, 30 October 1839
52 Ontario Archives, probate documents of Peter Robinson.
53 RP, J.B. Robinson to Arthur, 9 March 1841
54 RL, J.B. Robinson to Sarah Boulton, 30 October 1839.

CHAPTER 14 THE CANADA DEBATE

1 Sanderson *The Arthur Papers* I, J.B. Robinson to Arthur, 24 October 1838 319
2 Ibid. same to same, 23 November 1828, (at 394)
3 Ibid. same to same, 11 December 1838, (at 438)
4 RP, diary, December 1838
5 Sanderson *The Arthur Papers* II, J.B. Robinson to Arthur, 2 January 1839 (at 8)
6 Ibid. at 8
7 Ibid. I, J.B. Robinson to Arthur, 11 December 1838 (at 440)
8 RL, J.B. Robinson to Emma Robinson, 22 February 1839
9 RL, Peel to J.B. Robinson, 10 January 1839
10 Sanderson *The Arthur Papers* I, J.B. Robinson to Arthur, 19 February 1839 (at 47)
11 RL, J.B. Robinson to Emma Robinson, 22 February 1839
12 Sanderson *The Arthur Papers* II, J.B. Robinson to Arthur, 19 February 1839 (at 47)
13 Ged Martin *The Durham Report and British Policy* (Cambridge 1972) 29–42
14 RL, J.B. Robinson to Emma Robinson, 22 February 1839
15 Sanderson *The Arthur Papers* II J.B. Robinson to Normanby, 23 February (at 52–65)
16 Ibid. J.B. Robinson to Arthur, 19 March 1839 (at 88)
17 RP, diary, 1 May 1839
18 RL, Exeter to J.B. Robinson, 21 February 1839
19 Ibid. J.B. Robinson to Emma Robinson, 20 March 1839
20 Sanderson *The Arthur Papers* II, J.B. Robinson to Arthur, 24 October 1838 (at 519)
21 RL, J.B. Robinson to Strachan, 15 March 1839
22 Martin *The Durham Report* 38
23 RL, J.B. Robinson to Emma Robinson, 22 March 1839
24 MP, J.B. Robinson to Macaulay, 30 July 1839
25 RL, Colborne to J.B. Robinson, 29 July 1839
26 Sanderson *The Arthur Papers* II, J.B. Robinson to Arthur, 7 July 1839 (at 192)
27 RP, diary, 4 August 1839
28 Sanderson *The Arthur Papers* II J.B. Robinson to Normanby, 16 August 1839 (at 217)
29 Ibid. J.B. Robinson to Arthur, 17 October 1839 (at 283)
30 RL, J.B. Robinson to Sarah Boulton, 30 October 1839
31 Sanderson *The Arthur Papers* II, J.B. Robinson to Macaulay, 13 November 1839 (at 311)
32 RP, diary 16 December 1839
33 Robinson *Canada and the Canada Bil* 22

34 Ibid. 54
35 Ibid. 135
36 Ibid. 140
37 *Commentaries* I (London 1783) 154–5
38 Robinson *Canada and the Canada Bill* 145
39 Ibid. I 42–3
40 Terry Cook 'John Beverley Robinson and the Conservative Blueprint for the Upper Canadian Community' *OH* LXIV 94
41 Walter Bagehot *The English Constitution* (London 1867) 10
42 Barbara Tuchman *The Proud Tower* (New York 1966) 3
43 W.H. McNeill *The Rise of the West* (Chicago 1963): 'A comparatively broad suffrage permitted a large segment – in some colonies an abolute majority – of the adult male population to register its will in politics. This created an atmosphere strikingly different from the passive submission of their bureaucratic, oligarchic and ecclesiastical masters' (at 668–9).
44 *The Times* 30 January 1840
45 Sanderson *The Arthur Papers* III Arthur to Seaton 27 June 1840 (at 87)
46 Ibid. II, Thomson to Arthur, 29 March 1840 (at 475)
47 H. Scadding, *Toronto of Old* (Toronto 1878) 326
48 RL, J.B. Robinson to Sarah Boulton, 31 January 1840
49 Ibid. Hagerman to Robinson, 7 December 1839
50 Sanderson *The Arthur Papers* II Arthur to J.B. Robinson, 25 December 1839 (at 365)
51 RL, J.B. Robinson to William Robinson, 13 November 1839
52 MP, John Macaulay to Ann Macaulay, 17 December 1839
53 RL, J.B. Robinson to Sarah Boulton, 15 December 1839
54 *Spectator* 8 March 1840
55 *Hansard* LII 7 March 1840 at 1201
56 RP, diary, March 1840
57 Ibid.
58 *Hansard* LIV 29 May 1840 at 713
59 Ibid. at 732
60 J.M.S. Careless *The Union of the Canadas – The Growth of Canadian Institutions* (Toronto 1977) 208
61 RL, J.B. Robinson to Emma Robinson, n.d.
62 *British Colonist* 3 June 1840
63 *Patriot* 2 June 1840
64 Ibid. 5 June 1840
65 Fennings Taylor *Portraits of British Americans* (1865) as quoted in C.W. Robinson *Life of Sir John Beverley Robinson* (Toronto 1904)

CHAPTER 15   LORD CHIEF JUSTICE

1 Sanderson *The Arthur Papers* III, Thompson to Arthur, 13 June 1840 (at 79)
2 Ibid. Arthur to Seaton, 27 June 1840 (at 87)
3 Ibid. Thomson to Arthur, 16 August 1840 at 111
4 *Globe* 11 June 1844
5 RP, J.B. Robinson to Metcalfe, 9 March 1844
6 Ibid. Metcalfe to J.B. Robinson, 11 March 1844
7 John Forster, *The Life of Dickens* (London 1911), Dickens to Forster, 3 May 1842 (at 267)
8 BPP XVII, Metcalfe to Stanley, 17 April 1845 (at 4)
9 Ibid. Cathcart to Stanley, n.d. (at 14–15)
10 William Dendy *Lost Toronto* (Toronto 1978) 48; see also Toronto Land Registry Office Abstract Book, Park Lot 11
11 Lefroy *Autobiography*
12 M.L. Smith *Young Mr. Smith in Upper Canada* (Toronto 1980), diary of Larratt Smith, 26 November 1840 (at 47)
13 RL, Strachan to J.B. Robinson, 3 August 1845
14 MP, J.B. Robinson to Macaulay, 24 January 1843
15 MP, J.B. Robinson to Macaulay, 11 September 1843
16 JSP, J.B. Robinson to Strachan, 21 June 1850
17 RL, J.B. Robinson to Strachan, 9 January 1849
18 JSP, Strachan to J.B. Robinson, 31 May 1850
19 JSP, J.B. Robinson to Strachan, 17 June 1851
20 *The Church* J.B. Robinson to the Editor, 12 April 1842
21 Wilson *Clergy Reserves of Upper Canada* 159
22 JSP, J.B. Robinson to Stanley, 24 December 1841
23 MP, J.B. Robinson to Macaulay, 2 September 1842
24 RL, Airey to J.B. Robinson, 3 July 1849
25 *Hamilton* v *The Niagara Harbor and Dock Co.* (1842), 6 UCQB (O.S.) 381 at 399
26 32 Geo. III (1792), c.1 (UC)
27 (1846) 3 UCQB 27 at 28–9
28 *Plumer* v *Simonton* (1859) 16 UCQB 220. Not until a century later would the Canadian Supreme Court declare *Flureau* v *Thornhill* to be without any relevance in Canada: *AVG Management Science Ltd* v *Barwell Developments Ltd et al.* [1979] 2 SCR 43, 92 DLR (3d) 289.
29 *Lister* v *Warren* (1842) 6 UCQB (OS) 256
30 *Jones* v *Spence* (1845) 1 UCQB 367
31 *L'Esperance* v *Duchene* (1850) 7 UCQB 146; *Kimball* v *Smith* (1848) 5 UCQB 32
32 *Ross* v *Merritt* (1846) 2 UCQB 421
33 See also the provincial Seduction Act, 7 Wm. IV (1837), c.8

34 *Brown* v *Shea* (1848) 5 UCQB 141. See also *Crysler* v *Eligh* (1844) 1 UCQB 227: the mere statement of a condition and a breach did not enable the court to imply a breach of that condition.
35 *McAnany* v *Meyers* (1849) 5 UCQB 587
36 *Bagot* v *McKenzie* (1843) 6 UCQB (OS) 580
37 *Whitehead* v *(The) Buffalo and Lake Huron Railway Company* (1859) 7 Ch. 351 at 367
38 *The Buffalo and Lake Huron Railway Company* v *Whitehead* (1860) 8 Ch. 157 at 206
39 *Doe Anderson* v *Todd* (1845) 2 UCQB 82, at 87
40 *Leith* v *Willis (1836)* 5 UCQB (OS) 101, at 103
41 *Bank of Upper Canada* v *Bethune* (1835) 4 UCQB (OS) 165; see also *Stoner* v *Walton* (1842) 6 UCQB 190. Robinson rejected the English requirement to prove a legal marriage by producing the parish register and held instead that in Upper Canada the marriage could be proven by 'cohabitation and reputation.'
42 *Gardiner* v *Gardiner* (1833) 2 UCQB (OS) 520, at 552
43 Of fifteen reported cases in Trinity Term, 1860, ten referred to Canadian decisions or statutes. Of the fifteen reported cases in Easter Term 1831, only four referred to Canadian decisions or statutes.
44 F.J. Turner *The Frontier Thesis in American History* (New York 1947) 343
45 (1846) 2 UCQB 448
46 Ibid. at 450
47 *Turbervill* v *Stamp* 1 Salk. 13
48 (1868) LR 3 HL 330; 37 LJ Ex. 161, aff' LR 1 Ex. 265
49 (1872) 33 UCQB 128, at 140–
50 *Murphy* v *Dalton* (1884) 5 OR 541; *Clark* v *Ward (1909)* 2 Alta. LR 101
51 *Furlong* v *Carroll* [1882] 7 OAR 145 at 165; see also *Elder* v *Kingston* [1954] OWN 439, at 440, dismissing *Dean* v *McCarty* as one of the 'husbandry cases.'
52 Robin Winks *The Myth of the American Frontier: Its Relevance to America, Canada and Australia* (Leicester 1971)
53 Morton Horwitz *The Transformation of American Law, 1780–1860* (Cambridge 1977), quoting Justice Spencer: 'the doctrine of waste, as understood in England,is inapplicable to a new unsettled country ...' (at 55).
54 *Weller* v *Burnham* (1853) 11 UCQB 90
55 R.C.B. Risk 'The Law and the Economy in Mid-Nineteenth Century Ontario: A Perspective' *UTLJ* XXVII (1977) 403, at 407–8
56 *Browne and McDonell* v *Browne* (1852) 9 UCQB 312, at 314
57 David Gagan *Hopeful Travellers: Families, Land, and Social Change in Mid-Victorian Peel County, Canada West* (Toronto 1981) 26–9
58 *Chisholm* v *Proudfoot* (1857) 15 UCQB 203 at 210
59 P.S. Atiyah *An Introduction to the Law of Contract* 2nd ed. (Oxford 1975) 2–10
60 *Jarvis* v *Dalrymple* (1854) 11 UCQB 393 at 399

61 Horwitz *Transformation of American Law* 210

62 *Adams* v *Forde and McCauly* (1856) 13 UCQB 485; *McPherson* v *Cameron* (1857) 15 UCQB 48

63 (1847) 3 UCQB 377 at 379

64 *Bank of Montreal* v *Bethune* (1836) 4 UCQB (OS) 341

65 R.C.B. Risk 'The Nineteenth Century Foundations of the Business Corporation in Ontario' *UTLJ* XXIII (1973) 270, at 271–2

66 (1842) 6 UCQB (OS) 381

67 Ibid. at 387

68 Ibid. at 399

69 (1849) 6 UCQB 174

70 (1859) 17 UCQB 477

71 Ibid. at 485–6: 'There seems now indeed to be some appearance of a disposition in the courts in England to depart from the old current of authority in the very opposite direction, and to hold that a corporation, as long as they keep themselves within the proper sphere of their business, may without any express legislative provisions make themselves liable as upon special executory contracts ... and without binding themselves under their corporate seal.'

72 *Bradbury* v *Oliver* (1839) 5 UCQB (OS) 703; *Bank of Upper Canada* v *Boulton* (1850) 7 UCQB 235; *Reed* v *Reed* (1853) 11 UCQB 26

73 R.C.B. Risk 'The Golden Age: The Law about the Market in Nineteenth-Century Ontario' *UTLJ* XXVI (1976) 307, at 311

74 *Ewart* v *Weller* (1849) 5 UCQB 610, at 612

75 (1849) 5 UCQB 362

76 Ibid. at 368

77 See also *The Queen* v *Hespeler* (1854) 11 UCQB 222, at 227: 'Dr. Connor did indeed refer us to a passage in the very comprehensive American work of Angell and Ames on Corporations (693 and followig pages) which shews that in some of the courts of the United States this remedy has been extended ... but we cannot, for obvious reasons, adopt the authority of these decisions, in opposition to those of the English courts by which we are bound.'

78 *Boulton and The Town of Peterborough* (1858) 16 UCQB 380; applied in *Re Rex* v *Morello* [1936] OWN 473

79 *Charron* v *Montreal Trust Co.* [1958] OR 597 (CA).

80 (1850) 6 UCQB 424

81 (1856) 14 UCQB 213

82 RL, J.B. Robinson to Seaton, 30 March 1854

83 Horwitz *Transformation of American Law* 1

84 Ibid. at 255. Whether Horwitz is correct that a real transformation had occurred from eighteenth-century, law remains moot: see Stephen F. Williams 'Book Review' *UCLA L. Rev.* XXV (1978) 1187.

85 Horwitz *Transformation of American Law* 34–40
86 J.H. Beuscher 'Appropriation Water Law Elements in Riparian Doctrine States' *Buffalo L. Rev.* x (1961) 448
87 *Applegarth* v *Rhymal* (1827) Taylor UCKB 427, at 431, citing Blackstone's *Commentaries*
88 Horwitz *Transformation of American Law* 37
89 *McKechnie* v *McKeyes* (1852) 10 UCQB 37, at 48–9
90 *Buell* v *Read* (1849) 5 UCQB 546, and *McLaren* v *Cook (1847)* 3 UCQB 299, at 300: 'nothing short of a grant, or use for such length of time as will support the presumption of a grant, will entitle the proprietor of land on a stream to divert or *pen* back the water in such a manner as to occasion damage to those living above or below in the same stream.'
91 Horwitz *Transformation of American Law* 46–7
92 *Kerly* v *Lewis* (1842) 6 UCQB (OS) 207, at 209; Robinson's view of free competition: 'competition would at one time reduce the charge of ferrying so low, that no one would find it for his advantage to keep a sufficient establishment for that purpose and when this competition had driven all but one or two from the employment, then the power to extort would succeed ...' (at 210).
93 *Higgins* v *Hogan (1850)* 7 UCQB 401
94 *Churchill* v *Suter* (1808) 4 Mass. 156, at 161
95 *Fraser qui tam* v *Thompson* (1845) 1 UCQB 522
96 *Regina* v *Baby* (1855) 12 UCQB 346. *Gardiner* v *Gardiner* (1833) 2 UCKB)OS) 554, at 602: 'incongruities must present themselves in acting upon this statute, if we take the law of England as our standard, both as to form and substance; it cannot be otherwise. We have chosen to adopt the law of England; that has been our own act.'
97 *Hamilton* v *Niagara Harbor & Dock Co.* (1842) 6 UCQB (OS) 381, at 398
98 Risk 'Law and Economy' 431
99 Roscoe Pound 'The Scope and Purpose of Sociological Jurisprudence' *Harvard L. Rev.* xxiv (1911) 591
100 Durand *Reminiscences* 357
101 Ibid. at 356
102 *Doe Lowry* v *Grant* (1850) 7 UCQB 125, at 130
103 Sir A. Doughty, ed. *The Elgin-Grey Papers, 1846–1852* II (Ottawa 1937), Elgin to Grey, 17 December 1849 (at 566)
104 Ibid. J.B. Robinson to Bruce (governor's secretary), 3 April 1850 (at 645–6)
105 Ibid. Elgin to Grey, 3 May 1850 (at 642)
106 RP, Seaton to J.B. Robinson, 19 June 1854
107 BP, W.H. Blake to R. Baldwin, 18 September 1849
108 Ibid. W. Reid to R. Baldwin, 12 May 1849

CHAPTER 16   'IF I AM RIGHT THY GRACE IMPART'

The title of this chapter is taken from Alexander Pope's 'Universal Prayer.'

1 University of Toronto Library, J.B. Robinson to Seaton, 26 September 1850
2 W.L. Morton *The Critical Years: The Union of British North America 1857–1873* (Toronto 1977) 2
3 RL, J.B. Robinson to Strachan, 11 September 1850
4 RP, J.A. Macdonald to J.B. Robinson, 2 January 1861
5 Ibid.
6 Ibid. diary, 2 May 1851
7 MP, J.B. Robinson to Macaulay, 26 July 1852
8 MP, J.B. Robinson to Macaulay, 23 March 1843
9 RL, J.B. Robinson to Peter Robinson, 8 August 1837
10 J.J. Talman 'The Impact of the Railway on a Pioneer Community' *Canadian Historical Association Papers* (1955) 1, at 13; citing *Liverpool Journal*, reprinted in *Hamilton Gazette* 6 February 1854
11 *Hewitt v The Ontario, Simcoe and Huron Railroad Union Company* (1854) 11 UCQB 604, at 608
12 *Wilson v The Ontario, Simcoe and Huron Railroad Union Company* (1855) 12 UCQB 463 at 465–6
13 *Grimshawe v The Grand Trunk Railway Company of Canada* (1860) 19 UCQB 493
14 *Fulton v The Grant Trunk Railway Company* (1859) 17 UCQB 428, at 433
15 RP, Edmund Lally to J.B. Robinson, 10 August 1852
16 *Hill v The Ontario, Simcoe and Huron Railroad Union Company* (1856) 13 UCQB 503, 504
17 *Ward v The Great Western Railway Company* (1856) 13 UCQB 315, at 319; *Wallace v The Grand Trunk Railway* (1858) 16 UCQB 551; *Griffiths v Welland Canal Company* (1839) 5 UCQB (OS) 686: '... for anything tht may be thus done in strict pursuance of the power of the statute, no action may be maintained, for the statute makes it legal, and is a perfect defence under the general issue' (at 686).
18 Railways Act, Consol. Stst. Can., c.66, s.83
19 20 UCQB 202
20 Ibid. at 207
21 L. Friedman *A History of American Law* (New York 1973) 410
22 Gary Schwartz 'Tort Law and the Economy in Nineteenth Century America: A Reinterpretation' *Yale L. J.* XL (1981) 1717, at 1746
23 Ibid. at 1747
24 *Moison v The Great Western Railway Company* (1856) 14 UCQB 102; *The Streetsville Plank Road Company v The Hamilton and Toronto Railway Company* (1856) 13

UCQB 600, at 601: '... the Company will observe the restriction contained in the 5th clause ofthe statute 4 Wm. IV. ch.29, that they shall do "as little damage as may be in the execution of the several powers to them granted".'

25 *Campbell* v *The Great Western Railway Co* (1858) 15 UCQB 498

26 4 Wm. IV. (1834), C.29

27 *Renaud* v *The Great Western Railway Co.* (1855) 12 UCQB 408

28 Ibid. at 424

29 12 Vict. (1849), c.81

30 Robinson *Canada and the Canada Bill* 151

31 *Kruse* v *Johnson* (1898) 2 QB 91. This topic was brought to my attention by Mary Stokes.

32 *Smith* v *Riordan* (1838) 5 UCQB (OS) 647, at 649

33 *Re Barclay and the Municipality of the Township of Darlington* (1854) 12 UCQB 86

34 Ibid. at 91

35 *Peters* v *The London Board of Police* (1846) 2 UCQB 543

36 *Terry* v *The Municipality of the Township of Haldiman* (1858) 15 UCQB 380

37 *Scott* v *Corporation of Tillsonburg* (1886) 13 OAR 233

38 3–4 Geo. VI (1913), C.43, S.249

39 [1979] 2 SCR 212, 98 DLR (3d) 255

40 See note 31.

41 *Common Law Procedure Act* 19 Vict. (1856), c.43

42 *UCLJ* (July 1862) at 173

43 MP, J.B. Robinson to Macaulay, 26 July 1852

44 *Harper* v *Loundes* (1858) 15 UCQB 430

45 *Wells* v *Gzowski et al.* (1857) 14 UCQB 553, at 564

46 *Henderson* v *Dickson* (1861) 19 UCQB 592

47 BP, Blake to Baldwin, 27 January 1845: 'I [Blake] was deprived of the most effectual aid at Simcoe on account of a suit now pending before our inquisition.'

48 *Debates of the Legislative Assembly of the United Canadas* VIII 20 February 1849 (at 849–50)

49 BP, Blake to Baldwin, 27 January 1845

50 Ibid. R. Sullivan to Baldwin, 29 January 1845

51 J.D. Blackwell 'William Hume Blake and the Judicature Acts of 1849: The Process of Legal Reform at Mid-Century in Upper Canada' in David H. Flaherty, ed. *Essays in the History of Canadian Law* I (Toronto 1981) 132–74

52 BP, Blake to Baldwin, 7 September 1848

53 Ibid. same to same, 25 September 1848

54 Ibid. J.B. Robinson to Baldwin, 8 June 149

55 *McGann* v *Keyes* (1855) 12 UCQB 429

56 MP, J.B. Robinson to Macaulay, 20 July 1852

57 *Dougall v Long*, (1855) 5 Ch. 292; *A-G v McNulty* (1860) 8 Ch. 324

58 *Bouton v Jeffrey* (1845) 1 E. & A 111

59 (1852) 3 Ch. 379. 5 Ch. 1 (E. & A.), 5 CH. 108 (PC)

60 (1852) 5 Ch. at 29

61 Ibid. at 28

62 RL, Head to J.B. Robinson, 4 February 1855

63 *UCLJ* (March 1863) 62

64 RP, diary, 1855

65 N.A. Woods *The Prince of Wales in Canada and the United States* (London 1861) 255–66

66 Province of Canada Sessional Papers (1861) XIX (4), J.A. Macdonald to S.B. Freeman, 18 October 1860

67 UC Sundries, J.B. Robinson to Colborne, n.d. Only a few years earlier Robinson had interpreted the Separate Schools Act (1850, 13 & 14 Vict., c.48) to mean that where separate schools were established for black children, those children were barred from attending the common schools: *Re Hill v Camden* (1854) 11 UCQB 573. Nevertheless, the chief justice did not permit the interpretation of that statute to bar black children completely from obtaining an education. He decided that local trustees could not exclude black students from the common schools if no separate facilities existed: *Washington v Charlotteville* (1854) 11 UCQB 569. Those decisions of Queen's Bench did not sanction 'educational segregation throughout the province' (Jason H. Silverman and Donna J. Gillie 'The Pursuit of Knowledge under Difficulties: Education and the Fugitive Slave in Canada' *OH* LXXIV (1982) 94, at 102). Rather, they recognized the discriminatory policies imposed by the legislature.

68 *In the Matter of John Anderson* (1860) 20 UCQB 124

69 Ibid. at 174

70 Ibid. at 187

71 *Globe* 17 December 1860

72 Ibid. 19 January 1861

73 18 December 1860

74 Durand *Reminiscences*: 'Judge Robinson's ancestors came from a slave State, and the spirit of slavery may have been in him' (at 444).

75 R.C. Reinders 'The John Anderson Case, 1860–1: A Study in Anglo-Canadian Imperial Relations' *CHR* LVI (1975) 393

76 *Law Times* 12 January 1861 at 125

77 G.V. Laforest *Extradition to and from Canada* (Toronto 1977): 'The approach taken in Re Anderson seems to be the only logical one; the institutions and laws of the foreign country must necessarily form the background against which to examine events occurring in that country' (at 53).

78 H.R.S. Ryan 'Ex Parte John Anderson' *Queen's L. J.* VI (1981) 385
79 *UCLJ* (March 1863) 63
80 RP J.B. Robinson to Head, 16 March 1861
81 Ibid. Head to J.B. Robinson, 16 March 1861
82 24 Vict. (1861), c.36
83 RP, J.B. Robinson to Macdonald, 18 January 1862
84 Ibid. Macdonald to J.B. Robinson, 23 January 1862
85 *UCLJ* (July 1862) 172–3, and *Globe* 20 June 1862
86 *Globe* 20 June 1862
87 J.B. Robinson *Four Early Pamphlets on the Subject of the Confederation and Union of the Canadas* (Toronto 1967) at 23 and 40

EPILOGUE

1 Chap. 6, note 81
2 Sanderson *The Arthur Papers* I Arthur to J.B. Robinson, 19 April 1838 (at 82)
3 J.B. Robinson to Lord Bathurst, 1822, in *Four Early Pamphlets* 39–40
4 Robert Craig Brown *Robert Laird Borden: A Biography* II (Toronto 1980). Borden's government 'was not consulted about any significant aspect of the imperial government's war policy' (at 69).
5 Cook 'Robinson and the Conservative Blueprint' 95
6 Robinson *Canada and the Canada Bill* 144
7 J.B. Robinson to Lord Bathurst, 6 December 1824 in *Four Early Pamphlets* 54
8 *The Church* 12 April 1842
9 J.B. Robinson to Lord Bathurst, 1822, in *Four Early Pamphlets* 32
10 MP, J.B. Robinson to Macaulay, 11 September 1843
11 S.F. Wise 'Conservatism and Political Development: The Canadian Case' *South Atlantic Quarterly* LXIX (1970) 226 at 242
12 Carl Berger *The Sense of Power – Studies in the Ideas of Canadian Imperialism 1867–1914* (Toronto 1970) 103
13 RL, J.B. Robinson to Sarah Boulton, 30 October 1839
14 Colborne Papers, J.B. Robinson to Colborne, 11 June 1839
15 Ibid. same to same, 20 March 1836
16 RL, J.B. Robinson to Strachan, 8 April 1851
17 H.E. Read 'The Judicial Process in Common Law Canada' *Canadian Bar Review* XXXVII (1959) 265, at 276
18 RP, charge to the grand jury, 1837
19 *Morgentaler* v *The Queen* (1975) 53 DLR (3d) 161, at 168
20 E.Z. Friedenberg *Deference to Authority: The Case of Canada* (New York 1980) 54
21 UC Sundries, J.B. Robinson to Rowan, 25 December 1837

Index

The Osgoode Society was formed in 1979 to encourage research and writing in the history of Canadian law. Its efforts to stimulate legal history in Canada include the sponsorship of a fellowship, research support programs, an annual lecture on Canadian legal history, and work in the field of oral history. The Society will publish volumes which contribute to legal–historical scholarship in Canada, including studies of the courts, the judiciary, and the legal profession, biographies, collections of documents, studies in criminology and penology, great trials, and work in the social and economic history of the law.

DATE DUE
DATE DE RETOUR